STRANGERS AND PILGRIMS

STRANGERS AND PILGRIMS

A History of the
Anglican Diocese of Quebec
1793-1993

M. E. Reisner

ANGLICAN BOOK CENTRE
Toronto, Ontario

1995
Anglican Book Centre
600 Jarvis Street
Toronto, Ontario
Canada M4Y 2J6

Book design and typesetting: Willem Hart Art & Design Inc.

This book was commissioned by the Diocese of Quebec
of the Anglican Church of Canada in 1992.

Canadian Cataloguing in Publication Data

Reisner, M.E. (Mary Ellen)
  Strangers and Pilgrims

ISBN 1-55126-142-1 (bound)
ISBN 1-55126-116-2 (pbk.)

1. Anglican Church of Canada. Diocese of
Quebec - History.   I. Title.

BX 5612.C4R4 1995   283'.714471   C95-933074-7

These all died in faith, not having received the promises,
but having seen them afar off, and were persuaded of them,
and embraced them, and confessed that they were strangers
and pilgrims on the earth.

For they that say such things declare plainly that they seek a
country.

And truly, if they had been mindful of that country from
whence they came out, they might have had opportunity
to have returned.

But now they desire a better country, that is, an heavenly...

Hebrews 11:13–16

... sondry folk, by aventure y-falle
In felawshipe, and pilgrims were they alle

So hadde I spoken with hem everichon,
That I was of hir felawshipe anon...

Geoffrey Chaucer
The Canterbury Tales

Contents

List of Illustrations

Foreword

It is a privilege and an honour to write the foreword to this important and beautifully presented history.

Since becoming Bishop of the Anglican Diocese of Quebec in 1991, I have been profoundly moved by the importance of the long history of Anglican life in this Diocese. I have cherished the opportunity to celebrate many important anniversaries of its parishes and institutions. Most important for the life of the whole Diocese have been the 150th anniversary of the Church Society of the Diocese of Quebec in 1992, the 200th anniversary of the Diocese in 1993, and the 190th anniversary of the Cathedral of the Holy Trinity in 1994.

To celebrate the bicentenary of the Diocese in 1993, we chose "pilgrimage" as the overall theme for the various anniversary events. We focused on pilgrimage because of the way that word suggests an awareness of history and the past, of activity in the present and of journey into the future.

One of the projects of the bicentennial year was the launching of a major history of the Diocese. We were enormously fortunate that Mary Ellen Reisner agreed to take on the writing of the history. In her title *Strangers and Pilgrims*, she has picked up not only a significant New Testament description of the people of God, but also the sense which we recalled during the bicentenary that we are all pilgrims.

Our journey in the present and the new and difficult challenges to which God calls us in the future will be undertaken with clearer vision if we know the story of our past. We need to be reminded of the strength, devotion, and witness of so many people who have been part of our past. That story and the people of God responsible for it have been laid out for us in this volume.

I am grateful to Mary Ellen Reisner for the gift of this window on the life of two hundred years of Anglican ministry in the Diocese of Quebec.

† **Bruce Stavert**, *Bishop*

Preface

Strangers and Pilgrims is the first attempt at a general history of the Diocese of Quebec since 1893, when the Ven. Henry Roe prepared a 61-page booklet to celebrate its first one hundred years. Several early studies have shed much light on the pre-diocesan period and on the lives of the first three bishops. Little was available, however, for the reader in search of an overview of the Anglican Church in this Diocese since 1893 (and one could, in all fairness, push that date back an additional 30 years to G. J. Mountain's death).

Perhaps a special anniversary is necessary to spur on a project of this kind. Institutional history in general, and church history in particular, are rumoured to be "thin" and "dull," but nothing could be farther from the truth. Fascinating primary materials were ready to hand in the Diocesan Archives, and there was scope there, and elsewhere, for a whole series of lively volumes. The parishes themselves have often retained interesting and valuable records. A little persistence can bear rich rewards.

Authorized histories tend to be viewed askance by professional historians. Consequently, when Bishop Stavert approached me to take on this bicentennial history, I accepted on the condition that I would retain full scholarly control over the project, without interference either from individuals or from committees. The Diocese exhibited considerable trust in acceding to this, and I was granted sole responsibility for the research, its organization, and the preparation of the final text.

Although intended to be a serious study based on primary materials, *Strangers and Pilgrims* is addressed to the general reader as well as to the church historian. Notes and sources are given at the end of the book so as not to compromise the integrity of the text with footnotes. Individual chapters provide a thematic rather than a chronological picture of the Diocese, and every effort has been made to set events in context. To convey a sense of the texture of life in the Diocese at various periods, and to portray in concrete detail the challenges faced by individuals as well as their achievements over the years, I have prepared a sequence of "Windows," or vignettes. These afford glimpses of life in the Diocese from 1765 to 1993 on as diverse a series of subjects as might interest the reader: travel conditions, parish complaints, missions in the wilderness, synodical politics, local endowments, administrative nightmares, stories of heroism, tales of romance. Discovering, researching, and assembling this material was a joy and a challenge that I shall not soon forget.

In preparing a history of this kind, the inclusion of one detail seems to require sacrificing another; in the end, it was pertinence to the overall pattern that determined the choice. I made a particular effort to treat the Diocese in all the diversity of its components, and to resist the temptation to focus on the centre. However, in a project of this magnitude, omissions are bound to occur. I regret them and take full responsibility for them. Limitation of space made it impossible, for example, to trace the evolution of individual parishes, to discuss the range of institutions fostered by the Diocese, or to do justice to many of the men and women whose efforts have strengthened the Church here over so long a period. It is my hope that this beginning may encourage others to supply what I may have omitted and to succeed where I may have failed.

Acknowledgements

I wish to express my gratitude to the Rt Rev. Bruce Stavert for entrusting this project to me and for contributing in a variety of ways to its completion. It was Bishop Stavert who conceived of the history as a scholarly, and not merely commemorative, volume, and from the beginning he took the project under his wing. His availability for consultation and advice, as well as his unfailing personal interest and support throughout the preparation of the work, has eased my task immeasurably.

For giving me access to, and permission to quote from, archival material, I would like to thank the Rt Rev. Andrew Hutchison, Bishop of Montreal; Dr Richard Palmer, Librarian and Archivist, Lambeth Palace; Dr Gordon Huelin, Archivist and Librarian, The Society for Promoting Christian Knowledge; the Rev. Ian Pearson, former Archivist, Society for the Propagation of the Gospel; Ms Anna M. Grant, Archivist, Bishop's University Library; Mrs. Pamela Miller, Archivist, the McCord Museum of Canadian History; and Ms Teresa Thompson, Director, General Synod Archives, Toronto. The Rev. Canons Mervyn Awcock and Harold Brazel, former Archivists of the Quebec Diocesan Archives, gave every assistance. I am grateful to former Registrar Queenie Cazes for the wealth of her experience, and to present Archivist and Registrar James T. Sweeny. To Mss Joan Gibb and Helen Stuart of Church House, Quebec, I owe a special debt for their unfailing resourcefulness in supplying—virtually on demand—a multitude of helpful details.

I wish to thank the Ven. Robert A. Bryan for his generous permission both to quote from a number of unpublished texts he supplied and to reproduce several photographs from his own collection. His interest, enthusiasm, and advice have added materially to the whole book.

In February 1992, soon after taking on the history project, I wrote to every parish priest and chaplain in the Diocese (excluding military chaplains), as well as to several retired clergy (38 in all), soliciting their views on parochial and national church issues. I enclosed a detailed questionnaire addressed to the incumbent with the request that it be passed on to a layperson of long standing in each congregation under his or her care. Although I received several replies from clergy (10, to be exact), and managed to extract several others by telephone or in person, it was the laity who were most forthcoming in supplying information. Among these it was the outlying areas—Kawawachikamach, Sept-Iles, St Clement's Mission, the Magdalen Islands, parts of the Gaspé and areas of the Townships—that responded with particular generosity. To those who did so, I owe special thanks.

In addition to those already mentioned, many of the clergy provided invaluable assistance in a variety of ways. I would particularly like to thank the Very Rev. James Merrett; Archdeacons Richard Blyth, Peter Joyce, and Lynn Ross; the Rev. Canons Robert Jervis-Read, Curtis Patterson, Heather Thomson, Pierre Voyer, Ronald West, and the Rev. Canon Dr Ronald Reeve; as well as the Rev. Nelson Boon, Jacques Cloutier, Michael Hare, Ray Jensen, Ruth H. Matthews, John Morrell, Ronald Owen, Patricia Peacock, Stuart Pike, William Presnail, Janet Smith, Ailsa Spackman, Glenn Stone and Captain the Rev. Blair Ross.

All of the following lay people provided material help, some at considerable expense of time and effort. Many placed at my disposition items of great personal value and interest. For their various contributions to this volume, I wish to thank Alec Addie, Chris Ambidge, Ken Annett, Barbara Bignell, Christina Bobbitt, Byron Clark, Peter Clibbon, Marguerite Cotton, Graham Eglington, John Evans, Graham Jackson, Eleanor Blois Hall, Olive Harding and the late Richard Harding, Cecily Hinton, James H. Lambert, the late Jules Lord, Patrick Mallen, Barbara Matthews, Lottie McLaughlin, Fredi Meade, Clive Meredith, Doreen Mulcahy, Dorothy Phillips, Ruth Radley-Walters, Dorothy Shattuck, Phyllis and Terry Skeats, Beulah Smith, Rebekah Smith, Brian Treggett, Catherine Wark, and Mary Woods.

I gratefully acknowledge Dr Derek Booth's permission to reproduce a set of four maps, originally prepared by him for the Diocesan bicentennial souvenir booklet. Without their aid, the reader would often be hard pressed to locate many of the events in the ensuing narrative.

To Mr. Tony Price, who generously commissioned and donated the photograph for the cover design I am especially indebted. This window, given in memory of his grandfather, sets the tone in visual terms for part of the structure of *Strangers and Pilgrims*.

I owe a particular debt of gratitude to my husband, Dr Thomas A. Reisner, on whose criticism, advice, sharp eye and ear I have relied throughout this entire project.

Publication of *Strangers and Pilgrims* was made possible through generous grants from The Anglican Foundation of Canada, the Citadel Foundation, the Mathew Ralph Kane Foundation, and the Quebec-Labrador Foundation. To all these, I wish to convey my sincerest thanks.

List of Abbreviations

ANQ	Archives nationales du Québec
BAS	*Book of Alternative Services*
BCP	*Book of Common Prayer*
BCS	Bishop's College School
CCHS	Canadian Church Historical Society
CCS	Colonial Church & School Society
CS	Church Society of the Diocese of Quebec
DEC	Diocesan Executive Council
	(formerly Diocesan Executive Committee)
EB	*Encyclopædia Britannica*
ETA	Eastern Townships Archives
LPA	Lambeth Palace Archives
LR	Lay Reader
MDA	Montreal Diocesan Archives
OED	*Oxford English Dictionary*
QDA	Quebec Diocesan Archives
QDG	*Quebec Diocesan Gazette*
SPCK	Society for Promoting Christian Knowledge
SPG	Society for the Propagation of the Gospel in Foreign Parts
TM	Travelling Missionary
UCC	The United Church of Canada
USPG	United Society for the Propagation of the Gospel

PLATE 1A *The Royal gift of 1766 "for the use of the Episcopal Church of the Parish of Quebec." Each piece bears the arms and cipher of George III.*

PLATE 1B *The Royal gift of 1804, presented by George III to the Cathedral of the Holy Trinity on the occasion of its consecration.* (Photo credit: Public Archives of Canada)

"This Late Acquisition to the Crown": Beginnings of the Anglican Communion in Quebec

W hen Jacob Mountain, first Lord Bishop of Quebec, looked back in 1803 on his episcopate of 10 years' duration, he mourned the early days, long before his appointment, when the foundations of the Church in his Diocese had been laid. In a letter to the Archbishop of Canterbury, Mountain blamed what he regarded as the poor progress and inferior position of the Church of England in Quebec on "the total & unaccountable neglect of His Majesty's Institutions, for a long series of years." The claim was exaggerated, but it carried some truth. Until Letters Patent, issued 28 June 1793, created the Anglican Diocese of Quebec, such provisions as had been made for the spiritual welfare of Anglicans—or churchmen as they were called—in the Province of Canada were sparse and inconsistent. It was on this uncertain foundation that the new diocese was to be erected. Churchmen and the Church itself would continue to follow a chequered though interesting career as strangers and pilgrims in this new world.

The first Protestants to arrive in the new colony (the term Protestant being used at that time interchangeably, although not exclusively, for members of the Church of England) seem to have been an unpromising lot. General James Murray, Acting Governor during the *régime militaire* and civilian Governor until 1766, had ample opportunity to observe both the resident *Canadiens* and those of his own nationality who had arrived with the military or found their way to the new colony soon afterwards. Murray pointed a sharp contrast between the newly-settled Protestants and the resident Roman Catholics; the latter he found "frugal, industrious, and moral" as well as "zealous for their religion, though very ignorant." The former, with the exception of "a few half-pay officers," he described contemptuously as "traders, mechanics, and publicans, ... most of them were followers of the army, of mean education, or soldiers, disbanded at the reduction of the troops.... I report them to be, in general, the most immoral collection of men I ever knew; of course, little calculated to make the new subjects enamoured with our laws, religion, and customs."

"It would be more agreeable to suppress this painful testimony," remarked the Rev. Ernest Hawkins (the earliest historian of the Diocese of Quebec) when describing Canada's first glimpse of British Protestantism, "but it seems a duty to direct attention to the evils arising from the reckless and irresponsible manner in which, formerly, persons were selected for Colonial service." Writing almost one hundred years after Hawkins' book appeared, another church historian has singled out "the clash of culture" of two major groups within a single national framework as "the great Canadian theme." If this is so, the representatives of one of these groups, at the beginning of their confrontation, were off to a poor start.

The First Clergy: 1759-1768

Before 1759, the Church of England was as yet unrepresented in the 727,000-odd square kilometer expanse of territory that comprises the present-day Anglican Diocese of Quebec. In June of that year, the first Anglican clergy to penetrate its borders sailed up the St Lawrence or accompanied the land forces under General Amherst as chaplains to the British forces.

Of these chaplains, one had the distinction of performing the first Anglican service to be held in Quebec. Another appears to have given material aid in the form of military intelligence to the besieging army. That the calamitous defeat of General Montcalm, "a man of great ability and, for the age, nobility of soul" (as A.R.M. Lower has described him), may have been precipitated in this manner appears to have been a source of acute embarrassment to Philip Carrington, seventh Lord Bishop of Quebec. When he came to write his *History* of the Anglican Church in Canada, almost 150 years after the fall of Quebec, he alluded to these early events as follows:

> The first Anglican service in Quebec was taken by a naval chaplain, the Rev. Eli Dawson, in the Chapel of the Ursuline Convent; but there was a military chaplain whose name is worth mentioning, Michel Houdin, who was attached to the 48th Regiment.... He was a Québécois and had been Superior of a monastery in the city; but he had migrated to the American colonies, where he had entered the Anglican ministry, becoming Rector of Trenton, New Jersey. After the battle he wanted to leave, but General Murray commanded him to stay on because there was "no other person to be depended upon for intelligence of the French proceedings"... Did he show Wolfe the way up the cliff? It is not a very pretty question ...

To Carrington, raised as he was in the tradition of fair play, it was obviously distasteful that the treachery of a renegade rather than daring reconnaissance might have enabled a landing at Wolfe's Cove to take the enemy by surprise.

Houdin was actually Itinerant Missionary in New Jersey for the Society for the Propagation of the Gospel in Foreign Parts (known more familiarly as the Venerable Society or simply as the SPG). He had left his post to accompany the British troops to Canada. On 23 October 1759, he wrote anxiously from Quebec to the SPG, "intreating that his absence from his Mission might not bring him under the Society's displeasure ..." Houdin unwillingly remained until 1761 when he was transferred to the Mission to the French Refugees at New Rochelle, New York.

It is to the Rev. Dr John Brooke that credit should go for first ministering to the spiritual needs of the little band of civilian Protestants at Quebec. Brooke, like Dawson and Houdin, was a military chaplain, but he seems to have arrived some time after 18 September, the date of the battle. From the outset, his knowledge of French was an asset, as many of the soldiers wished to take Canadian wives and, although most applied to local priests, a few sought out a Protestant clergyman to perform the ceremony. As Frances Brooke, the chaplain's wife, complained to the authorities in 1765, "the discharged soldiers every Day turn papists: else the priests will not marry them. Some will be married by Mr Brooke, who [can] marry & bury in French." On 27 December 1760, Dr Brooke had been appointed chaplain to the town of Quebec and parish priest to all His Majesty's Protestant subjects in the Government not belonging to particular regiments.

Because he enjoyed General Murray's "approbation ... upon a twenty year's personal acquaintance," which was undiminished with the Governor's "particular observation of his conduct in the exercise of his function for upwards of a year in this place," one might suppose that Brooke would have been speedily placed on a permanent footing by the Home Government. Indeed, the "Chief Justice, Civil Officers, Merchants and others of the city and province of Quebec" dispatched a petition to the SPG that the Society adopt Brooke as their Missionary. This, they argued, would allow him to sustain a "respectable appearance" and thereby increase his "usefulness amongst a clergy and people Strangers to our Nation and prejudiced against our faith and Religion." With their petition went Murray's personal recommendation; such an appointment "is as much my desire as theirs," he urged. Nothing came of this appeal.

When the first permanent pastoral appointments for the civilian population of Canada were made in 1768, "a very unfortunate, though well-meant, policy was decided upon by the authorities," namely to wean the

Canadiens from Roman Catholicism and win them to the Church of England by situating French-speaking Protestant clergy, with generous Government stipends, at Quebec, Montreal, and Trois-Rivières. These clergymen were, respectively, Francis de Montmollin and David Chabrand Delisle (both Swiss Calvinists), and the French-born Legère Jean-Baptiste Noël Veyssière, a former Recollet priest (recently converted). The Colonial Government's ill-advised plan was soon to be abandoned, but not before the appointment, for their lifetimes, of clergy who were not only unable to officiate in the English language but also largely unfamiliar with the doctrines and ritual of the Anglican Church. The needs of the English-speaking Protestants, who had hitherto received no encouragement or support—even to the extent of being granted a church for their exclusive use—seemed left to one side (see Window 1).*

Neither Murray nor Sir Guy Carleton (the latter became Governor in 1768) believed in interfering with the "religious attachments" of the French Canadians. Carleton, under whose tenure of office all three new clergy were appointed, was loath to honour the Royal Mandamus each had procured. The Governor dispatched a curt letter to the Earl of Hillsborough, who, as president of the Board of Trade, was the official responsible. The terms of the Mandamus as such, he pointed out, "have occasioned no small difficulty" in civil matters and, if extended to ecclesiastical property, would deprive the *habitants* of their parish churches and their priests of their tithes. This hardship, Carleton clearly implied, ought not to be imposed upon them. In a letter to Richard Terrick, Bishop of London, he stated that, in his judgement, the Government's policy of dispatching Protestant clergy to convert the local population from "their old attachments ... in which they have been trained and educated from their earliest Infancy" was a mistake. He also informed the Bishop that he had himself instructed these new men "to avoid religious Disputes, which can never bring about a Reformation, and may tend to create ill Blood, and to breed a Discontent, not easily to be got the better of."

Carleton was not altogether without sympathy for some of the Protestant clergy he encountered. Dr Brooke, for example, of whom, since the time of his arrival (as the Governor affirmed to Bishop Terrick) he person-

---

* From time to time the reader will be invited to consult "Windows," brief vignettes on a variety of subjects, collected at the back of the book. In this particular case, the first part of Window 1 provides more detailed information about the situation in which the first Quebec Protestants found themselves.

ally had not had the least reason to complain, was now—since the arrival of de Montmollin at Quebec—deprived of his position and about to leave the country after "having served the Protestants of this City as their Curate and Minister for eight years past, without any Allowance for the same." The Governor's indignation at this treatment seems more on behalf of the man than his calling, however.

One might assume from Carleton's treatment of the Home Government's appointed clergy "newly come over" that he harboured some active prejudice against the Church, but he appears, like Murray before him, to have been merely indifferent to religion. Both were more concerned with the practical problem of winning the *Canadiens* to the King's interest. "To conciliate their Affections by a strict, steady, and impartial Administration of Justice" seemed more desirable to Carleton than the introduction of potentially turbulent religious controversialists. The Governor was impatient of the pretensions and troublesome demands of these most recent representatives of the Church of England, particularly of the Rev. Francis de Montmollin at Quebec. De Montmollin seems to have insisted that a particular church building, which had been damaged in the war and was "now almost repaired at a considerable expense" by the French population, be turned over to *him*. The angry Carleton—as he fulminated to the Earl of Hillsborough—retorted that such deprivation amounted to "Violence, Injustice, & Breach of Treaties," only to receive the clergyman's retort "that Louis the 14th had not kept his Treaties with Protestants, [and] he therefore sees no reason why we should keep ours with Roman Catholics."

"The Liberty of the Catholic Religion"

In 1763 the position of a Roman Catholic majority in a British colony was a peculiar one. In Britain there were considerable restrictions on anyone who did not profess to be a member of the Church of England. Under the Test Acts, all persons holding any office, civil or military, had to take the oaths of supremacy and allegiance and subscribe to a declaration against transubstantiation. Within three months of being admitted to office, they were required to receive the sacraments according to the rites of the Church of England. Conscientious Roman Catholics were thus excluded from public office or commissions in the armed forces until passage of the Roman Catholic Relief Act in 1829. Dissenters, who could readily subscribe to the declaration against transubstantiation, were freed in 1828 from the necessity of receiving the sacraments as a condition of taking office. It was not until the repeal of the Corporation Acts in 1871, however, that Roman Catholics or Dissenters who had completed a course of university study would be granted degrees at Oxford or Cambridge. Such restrictions on personal freedom based on religious belief and practice were usual in Europe during that period, however. On the eve of the Revolution in France, as Alec Vidler remarks, "the Catholic Church had no rivals, for since the revocation of the Edict of Nantes [in 1685] Catholics alone had the right of citizenship."

When the Treaty of Paris was signed on 10 February 1763, its fourth Article stipulated that "His Britannic Majesty ... agrees to grant the liberty of the Catholic religion to the inhabitants of Canada: he will consequently give the most effectual orders that his new Roman Catholic subjects may profess their religion according to the rites of the Roman Church, as far as the laws of Great Britain permit." It appeared that, while the Roman Catholics in the colony would enjoy a degree of toleration, they were not intended to be altogether exempt from the restrictions that applied to their co-religionists in Britain.

In England at the end of the eighteenth century the Roman Catholics—"commonly known as 'the Romish dissenters' or 'the papists'—were a tiny minority, about one percent of the population." Papal jurisdiction was not countenanced by the authorities. The so-called "Catholic Committee," consisting for the most part of influential Roman Catholic laymen, was apparently prepared to go a long way to win relief from their disabilities under the law. "With this end in view, they proposed to repudiate subversive beliefs they were supposed to hold—the power of the pope to depose an excommunicated ruler or to approve his assassination, the doctrine that 'faith is not to be kept with heretics', and the infallibility of the pope." Besides the removal of disabilities, "they wanted a normal diocesan constitution to be restored with the election of bishops and even a royal veto." As a result, in 1791 the Government passed a bill relieving from a number of vexatious disabilities those Roman Catholics who rejected the temporal authority of the pope. It was not until 1851 that a Roman Catholic hierarchy was restored in Britain.

When the British converts of the 1840s—drawn to Roman Catholicism in the wake of the Oxford Movement—were to examine the attitudes held by those born to the faith, they judged them harshly. Centuries of distrust had made the old believers timid, conservative, austere, and restrained; not drawn to pro-Roman custom and devotion; wanting "to seem English"; and, as one uncompromising convert accused, "moving in society without being known as Catholics."

In sharp contrast with English Roman Catholicism, the Quebec Church had been enjoying "all the aspects of a full-blown diocesan organization" for more than a century. Furthermore, the Quebec Catholics were loyal primarily to Rome, not France. François de Laval-Montmorency, who arrived in New France in 1659, had reinforced the powerful ultramontane influence that the Jesuits and the Ursulines had already implanted. Wishing to seek "freedom as a bishop in the New World from all Gallican restrictions," he had sought his appointment from the pope, rather than from the king. Consequently his consecration had not been by the hand of the Gallican Archbishop of Rouen, who claimed jurisdiction over ecclesiastical appointments in the colonies, but by the papal nuncio in Paris acting in cooperation with two French bishops.

"Elsewhere in the history of Christianity," writes Owen Chadwick in his study of the Victorian Church, "it has been observed how a state, which by conquest or inheritance or accident acquires a new and large population practicing a different religion from the religion of the old population, is forced to modify its religious policy if it wishes to survive as a state." Murray and Carleton were fully aware of the need to be pragmatic and not doctrinaire if Canada was to remain governable. Thus it was that Roman Catholics enjoyed a whole range of freedoms in Canada that their brethren in Britain would wait many years to achieve.

"Lopt of Episcopacy": The Church of England in America, 1759
At the time of the fall of New France, the position of the Church of England in North America—that is, in the Thirteen Colonies—was an awkward one. Without a resident bishop anywhere outside the British Isles, all the Anglican clergy, military chaplains excepted, fell under the jurisdiction of the Bishop of London. Thus there was no one in the colonies empowered to ordain priests, to confirm baptized persons, to undertake visitations, or to consecrate churches and burial grounds. No supervision or guidance of the clergy was possible except through transatlantic correspondence. There were no ecclesiastical courts to enforce clerical discipline.

For some years, American churchmen had tried to secure the consecration of a bishop for the Thirteen Colonies, but without success. The founders of New England, after all, were Protestant Dissenters "fleeing an Anglican Jacobean England of whose 'reformation' they had despaired." The very thought of transplanting an Anglican hierarchy to any of the Thirteen Colonies was, to many, a betrayal of the distinctive American religious tradition. With New France now under British rule, and religious toleration granted under the Treaty of Paris to her Roman Catholic inhabitants, an episcopal

The Bishops of Quebec during the Nineteenth Century.

PLATE 2   *From the* Quebec Diocesan Gazette, *January 1901. Bishop Dunn resigned his office in 1914 and died aboard ship while returning to England that same year.*

system of church government *had* finally taken its place in British North America. In spiritual matters, New France had been governed by its own resident bishop since 1658, had enjoyed the benefits of a seminary since 1663, and was well supplied with locally trained as well as European priests. Such an anomaly could hardly fail to draw attention to the plight of the national church of Great Britain in America.

On 20 February 1767, the Bishop of Llandaff preached a sermon before the members of the SPG in the London church of St Mary-le-Bow, pointedly and publicly drawing attention to the state of the Church of England abroad. "The want of Bishops (in America) hath been all along the more heavily lamented," he pointed out, "because it is a case so singular, that it cannot be parallelled in the Christian world.... All sects of Protestant Christians at home ... have the full enjoyment of their religion. Even the Romish Superstition, within a province lately added to the British dominions [*i.e.*, Canada], is completely allowed in all points; ... only the church here by law established ... exists only in part, in a maimed state, lopt of Episcopacy, an essential part of its Constitution."

The consecration of *any* bishop, however, let alone of a bishop for a new diocese, was not strictly an ecclesiastical matter. Letters Patent and a Mandamus from the Crown were required. The Church of England hierarchy "was not free to act on its own initiative. The bishops were all appointed by the king and subject to political pressures ... They were amenable to king and parliament for their official and personal conduct. George III did not hesitate to intervene directly into ecclesiastical appointments when he wanted a favourite appointed." Thus, in 1759 the Church of England was reduced to a condition of subservience to the Government. As far as the appointment of a hypothetical bishop for America was concerned, there was no precedent for such an action. It was thought that a special Act of Parliament would be required to do so, were such an appointment thought to be desirable. The support of spiritual authority was helpful, but it was with political forces and party interest that the real power lay.

Such subordination had not always been the rule. As early as the thirteenth century, the spiritual leaders of England had met in convocation for purposes of discussion and self-government. To do so, they were assembled by the Archbishops of Canterbury and York within their ecclesiastical provinces by means of royal writ, and had sat concurrently with Parliament. Convocation consisted of two Houses: an upper House composed of the archbishops and bishops, and a lower House of the deans and archdeacons of each cathedral, a few other specified officers, and two beneficed clergy from each diocese. Early in the eighteenth century, the lower House became contentious over several issues, finally challenging the authority of the upper House and the archbishops. In 1717, convocation was virtually shut down by the Whig government under George I, when, after a particularly disputatious session, it was prorogued in accordance with a Royal writ and the requisite licence to reassemble was not forthcoming. This state of affairs was to continue until 1861, almost 25 years into the reign of Queen Victoria.

The acquisition of a large territory already settled exclusively by members of a religious denomination that was tolerated only within strict limitations in Britain made it politically expedient to introduce a full-fledged Anglican establishment to counterbalance and outrank it. The appointment of a colonial Bishop of the Church of England was now inevitable.

"The Proposal of Appointing Bishops": Where and When?

There was a good deal of speculation about how best to establish the Church of England in the new colonies. Although Halifax was finally settled upon as the first See City in British North America, this was by no means an obvious choice from the outset.

The city of Quebec, with its strategic setting and romantic history, had already captured the imagination of the people of Great Britain. It was, moreover, the administrative centre of Roman Catholicism in New France. Thus, at first, Quebec seemed to be the logical choice. As one British clergyman observed in 1765, "Quebec being [a Roman Catholic] Episcopal See, if a Popish Bishop continues to preside there over his Clergy, & no Episcopal Clergy, on the Protestant Side, be sent over, but of an inferior rank, the Protestant cause must unavoidably suffer by it." In the same year, Dean Tucker of Gloucester, using the economic argument, asked "whether a Church of England Bishop might not be settled at Quebec at less Expence, & with more Facility than any where else?" He even suggested that Quebec might be a convenient base from which the needs of the Thirteen Colonies could be met; that is, whether "this Bishop of ye new Colony might not ... ordain Priests & Deacons for ye Episcopal Congregations of New England, New York, &c? or whether such Candidates might not come to him to Quebec much more conveniently & expeditiously, than take a Voyage to England." If the first bishop for British North America had been consecrated within 10 years of the Treaty of Paris, it is quite likely that he would have administered his diocese from Quebec. As it was, the American Revolution intervened in 1776 and Samuel Seabury, grown weary of petitioning the Archbishop of Canterbury and the English bishops, had himself consecrated not at Lambeth, but in Aberdeen. Thus, in 1784 the first Episcopal bishop in North America was consecrated by three nonjuror bishops of the Scottish Episcopal Church.

"Jurisdiction, Spiritual and Ecclesiastical": 1787-1793
Until the appointment of Charles Inglis by Letters Patent—dated 9 August 1787—to the first bishopric to be erected by Parliament outside the British Isles, episcopal authority over all the colonial clergy was vested in the Bishop of London; thus, in Church matters, Canada was first administered from Fulham Palace and secondly from Halifax until the appointment of Bishop Jacob Mountain as first Lord Bishop of Quebec in 1793.

British North America in general, and the Diocese of Nova Scotia in particular, was fortunate in its first bishop. Inglis, although a native of Ireland, had lived and worked in New England since 1755. He was familiar with the realities of life in the colonies. As a former schoolmaster in Pennsylvania before his ordination, and later Acting President of King's College, New York, he retained a lifelong commitment to education. As a priest and missionary of the SPG, he understood the need to travel far afield to serve a scattered flock. Church building formed part of his experience, too. Furthermore, he had attended and knew the value of gatherings of the colonial clergy. By the same token, in England, he had experienced the frustrations of waiting out the bureaucratic procedures of both church and state authorities.

The vast Diocese over which Inglis held sway was defined by two Letters Patent. It included Nova Scotia, New Brunswick, (what is now) Prince Edward Island, Newfoundland, Quebec, and Upper Canada. Immediately after arriving at Halifax on 15 October, the Bishop set about planning a visitation of his clergy, first in Nova Scotia, then in New Brunswick. By 1788, he had completed both these undertakings.

One might expect the western portion of the Diocese to have suffered neglect while Inglis consolidated his position at home, but this was not the case. From his arrival at Halifax, the Bishop's biographer points out, he had continued to correspond with Sir Guy Carleton, but knowing "so little of Quebec and its people, he felt himself at a loss to advise the Governor-General on the disposition of missionaries there." He "wanted to appoint ecclesiastical commissaries, but did not know who would be the most effective." Despite distances and difficulties, Inglis decided to devote the summer of 1789 to visiting Canada. On 13 May of that year he set sail aboard the frigate *Dido* for the city of Quebec.

After a week at Charlottetown, the *Dido*, which had been placed at the

Bishop's disposal by the Governor of Nova Scotia, prepared to enter the Gulf of St Lawrence, but, on 1 June, "was driven by bad storms to take refuge in Gaspé Harbour on the eastern shore of French Canada." Inglis profited by the occasion to visit the scattered settlements in the vicinity, "which consisted of men from Wolfe's army, merchants from the Channel Islands, a few Loyalists, and the usual fleets of whalers and fishermen."

The Bishop was clearly interested in people, their history and circumstances. Ashore, he took care to visit the local magistrates and to learn the names and livelihood of at least some of the inhabitants. At "Gaspé and Pierce Island," he found "500 souls in a state of heathenism, chiefly papists and protestant dissenters; few members of the Church of England." There was "no place of worship." The entry in his diary for 4 June describes landing on the east side of Gaspé, where he saw "flakes and stages for curing cod. Mr. LeMesurier, a trader in the fishery, lives here and had 4,500 quintals of fish last year. Several brothers of this name, natives of Guernsey, deal in fishery business and ships arrive with stores, returning with fish for Europe. 100 fishermen from Guernsey are brought over for the summer." He also noted the poor prospects for agriculture ("Rocky shores mostly plaster of Paris. Soil resembles pulverized plaster of Paris").

On 10 June, Inglis landed at Quebec, as his diary records, "under a salute of 11 guns, and was received by artillery officers, the clergy and a curious multitude." On the same day, he met with the Governor-General and "had the first of many 'warm' discussions with Dorchester over the state of the Church in Quebec; ... [Carleton's] policy of conciliating French Canadians ... meant he was unprepared to countenance any measures forwarding the interests of the Church, if he believed they would offend the Catholic hierarchy." Inglis found only one Protestant church erected in Quebec, and that Presbyterian; there were 11 Protestant clergy, of whom three were Dissenters. By contrast, the Roman Catholics "had 200 priests and more churches than they needed." The "old Anglicans" who had arrived with the military had grown accustomed to using whatever Catholic churches were made available to them, even to the ministrations of their French Swiss clergyman, but the newly-arrived Loyalists from the former American Colonies found both these provisions intolerable. Not only were de Montmollin's sermons incomprehensible; the forms and ritual he employed did not conform to those of the Church of England.

Inglis, himself a Loyalist, deemed the present incumbent to be of no use to the English Protestants at Quebec, and tactfully persuaded him to continue to enjoy his Government stipend but to allow the Rev. Philip Toosey, a military chaplain on the spot, to minister to the congregation. As Inglis found, the same situation prevailed at Trois-Rivières with Veyssière; he was not able to persuade *him* to take an assistant, however. "[I] did not understand one twentieth of his sermon," the Bishop noted in his diary on 28 June. "Strange policy to appoint such Clergymen. Most effectual way to degrade our church and the protestant religion. Not one Canadian convert; impossible that there should be any."

On 5 August, Inglis held the first Visitation of the clergy in the Canadas. In order to see as much of his Diocese as possible, the Bishop had himself travelled as far west as Coteau-du-Lac, in the present-day Diocese of Montreal. Now all his eight clergy were gathered together at the Recollet Church in Quebec. Those from beyond the Ottawa River had travelled nearly four hundred miles to get there.

His Charge to the clergy, which he read on the opening day, gave Inglis the opportunity to make clear that he intended to remedy the general laxity in ecclesiastical matters that he had found not just in the Canadas but throughout his Diocese. His injunctions to the clergy, which he read to them on the following day (and had printed up for distribution), were concrete, specific, and clear. The clergy were to be "exemplary in their lives" and diligent in their duties; he bade them to "punctually observe the Rubrics contained in the Book of Common Prayer" and "wear their proper habits." Other injunctions dealt with the frequency of Divine Service and of Holy Communion, the regularizing of questionable baptismal practices, and the catechizing of children in church. The appropriate uses to be made of money collected at the offertory and the services for which fees might or might not be demanded were also laid down. Wardens and a Select Vestry were to be chosen every year at Easter, and no "strangers who appear in the character of clergymen" were to be permitted to do duty for them without showing proof of ordination ("letters of Orders") and displaying regularity of life and morals.

The Visitation, besides gathering the clergy in one place, provided Quebec Anglicans with the opportunity to draw together in a show of spiritual strength (so to speak), a sense of solidarity normally confined to the French-speaking community. A week after his arrival, Inglis had witnessed "4,000 Canadians assembled in [the Roman Catholic] Cathedral for procession on [the] Octave of Corpus Christi." The numbers *he* could command were far more modest: 130 confirmed on 8 August, "including two of the Governor's sons and some dissenters," and 110 at the Sacrament on the day following. It was seen to be significant that Lord and Lady Dorchester were among the communicants.

In 1765, Frances Brooke had complained that the Roman Catholics "dislike our church principally for want of music & shew." When (in 1893) the Rev. H. C. Stuart, incumbent at Three Rivers, set out to trace the progress of the Church of England in Quebec between 1759 and 1793, he described the impact of Inglis's coming with a sense of drama. "The visit," he wrote, "was a very important event. Its beginning and its ending were marked by an enthusiasm seldom witnessed in modern days. There were the acclamations of joy on the part of the populace, accompanied by the glitter of military ceremonial and the roar of artillery." Here was a show of strength at last.

On Sunday, 16 August, Inglis preached a farewell sermon at the Recollet Church and embarked on the sloop *Weasel* for Halifax the next day. His journey to Quebec had enabled him to see and counsel his clergy, to go some way towards providing suitable places of worship, and to furnish a degree of local supervision by appointing commissaries for the western and eastern districts in the persons of John Stuart and Philip Toosey, respectively.

Inglis was never to return to Quebec. His first impressions, keenly observed and carefully noted, were particularly appropriate to the nature and character of the future Diocese of Quebec. It was the fishermen of the Gaspé coast, not the snugly-housed citizens of Quebec, that the Bishop first met here: isolated, independent, struggling to survive. In 1934, Lennox Williams, sixth Lord Bishop of Quebec, in a description of St Clement's Mission on the Lower North Shore, was to observe: "the Diocese of Quebec covers a huge area. Although not so large as it was when it was first created in 1793 ... [it] is still nearly one thousand miles from east to west and three hundred and fifty miles from north to south. It is so large and the Church people are so scattered that it may fairly be said to be a Missionary Diocese."

"The Maintenance of a Protestant Clergy": 1791-1793

The Constitutional Act of 1791 changed the religious climate considerably. It divided the colony into Upper and Lower Canada with separate Governors and Assemblies for each. Whereas the Governors of what had now become the Lower Province had obstructed the establishment of Protestant institutions, the newly-appointed Lieutenant Governor of the Upper Province immediately began campaigning for the appointment of a bishop for Upper Canada. Even before leaving Britain to take up his post, John Graves Simcoe was writing to the Colonial Office, proposing as his candidate the Rev. Samuel Peters—a Loyalist, "late of Connecticut," towards whose episcopal stipend he offered £500 from his own income. Meanwhile, Bishop Inglis, as soon as he heard the provisions of the Act, wrote to Archbishop Moore proposing that, as the appointment of a second colonial bishop "was a virtual certainty," the Rev. Jonathan Boucher be chosen for the office; he also warned the Archbishop to be on his guard against Samuel Peters.

Boucher, a former rector of Annapolis, Maryland, was (like Inglis and Peters) a Loyalist. With the outbreak of hostilities, he had returned to England and had become vicar of Epsom, Surrey, in 1784. A respected scholar and philologist, Boucher was considered to be one of the most eloquent preachers of his day. Since Inglis's appointment to the See of Nova Scotia, "Boucher had never ceased urging Inglis and Seabury to act together to preserve in America the mission of the 'Holy Catholic Church,'" but the prospect of returning to North America did not appeal to him. As he survived the erection of the new diocese by only ten years, it may have been just as well that he had resisted nomination. However, if Boucher *had* become bishop of the Canadas, Inglis's biographer theorizes, "closer relations might have developed between the struggling American Protestant Episcopal Church and the largely Loyalist Anglican Church emerging in British North America." Unfortunately, "Inglis's well-known preference for American clergy was causing murmurs in London, where he was accused of giving 'too much encouragement and invitation to American-bred Divines.'"

Lord Dorchester's candidate was the Rev. Philip Toosey, Bishop's Commissary for Lower Canada. Now that Boucher was not in the running, Inglis joined in adding a warm recommendation to that of the Governor. Toosey— "a Clergyman from Sussex" and a keen agriculturist, as Mrs Simcoe described him in 1791—had been given permission to absent himself from his duties in Quebec to press his candidacy in England, where Peters had already spent two years lobbying on his own behalf.

In a Memorial dated 13 March 1793, Toosey stated that he had served as Bishop's Commissary since 1789 without salary, that he had an intimate knowledge of both Canadian provinces, and that he had "come to England, on the suggestion of the Bishop of Nova Scotia, in the hope that a salary and certain powers might be attached to his office, or that he might be appointed Bishop of one of the Provinces of Upper or Lower Canada, where he could organize Church establishments in the new Townships." In England, Toosey managed to attract powerful supporters: among them, the Bishop of Lincoln, the Bishop of London, and the Archbishop of Canterbury. The choice had ultimately to meet certain political requirements, however, and, with the Governor of each province in Canada proffering his own candidate, it was

PLATE 3 *The Bishops of the Diocese in the twentieth century:*

Top row, left to right: Lennox Williams, 1914-1935, Philip Carrington, 1935-1960
Russell Brown, 1960-1971
Bottom row, left to right, Timothy Matthews, 1971-1977, Allen Goodings, 1977-1990
Bruce Stavert, 1990-

(Photos courtesy of the Quebec Diocesan Archives)

unlikely that either one would be acceptable.

In the face of an apparent stalemate, George Pretyman, Bishop of Lincoln, who had hitherto supported Toosey, put forward a compromise candidate in the person of his own Examining Chaplain, the Rev. Jacob Mountain. An endorsement from Pretyman carried considerable weight. He had been William Pitt's tutor at Cambridge, and from 1783—the year in which Pitt became Prime Minister—until 1787, when Pretyman became bishop, he had served as his private secretary. Pretyman's "close friendship with the young statesman never faded," and until Pitt's death in 1806, "the greater part of Pitt's ecclesiastical patronage was exercised in accordance with [Pretyman's] advice." Mountain, himself a Cambridge graduate, was known to Pitt from their college days. Faced with the dilemma of two rival candidates and encouraged by the nomination of his old adviser, the Prime Minister not surprisingly chose a compromise candidate as first Lord Bishop of Quebec.

Thus it came about that Jacob Mountain, a man of refinement and sensibility—an English gentleman, scholar, and eloquent preacher, who held several livings and enjoyed good prospects for advancement at home—set out to found a new diocese on the pattern of the eighteenth-century churchmanship he had always known. Unlike the candidates he had displaced, Mountain had *no idea* that the Church in the Canadas was, or should be, required to adapt itself to local circumstances.

"To a clergyman who will transplant himself & Family into Canada," remarked an English clergyman in 1765, "it is a point of no small concern to know what footing Religion is to be upon in that New-world." A mere five weeks after Mountain's consecration in Lambeth Palace Chapel "to be Bishop of the Bishop's See of Quebec and its dependencies ... during his natural life," he and 12 of his family members set sail from the Downs aboard the *Ranger* for Quebec. On 1 November 1793, as the new bishop prepared to disembark to take up his duties, Mountain envisioned nothing less than his ready installation as the spiritual leader of the Established Church in Canada. In his mind—as borne out in the Letters Patent erecting his See—the ultimate spiritual authority in worldly matters for the colony was to be "the Archiepiscopal See of the Province of Canterbury" and "the Most Reverend Father in God, John, Lord Archbishop of Canterbury, Primate of all England and Metropolitan."

An attempt to settle at least some of the religious questions prevalent in the Canadas had been made in the recent Constitutional Act, and seven of its 50 sections dealt with ecclesiastical affairs. The provisions of the Quebec Act of 1774, which had allowed considerable autonomy to the Roman

Catholic Church (including the collection of tithes by its priests), were maintained in the Act of 1791, but the position of the Church of England was strengthened. The Act of 1774 had made a general provision for the "encouragement of the Protestant religion, and for the maintenance and support of a Protestant Clergy"; the new Act, however, specified how the funds to do so were to be raised. Lands were to be appropriated in each province, the allotment of which was to be in the hands of the Governor. The "rents and profits arising from these allotments" were to be applied "solely to the support of a Protestant Clergy." Provision was also made for erecting and endowing "Parsonages or Rectories" and installing incumbents in them, subject to the "right of institution and ecclesiastical jurisdiction of the Bishop of Nova Scotia." Setting aside one-seventh of the land in each township as it was surveyed would seem to have put the Church in the Canadas on a firm footing at last. As Carrington asserts, "the provision of land was, of course, the normal method of endowment ... so that it was not unnatural that the Church should be provided for in this way." Unfortunately, the plan had fundamental flaws.

It may be argued on the one hand that from the time of the Conquest "it was distinctly understood in the Imperial Parliament that the Anglican Establishment was to be the National Church" in Canada; it has been equally maintained on the other that, although it may well have been their *intention* to give the Anglican Church the prestige of establishment, the Government failed to make this crystal clear.

The problem was partly one of terminology. "Protestant clergy," to Anglicans, applied exclusively to clergy of the Church of England. In the Anglican view, such Nonconformists as the Presbyterians—although their church had been recognized as the Established Church of Scotland since 1707—to say nothing of the Methodists, Baptists, and a multitude of other Protestant sects, were not intended to benefit from the Clergy Reserves, as these lands were called.

The provisions of the Constitutional Act seemed to bear out the Anglican claim. Section 39, for example, states that incumbents to be granted Rectories endowed from the Clergy Lands were to "enjoy them as fully as do the Incumbents of Parsonages in England," yet it would have been unthinkable to install any but Church of England clergy in an English parish. Similarly, placing all such presentations under the jurisdiction of a Church of England bishop would have been an odd thing to do if Dissenting clergy had equally been intended by the Act.

Although the provision of land to support religious institutions seemed a practical plan at the time, in fact "it was long before this became effective, and by then it was the subject of fierce political controversy." In the meantime, the Roman Catholic Church, with its finances assured by state-recognized tithing, had achieved the status of virtual establishment in Quebec. When Jacob Mountain arrived from England with the understanding that he was to be bishop of the Established Church, of which he always maintained there could be only one, "he immediately proceeded to put the other churches in what he conceived to be their proper places." It was his unswerving belief in the exclusive rights of the Church of England that set the course of Mountain's episcopate.

"If he had come to the Canadas simply as a missionary bishop, to perform episcopal functions which are expected in the twentieth century," Mountain's biographer remarks, "then his record, in a few respects, might be viewed with some impatience." It was with an essentially unworkable ecclesiastical policy on the part of the Government, and an almost entirely inappropriate image of the eighteenth-century English bishop in his mind that Mountain strove to fulfil his mission. When this is understood, "his conduct appears to be coherent and correct, and he himself emerges as a man of stern loyalties, inflexible determination, unfailing resource, and outstanding ability."

Territorial Limits of the Diocese of Quebec: 1793 and 1993

When the Diocese of Quebec was erected by Letters Patent (dated 28 June 1793), the Bishop of Nova Scotia's Commission for Quebec, which had been issued on 13 August 1787—to be held at the King's pleasure—was revoked. Thus Jacob Mountain, appointed to the new See by the same Letters Patent, became responsible for "the Provinces of Lower and Upper Canada and their Dependencies"; that is, the territory west of Labrador and north to the domain of the Hudson's Bay Company; the Magdalen Islands, and Anticosti in the Gulf of St Lawrence, the Gaspé Peninsula (excluding New Brunswick), southward to the border of the United States, and westward to the shores of Lake Superior.

This vast Diocese was to be successively reduced in size, first by the erection in 1839 of the Diocese of Toronto (which was, in turn, further divided into the Dioceses of Huron, Ontario, Ottawa, Algoma, and Niagara) and later by that of the Diocese of Montreal.

When the latter was erected in 1850, the Letters Patent revising the boundaries of the old Diocese stated "that the limits thereof should ... in future comprise the Districts of Quebec, Three Rivers and the Gaspé only."

It was soon discovered, however, that "a certain District in the province of Canada, called the District of St Francis, was ... unintentionally omitted from the said Dioceses of Quebec and of Montreal, and from each of them, and is not now included in any Bishoprick or Diocese." It was therefore necessary to repair this flaw in the Letters Patent and redraw the border with the orphaned district being reincorporated into the Diocese of Quebec. Within this territory, so narrowly reclaimed, lay the site of the reigning bishop's dearest project: Bishop's College, Lennoxville, a training ground for locally bred clergy that had been in operation for a mere nine years. Thus, by an Order in Council dated 21 February 1853, the western boundary of the Diocese took on its current shape.

On the east, the Diocese had shared a border with the original Diocese of Nova Scotia. In 1839, coincidentally with the erection of the Diocese of Toronto, the Diocese of Newfoundland, which included Labrador, was carved out of the Diocese of Nova Scotia. Currently the Diocese of Quebec, north of Blanc Sablon on the Labrador Peninsula, is bounded by two dioceses: Western Newfoundland, and Eastern Newfoundland and Labrador, two of the three bishoprics formed in 1976 from the original Diocese of Newfoundland. Across the Baie des Chaleurs lies the Diocese of Fredericton, created as a separate diocese out of Nova Scotia in 1845. The civil provinces of Quebec and New Brunswick are adjacent, but the hinterland through which the diocesan boundary runs is devoid of parishes; these dioceses, therefore, do not seem to be regarded as bordering one another.

On the American frontier, the Diocese of Quebec shares a long tradition of border ministry predating the erection of two neighbouring Sees, the Episcopal Dioceses of New Hampshire and Vermont.

The Diocese of Moosonee, erected in 1872, fixed part of the frontier to the north in a great circular sweep just south of Lake Mistassini. The erection of the Diocese of the Arctic in 1933 gave separate jurisdiction to the far north, bordering that of Quebec just south of Schefferville. The latter community, although part of another diocese, has in fact been administered by the Diocese of Quebec.

Thus, the Diocese of Quebec entered its two-hundredth year with boundaries that had been fixed for a mere six decades, bordered directly by five Canadian and two American dioceses. It had taken 140 years and more than five episcopates to settle its present dimensions.

Although it has lost much of its original land mass to other episcopal jurisdictions, the Diocese of Quebec is still one of the largest in the country. Of the 30 Anglican dioceses in Canada, only those of the Arctic,

Keewatin, Moosonee, and the Yukon cover a larger area each than does Quebec. Of these, the largest population and the highest degree of urbanization are to be found in the Diocese of Quebec, but the number of Anglicans within its borders gives no sign of this advantage.

"How many may you be?"—Anglican Population in the Diocese of Quebec
It is not surprising that the Anglican (and indeed the Protestant) population in Quebec should be relatively small. The port records speak for themselves. Although some 32,000 immigrants from abroad disembarked at Quebec in 1846, for example, it is estimated that perhaps 1,900 remained in the lower province, while about 26,000 went on to Upper Canada, "and possibly one-fifth of all passed on to the United States."

At first glance, it seems odd that settlers would not wish to establish themselves where the wilderness had been broken and in the vicinity of such amenities as an established colony had to offer. Yet a glance at some of the guides and handbooks available to British settlers may explain why so many immigrants hardly paused at Quebec on their journey "up the river." Adam Fergusson, a Scottish advocate and director of a Highland emigration society, visited the Canadas and the United States in 1831 to collect information on local conditions. In his book of practical advice for would-be settlers, he wrote:

> Notwithstanding ... the many advantages which approximation to the sea-coast holds out, I should certainly not consider Lower Canada likely to realize the hopes of British settlers....
>
> To many, the difference of religion, and scarcity of Protestant churches, will prove a drawback. To many more, the preponderance of the French language, laws, and manners, will create a serious obstacle. Nor am I aware of any existing circumstances, in the Lower Province, which can be said to counterbalance these objections.
>
> It is no doubt true, that many individual instances of prosperity are to be met with in Lower Canada, among agricultural settlers from Britain and Ireland; but these must be viewed as exceptions, and not followed as a rule.
>
> Even the land-measure will somewhat tend to embarrass a stranger, as it is the *arpent* (about one fifth less than the English acre) which is in use, and the tenure and titles of his property will still more perplex him.

As the prospect of freehold ownership of land was one of the main attractions of the New World, most settlers in the Canadas preferred to forego the uncertainties of land tenure under the seigneurial system in the lower province. Furthermore, Upper Canada, as one historian has put it, "might be expected to develop a society basically similar to that of England." In fact, population movements from established settlements to the west and to the south have been of perennial concern in the Diocese of Quebec.

Twenty years after Fergusson's assessment of the relative prospects offered by the upper and the lower province was published, Bishop G. J. Mountain was to plead with the SPG that the uniform reduction of support to clergy in the Canadas was inequitable. In 1851, the wheat crop in Upper Canada amounted to 15.33 bushels per inhabitant, he pointed out, while in Lower Canada the per capita yield was only 3.46 minots (eight minots equalling nine bushels).

> Most of the Church of England missions in this diocese [the Bishop argued] are either in back-wood settlements, often with desperately bad summer roads, or among the fishing-settlements of the Gulph. With reference to the former class of missions, the proportion of the emigrants who remain in this part of Canada consists largely of those who are too poor to proceed farther. And it is notorious that if they become a little prosperous they are constantly prompted to move westward, and thus plant themselves out of the limits of the diocese.

Population movements within the Diocese itself, often prompted by economic factors, would frequently strain the resources of rural communities. Effects were particularly felt where settlements were small. This was the situation described by the Rev. Louis Wurtele in his annual report to the Church Society on the sorry state of his mission at Acton Vale in 1866:

> The circumstances that have affected the Township of Acton for the last two years have been of a very depressing nature.
>
> There are so many vacant houses at the present time, that compared with what it was three years ago, Acton Vale might be called "The deserted Village."
>
> No more than half the houses are occupied, and these mostly by women and children, their husbands being obliged to seek employment elsewhere.
>
> Under such circumstances, it would be unreasonable to expect much [in the way of paying the Diocesan assessment] of this Mission.

Before the prosperity of Acton had begun to decline, the congregation had contracted a debt of $600 to secure a parsonage for their missionary. As there was still a debt of $380 outstanding on their church, the "thirty Protestant families" of the mission found themselves hard pressed.

With the growth of towns and cities, young people were increasingly drawn away from their rural parishes. This was particularly true of the Eastern Townships, traditionally a Protestant stronghold in the predominantly Roman Catholic province of Quebec. The Rev. C. B. Washer's account of his mission at Bury, for example, is far from untypical of reports from the countryside at the turn of the century. As he wrote to the Church Society in 1901, all three of the churches in his mission of Bury had sustained losses during the year.

> [At St Paul's] ... The removal of Mr. Josiah Boydell and family from the Mission is regretted on all hands. They were hearty helpers in every good work. Who will take their place?

> [At St John's] The Church population of this district is still small, with a tendency to diminish.

> [At St Thomas'] No increase of Church population; natural increase in size of families counterbalanced by the removal of persons old enough to go away.

The grim tale of a declining Anglican population formed part of Archbishop Carrington's retrospective of his quarter-century episcopate. Yet in his monthly letter for April 1960, written on the eve of his retirement and printed as usual in the *Diocesan Gazette*, he handles the subject more as a fact of life than as grounds for discouragement.

> Of course I was faced with the problem of dwindling members in some parts of the Diocese, and the fear was commonly expressed that the English population was diminishing so fast that there was really no future for us; it was represented that churches would be closed and numbers decrease. Churches have indeed been closed in country districts from which our Anglican population has moved away, and this is always a painful thing; but it is more to the point to thank God that they served their purpose during the time when they were required.

He went on to remind the reader that while some 20 churches had indeed been closed, "more than twenty new churches have been built or are in process of building" (see Window 36). The thrust of his remarks brings home the fact that there seems always to have been, in this diocese, a preoccupation with numbers.

> I came across a doleful statement of Bishop Mountain [Carrington continues], made by him a hundred years ago, in which he saw the future in the darkest

possible terms, and predicted the decline of the church. At that time there were about 25,000 Anglicans in the Diocese, and it has continued at that level ever since. Previous to the war of 1914-1918 it was 25,000, but sank to 22,000 during the war; but between 1918 and 1935 it came up to 25,000 again. During the last war it sank again to 22,000; but this year I note it is increasing again. I believe it will reach the old level.

Early in the 1890s, during Bishop Andrew Hunter Dunn's episcopate, the Church Society began to include yearly statistics of the "total number of souls" on parish rolls throughout the Diocese as a regular part of its annual reports. Based as they were on returns filed by individual parishes (some of which, it is noted, neglected to report), the figures leave something to be desired, but they are certainly more reliable than the Census. In 1894, these Church Society statistics fixed church membership at 21,398, with the figure dipping to 19,992 in 1901 and rising to 22,514 in 1911. This range is maintained steadily (with the exception of a drop to a low of 17,921 in 1920), into mid-century, when membership rose to 23,196 in 1952. Thereafter, a steady downward slide is discernible, beginning with 1970 when numbers fall to 17,600. Before the decade was out, the rolls registered 11,810. By 1983, membership had fallen below 10,000 souls, but rose the following year to 10,053 and continued to make modest gains until 1987 when it dipped again, to 9,587.

The highest proportions of Anglicans in the general population within the Diocese of Quebec have traditionally resided in particular areas. They appear to be concentrated in such outlying regions as the Lower North Shore, the Gaspé Peninsula, and parts of the Eastern Townships. Given the overall trend, especially among young people, of migration away from economically depressed rural areas, it is not surprising that many Anglicans have moved on to urban centres in other dioceses. Political uncertainty has played a role as well in decreasing the numbers of Anglicans in the Diocese. Whereas, according to the *Anglican Yearbook* for 1992, the neighbouring Diocese of Fredericton, with a territory one-tenth the size of that of the Diocese of Quebec, reported 41,329 Anglicans on its parish rolls, Quebec recorded 9,364 members for the same year.

By its more severe critics, the Anglican Church in Canada has been painted as "snobbish and wealthy, ... its clergy content with the comfort of the towns and unwillingly to face the rugged life of itinerants in the deep bush." Canadian Anglicans have not infrequently been regarded as claiming for themselves a position of privilege, not only in religion, but socially and politically as well. Yet circumstances clearly alter cases. While, as Nancy Christie suggests, "in Upper Canada the privileged position of the Anglican church more accurately reflected the reciprocal relationship between church and state in England," the same Church foundered in the Maritimes largely because of "the smug assumption ... that the traditions and rituals of the Anglican church need not be adapted to colonial circumstances."

Each diocese has been shaped by its peculiar history. The situation in Quebec was quite different from that in the Maritimes or Upper Canada. Jacob Mountain, it is true, attempted to impose his own rigid view of a religious Establishment, but his successors could show remarkable sensitivity to local conditions. Anglicans have always formed a small segment of the population in this province; throughout its history, the Diocese has invariably had to struggle to maintain itself. "Despite the fact that many English-speaking Loyalists settled in Lower Canada, it was apparent by the beginning of the nineteenth century that Protestantism was destined, in that province, to be a minority religion." Knowledge and acceptance of this fact of life have done much to shape the destinies of the Diocese of Quebec.

PLATE 4   *St James' Church, Trois-Rivières, formerly a Recollet chapel, is the oldest Anglican church building in the diocese.*

CHAPTER II

Branches of the Vine:
A Glance at Anglican Polity and Party

Since the time of its first foundation in North America," writes A. R. Kelley, "the Church of England has been known by various names, some official and others popular." The term "Episcopal," although now seldom used in Canada, was employed in a variety of eighteenth-century documents referring to the Church, and persisted well into the nineteenth century in this country. The expression "The Established Church" was sometimes used, but correctly so only in Nova Scotia, where the Church of England enjoyed this legal status. Kelley traced the appearance of the word "Anglican" to describe the Church and its doctrines to the Tractarians, "who spoke of Anglican Orders" in the 1840s. Officially, however—from 1801—the Church was known as "The United Church of England and Ireland"; this ceased to be the case with the disestablishment of the Church of Ireland in 1871.

From the earliest years of the twentieth century, there were moves to provide the Canadian Church with a distinctive name of its own, but all efforts failed until 1921, when General Synod (rather lamely) adopted the title "The Church of England in Canada." Popularly, however, the term "Anglican" had already taken root to describe organizations within the Canadian Church—the Anglican Young People's Association, for example, formed in 1902. Although there was resistance to any further change for some time, by mid-century "a general feeling" had arisen that, "since the church was popularly and universally known by the title 'Anglican,'" and because "the Canadian sense of self-identity was stronger than ever before, ... persistence in retaining the old name would be foolish." In 1955, the Church officially adopted the name "The Anglican Church of Canada."

No sooner had the name been changed than it seemed to pose problems. Fears were voiced that the designation "Anglican" (or *anglicane*, as it translates into French) was suggestive of an "English" church, ethnocentric and unwelcoming to non-English speakers. The name seems to have created no difficulty among Anglicans within the Diocese of Quebec. From outside Quebec, however, came the impulse for further adaptation of the name, at any rate as it appeared in French; this move, as one churchman at least has suggested, was intended to appease the forces of nationalism. "As nationalistic feeling grew in Quebec, it was found that Anglican Church was not a popular title. Our French title is, therefore, l'église episcopale du Canada," remarked J. G. McCausland.

This change, presumably meant to ease *their* position, was far from welcomed by Anglicans in the Diocese of Quebec. As the preamble of a Resolution taken at the 1987 Diocesan Synod makes clear, there was "considerable resistance on the part of both clergy and laity to the change of designation," particularly because "current language legislation in Quebec would make the French designation the official designation." It was therefore moved that

> [t]his 70th Ordinary Session of the Synod of the Diocese of Quebec hereby registers its dissidence with General Synod's designation in French of the Anglican Church of Canada as "l'Eglise Episcopale du Canada" and respectfully requests the Bishop to advise General Synod of the same and to take any other action he may deem appropriate.

The Resolution was adopted unanimously.

Some confusion still persists about the name. It is perhaps worth noting that the 1995 Telephone Directory for Quebec City and Region lists two of the three Anglican places of worship in Greater Quebec under the designation *Églises: Anglicane:* "St Michael's Church," Sillery, and "Cathédrale Episcopale de la Ste-Trinité." Under a separate heading, all its own, is "Trinity Church," Ste-Foy: *Église Episcopale.*

Worthy of All to Be Received

Granted that the Anglican Church of Canada as an autonomous member of a worldwide communion has certain characteristics peculiar to itself, it seems reasonable in any examination of what an Anglican believes and does, to proceed with at least some reference to the stock from which the Canadian communion springs.

In the 1960s, Paul Ferris, writing as a layman and "an outsider," produced what may be called a "fair but critical" examination of the Church of England. In preparing for the task, and in attempting to get a feel for the Church, he talked to a wide spectrum of the clergy: bishops, curates, industrial chaplains, and university theologians. Yet, having done so, far from gaining a clearer, more cohesive picture of the institution, he was increasingly struck by its "careful" and "uninstitutional" vagueness. "Going from one clergyman to another," he observed, "it's sometimes hard to believe they inhabit the same Church; 'diversity' becomes contradiction."

> Only an idiosyncratic church with its roots in the obstinacies of the English temperament could survive the tensions [Ferris concluded]. "The Anglican theological position," a clergyman reminded me, "has been to secure general agreement on primary matters and to let the rest go by private assent. Elizabeth I's statement about not making windows into men's souls is a good one."

The wide spectrum of belief and practice in the Anglican tradition has been traced, at least in part, to a peculiarity in English law. Once inducted, an incumbent in England has traditionally been virtually unremovable from his "living" by civil or ecclesiastical authority.

> The result of this has been the development within the Established Church of a most startling diversity of doctrine and ritual practice, varying from what closely resembles that of the Church of Rome to the broadest Liberalism and the extremest evangelical Protestantism. This broad comprehensiveness, which to outsiders looks like ecclesiastical anarchy, is the characteristic note of the Church of England; it may be, and has been, defended as consonant with Christian charity and suited to the genius of a people not remarkable for logical consistency; but it makes it all the more difficult to say what the religion of Englishmen actually is, even within the English Church.

Writing shortly after the turn of the century, the Rev. William Hunt (a President of the Royal Society and historian of the early Church) furnished a basic definition of the Church of England, centred on its history and its doctrines as prescribed by Parliament.

> The Church of England claims to be a branch of the Catholic and Apostolic Church; it is episcopal in its essence and administration, and [in England] is established by law in that the state recognizes it as the national church of the English people, an integral part of the constitution of the realm. It existed, in name and in fact, as the church of the English people centuries before that people became a united nation, and, in spite of changes in doctrine and ritual, it remains the same church that was planted in England at the end of the sixth century.

Its doctrines, he continued, "may be gathered from its Book of Common Prayer as finally revised in 1661, ... from the XXXIX Articles, published with royal authority in 1571; and from the First and Second Books of Homilies of 1549 and 1562, respectively, which are declared in Article xxxv to contain sound doctrine."

In Canada, as in Britain, it was customary that all candidates for Holy Orders, before ordination and after satisfying the examiners as to their knowledge of Scripture and the doctrines of the Church, subscribe formally to the Thirty-nine Articles, and promise to conform to the Liturgy as well. The Quebec Diocesan Archives preserve copies of the forms signed by hopeful ordinands and those clergy about to be licenced within the Diocese. In the early days, each transcribed the whole formula, with date and signature, in a book set aside for that purpose and retained by the bishop. The following entry from the Diocese Book is typical:

> I John Butler now to be licenced to the Mission of Kingsey & parts adjacent in the County of Drummond & District of St Francis in the Diocese of Quebec do willingly & ex animo subscribe to the Thirty-nine Articles of the Church of England & to the three Articles of the Thirty-sixth Canon & to all things that are contained in them, this third day of March in the year 1843.
> [signed] John Butler
> I do declare that I will conform to the Liturgy of the United Church of England & Ireland as it is now by Law established.
> [signed] John Butler

An oath of allegiance to the Crown was taken at the same time but recorded elsewhere. It was not for nothing that the Anglican clergy were regarded as a bastion of loyalty to Her Majesty and Her Majesty's Government.

In 1883, the Diocese adopted printed forms with appropriate blanks for candidates' signatures. The text was considerably revised in 1889. For the first time, the apostolic nature of the ministry was to be specifically subscribed to, and there was new stress on the force of "lawful authority." By 1866, the promise to conform to the enactments—past and future—of Diocesan and Provincial Synod had been added to the ordinand's pledge. One of the new forms, completed in 1889 and pasted into the Book of Subscriptions, illustrates these changes in emphasis:

> I Edwin Weary now to be licenced to the mission of Rivière du Loup do solemnly make the following declaration. I assent to the Thirty-nine Articles of Religion, and to the Book of Common Prayer, and of the Ordering of Bishops, Priests and Deacons; I believe the Doctrine of the Church of England as therein set forth to be agreeable to the Word of God; and in Public prayers and administration of the sacraments I will use the Form of the said Book pre-

scribed, and none other, except so far as shall be ordered by lawful authority.
[signed] Edwin Weary

I Edwin Weary do willingly subscribe to and declare that I assent to, and abide by the Canons which have been or shall be from time to time passed by the Provincial Synod or the Synod of the Diocese of Quebec.
[signed] Edwin Weary

In 1896 the enactments of General Synod were added to the list as well.

Although the Thirty-nine Articles, which were drawn up at the height of Protestantism after the Reformation, remain "on the books," High churchmen and Anglo-Catholics object to their Protestant bias and largely disregard them in the performance of their priestly functions. It is chiefly the Evangelical (or Low-church) wing of the Anglican Church that regards the Articles as having more than "historical interest" in the Church today. Pledges of adherence to the Articles (as specified in the declarations shown above) have been modified to require merely the "general assent" of ordinands. Today in the Diocese of Quebec, candidates for Holy Orders are no longer examined on the Articles at all.

Meanwhile, towards the end of the nineteenth century the question of Christian Reunion had come into prominence. Leaders of the worldwide Anglican Communion, meeting at the Third Lambeth Conference, "attempted [finally] to define those standards of historic faith and order which Anglicans should maintain as fundamental." The result, called the "Lambeth Quadrilateral," pointed to four essentials: the Bible, the creeds and general councils of Christendom, the ancient sacramental order, and the apostolic type of ministry, bishops, priests, and deacons – "points," Carrington suggested, "on which all Christians had happily agreed together for so many centuries."

For the individual Anglican, however, the Lambeth Quadrilateral has probably had little impact. To most laymen, the Prayer Book and the liturgy have been the chief distinguishing features of Anglicanism. The first Anglican missionaries coming upon scattered churchmen in the wilderness spoke of the effect on these hearers of the old familiar forms. In 1820, for example, the Rev. John Suddard, SPG Missionary at Gaspé, reported to the Society in London, as follows:

It is highly gratifying to witness the satisfaction communicated to these several settlements by the visits and residence [on the Gaspé peninsula] of a Minister. Several elderly men, who in their youthful days had attended the church service, hearing the same prayers once again under similar circumstances, were so affected, that they declare language ineffectual to convey their feelings.

To others unfamiliar with the Anglican tradition, the liturgy and psalmody were to be powerful incitements to join the Church. While still a parish priest, the future Bishop Stewart found congregations among people where there were

> neither churches nor Prayer Books, nor any that knew how to use them, except only two families. The people were as much Strangers to sacred music as they were to the use of the Prayer Book. The latter he could himself teach, and did teach to many; but in the former he had no skill. So sensible, however, was he of the value of Psalmody in the worship of God, that he soon procured a good teacher of sacred music ...

The combined impact of these aspects of the liturgy was not lost upon the worshippers. Jacob Mountain, while on a confirmation tour of the Eastern Townships in 1809, confessed in a private letter that he was not equal to expressing the effect that "this truly devotional music" in Stewart's church had had upon him "otherwise than by saying, that if you had been with me I am sure you would have wept outright."

The centrality of the Book of Common Prayer (BCP) as the mainstay of Anglican worship was to persist unchallenged for many decades. More than 150 years after Bishop Mountain had been so moved by a rendition of the service in a simple country church, Archbishop Carrington (who was prominent in framing the "renewed" Prayer Book of 1962) paid tribute to the place of the liturgy in the life of the Church. "[It] is mainly through the Prayer Book services that the Anglican Church builds up the spiritual life of its people and witnesses to its special tradition," he maintained.

In nineteenth-century Canada, the Church of England was "almost alone" among Protestant churches in retaining its unity:

> It was not because of an absence of differences, for at times the divergence between the high and low church parties threatened a division. Three main factors prevented a schism. Organizations and discipline were two, but were not peculiar to the Church of England. The unique binding force was the prayer book.

It remains to be seen whether the Book of Alternative Services (BAS), introduced experimentally by virtue of a 1983 Resolution passed by General Synod, will displace the Book of Common Prayer in the affections of Anglicans, or provide a defining and unifying focus to Anglican life, as the

BCP has done.

Methods of introducing the BAS have varied widely from diocese to diocese. In 1985, the Diocesan Doctrine and Worship Commission produced guidelines (publicized in the *Quebec Diocesan Gazette*) for the use of the BAS in the Diocese of Quebec:

> Perhaps the most important question in the minds of most people is, Who decides whether a congregation uses the Prayer Book or the Alternative Services? Without laying down hard rules about the **method**, the statement provides that such decisions are to be made **jointly** by the Minister and Congregation using procedures which are mutually acceptable to arrive at those decisions.

In the absence of figures to establish the extent to which either the BAS or the BCP has served consistently for parish use in the Diocese since 1985, it is difficult to assess the balance of opinion on liturgical change at the parish level.

In 1988 the Diocesan Executive Council (DEC) drew up and forwarded to General Synod a Memorial on the subject of the BAS, "requesting the appointment of a commission, separate from the Doctrine and Worship Committee, to review the Book, in relation to its theological comprehensiveness, its liturgical adequacy, and its literary style." This suggests caution. It must be pointed out, however, that the Prayer Book Society of Canada (PBSC), which has opposed the replacement of the of BCP by the BAS because of the latter's theological, liturgical, and literary inadequacies— precisely those areas mentioned in the DEC Memorial—has few adherents here. In 1995, the PBSC claimed a scattering of individual members in the Diocese of Quebec, and the establishment of only one branch there. Episcopal preference, which according to the guidelines of the Doctrine and Worship Commission is to determine the form used for the Offices of Confirmation and Ordination, has favoured the BAS since 1991.

"A most startling diversity": The "Many Mansions" of Anglican Tradition
To understand developments in the Diocese of Quebec since its founding, account must be taken of the changing visions of the Church by those who strove to build its institutions and spread its influence.

When the first resident bishop to the Canadas was preparing to depart for Quebec to assume his new duties, the Church in England had been experiencing a long period of aridity and decline. The French Revolution in 1789 had served principally to stiffen the conservatism of the English and, as Vidler remarks, "to postpone the pressure for reform in Church and State which everywhere made itself felt sooner or later in the nineteenth century." Had it not been for this reaction, "parliament might have been reformed, the dissenters, Catholic and Protestant, freed from their disabilities, and the slave trade abolished a generation earlier than they were."

Except for the stirrings of the eighteenth-century Evangelical Revival under such powerful leaders as the Wesleys, William Wilberforce, and others, the Church of England was, in spirit, "dry, commonsensical, averse to 'enthusiasm,' acclimatized to the Age of Reason." Abuses were rife; "pluralism, absenteeism, sinecures, extremes of clerical poverty and wealth went unchallenged." Since the accession of the Hanoverian line in 1714, a growing slackness had marked the performance of clerical duties. Daily services were discontinued, holy days unobserved, and Holy Communion celebrated infrequently. Even the realm's great churches were affected, as S. H. Nicholson (writing on English church music) makes clear:

> Cathedral music reached its lowest ebb in the latter part of the eighteenth and early nineteenth centuries. Little interest seems to have been shown in the choirs, which were allowed to get into an appalling state of slackness. In London, for instance, the same person often held a lay-clerkship at different places like the Abbey, St. Paul's and the Chapel Royal, and did duty either himself, or quite as often by deputy, in all three places. Thus, even as late as Queen Victoria's coronation [in 1838], of the three chief London choirs … only one in fact existed—

With such visible widespread evidence as decaying church buildings, starveling curates, and the neglected poor, the stewardship of the clergy was generally held in low regard. Advancement in the Church depended more on sound Whig principles than on learning or on spiritual gifts. The tone of the household in a well-bred English clerical family of the period is perhaps best pictured through the recollections of James Anthony Froude, born in 1818. His father, the subject of the following description, was Rector of the parish, Archdeacon of Totnes, and a Justice of the Peace. He enjoyed "a moderate fortune of his own," and belonged to the landed class:

> His children knew him as a continually busy, useful man of the world, a learned and cultivated antiquary, and an accomplished artist. My brothers and I were excellently educated, and were sent to school and college. Our spiritual lessons did not go beyond the Catechism. We were told that our business in life was to work and to make an honorable position for ourselves. About doctrine, Evangelical or Catholic, I do not think that in my early boyhood I ever heard

a single word, in church or out of it.... [The Church] did not instruct us in mysteries, it did not teach us to make religion a special object of our thoughts; it taught us to use religion as a light by which to see our way along the road of duty.

Jacob Mountain was much this sort of person: cultivated, urbane, having a high sense of position and a low view of "enthusiasm" (that peculiar brand of "ill-regulated or misdirected religious emotion" associated with the Evangelicals). He was, as his son George recalled, "thoroughly averse from all flourish or ostentation in religion" and "friendly ... to all exterior gravity and decorum in sacred things." Like Archdeacon Froude, family concerns loomed large for Mountain, and he gave much care to the rearing and education of his sons (see Window 4). Such men were "High churchmen" in that they were, as Vidler defines the type, "jealously concerned to preserve the property and privileges of the Church as a national institution. They were politically, rather than theologically, High Church."

To his critics, both recent and contemporary, Mountain made an unsuitable Colonial Bishop. More concerned with questions of precedence in Council, display at levees, political intrigue, and personal (or family) aggrandizement than he was "with the spiritual interests of the backwoods settlers committed to his care," both his habits and his manners were appropriate "rather for an English Bishop than a Missionary Bishop of Canada."

If, in retrospect, one tends to criticize Mountain for pouring his energies into letters of complaint to Government about "the respectable establishments, the substantial revenues, & the extensive power & privileges of the Church of Rome," rather than into appeals to private donors (as his successor, Bishop Stewart was to do), one ought to remember that Mountain was merely calling upon the authorities to fulfil the compact between Church and State that was held to exist in the society of his day.

To the modern reader, it may seem incomprehensible that Mountain, who penned constant pleas that clergy be sent to serve his Diocese, retained as "Evening Lecturer at Quebec" (from 1800 to 1811) the newly-ordained John Jackson, while groups of settlers in the hinterland remained unserved. By the standards of the day, however, maintaining the semblance of an entourage at Quebec must have seemed more pressing than dispatching to the wilderness a man "whose character [in Mountain's words] had obtained the approbation of persons of the greatest respectability here." One must take a similar view of the Bishop's plea for the dignity of a Dean and Chapter at Quebec before the majority of the outlying settlements of his Diocese had either church or missionary.

PLATE 5A *Interior of the Cathedral of the Holy Trinity dressed with evergreens, Christmas, 1896. Note the old regimental colours of H.M. 69th Regiment deposited here in 1870.*

PLATE 5B *Some of the Archbishops and Bishops who attended the Consecration and Enthronement of the Rt Rev. Lennox Williams, 25 January 1915.* (Photo credit: *Church Life*, Toronto)

Although he undoubtedly laid down foundations on which others could build, Jacob Mountain seems never to have modified his eighteenth-century concept of the Church or of its relation to the state. As his biographer concludes:

> It was to government that the Bishop looked for clergy, for clergy stipends, for assistance in church building. It is no matter for wonder that when Portland was replaced, when Pitt died, when Roman Catholic opposition hardened, and when administrations arose, both in England and in the Canadas, who "knew not" Jacob, he found it difficult to adjust himself to realities and continued to dream of an Establishment which was never to have a substantial existence.

Jacob Mountain was a churchman of the early eighteenth-century type, a "High" churchman, but not as that appellation would be understood in the context of Tractarianism and the Oxford Movement of the 1830s. *His* branch of the Church of England, if not exactly "asleep," was "only slowly and in parts rousing itself into activity."

The division into religious parties that characterized the controversial elements of mid-nineteenth-century churchmanship was quickly transplanted into the colonial setting. The Diocese of Quebec soon had its share of Tractarians and Evangelicals, some of whom were to engage in more or less acrimonious debate.

The third party, the Liberals or old Latitudinarians, do not seem to have been represented, at least among the clergy, for many years, but would later emerge in the guise of Modernists. Many clergy of course were only moderately influenced by one party or another, but to grasp the impact on the Diocese of this ferment in the Church at large, it will be useful to glance briefly at the divisions of greatest moment here.

The Tractarians saw the Church as distinct from and more ancient than the State. They claimed to inherit, "through the continuity of an episcopate which derived its sacred authority unbroken from the Apostles, the true tradition of a Catholic, sacramental, priestly church," and to be heirs to the party "represented in the eighteenth-century by the Non-jurors who had refused to take the oath of allegiance to William III by reason of their belief in the divine right of anointed kings." Through the influence of such men as Jasper Nicolls (first principal of Bishop's College), whose student life at Oxford had coincided with the movement, Tractarianism was to have a profound effect; Bishop's was to have an impact on the Diocese and on the Church in the Canadas as a whole, as "an important exponent of Anglican theology ... a frontier outpost against the forces of Methodism, Evangelicalism and

Liberalism."

Other clergy in the Diocese who were deeply imbued with Tractarian principles included Armine Mountain (Bishop G. J. Mountain's son) and Henry Roe. To the High church sympathies young Mountain would have acquired at home were added the influences of his student years at Oxford, centre of the Tractarian movement. Roe, for his part, was among the first students trained at Bishop's College, and, after more than 20 years as a parish priest, became Dean of Divinity there.

Although an avowed Tractarian, Roe could still value those whose churchmanship differed from his own, as his fine tribute to the Rev. C. P. Reid (who had Evangelical leanings) amply shows. The more distressing, then, was a savage assault, launched in 1858 by the Evangelical clergyman Gilbert Percy, on Roe and his ministry.

In a pamphlet addressed to his congregation at St Matthew's Chapel, Quebec, Roe's efforts to meet Percy's accusations make clear the animosity of the latter's attack. After conceding that "there is not a single Clergyman in the Diocese who is more Romanistic in his doings, feelings, and tendencies" than he, Roe denied the thrust of Percy's attack (which had been printed in the local Press under the guise of a letter to the Bishop):

> I am accused of being a "modern innovator," of striving "to introduce Oxford novelties and to revive exploded superstitions,"—of "an insane desire for the revival of practices long obsolete," ... and of having thus "excited divisions, given origin to doubts, and stirred up strife in the congregation of the Lord." These are grave charges,— I challenge the world to fix one of them upon me,—to point out a single instance, in my teaching or my doings in which I have stepped out of the line of honest or even moderate churchmanship, or have gone beyond or beside the teaching of the Prayer Book, or the unanimous voice of our great divines....The prayer book to which (in common with Dr. Percy) I have so solemnly declared my "unfeigned assent and consent," I confess, I thoroughly believe and love, and to teach and carry out the system of religion laid down in it, is the object of my life. But an innovator in doctrine, or an introducer of novelties in ritual matters, I am not and by the grace of God, I never will be.

To Roe's pamphlet, dated 10 May, Percy rattled off a rapid reply three days later in the form of a letter to the Editor of the *Quebec Gazette*, in which he referred to Roe, incongruously enough, as a "mousing owl," "letting fly his little harmless bird-bolts." "I shall not suffer myself to be driven by any such petty annoyances from the height on which I have planted my standard," Percy concluded. "I have set my foot upon a rock of truth—the broad platform of PROTESTANTISM—and there I bide the Issue." Such was the flavour of the times, and each party claimed to represent the authentic practice of the Church of England.

The Evangelicals, for their part, had entered a period of spiritual renewal considerably before the emergence of the Oxford Movement, and had responded to the lethargy of the eighteenth-century Church in a more personal, less institutional, way. As John Henry Newman described the tradition in which he had himself been raised, the Evangelical party traced its roots to the Puritans:

> To them the Scriptures, rather than the Church, were the embodiment of the revealed truth. The Bible contained all that a man needed for salvation. The gospel had but to be preached; the sinner to be converted. Thenceforward he was in a direct personal communion with God, and in perfect assurance that he would be saved. No priest, no mystical rite, had any office or function to perform between him and his maker.... Men must meet to praise and to pray and to be wrought upon by preaching. Baptism and the Lord's Supper were symbolic and commemorative acts, enjoined by Holy Writ.... The keynote of Evangelical Christianity was enthusiasm, in the literal sense of the word. The converted sinner was filled with God, and he carried his conviction of God's presence into every moment of his daily life.

Because they believed that the winning of further souls was the duty of all faithful people, it was, not surprisingly, "the Evangelical party which maintained all the Biblical Societies and most of the associations for Protestant Missions throughout the world." By contrast, the Society For Promoting Christian Knowledge (SPCK) and the SPG, both of which made an incalculable contribution to the colonial Church, were born of the old-fashioned High church, and traced their founding (in 1698 and 1701, respectively) to the reign of William III.

Although clergy of firm Evangelical conviction have not been lacking in the Diocese of Quebec and have even held offices of importance—Isaac Hellmuth was a member of the faculty at Bishop's College from 1845 to 1853, Gilbert Percy was secretary of the Church Society from 1855 until 1860—theirs has seldom been the dominant voice. During G. J. Mountain's episcopate, Hellmuth, E. W. Sewell and W. L. Thompson, all of this party, attempted (without success) to build into the Diocesan Synod, then being formed, a distinctly Protestant bias. If successful, this would have reduced the authority of the bishop by eliminating the episcopal veto and giving his vote no more weight than that of any other clergyman's (see Window 15). The much-publicized activities of the Evangelical Colonial Church and School Society (CCS), which chafed under episcopal authority (see Window 10), caused some to regard all Evangelicals as intractable and divisive, but there were many faithful clergymen of this calling whose zeal and simple piety made them particularly acceptable to the people whom they served (see Window 12).

Fitting individuals into neat compartments is not always easy or even desirable, and there may not be agreement among those who seek to do so. H. H. Walsh, for example, has identified Charles James Stewart with the Evangelicals, whereas Jacob Mountain, who disliked that brand of churchmanship, specifically absolved Stewart of "the least appearance of enthusiasm." T. R. Millman, his biographer, observed that it was "difficult to attach any label to Stewart's churchmanship," save that he "stood in the great central Anglican stream of tradition."

Among the documents preserved in the Quebec Diocesan Archives is a powerful and earnest sermon, a fine example of Evangelical preaching, which was delivered at the opening of Diocesan Synod by Bishop J. W. Williams in 1888 and published by request. Although in some respects it touches on subjects more regularly emphasized by the High than the Low church party (the frequency of receiving the Sacraments, for example), the sermon presents a distinctly Evangelical concept of the ministry. The following passage deals with pastoral visits:

> Very often, that spiritual character, which we shrink from impressing upon our visit, is just what those visited expect and desire. Begin, and a spiritual confidence will grow up, that will bring you and your parishioners close together soul to soul. And then it is, when souls touch, that the divine spark of converting grace passes between them.
>
> And here we come to that other point upon which I proposed to speak—the state of our own personal religion. To kindle others, we must burn ourselves. The preaching and the teaching of a clever man, who has prepared himself by human means, and natural industry, may dazzle and delight, inform and instruct, but the breaking out into voice and utterance of a life that is "hid with God in Christ," converts and saves the soul. A life lived in secret communion with God is the mightiest instrument God is pleased to use for the salvation of souls. Instruction is not everything, and precepts touch but single points; exhortation by repetition loses its effect; and denunciation only irritates; but a holy life is never ineffectual—its influence is freshened and deepened by every renewal of contact; and it takes hold by a thousand points....
>
> A letter was once written to an old clergyman, whose ministry had been greatly blessed. "My people," said the writer, "are cold and heartless; tell me how I can effect a revival of religion in my parish."

The answer was brief—"My brother," he said, "revive thyself."

If, in prayer and devout meditation, our life be spent in the perpetual renewal of our own spirituality, we are in the very best way of preparation for doing the work of Evangelists—for making full proof of our ministry—for converting souls to God.

Related to Tractarianism was a movement within the Church that soon came to be known as Ritualism. To think of the Oxford Movement *itself* as a ritualistic movement, however, would be (in Faber's view) "a gross error." Ritualism, he maintained, "became the mark of the Anglo-Catholic party which grew up in the Church after the Oxford men had done their work. The Tractarians were concerned with invisible, not visible things" (see Window 19).

The original Tractarians, as Vidler pointed out, "were quite content with the Book of Common Prayer, and were punctilious in observing its directions." In it "they were delighted to find," as Chadwick noted, "provision for daily service, private confession, weekly celebration of the sacrament, and splendid ornaments if the ornaments rubric of the prayer book were correctly understood." With fresh eyes they observed that parts of the service could be "said or sung."

Then, about 1840, began the "startling impact" on the worship and adornment of parish churches, ending in riots among the laity and, in some cases, prosecutions of the clergy for employing "unfamiliar rites and ceremonies." Many of the practices for which the nineteenth century Ritualists were denounced have become so much a part of present-day Anglican worship that it seems useful to furnish a catalogue of them (this one supplied by Vidler). Ritualism then was seen to be manifested in the use of any or all of the following as part of the service of the Church:

> altar lights, vestments, wafer bread, the mixed chalice (mixing a little water with the wine at the communion), making the sign of the cross, incense, genuflexions, preaching in a surplice instead of a black gown, surpliced choirs, much singing and chanting, the use of holy water, fixed stone altars instead of movable wooden ones, crucifixes and statues, cultus of the Virgin Mary and Saints, reservation and adoration of the eucharistic sacrament, and auricular confession.

In 1860, the English Church Union was formed to uphold High church doctrine and ritual, as well as to assist clergy prosecuted for either cause. In 1865, largely to put down such doctrine by prosecution, the Church Association came into being. In the famous *Lincoln Judgment* of 1890, the Bishop of Lincoln was charged by a parishioner and tried for a number of "illegal

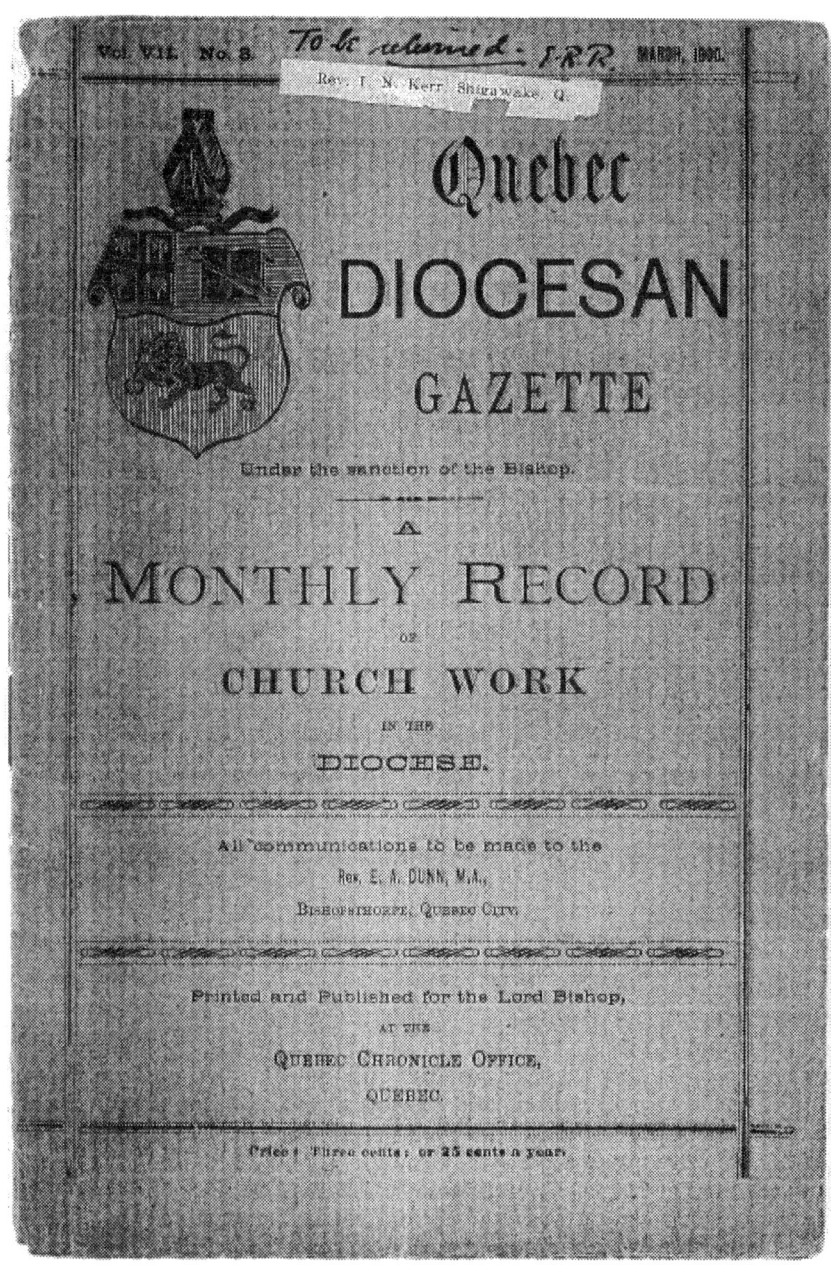

PLATE 6   *The earliest format (15 x 22 cm) of the* Quebec Diocesan Gazette, *founded in 1894 by Bishop A. H. Dunn and still in publication. Note the printed subscriber's label on the cover.*

practices." Although acquitted of several, he was condemned for mixing water with wine in preparation for Holy Communion, for consecrating the elements out of view of the congregation, and for making the sign of the cross in the air in benediction. The Archbishop of Canterbury, who personally heard and decided the case, did not pronounce any sentence, but the Bishop, for his part "conformed his practice to the judgment from the date of its delivery." Other clergy were less obedient. The Archbishops of Canterbury and York and the Bishop of London, who all tried to stem the tide of Ritualism, were unable to maintain discipline or keep practice within acceptable bounds.

In the Diocese of Quebec, all the glories of Ritualism burst upon the scene in 1892 with the arrival of its fifth Lord Bishop in the person of Andrew Hunter Dunn. Although such noted Catholic churchmen as Charles Hamilton, George Thornloe, and Frederick George Scott (all Bishop's graduates) had served "to raise the dignity of worship" within their spheres of service, it was Dunn himself who advanced the Catholic temper in the Diocese as a whole.

Dunn came to Quebec from the large London parish of South Acton, where he had built up an extensive congregation of "those who had been led by the Oxford Movement to desire fuller teaching in the faith than could be obtained in most churches." Although a man of great tact and charm, Dunn faced some initial resistance from both clergy and laity in his attempts to bring religious practice in his Diocese more into line with trends in Britain. An excerpt from a letter he wrote in 1897 to one of his former parish workers serves to show his considered approach to affecting change. The correspondent had obviously sought the Bishop's advice on a matter of ritual:

> As to a Processional Cross or Banner [Dunn replied], nobody cares more to add to the dignity of our worship than I do, and if it were a mere question of ministering to a regular congregation I should soon educate them up to this, and much more, and then have the things, but it is worthy of remembrance that every week there are new-comers, and it is just the Processional Cross in many of these new-comers' eyes which settles them not to come again, whereas they would have thought nothing of a surpliced choir and a processional hymn, and would have come again. The question therefore arises, Is the added dignity worth having at the cost of not being permitted to rear in good Church teaching and Church associations this and that soul ... if it were not for that Cross? But, of course, public opinion is continually advancing, and I am a long way off, and cannot judge as well as I could when on the spot.

Although he encountered determined opposition "and many difficulties, especially from the extreme low-church party," admitted the Bishop's protégé and friend, R. A. Parrock, Dunn succeeded remarkably well in "educating them up" (see Window 27). Parrock, who had been invited to join the Bishop's household (as Domestic Chaplain and tutor to Dunn's sons) upon completion of his studies at Cambridge, was afterward appointed Principal of Bishop's College, thus ensuring that upcoming clergy would be reared in the appropriate Catholic tradition.

Some proponents of Ritualism, unfortunately, were less mindful than the Bishop of the impact their practices might have on the sensibilities of their parishioners. In or about 1907, the Rector of St Matthew's Church, Quebec (who had served the parish since 1891), appears to have introduced some new element into their worship that upset a large number of the congregation. It is difficult to be certain what exactly the trouble was, but a printed petition in the form of a letter dated February 1909 makes it clear that it centred on ritualistic innovation. The priest in question was F. G. Scott.

Scott had already encountered opposition to his churchmanship in a previous parish, but this had come from a congregation of a temper quite different from that of the traditionally High-church people at St Matthew's, and had occurred in J. W. Williams' episcopate, a bishop not much given to Ritualism.

Then, in 1909, having been unable to make any headway with their grievances at St Matthew's, the two current churchwardens, the two sidesmen, together with three former churchwardens (accounting collectively for more than thirty-two years of service to the parish) presented a written appeal to their rector. In it they reasoned as follows:

> We do not think it the part of wisdom to indicate in detail what we may severally imagine to be the causes for the present unhappy state of things; possibly we might not even agree amongst ourselves were we to attempt the task. We only know that we have not ourselves the power to remove those causes, and therefore we appeal to you.
>
> We admit fully that the privilege and the responsibility for the conduct of the Services, and for the teaching to be given—so long as they are in accord with the Prayer Book and with Church of England doctrine—are yours alone. But if an uncompromising insistence on changes, perhaps harmless in themselves, is found to be spoiling temper, spoiling home-peace, and so spoiling religion itself; if the old, and the weak—whether in body or in spiritual understanding—are found to be incapable of appreciating, and joining with heart and soul in the Services as at present conducted, can no place, we would plead with you, be found for that highest Christian grace of Charity, which might tend to restore peace, and so let Patience have her perfect work amongst us?
>
> We willingly allow that misunderstandings and misconceptions may have

much to do with our existing troubles; if so, we would rejoice to have them discovered and removed. But how can this be done? We seem to recognize in you an unwillingness to discuss these things with your own people; would you not, then, be willing to take counsel with others of like experience with your own, say with the Lord Bishop of Ottawa [Charles Hamilton], the Rev. Canon Allnatt, and the Very Rev. Dean Williams, your immediate predecessors in the Rectory of St. Matthew's, or with some others of the Bishops and Clergy, in whose advice both you and we could have implicit confidence? We would gladly bid you God-speed in this or any effort you may make to restore confidence and peace to that congregational life which we have received from our fathers, and which, with God's help, we would hand on unbroken to our children.

Scott's reply, dispatched to the wardens on the day he received the petition, was brief and blunt. Although he conceded that the petitioners had been "actuated only by the highest motives," nevertheless he felt himself bound by what he believed to be "the best interests of the Church." He declined to accede to any of their requests. Scott's sense of rectitude was uncompromising. On the subject of ritual, he had nailed his colours to the mast in the parish paper (the *S. Matthew's Church Messenger* of January 1908) where it was stated of the Eucharist that "no splendour of decorative ritual can be inappropriate in order to accentuate and to honor this authoritative spiritual trysting-place between the risen Lord and His Church."

Under such circumstances, there was little that the parishioners could do. Protests to the Bishop would have been a possibility, and Scott's former parishioners at Drummondville had received a sympathetic hearing from Bishop Williams when they had laid complaints. On that occasion, however, Scott (like the English Ritualists who resisted admonitions from their Bishops), had followed his conscience and defied his Diocesan (see Window 23).

Other parishes resisted Ritualistic advances through symbolic gestures, such as refusing to pay for wafer bread or walking out of the church if candles were lit (see Window 34). Withdrawing from the congregation was a parishioner's ultimate protest, but within the Diocese of Quebec, there were few centres that offered an alternative Anglican Service. In 1892, in his first Charge to Synod, Bishop Dunn spoke to this problem and the accommodations that circumstances might require:

As to the manner of conducting service, I am very glad to know that we, who have a goodly heritage,—we, who are a part of the great Anglican branch of Christ's Holy Catholic Church, have permitted to us, by the highest ecclesiastical authority,—a wide diversity of method, so that in cities and other populous places, where there are several churches, a Table can be spread for all, and consequently congregations which enjoy different methods should be content to differ in such matters, and instead of distraction and jealousy, each should delight in honoring and commending the other for its especial virtues and good works. In country parishes, the matter stand[s] on rather a different footing, and it is certainly the duty of every clergyman to put aside, to a great extent, his own predilections and carefully to consider what, on the whole, is best for the whole body of people committed to his charge.

In Quebec City, there were several churches, each representing a distinctive brand of churchmanship. In a series of reminiscences printed in the *Diocesan Gazette* in 1964, a 99-year old Quebecer recalled laconically a past conflict over ritual. "I attended the Cathedral for twenty-five years," she wrote. "Then, they brought in new forms which I did not like, so I changed to Trinity."

Bishop Lennox Williams, who was elected sixth Lord Bishop of Quebec in 1914, appears to have been a man of peaceful disposition. He valued the comprehensiveness of the Anglican tradition and deplored the existence of factions within the Church (see Window 31). In 1932, when plans were afoot for celebrating the centenary of the Oxford Movement the following year, there was anxiety that the event would rekindle old party divisions and exacerbate existing ones. The following excerpt (from an article by the Rev. Charles Eardley-Wilmot, editor of the *Diocesan Gazette*) reflects this mood, and describes the care with which organizers were chosen and their mandates defined:

> It will be the aim of the Committee appointed by the Bishop ... to carry on a campaign of instruction concerning the Oxford Movement and its forerunner, the Evangelical Revival, and the debt that the Church to-day owes to them. Enough has been said, we hope, to commend the subject to churchmen of all schools of thought. There are to-day, as there have always been, different views held by men of unquestioned loyalty to the Church and the Prayer Book. These differences are largely a matter of emphasis, and it is the glory and the strength of our Church that she can include in her communion different types of churchmanship.... It must be admitted that the growth of the Oxford Movement has often resulted in much bitterness of feeling between "High" and "Low" Churchmen,—between Evangelicals and Anglo-Catholics, so-called. The last thing to be desired is that our observance of this centenary in the diocese should be a party matter. It is a great and glorious opportunity for promoting unity ...

Like his predecessor Lennox Williams, Bishop Carrington disliked the appearance of party spirit, but unlike Williams he was (according to his biographer) "an iconoclast of the first water." As the incoming Dean of Divinity at Bishop's, he encountered a residual "Anglican pre-Raphaelite" spirit, noted for "its earnestness and ceremonial zeal." This was no doubt the legacy of Rocksborough Remington Smith, a former Dean of Divinity, who had left Bishop's in 1926 on his election as Coadjutor Bishop of Algoma. Carrington's approach to theology and religion raised an element of opposition among students "who had known the previous regime." He met student challenges to his orthodoxy with wit and flair, however; nor was he behindhand in demolishing any sort of party pose he encountered:

> His most caustic verbal assaults [his biographer notes] were reserved for certain kinds of Anglo-Catholic or Bible fundamentalists or the *unco' guid*; whenever, in fact, he encountered intolerance or sham or insincerity wearing a religious label.

More than one of Carrington's ordinands, known to him personally as students at Bishop's, recalled having been cautioned on ordination day against too much zeal in any extreme of churchmanship. Carrington's epithet "he was no party man," when applied to a member of the clergy in his history of the Anglican Church in Canada, strikes one as praise indeed.

Although one former student, Fr John G. McCausland, recalled thinking of the Dean as representing "the new theology" and expounding "modernist or liberal views," this may well have been prompted by the obvious contrast between Carrington's more contemporary brand of thinking and Principal A. H. McGreer's old-fashioned "state-church Anglicanism." Far from endorsing Modernism, however, Carrington appears to have regarded the German critics, who had made such an impact on post-World War I theology, as both negative and divided. Colin Cuttell, himself prepared for ordination by the Dean, remarked on Carrington's utter confidence in the credibility of the gospels—the result of his study of Scripture—and his ability to dismiss completely "the prevailing mood of scepticism."

> This quality of conviction and superb confidence followed him all his days. And he always dealt summarily with the "destructive critics" who said that the Resurrection and the miracles were "past already," pious legends, part of the assimilated folklore.... [He] said that this facile view was now impossible to accept because we now know the gospels to be so early. There had been no time for legends to arise ...

When he became Bishop, and later Archbishop, Carrington did not

PLATE 7 *Advertising pages such as this May 1899 flyleaf of the* Quebec Diocesan Gazette *would usually have been discarded when the monthly numbers were sent to the binder.*

abandon scholarship, and his theological interests could not fail to have an impact on his episcopate. This period (1935-1960) coincided with the cultivation in Britain of what was called a "biblical theology." It was supposed, Vidler observed, "that the storms of the age of Liberalism and Modernism had been safely weathered and that theologians could concentrate again on the positive exposition of their faith and its corollaries." Carrington's views and interests appear to have corresponded with this trend.

If the *Diocesan Gazette* is any indication of the impact Modernism may have had on the Diocese, there were few (if any) questionings or anxieties in the air. Carrington's positive, energetic presence dominated the publication, not only through his episcopal letters, but through articles, reviews, and accounts of Visitations and excursions. After the war was over, articles by returning padres testified to the instances of faith and selflessness they had seen, whether in action or among the casualties. The Rev. A. V. Ottiwell, who had left his parish of Coaticook in 1941 to serve with No. 8 Canadian General Hospital in France and Belgium, wrote feelingly of what might be learned from such an experience:

> [T]he consciousness of faith expressed by men who have felt the experience of something "other" than themselves in time of war, not alone in times of danger, and of a guiding, strengthening and over-ruling power, is something which we must pray will be quickened and developed, so that they may serve as well in peace as in war.

In addition to the usual parish and W.A. news, and a good deal of emphasis on camping for boys and girls (see Window 35), the *Diocesan Gazette* contained considerable matter for reflection. The Dean of Divinity of Bishop's University prepared "A Message For Lent" for the appropriate 1952 issue. Sermons or Addresses were sometimes printed (in whole or in part): "The Marks of the True Shepherd," preached at the ordination of J. A. Secord at the Cathedral, for example, or "The Bible and the Ministry of the Word," a talk by the visiting Archbishop of York, given to the clergy at Quebec. The Rector of Drummondville contributed a short piece entitled "Christian Teaching and Antisemitism" to the Lent issue of 1958.

The publication of well-written, original contributions in the *Diocesan Gazette* raised its stature and educated its readership. It presented the Diocesan clergy as learned men with things to say. James R. Brown, the author of "Christian Teaching and Antisemitism," for example, was an Oxford graduate. He had spent three years of further study on Semitic languages on a research fellowship made available for Christian clergy at a rabbinic theological college in America. Besides producing articles on the Old Testament, he had prepared the Forward Movement pamphlet, *Christians and Jews.* Carrington seems to have been able to attract a number of extremely well-qualified men to serve his diocese. Indeed, in view of his worldwide reputation as a New Testament scholar, this is hardly surprising.

If elements of "death-of-God" theology were present in the Diocese, they were not conspicuously so. The Rev. Ernest Harrison who, as Michel Despland has pointed out, was to elicit a response from some Anglicans that was "strongly reminiscent of heresy trials," had entered the Diocese in 1953, and was invited to join the editorial board of the *Diocesan Gazette* in 1957. Although he contributed a large number of articles, such as "Christmas: Natural and Supernatural," "The Unjust Steward," and "General Synod High Spots and Low Spots," all mildly suggestive of things to come, they seemed harmless enough at the time. Discussions in print of "such controversial topics as the eclipse of the Bible, the death of God, ... the parish of the future ... [and] the so-called 'new morality'" would burst upon the public only after Harrison had left the Diocese and Carrington had retired.

While Carrington's churchmanship defied a label (his biographer, perhaps in desperation, described him as an "Evangelical Catholic"), that of his successor Bishop Russel Brown posed no such problem. A deeply spiritual Catholic churchman, he guided the Diocese into the ambiguous and increasingly fragmented world of the 1960s.

The *Diocesan Gazette* reflected the changing approach to forms of worship that were evident elsewhere: folk instruments appeared in church, new liturgies were described. The Rev. Norman Pilcher contributed an article on the Liturgical Movement.

Articles on clergy working closely with medical practitioners—whether as counsellors alert to the psychiatric needs of their parishioners or as spiritual care-givers cooperating with hospital staff—projected a contemporary image of the Church. The clinical pastoral training movement had taken early root in the Diocese, and Bishop's, in collaboration with the Sherbrooke Hospital, claimed to be the first university in Canada to have set up a programme of clinical pastoral training "as a regular part of its divinity course, exclusively for divinity students."

> It is no longer adequate to deal with the problems of people only in terms of sin and repentance [the Rev. Prof. W. P. Zion maintained]. Future priests are called not only to study the personality sciences, but to obtain knowledge to enable them to identify and act helpfully in relation to mental illnesses. This is not to give them the task of major psychotherapy.... [I]t is to provide them with

tools which may be used so that they will not stumble and actually harm disabled souls. Just as important, however, is such knowledge for working with the normal person. A pastor cannot dismiss a knowledge of interpersonal dynamics, group processes, and the emotional responses of people and successfully reach out to his flock.

Theological education was re-examined and expanded. "A strong case can be made for the inclusion in the theological college syllabus of psychology, science, sociology, educational theory, ancient or modern languages, political science—or indeed any topic of honest human inquiry," wrote the Rev. Professor J.D.F. Anido, Diocesan Chairman of the Board of Religious Education.

This was a period of theological controversy. In 1963, the Canterbury Association at Bishop's (by this time, a largely interdenominational group) was examining *Honest to God*, the explosive best-seller by the Bishop of Woolwich. By 1965, the General Board of Religious Education (GBRE) in Toronto had commissioned *The Comfortable Pew* (with a preface by Ernest Harrison). Perhaps in deference to her former colleague on the editorial board, the editor of the *Diocesan Gazette* claimed to have "followed the stormy course of events" leading up to the publication of the GBRE's venture, "with warm, though perhaps silent, sympathy and encouragement." Prominent American sociologist of religion Peter Berger "dismissed the book and the controversy around it as 'the relevance bit comes to Canada.' Another reader called it 'an ecclesiastical *Fanny Hill.*'" In Quebec City, a layman ventured some positive comments in a detailed, mixed review entitled "Uncomfortable Spew?"

Some of the Diocesan clergy began voicing their anxiety about the impact of the self-appointed demythologizers of the faith. If all the so-called "stumbling blocks to the modern mind" were expunged from religion, the Rev. J.D.R. Franklin predicted, it "would do more in a single generation to destroy the Christian religion than all the persecutions of history." He also expressed his doubts that "a Cross-less, joyless, powerless, painless Christianity, bereft of all hope for salvation, would appeal to anybody at all." Preaching at an Ordination Service at the Cathedral in 1965, Dr Sidney Jellicoe, Dean of Divinity at Bishop's, attacked the principle of tailoring the Church to the times.

> Though **particulars** may differ, the Church, the world and its inhabitants, have not essentially changed; nor has the Mission of the Church, or the world's disposition to the reception of that mission, altered in any way....

For this reason, any attempt, in the supposed interests of evangelism or of commending the Gospel, to accommodate the Word to the interests and temper of an age, or even to attempt to express it in terms of any contemporary philosophy, is a cardinal error. At best it can but substitute the part for the whole; at worst it can serve only to veil the uncompromising claim: "As the heavens are higher than the earth, so are my ways higher than your ways, and my thoughts than your thoughts."

Dean Jellicoe's sermon was printed by request. Among the five young men ordained at this impressive ceremony was Bruce Stavert, hitherto Deacon in charge of Schefferville.

Just as Carrington appears to have used the *Diocesan Gazette* to infuse his people with a sense of purpose and confidence, Bishop Brown seems to have encouraged his clergy to write articles to "educate them up" (in Bishop Dunn's phrase). Both Church Music and Church Architecture formed a series of contributions, but perhaps the most striking was a five-part monthly sequence beginning in September 1963. Entitled "Churches and Ceremonials or Rubrics and Ritual," it was contributed by the incumbent at Magog and generally appeared on the front page.

In this series, the writer proposed to describe "an Anglican Church ... which is a composite of all Anglican Churches whether in England or East Africa, America or Australia or the East Indies or West."* Details included stoups for Holy Water, Altar Crucifixes, an all-boys choir in purple cassocks ("we are fortunate that we do not have to rely on female voices"), Acolytes, Incense, and Sanctus bells. "[A]t the end of each side aisle in this our composite Church," he directed, "there is an Altar. The one on the right with its blue furnishings obviously under the patronage of and dedicated to the Blessed Virgin Mary; the other, in black and silver, for the offering of Holy Sacrifice for the holy dead."

Two interesting items appeared in the March 1964 issue. One was a disgruntled letter from "An Anglican, Rivière du Loup," citing Article XXII ("Of Purgatory") of the Thirty-nine Articles and challenging "the Roman Church to prove that they are right" from Scripture. "If they cannot prove that they are right," the correspondent concluded, "this would be a big victory for the Anglican Church and other Protestant churches who like the Anglicans have no belief in 'Purgatory.'" To this outburst was appended an editorial reprimand that "in the attempt to unify Christendom, all these matters must be

---

* The author of the series had come to the Diocese of Quebec from that of Barbadoes where he had served for several years as curate at St Michael's Cathedral.

examined." The second item, incongruously enough, took the form of an editorial wail deploring the supposed indifference of readers to material published in the *Gazette*. "Are we publishing a paper by the clergy for the clergy? Even they are remarkably silent about what appears in print. But we hope we are publishing for YOU, important members of the Anglican Church."

During the same period there were signs of willingness, on the part of some, to be more open and less exclusive in the administration of the Sacraments. In 1967, T. J. Matthews (then Archdeacon of St Francis) expressed this unequivocally when he spoke of the priest reading the Exhortation before celebrating the Eucharist:

> He has the right to expect that the Anglicans who draw near are confirmed because our rule applies to them. But the others—members of other denominations—who join with us in worship, what right has he to deny them the Sacrament? It is not his Sacrament. It is not even an Anglican Sacrament. It is a Sacrament of the Church.
>
> What I am saying is that while the Anglican Church has the right to regulate its own communicant members; and similarly the United Church and Roman Catholic Church theirs, I question the right to regulate each other's communicant members.... As far as the Anglican Church is concerned, to invite every penitent person present to draw near and take the Holy Sacrament to his comfort, and then resent or even resist a general acceptance of the invitation, is downright hypocrisy. This kind of thing was all right in a secret society, but not any more.

Matthews explained his present position, in part, by recounting an anecdote. A fellow-priest had written an irate letter to the Archdeacon expressing his annoyance at seeing Matthews—duly robed—together with an Anglican clergyman and the United Church Chairman of Presbytery (these two attired in business suits) assisting in the Sanctuary at an ecumenical service:

> I understand this cleric's preoccupation with vestments and ceremonial—and, indeed, his love of beauty in form and order. I was raised in the Catholic tradition too.
>
> But I have learned to recognize things about the Anglican Church besides the "dignity of its worship." I think it has been noted for its false loyalties, its inherited and built-in prejudices, its whiteness, its rightness and its remoteness. I know how dreadfully dull it can be—and irrelevant.
>
> At the same time I am fiercely proud of the Anglican Church—I love it; not only because of its fine old traditions ... but for its great new courage ... because there are people in it today who just will not allow the Church to stay the way it is.

PLATE 8A   *The S.S. Colon landing Bishop A. H. Dunn at Pointe Bleue Rocks, July 1905.*

PLATE 8B   *Cree Lay Reader Joseph Gunner, Bishop Dunn, the Rev. Philip Callis, Maggie Robertson, and "Old Charlie" Robertson, with parishioners and visitors in front of the Church of St John the Divine, Pointe Bleue, July 1901.*

On Bishop Brown's retirement in 1971, T. J. Matthews was elected in his place. As had occurred more than once in the history of the Diocese, the new episcopate sharply contrasted with the old: in churchmanship, priorities, and style.

However influential they may be, bishops do not exclusively determine the quality of churchmanship within their respective dioceses. To be sure, a long episcopate—and in the Diocese of Quebec the average has been 20 years—would leave its imprint on the diocese. It would show itself in the recruitment of a certain type of clergyman, and, in earlier days, in the choice of professors appointed to the theological college. But other factors must be seen to play a part as well.

In 1892, within three weeks of docking at Quebec, Bishop A. H. Dunn made a whirlwind episcopal tour—confirming, preaching, chairing meetings, dedicating churches and altars, lecturing, catechizing, and meeting his people. Writing in a missionary journal about his first impressions of the Diocese, Dunn remarked that "he was struck, first and foremost, with 'the warmhearted kindliness of everyone, everywhere,' and also that 'in the face of a powerful Roman Catholicism, the clergy and people were, for the most part, strong Prayer-Book Church-people.'" Clearly, the dominant presence of Roman Catholicism in Quebec has had its impact on the attitudes of the individual in the parish pew. In 1993, when it was casually suggested to one of the clergy recently recruited from outside the Diocese that Quebec was said to be "a High-church Diocese," his rather wistful reply was, "Yes, but the *people* aren't." Whether this assessment is accurate or not, it has much to say about the Anglican tradition generally, and about the form that it has taken in the Diocese of Quebec.

PLATE 9A *Left to right: Bishop Bruce Stavert and the Rt Rev. Narciso Ticobay, Bishop of the Episcopal Diocese of the Southern Philippines, during the latter's visit to the Diocese of Quebec in 1991.* (Photo credit: Lynn C. Ross)

PLATE 9B *Visiting parishioners: Harrington Harbour. The Rev. Robert A. Bryan and George Ransom, 1978.*(Photo credit: Candace Cochrane)

CHAPTER III

The Road to Autonomy

One of the greatest practical problems faced by the Anglican Church (in the Diocese of Quebec and elsewhere) has been the seeming unwillingness of its adherents to accept the principle "that churches should be supported by their members rather than look to the State for aid." By contrast, as Carrington has pointed out, individuals belonging to other denominations had brought the spirit of voluntarism with them into the Diocese—the notion of relying upon their own resources:

> The American Methodists and other independent religious bodies brought in a distinctive contribution in the idea of a Church which was free from entanglements with the State, and organised from the ground up on a voluntary basis. This was their contribution, and the Anglican Church had to learn the lesson, as its sister-church in the States had already done.

The Piper and the Tune

Initially Anglicans, from Jacob Mountain down through the ranks, thought that provision by Government would (and ought to) supply the fledgling Diocese of Quebec with funds and clergy, as well as ensure the Church's predominance and prestige.

Early on, the special constitutional status of the Church "at home," and fear of the "democratic thinking" fostered among dissenting Protestants, led British officialdom to view state support of the Church as a matter of political expediency. Following the American Revolution, sectarianism became "identified with republicanism, and Anglicanism with loyalty to the British crown; therefore, the obvious way to retain what was left of British North America ... was to establish an imperial church to teach proper respect for British institutions."

To those charged with looking after her welfare, it soon became clear, however, that Government was not meeting the needs of the British North American Church, and that some other source—both of clergy to serve and of funds to sustain them—would have to be found. Rescue came in the guise of the SPG. In 1801, after consultation with Bishops Mountain and Inglis, the Society presented "a strong memorial" to the Government at Westminster, "urging the need that it should do more than 'reserve' land of no present value." Pointing to the "the wealth and privileges of the Roman Church (whose patronage in Canada it reckoned to be worth £40,000 to £50,000)," the Society suggested that some of the Jesuit and Sulpician lands, then in Government hands, should be turned to the benefit of the Anglican Church. Although little came of this proposal, in 1813 the parliamentary grants towards the maintenance of clergy in the Canadas (hitherto in the hands of the Governors) were entrusted to the SPG. For the next twenty years the Society allocated these funds, adding £50 of its own money to each £150 received from the Government.

The state had begun by expending large sums on sustaining the work of the Anglican Church, but about 1830, the Government's attitude toward every aspect of colonial administration began to change. There was an increasing unwillingness to continue the expenditure hitherto lavished upon them for maintenance and defence. "In 1832," as the SPG reported of the colonial Church, "the British Government began to withdraw the annual grant, amounting to £16,000, which, from the year 1813, it had applied towards the maintenance of the North American Clergy. A great additional burden was thus thrown upon the Society." The Government did not totally abandon the Church, however, or renege on the responsibilities it had earlier assumed. Until Bishop G. J. Mountain's death in 1863, the bishop's salary (amounting at that time to £1,990 annually) was supplied by vote of the Imperial Parliament.

Perhaps because of the prevailing uncertainty, the SPG experienced some difficulty in attracting clergy for missionary work abroad, and its Annual Reports, widely distributed in Britain, began to carry detailed accounts of the advantages and financial safeguards on which missionaries "adopted by the Society" could depend (see Window 5). Each clergyman was sent out to fill a particular post. He was promised a church, a parsonage, and usually a glebe, in addition to receiving a pledge from the people for a certain sum to be paid towards his support. His stipend, the Society announced, would amount to £150 at least. In return, the clergyman was expected to report to the Society on the progress of his mission at least once a year. It would not have been surprising if many of these men—who were recruited, examined, adopted, and paid by the SPG—thought of themselves as missionaries of the Society rather than as subjects of the Diocese. Indeed, even the laity came to think of the SPG as the real religious authority in the Diocese, as the following excerpt from the 1803 *Abstract of the Society's Proceedings* laconically suggests:

> The cause of the people of Paspebiac (or Gaspé) having applied to the Society for a Missionary, previously to their communicating their intention to the Bishop of Quebec [Jacob Mountain] has been explained to his satisfaction: and they have received from him full instructions of what is expected to be done on their part by Government and the Society.

The SPG depended on private donations and bequests for the bulk of its funds, and as applications for support from an expanding colonial Church multiplied, the Society pressed its needs increasingly on the British public. A particularly effective means for this was the SPG's *Annual Reports*, in which the human context of their benevolence was conveyed to would-be patrons through printed selections from the more interesting communications sent from the field by their missionaries. Whether this particular approach can be credited for it or not, the Society was able to increase significantly the sums collected and, consequently, its expenditure on missions.

> With respect to the voluntary contributions, which form at present two-thirds of the disposable income of the Society [stated an SPG financial report published in 1828], it is gratifying in the highest degree to the Committee, to remark, that this source of income, which produced in 1814 £444 13s 6d, and in the year 1820 no more than £1458, has in the year 1827, produced no less a sum than £7833 6s 10d (including legacies to the amount of £1168 18s), a circumstance which proves most clearly, that the objects of the Society, both in North America, and in the East Indies, are viewed by the public with a degree of interest which has continually increased. At the same time it must be remembered, that the whole expenditure in the last year, notwithstanding the additions made to the voluntary contributions, exceeded the income by £5710 7s 6d.

Jacob Mountain, although gifted with an eye for incident as well as fine descriptive powers, seems to have saved these talents for his private correspondence (see Windows 2, 4, & 8). By contrast, Charles James Stewart was well aware of the importance of publicity. While serving as Travelling Missionary in the Diocese of Quebec, he had made it a point to file prompt and detailed reports to the SPG, from which the Society frequently quoted. When Stewart became Bishop, he took care to assure himself that his clergy's communications with the Society were well and fully prepared. Such intermeddling with what had hitherto been a private relationship between the Society and individual missionaries, however, was bound to provoke some resentment. Although Stewart probably did not mean to be officious, some clergy took offence. As the Rev. James Reid (in 1849) confided to his diary:

> Soon after Bishop Stewart was promoted to the See of Quebec, a circular was sent to the Clergy, requiring them to send for his inspection, all their annual notitias.* This request no doubt made them all feel little in their own eyes; and without pretending to know how they have managed their notitias since that order, I suspect they have done, as I have done, sent none at all since. This appears to be corroborated by the fact that the present Bishop [G. J. Mountain] reports for the whole, and makes no complaint of omission on the part of the clergy.

Reid was in a position to know that Stewart was serious about inspecting reports. In 1828, the Bishop had sent a message through Reid to a neighbouring clergyman "request[ing] him in future to enclose [the Report] open in a cover directed to me, Civil Secretary's Office, Quebec." The following year Reid himself was reprimanded for the content of his annual letter to the SPG. The Report was returned to him with the following comments: "I wish you w^d write a more full & correct Report for the Society. Might you not mention the School in your village, & enlarge a little on the prospect of the increase of the Church ... The Society wishes for interesting reports which they may publish."

Despite the resentment of some, however, the letters from missionaries to the Society continued to provide much useful information about the progress made by the churches in the Diocese. In December 1840, Charles Peter Reid (James Reid's son) sent a detailed description of his work to the Rev. A. M. Campbell (Secretary of the SPG), his third letter that year to the Society. In March, he had been transferred from Victoria in the Township of Bury. It seems that in Victoria "the temporal prospects of the settlement" were poor. The number of families had declined from 350 to 186, and the remaining population was in an "unsettled & dissatisfied" state of mind about their future. Consequently, the Bishop had repositioned his clergy, directing a newly-ordained deacon (William King) to Bury, and the more experienced priest (Reid) to Compton (previously a mere "appendage of Hatley"), as its first resident missionary.

---

* *notitia parochialis* = the annual number of baptisms, marriages and funerals performed in the parish.

Compton was then populated almost exclusively by American settlers who were, Reid admitted, "generally prejudiced against the church;" but, he hastened to add, this was "more from ignorance of her doctrines than any other general cause." Evidently pleased with the advances he and the people had been able to make during his brief period of residence, he then proceeded to set out the details of their accomplishments:

> The Church edifice, which was fast going to ruin has been thoroughly repaired, and the outside painted white:—[T]he pulpit and desk have been decorated with handsome hangings,—the communion table covered with a suitable cover,—the pulpit stairs & chancel floor carpeted,—arrangements have been made to procure a transparent painting to place in the large window over the altar,—we are shortly expecting the arrival of a font for Baptisms & vessels for the altar, that the Lord Bishop of Montreal [G. J. Mountain] has kindly engaged to procure for us,—and before the end of the next summer there is every present probability—that the inside, as well as the outside, will also be handsomely painted.

A description such as C. P. Reid's brings home the great difficulties in the small communities of procuring the simplest of "decent furnishings" for their churches. It was hard for struggling settlers to come by ready money to purchase what they could not make.

Besides the SPG, another source of aid from overseas was the SPCK. A publisher of religious books and tracts, it had an elaborate distribution system, both at home and abroad, whereby subsidized packets of Christian literature were available to those who wanted them. In the Canadas, they furnished vast numbers of Bibles and Prayer Books to those unable to pay for them, as well as altar books for churches that otherwise would have had to do without. The nucleus of many a Sunday school library—perhaps the only educational resource in a wide area—can frequently be traced to a grant from the SPCK. In addition, the Society gave financial aid for the building of churches (see Window 21).

Like the SPG, the SPCK encouraged self-help, and expected those who received their grants to demonstrate a willingness to raise subscriptions locally. Quebec was urged to follow the lead of the Maritimes and found a Diocesan Committee of the SPCK. By 1819 it had done so (see Window 7). The following is an excerpt from the Annual Report of the parent society:

> In the Diocese of Quebec, the first Annual Report of the Diocesan Committee

at Quebec has been received. The Committee express their sense of the readiness with which all classes have come forward in support of the design ... They state that it was in compliance with directions received from the Lord Bishop of the Diocese, that the public attention was first called to the formation of the Society; and it was commenced, upon the spot, under the auspices of the late Governor in Chief (Sir John C. Sherbrooke) who had extended the same countenance upon a former occasion to the Diocesan Committee in Nova Scotia.... It appears that the number of the Members of the Society who join this Diocesan Committee amount to 95. This Committee thankfully acknowledge the very expeditious compliance with their order to the SOCIETY for Books. These Books have been chiefly distributed among the poorer classes of Protestants in Quebec, and the vicinity; a few have been sent to the new settlement at Val Cartier; a certain number have been dispersed among the Drummondville settlers; and others have found their way into different parts of the Eastern Townships, where the Committee state, vast quantities might be circulated with excellent fruit.

In 1827, the Committee reported that in the previous 18 months it had distributed "500 Bibles, and 15,000 Prayer-Books, procured by His Majesty's Government from the PARENT SOCIETY" to various parts of the Diocese. Under their auspices, a branch of the National School System for the education of the poor had been recently established in the city. It was described as "in a flourishing condition" and was attended by 125 boys and 105 girls. Of these, the report noted, "about 160 belong to the Church of England, and the remainder are divided in nearly equal portions between the other Protestant denominations collectively and the Church of Rome." The Committee also stated that a collection of £115.5.2 "was made in May 1827, at the Cathedral Church, in aid of the funds of the SOCIETY and the schools."

The SPCK continued to award grants to the Diocese of Quebec well into the twentieth century primarily for books, church building, and theological studentships. In 1901, the Society's Minute Books quote from an application, duly countersigned by Bishop Dunn, from the Rev. G. P. Pye of Labrador:

You may know [Pye explained] that our Canadian Labrador is simply the north shore of the Gulf of St Lawrence, about 435 miles long. Here we have about 24 stations, most of them small, but 3 considerably larger than the rest. At these there is fairly regular Sunday worship, the other places being visited on weekdays. At two of these 3 stations with your kind help we have built 2 churches, viz., at Mutton Bay and Harrington Harbour. And now we want to put up a little C^h at the 3rd [St Paul's River], where we always have a resident minister & school teacher for the 6 or 7 months covering the winter.

The Society voted £20 to aid the building. According to Pye's report to the Church Society, the people had put in the foundation and the frame the previous year, and, "on the 12th August [1901], Mr. John Côté began work and built the church in two months."

In 1908, the SPCK donated books to the amount of £11.2.4 in answer to requests from the Rev. A. E. Burgett for his congregations at Montmorency Falls, Lac Beauport, and St Paul's (Quebec), and from the Rev. A. H. Robertson at Cookshire. A set of Communion Service Books, such as that received by St James's, Lac Beauport, would have cost the congregation £1.1.8.

Bishop's College was also a beneficiary. An annual grant of £500 for two successive years was voted by the Standing Committee of the SPCK in December 1842 "towards the establishment of a *College at Lennoxville.*" In 1847, it voted an additional sum up to £1000 as a sort of "matching gift," "in order to double such amount as may be contributed henceforth from other quarters." For more than 50 years the SPCK awarded the College generous grants, including the endowment of a Professorship of Pastoral Theology in 1892.

The Diocese celebrated its centenary in 1893, still drawing on overseas support from the SPG. The Clergy Reserves, which were to have supplied the financial needs of the Church, had been alienated by the Canadian Legislature in 1855. Although the stipends of clergy whose appointments predated the withdrawal of grants were secure until they retired or died, no funds to replace them or to deal with the needs of new settlements were to be forthcoming. To establish a fund from which the ministry could find support, the clergy with such life interests were persuaded to commute them, on the understanding that the responsibility of providing for them would be assumed by the Diocese. In Upper Canada the commutation represented a tidy sum (£222,620), but in Lower Canada it came to no more than £10,500. This sum was paid to the Diocese by the Government in 1857, in debentures valued at $53,341.59.

In 1858, the SPG reduced its grants further and cut off subsidies for building. Another blow fell with Bishop Mountain's death in 1863, when outside payment of the bishop's salary ceased. Because there was only a single self-supporting parish in the entire Diocese as late as 1862, Mountain—who happily had private means—had routinely expended the whole of his own salary "in augmenting the incomes of the city clergy." Thus, on the Bishop's

PLATE 10A   *The Rev. Sydney Meade, with a komatik, at St Augustine River.*

PLATE 10B   *The M.V. Hollis Corey, the last of the diocesan Mission Boats, in the summer of 1966.* (Photo credit: E. O. Miller, Jr)

death, the Quebec City parishes "lost and had to make good to the clergy, at once, $3,000 a year."

Although Mountain's leadership undoubtedly sustained and strengthened his diocese in spiritual terms, "he was not supposed very greatly to excel as a man of business, a financier, or a *manager* of other men—he dwelt too much in the higher regions of the Christian life for that." Fortunately for the temporal well-being of the Diocese, J. W. Williams (Mountain's successor) *was* a capable financial administrator, and, like Bishop Stewart, a strong believer in self-help. Williams started a parochial endowment scheme like that adopted by the Diocese of Montreal and pressed forward the mandate of the Diocesan Board (whose organization had been completed in 1862) to work towards supporting the clergy through local means.

In 1888, the SPG again reduced its grant to the Diocese, this time by half, but under Williams' able guidance the Diocese had gained in strength and confidence. That same year, the 25th anniversary of his consecration, Williams delivered an Address to the 18th session of the Diocesan Synod in which he reviewed the achievements of his episcopate. He had, he said, confirmed 11,176 individuals, ordained 47 deacons and 43 priests, and consecrated 37 churches. A trust had been created to provide pensions for aged or infirm clergymen, and the capital of the fund into which parochial assessments were paid had risen from $3,000 to $17,500. The number of self-supporting parishes had increased from one to sixteen.

> Such [he reminded the Synod], during the last twenty five years, has been the Church's growth in outward and visible form; and I would gladly believe that she has made like progress in inward and spiritual grace; but the volume and intensity of the Father's love it is not easy to estimate and impossible to exhibit; the grace of our Lord Jesus Christ cannot be expressed in figures; and the fellowship of the Holy Ghost is not susceptible of tabular statement. The means of grace we have endeavoured to use. And, so far as human eye can judge, our use of the means has not been unfruitful.

In 1893, Archdeacon Henry Roe paid tribute to the "life, energy and progress" of a Diocese that had resolutely pulled itself out of a position of almost total dependence on external aid and had become self-supporting. This achievement he attributed to the financial organization implemented in Williams' episcopate and known as "the Quebec system."

The main features of "the Quebec system" are—(1) An equitable assessment, graded according to means, of the amount to be paid by each mission towards the stipend of its clergyman; (2) The payment of this assessment, not directly to the clergyman, but to the Diocesan Board of Missions; (3) A simple but effective means of enforcing its regular and punctual payment; and (4) The payment of the entire stipend of the missionary by the Diocesan Board.

In 1963, Carrington described this procedure in his *History* as still in operation in the Diocese, "without change," over a hundred-year period.

As far as I know [he remarked], it has been followed in only one other Canadian diocese, that of Montreal, where Bond was strongly in favour of it; but it was heard of to the ends of the earth. It was in operation, for instance, in at least one diocese in New Zealand, and my stipend in my country mission in that diocese came to me regularly once a month under what was called there "The Quebec system."

As for the "simple but effective means" of enforcing the "regular and punctual payment" of assessments, its particulars were defined by Canons VII and IX under the Constitution of the Synod in 1888. Section 5 of the latter outlines the consequences of failing "to meet the requirements of the Diocesan Board":

Whenever the Diocesan Board finds that the fault is in the people, it shall be the duty of the Board to insist upon payment ... and in the event of their still declining, the Board shall remove the Clergyman ... and in every such case the Board shall not, unless they shall see special cause, make any grant to aid the mission in default to obtain another Clergyman, until every mission, which is willing to meet the requirements of the Board, has been supplied with the ministrations of the Church, and the money given to the Clergyman to enable him to remove has been refunded to the Board by the mission.

When A. H. Dunn succeeded Williams as bishop, the Diocese—though virtually self-supporting—was still receiving about $5,000 in aid from the SPG. Dunn, who "fully understood the Society's wish to turn its grants to other uses," proposed to his first Synod in 1893 that it voluntarily "give up by the end of the century, the large sum ... which we at present receive from that most noble organization, the venerable Society for the Propagation of the Gospel in Foreign Parts," as one element of the Centenary Thanksgiving Celebrations. This the Diocese faithfully accomplished:

Three special objects were, however, still maintained for a time: grants to ordinands training at Lennoxville, a share in the stipend of a chaplain for the Marine Hospital at Quebec, and a stipend for the missionary at lonely Blanc Sablon, the furthest point on the South Labrador coast in the Province and Diocese of Quebec. This, and the equally lonely Magdalen Islands, ... had been a particular care of the Society.

Thus at the turn of the century the Diocese of Quebec finally severed its apron strings and assumed financial responsibility for its own affairs. It had in the meantime achieved administrative autonomy—some 40-odd years earlier—in a manner equally peculiar to itself.

"Thought For the Morrow": Steps towards Self-Rule

Until the institution of synods in British North America, virtually all the power in the Church was vested in individual bishops whose appointment in turn was in the hands of the Crown. They were, as Glazebrooke puts it, "in positions of isolated power, so that much depended on their personal attributes."

From the earliest days, bishops on occasion delegated their authority to commissaries (as Inglis did with Toosey in Lower Canada). G. J. Mountain was the first archdeacon in the Diocese of Quebec, undertaking visitations and acting as standing assistant both to his father and to Bishop Stewart. Visitations of the Clergy, at which all diocesan clergy foregathered in one place to hear the bishop deliver his instructions or advice, had some of the qualities of a synod, but no regulatory status. No provision whatsoever was made for lay participation.

In 1832, when the annual parliamentary grant to the SPG "was threatened with extinction," it became obvious that some form of self-government for the Church in the Canadas would have to be instituted. Invoking precedents from Scotland and the United States, John Strachan (then Archdeacon of York) urged Bishop Stewart to convene annual meetings of the clergy, but to no effect. The first step in the direction of self-regulation was to be the founding of Church Societies, pioneered in Nova Scotia and New Brunswick by Bishop John Inglis (in 1836 and 1837, respectively). In 1842, the Dioceses of Toronto and Quebec followed suit, the two Societies being duly incorporated by a single Act of Parliament.

As these associations [Millman points out] were not proper synods and had no power to enact canons their creation posed no problem for English civil and ecclesiastical authorities. They were to some extent precursors of synods in that they enabled the laity to assist.the clergy in raising money for missions and for religious education and in managing the church's temporal affairs. Without a doubt they were successful in giving new energy to the church's administration.

Like the SPCK, the Church Society of the Diocese of Quebec encouraged the formation of District Associations whose members were to subscribe an annual fee (in 1842 it was 5s) in support of the stated purposes of the Society. This sum was purposely set low to attract wider support in the country districts; to be eligible for election to the Corporation, however, subscribers were expected to pay 25s per annum, or £12.10.0 for life membership.

The Central Board in which responsibility for managing the Society was vested was to consist of a president (the bishop), vice presidents (representing in part the chairmen of the District Associations), and a committee of no fewer than 12 clergymen and 12 laymen, to be chosen annually at the General Meeting of the Society. Eleven members at any meeting sufficed for a quorum.

The establishment of the Church Society represented a great advance in the distribution of power, even though the Society was far from democratic in conception. Thus, in its early years, the chairman of a District Association was *ex officio* "the Senior Clergyman holding a Pastoral charge" within its boundaries; his appointment had nothing to do with his abilities or his interest in the organization. The Lay Committee, from which the real financial support and expertise of the Society were expected to come, was to "consist of such Members as the Central Board shall appoint at their first meeting." Furthermore, the bishop's sanction was "necessary for the completion of all important acts of the Society, and especially for the revocation or alteration of the standing rules, and for the making of any addition to them."

The objects of the Church Society were five-fold:

First—Missionary labour, including the creation of a fund towards the augmentation of the stipends of poor Clergymen—towards making a provision for those who may be incapacitated by age or infirmity, and for the widows and orphans of the Clergy.
Second—Education, and Day and Sunday Schools.
Third—Assistance, where it may be necessary, to those who may be under preparation for the ministry of the Gospel.
Fourth—Circulation of the Holy Scriptures, the Book of Common Prayer, and such other Books and Tracts as shall be approved by the Central Board ...

Fifth—Aid towards the erection of Churches, &c., Parsonage Houses, and the management of all matters relating to the endowment of the same.

Parishes were initially free to retain for local purposes three-quarters of the funds collected by the treasurers of the District Associations, provided the projects conformed to the objects specified in the Constitution of the Society. Not surprisingly, individual donors were likelier to give money to meet specific needs, such as enclosing the graveyard, roofing the parsonage, or procuring a harmonium for the church, than to contribute to the general fund. Many donations were earmarked for such specific uses. The amount remitted to the Society was consequently found to be a trifling one, and parishes were soon instructed that they must not retain more than one-half of the funds collected through the District Associations. Faced with ever-increasing appeals from needy settlements with few resources of their own, the Society cast about for other sources of revenue and, from 1845, instituted the practice of requiring annual sermons to be preached in aid of its various projects:

One sermon at least [By-law XI specified] shall be preached during the year within the limits of such Parish, Station, or Chapelry, on such Sunday as the Bishop shall appoint, in favour of some one or more objects of the Society; and a collection shall then be taken up in aid thereof, the proceeds of which shall forthwith be remitted to the Treasurer ... of the Society; any Parish, Station, or Chapelry in which such sermon shall not have been preached, shall not be considered entitled to any grant or benefit from the Society, until a sermon shall have been so preached.

This no doubt provoked some grumbling, as did the begging circuits most clergy were obliged to make to secure annual subscriptions from their parishioners. The central management and apportioning of endowments could likewise be an occasion of friction between some parishes and the Central Board (see Window 20). Yet, generally, the Church Society seems to have functioned well.

An incidental benefit of the Society's operations was the free flow of information its annual reports made possible. From the beginning, these included a record of the award of grants made by the Central Board, the reports of the District Associations (and later of individual parishes), the occasional extract from Travelling Missionaries' journals, as well as membership and subscription lists for the entire Diocese. The following sample (excerpted from the Megantic District Association Report for 1850-1) illustrates the storehouse of minutiæ afforded by the Society's publications:

> The Secretary reports having been present at the Annual Meeting of this Association, held at Pointe Levi, on the 8th January last, and having been much gratified by the lively interest manifested on the occasion.
>
> At this period, the Megantic District Association was without a code of By-Laws, and much inconvenience, as might have been expected, had been the result....
>
> £83 13s 10d have been raised within this District, on account of the Society (shewing an increase over last year)—and £155 8s 1d for various local purposes. Total £239 1s 11d.
>
> The Mission of East Frampton is at present busily engaged in rebuilding in stone, and in a substantial style, the Church which was destroyed by fire in the spring of last year. It is expected that the building will be roofed in by the 1st September next.—In the Rev. W. King's extensive mission, several works are in contemplation, towards which money and labour have been promised, and among them a new stone Church ... at Cumberland Mills, the site of which, together with 200 acres, and £100 in money, were a gift from the late E. Harbottle, Esq.—In the Mission of New Ireland, £30 per annum has been engaged to be raised by the congregation of the second Inverness Church, should a resident Clergyman be established among them.—It is gratifying to be able to add that a remittance has been received this year, for the first time, from the residents at Grosse Isle [the Quarantine Station], amount £7, in addition to the sum above reported.

With the formation of diocesan synods, the functions hitherto assumed by the Church Societies were for the most part submerged in these organizations. Within Canada, only Prince Edward Island (a dependency of the Diocese of Nova Scotia) and the Diocese of Quebec have retained these Societies for the care of their missions.

In the Fall of 1849 it became clear that the long-hoped-for division of the Diocese of Quebec would finally come about with the erection of the See of Montreal. With this end in view, Mountain had retained his title of Bishop of Montreal, granted when he was consecrated suffragan bishop in 1836 and under which he had continued to administer the Diocese of Quebec even after he succeeded to the episcopate on Bishop Stewart's death. With the erection of the new diocese, new Letters Patent would be issued to appoint him to the remaining territory of his See, and restoring to use (after a lapse of 14 years) the traditional title of Bishop of Quebec.

But who would be the *new* Bishop of Montreal? As the British Government had become increasingly unwilling to intervene in the internal affairs of the colonies, it was feared in some quarters that the selection would be made by the Governor, Lord Elgin. Although popular among the Liberals, Elgin had incurred the virtual detestation of the Tories for his stand on the Rebellion Losses Bill. Most Anglicans were Tories. Although Elgin was an Anglican and (as Governor General) Patron of the Church Society, he seems to have been regarded by most churchmen as "unsuitable" to name a bishop.

In an effort to secure a say in this new appointment, some of the Diocesan clergy took the initiative to assemble their fellow clerics in order to select one of themselves as a nominee for episcopal appointment. John Bethune, Rector of Christ Church, Montreal, was the leader of this movement. Although within the decade G. J. Mountain would be struggling to organize a synod (an institution which in due course would elect his successor), in 1849 the Bishop was totally averse to such a seemingly unprecedented procedure.

"It is thought, in some quarters," Mountain observed acidly in response to Bethune's action, "that the Clergy ought to elect the Bishop, or which amounts to nearly the same thing, to be consulted, in a body, about the appointment—movements are known to have been made in this direction." Bethune's initiative, which had foundered before Mountain heard of the intended assembly, incurred his displeasure and received the following reprimand:

> Now, with respect to the election of Bishops, it is, in the first place, perfectly well known that such is not the actual practice of the Church of England ... [I]t is both idle and mischievous to contend against the exercise of the power of appointment, in the particular instance, or to raise a clamour and excite a prejudice against the proceeding.

Mountain was later to modify this view, but he seems never to have regarded the principle of electing bishops with equanimity. In 1861, in his Address at the opening of the Third Diocesan Synod, he made the following observations:

> In our own particular case in this Province,* the principle of elective bishops has been introduced. Not that it has been made compulsory: we are left free to choose our own method, in each Diocese, ... and might leave the nomina-

---

* Since the previous Synod, Bishop Francis Fulford of Montreal had been appointed Metropolitan to oversee the newly-constituted Ecclesiastical Province of Canada.

tion, if we saw good, in the hands of the Sovereign. But we may consider it, in a manner, as a settled point, that all the Bishoprics will be elective; and the day cannot be very remote when occasion will be given to put this principle in exercise within the Diocese of Quebec. I hope the Clergy and Laity will be prepared, when that day shall come, to act with a single eye to the glory of God, ... with an inviolate spirit of charity and forbearance; with an utter repudiation of all worldly intrigue and partizanship, ... [and of] every thing, in short, which is described by the word *electioneering* in the transactions of popular government in the world.

Besides the "evils and dangers ... incident, generally, to the elective principle," Mountain cautioned against the unbridled use of the legislative powers granted to the Synod:

It is, in my apprehension, very important in young institutions, like that in which we are here engaged, to avoid the vice of continually accumulating legislation.... It is better to bear some slight inconveniences and to forego some slight advantages, ... than to open the way to a sort of habitual agitation, a periodical fever of change, which would place us upon an unquiet and fluctuating basis, where we should feel nothing to be certain, nothing to be stable and solid, and which would also involve the serious evil of engrossing a large portion of that scanty time, which, under the peculiar circumstances of this Diocese, is all which is open to the disposal of business by the Synod. Nothing can more embarrass and obstruct our proceedings than such a tendency as this.

In view of Mountain's apprehensiveness about almost every aspect of synodical action, it might seem odd that he had been a prime mover in paving the way for the formation of synods in Canada. The Conference of Bishops at which this course of action was fixed upon was convoked by him and held at Quebec in 1851. After a week of deliberation, the five bishops in attendance issued a general declaration that they would seek to enlist the support of the Archbishop of Canterbury to secure the appointment of a Provincial Metropolitan to oversee "the North American dioceses," and to establish the right of "the Bishops, Clergy and Laity of the Church of England in each diocese" to "meet together in synod."

When a conference of overseas bishops gathered in England in 1853, it was Mountain as senior prelate of British North America who carried to it the message of the Quebec Conference. Bishop Broughton of Sydney, Australia, who had been consecrated with Mountain 17 years earlier in Lambeth Palace chapel, presided at first. The conference endeavoured to secure the enactment of a Bill to legalize synodical government in the colonies. Broughton died in the course of the proceedings, however, and it was Mountain who took his place in the chair. The remaining bishops—of Newfoundland, Antigua, Cape Town, and Nova Scotia—worked on under his leadership, seeking the support of "different persons in authority, ecclesiastical as well as civil."

As matters turned out, legislation was not to be forthcoming in Britain, and the instruments drawn up in the Canadas were flawed. Mountain himself was sorely tried in establishing a synod in the Diocese of Quebec (see Window 15). The emergence of Canadian synodical government, a complex and difficult matter, has been the subject of several good studies, and consequently need not be dealt with here at length. Some brief manifestations of Synod in action in this diocese will be of interest, however.

Moving in Mysterious Ways: The Election of Bishops
On 4 March 1863, a special session of Synod was convoked for the purpose of "electing a successor to the See," which had fallen vacant with the death, on 6 January, of G. J. Mountain in the 27th year of his episcopate. Although an election had already preceded the appointment of two Canadian bishops—Benjamin Cronyn of Huron in 1857 and John Travers Lewis of Ontario in 1861—the experience does not seem to have eased the difficult first steps taken in the Diocese of Quebec towards implementing that particular aspect of self-government.

The rules laid down by Synod for the election of bishops were intended to ensure overwhelming endorsement by the membership of the successful candidate, but they virtually guaranteed a lengthy contest—if not a deadlock—should there be several nominees for the office. According to Article 9 of Quebec's *Constitution of the Synod*: "when the See shall become vacant ... no election [of a new bishop] shall take place unless three-fourths of all the Clergy and Lay Representatives, respectively, of the Diocese, shall be present to form a quorum." Furthermore, a majority "consisting of not less than two-thirds of each order present" was necessary for a choice to be made.

Although distances were great and travel costly, the requisite number of clergy and lay delegates *did* duly assemble at Quebec for a projected two-day session. More than one full day was consumed, however, in wrangling over procedure. Would balloting be "silent" or would "permission be given to members to address the meeting, avoiding all invidious remarks," before balloting? Would names be proposed or would members just write their preference on their ballot? Would each ballot bear a single choice or could it "bring forth all names desired by each member?" There was even an effort to sidestep an election altogether by one amendment, moved by E. J. Hemming and seconded by James Bell Forsyth (both lay delegates):

> That, inasmuch as it is desirable ... that a contested election for a Successor to the vacant see of Quebec should if possible be avoided, a Committee of Conference, consisting of clerical delegates and lay delegates, fairly representing the different opinions held by the various members of this Synod, be named for the purpose of conferring together and ascertaining whether they can unanimously recommend ... any nominee duly qualified to fulfil the high office of Bishop in this Diocese ...

Nor was the composition of this committee to be left to chance, for the names of all 12 of its members formed part of the amendment. It was defeated.

The record of these proceedings is particularly interesting in that it shows the dominance of the position held by the See city's representatives. Of the 11 clergy serving the City (at the Cathedral, in churches, chapels, and chaplaincies), all were present and voting. Besides the eight lay delegates the City and district parishes were entitled to send to Synod, the Quebec City laity had gained a disproportionate voice by securing their appointment as delegates for outlying parishes. Forsyth, the seconder of the above amendment, was acting as lay delegate for St Paul's, Gaspé Basin. In civilian life, Forsyth was in fact a prominent merchant of Quebec, a member of the Central Board of the Church Society, and a parishioner at the Cathedral. It is worth noting that eight of the twelve-man committee he endorsed (four of the clergy and four of the laity) were drawn from among the representatives of the city of Quebec and vicinity.

Balloting did not begin until the second day. The front-runners appeared to be the Rev. Armine W. Mountain, Rector of St Michael's, Sillery, and the Rt Rev. David Anderson, Bishop of Rupert's Land since 1849. Eight other names came up from time to time. Because there was no provision for eliminating candidates with negligible support—or even to prevent new names from being introduced at any time throughout the balloting—little progress was made for some time. For the first three ballots, Mountain led in both houses, and from the second through the fourth he received the requisite clergy votes for an election. There was apparently unshakeable support for Anderson among the laity, however, and when this became obvious to the clergy, they appear to have lost heart for a time. As the proceedings wore on, a number of clergy ballots began to call for reference to Canterbury, York,

London, or merely "to England." For whatever reason, the clergy clearly did not want Anderson, and he never received more than 11 of a required 42 votes from that quarter.

Then, slowly, the Rev. J. W. Williams, Professor of Belles Lettres and Rector of the Junior Department of Bishop's College, began to gain support. In the first ballot he had received only two clerical and three lay votes; by the eighth ballot he was leading in both houses, but was still far short of the majority required in either. By the ninth ballot he had secured the necessary lay vote, but the clergy were slow to swing their support. Finally, on the eleventh ballot, Williams received the requisite 28 clergy votes, with 12 hold-outs for Mountain and a single vote for Canon Thompson whose name had appeared out of nowhere on the previous ballot. The laity, meanwhile, had given Williams 52 of their 62 votes. After this hotly-contested election, the Rev. Henry Roe, seconded by Mr H. S. Scott, moved "that the election be unanimously concurred in," which was "carried by all standing."

Thus began a long tradition of episcopal succession passing to a surprise candidate, following determined resistance (in one house or the other) to the apparently favoured choice. On Williams' death in 1892, in the 29th year of his episcopate, the same sequence was replayed. From the first ballot, the Rt Rev. Charles Hamilton, Bishop of Niagara (and former Rector of St Matthew's Church, Quebec) was far and away the favourite in both houses, but the lay vote was divided between Hamilton and Canon Thornloe, Rector of Sherbrooke, who was later to be elected Bishop of Algoma and, eventually, Metropolitan of Ontario. There was an initial show of support for Henry Roe as well. The clergy did not seem much interested in Thornloe or Roe, and had voted the required majority to Hamilton by the second ballot. No progress toward consensus was made, however. By the 11th ballot the lay vote recorded 49 for Hamilton and 31 for Thornloe, with 61 needed for an election.

Then, as had been the case in the election of 1863, a compromise candidate in the person of the Rev. A. H. Dunn, Vicar of All Saints', South Acton, in the Diocese of London, began to attract support. On the first ballot Dunn received a mere five votes, one from the clergy and four from the laity. When (by the 12th ballot), it became obvious that the houses were hopelessly deadlocked, the clergy flocked to Dunn in the 13th round, their support rising from 9 votes on the previous ballot to 34—enough for a majority in that house. The laity were quick to follow suit, and on the 14th ballot accorded 61 votes (three more than the number by then required for an election) to Dunn; Thornloe received 23, while Hamilton had sunk to two.

PLATE 11A *The congregation of Christ Church, Brompton, in 1950, with their minister the Rev. Arthur Ottiwell, Rector of St Paul's, West Sherbrooke.*

PLATE 11B *The Stubbert family at their lobster fishing camp at Coachachou near Wolf Bay, with the Rev. Robert A. Bryan, after a Service of Holy Communion, 1978.*
(Photo credit: E. O. Miller, Jr)

Once again an unforeseen selection had been made; yet Williams and Dunn would turn out to be among the most energetic and "productive" bishops the Diocese has ever known. At the time of his election, Williams' experience in Canada had been confined to college life, while Dunn, for his part, had never set foot in the country.

In the matter of episcopal elections, several Synods have shown themselves recalcitrant. On two occasions Synod has failed to elect anyone. In 1909, during Dunn's episcopate, a canon was enacted to provide for the election of a coadjutor bishop—should the bishop request it of the Executive Committee in writing, or in the event of his becoming incapacitated "by mental infirmity, age, or other permanent cause" from discharging his episcopal duties. The canon stipulated, moreover, that two-thirds of Synod had to approve a resolution to the effect that such a course of action was necessary, and that an adequate stipend should be provided for the coadjutor. Dunn obviously hoped to call this canon into play at once; but the Synod of 1910 refused to endorse the "necessity" of such a course of action.

In June 1911, Synod was called again to entertain the same request. This time the resolution to proceed received the requisite support in both houses; it was the election itself that posed problems. Since the previous Synod, Dunn had brought over from England the Rt Rev. Walter Ferrar, formerly Bishop of Antigua. Dunn had licensed Ferrar as "Assistant Bishop," a title not accorded by Synod and having no official status, but one which marked him as the heir apparent, in the Bishop's eyes at least. According to the canon, the coadjutor would succeed automatically once the See had become vacant; the election could not be regarded as a mere temporary stop-gap.

As the balloting record makes amply clear, neither the clergy nor the laity seem to have fancied Ferrar, and 15 names besides his appeared on the first ballot. Lennox Williams, Dean of the Cathedral, made a strong showing in both houses, but Synod seemed disinclined to favour anyone. By the 11th ballot, Ferrar finally received the requisite lay vote, but the clergy remained aloof. When, on the 15th ballot, the Assistant Bishop—who had never received more than 35 of the requisite 42 votes—began to *lose* support, the laity voted with their feet and quorum was lost. A final attempt the next day to resume with a 16th ballot also ended in failure, and Synod went on to other business. The project was given up altogether, and when Dunn resigned in 1914 due to ill-health, there was no successor in place.

The second failure to elect occurred in 1976, when Bishop Timothy Matthews requested the election of a coadjutor bishop. Procedures had altered very little in the interval. Quorum was now set at two-thirds, but the required two-thirds majority for election remained unchanged. There were still no formal rules, and custom had evolved few practices to facilitate a choice. No new names could now be introduced after the first (nominating) ballot, but the names of candidates with negligible support (even those who had disappeared entirely for a round) were not eliminated unless they themselves requested it. There was by now some effort made to provide information about nominees from outside the Diocese:

> In accordance with a prior resolution of the Executive Committee [reads the Journal of Synod], the Clerical Secretary read from "Crockford's Clerical Directory" or the "Directory of Episcopal Clergy" as the case may be, the standard information regarding each of those clergymen whose names appeared in the first ballot, but who are not members of this Diocese.

On this occasion, everything possible to guide the spirit of Synod to consensus seems to have been done. On the night before the election, "a group of Young People from the Quebec Deanery had kept an all-night vigil of prayer for Synod in All Saints' Chapel from 10:00 p.m. Thursday until 8:00 a.m. Friday." The election was held in the Cathedral itself, "within the context of the Holy Eucharist," as the Bishop reminded the members in his Charge. The envelopes containing the ballots and listing the nominations were placed on the Altar, "together with the offerings of the congregation." The second ballot was called after "Gloria in Excelsis," and "during the latter part of the afternoon (after the ninth ballot) a group of singers in the galleries broke into the spontaneous singing of modern hymns during the pauses between some of the ballots." All was to no avail. After the 15th ballot the Bishop declared "No Election" and called for a motion to adjourn.

It is worth noting that at the electoral Synod following each of these failed elections (in 1914 and 1977, respectively), the choice of a bishop was made with ease. The Very Rev. Lennox Williams was elected on the second ballot, and the Very Rev. Allen Goodings on the fifth. At the latter election, provision was made to eliminate names "simultaneously low in both houses." The procedures laid down at the 1990 synod were designed to urge the members more firmly towards a consensus; it was stipulated that "the name of the candidate receiving [the] lowest number of votes in both houses simultaneously, shall be withdrawn," a practice which could (and did) produce in due course a ballot with a single candidate, in contrast to previous elections. The majority accorded on this occasion far surpassed the two-thirds required in each order, but the regulation as it was applied favoured election by default.

Another regulation, long overdue, was also added in 1990: that the nomination of persons not resident in the Diocese or not present at Synod "must have the written consent of the nominee." The utility of this provision becomes clear in light of the following incident. In 1900, Lennox Williams, then Dean of the Cathedral, was informed by telegram that he had been elected Coadjutor Bishop of Ontario with the title of Bishop of Kingston and with right of succession to the See of Ontario. The following is an excerpt from his reply:

> I shall not lay stress upon the feeling of my own unfitness for such a high and responsible position, for fear of seeming to be guilty of cant, and still worse, of a lack of trust in God, but nevertheless I feel it very keenly.
>
> Apart, however, from this, that which has chiefly led me to the decision at which I have arrived is the conviction which has been growing stronger and stronger, ever since I first received your telegram, that I have taken up a work in this Cathedral which I dare not yet lay down....
>
> It would be impossible for me to explain the circumstances and conditions connected with my acceptance of this charge. Let it suffice to say that I conscientiously believe it to have been God's will that I should enter upon this work. I have been here just one year, and having met with unusual willingness on the part of the congregation to sink differences and preferences, and to co-operate for the welfare of the Church, I feel in honour bound to remain until the work thus happily begun, but only just begun, is on a more solid basis. Believing and praying that God will guide your Synod to a right choice, I remain,
>
> Very sincerely yours
> Lennox Williams

By resolution of the 1990 Synod, the DEC was instructed "to strike a Task Force which would evaluate the present process of Nomination and Selection of a Bishop and further investigate additions and alternatives to the existing process." At the time of writing, the Task Force had not filed a report. There are at present still no standing rules governing the election of bishops to the See of Quebec.

"An Obviously Desirable Innovation": Extending the Franchise to Women
On 29 October 1920, Canon XVII—*Of the Temporalities of the Church in this Diocese*—was amended by the Lieutenant Governor in Council to extend the right to form part of the Vestry of free Churches to "all those ... female members of the Congregation, of the full age of twenty-one (21) years ..."

In his Charge to the Synod of 1934, Bishop Lennox Williams "pre-

PLATE 12A A.Y.P.A. Conference, Quebec Lodge, 1945.

PLATE 12B Senior Girls' Camp, Fort Haldimand, Gaspé, 1949.

sented the question of the desirability of giving women representation in the Synod." This subject, as the Bishop pointed out, had been prompted by a resolution adopted at the Lambeth Conference of 1920 that "women should be admitted to those Councils of the Church to which Laymen are admitted, and on equal terms. Diocesan, Provincial or National Synods may decide when or how this principle is to be brought into effect."

The notion met with determined resistance although the subject of extending the franchise came up regularly at Synod, especially after World War II. For three consecutive Synods the Very Rev. R. L. Seaborn was to move, seconded by Mr S. A. Meade, that the canon barring laywomen from representing their congregations at Synod be amended. Parishes were consulted and of the 31 returning replies, 19 were in favour of the motion. In 1951, "after a spirited debate the motion was defeated by a standing vote by orders—Clerical: for 13, against 25; Lay: for 29, against 21." In 1953, Archbishop Carrington remarked rather testily in his Charge that "the admission of women to membership in this Synod has been more than once rejected on the floor of this house. It may interest you to know that the Synod of Toronto has taken this step, and that 17 women have been elected as members." He might also have mentioned that women had been "duly appointed" as delegates to General Synod since 1946 when Mrs R. E. Wodehouse, Dominion President of the W.A., had taken her seat to represent the Diocese of the Yukon.

In 1963 and 1965, despite continued opposition (duly recorded in the Synod Journal), the necessary ratification at two consecutive Synods was at last secured. Among those supporting the motion were Archdeacons John Comfort, Guy Marston and T. J. Matthews, Canon W.H.M. Church, Chancellor H. E. Grundy, Q.C., and Dr D. C. Masters. Of the original movers, Seaborn had left the Diocese in 1958 on his election as Assistant Bishop of Newfoundland and Bert Meade had died, aged 79, in 1961. Finally, at the 1968 Synod, Bishop Brown welcomed the first female delegates (15 of whom were present) with characteristic courtesy:

> It is significant that at this Synod, at which we recognize the change in name of our national women's organization from "Woman's Auxiliary" to "Anglican Church Women," we should also welcome as full delegates to our Synod— women from various parts of the Diocese. Their presence here to-day makes one wonder why in the past there should have been any debate about such an obviously desirable innovation.

It would appear, however, from the Report of the Committee on the

Bishop's Charge, that the innovation had gone down hard. "We consider with you My Lord that it is cause for delight that women delegates are present," it began. "While some members of your committee, notwithstanding retain reservations on the feminine presence here, yet none of us you may be sure withholds his hearty concurrence that Synod has admitted women delegates." Far from taking the lead from the Bishop in making the best of a *fait accompli*, the committee's stipulated "reservations on the feminine presence," its avowals of "delight" and "hearty concurrence," strike one as somewhat less than sincere—a fine instance of what might be termed as "Anglicant."

In 1969, the Diocese sent as its first youth delegate to General Synod a Quebec high school senior, Jane Corkran. In an article highlighting her experiences there, she outlined the measures taken to broaden future representation:

> Many other issues were presented ... but to me one of the most important was the resolutions concerning youth.... A great step was taken ... in that fifteen young people will be chosen for the next General Synod in 1971 where they will be full members with a right to vote if this resolution is passed again.... Along with this resolution another was carried allowing adequate representation by youth on the standing committees of the Anglican Church of Canada.

The introduction of wider representation at Synod, whether at the Diocesan, Provincial, or General Synod level, was bound to have some impact, but in the Diocese of Quebec the shock appears to have been minimal. Women's names began to appear among those appointed to serve on Diocesan committees, councils, and boards, initially showing particular strength on the Diocesan Council for Social Service. As for raising a distinctive voice, however, it would be the youth delegates who would rattle the windows and call for appreciable changes.

At the Diocesan Synod of 1974, for example, although the three youth delegates in attendance had no vote, the Report they filed (printed as "Appendix K" of the Synod Journal) could not have failed to raise uncomfortable questions among the regular members. The Report, which was brief and to the point, consisted of three resolutions passed at Youth Synod, a declaration of support for the ordination of women to the priesthood, and

> a statement of sentiment which Youth Synod has requested be forwarded to Diocesan Synod and General Synod.
> We the members of this Youth Synod of the Diocese of Quebec are concerned

that the institutionalized church has lost its bearings when it spends as much time on such issues as church union, the ordination of women, and initiation rites.*

It is our opinion that the most important matter is the revitalization of the church. We need to develop a strong supportive Christian community so that Christians can be given a strong spiritual renewal to help them take on the labours of the world.

Topics such as capital punishment, euthanasia, starvation and ecology are also of great importance because they deal with human lives.

Although General Synod had made provision for youth representatives in the 1970s, it was not until 1990 that the Diocese of Quebec enfranchised its own youth delegates at home.

Autonomy came to the Canadian Church largely through the formation of Diocesan Synods. "The next step," as Carrington pointed out

was the appointment of a Metropolitan (or presiding bishop), and the formation of a "Provincial Synod" to include all the dioceses, so creating an autonomous and national Church order, which would no longer be dependent on the British government and on the Archbishop of Canterbury for episcopal consecrations and for other acts and decisions on a higher level than that of the diocese. It would also draw the much-too-independent dioceses into a common bond of order and self-government.

The "common bond" was not to be achieved nationally, however, until the formation of General Synod in 1893.

"Decisions on a Higher Level": The Diocese of Quebec in Perspective
In the national context, the Diocese of Quebec—as one of the smaller dioceses in Canada in Anglican population and numbers of licensed clergy, if not in territory—has stirred little water. Where decisions of General Synod have determined policies, priorities, and discipline, the Diocese of Quebec (which, like other minority jurisdictions, operates within a framework peculiar to itself) may well have experienced a diminution in autonomy. Its voice in proceedings is very small: "The [General] Synod's members have always represented dioceses, whose appropriate authorities have selected their clerical and lay representative. Each diocese has heretofore been entitled to a number of representatives of each of the two orders based on the number of licensed

---

* These were the three main issues under discussion at Synod that year.

diocesan clergy.''

Dissatisfaction about representation at General Synod among members of the Ecclesiastical Province of Canada (within which Quebec has long since been among the weakest in number of licensed clergy) led the provincial synod of that province to make a presentation (in 1987) to the National Executive Council: "It asserted that membership based on numbers of licenced clergy is wrong; the clergy are not the Church; the whole people of God make up the Church; all have a ministry and not the clergy alone."

In response to this, a Task Force was set up which accepted the claim of Provincial Synod and recommended a change in diocesan representation at General Synod. Although the resolution embodying the Task Force's recommendations received General Synod approval in 1989, the required second ratification in 1992 was not forthcoming. Had the resolution passed, no diocese would have been represented by fewer than two—or more than nine—members of *each* order, plus the bishop and a youth member. By way of discouraging support for the measure, it was shown in debate that under this new model "the size of synod would increase from 224 to 258" members. In the wake of a series of amendments to the resolution,

> one delegate pointed out the synod was trying to rewrite one of its founding documents on the floor, and moved referral back to the organization committee. Synod agreed.
>
> The organization committee was asked to explore alternate models of representation, including equal representation from each diocese.

To the 1992 assembly, the Diocese of Quebec had sent a delegation of eight (four men and four women): three clergymen, three laywomen, one youth delegate, and the bishop. In the unlikely event of the adoption of the "equal representation" model, Quebec would be among the dioceses with most to gain.

CHAPTER IV

Within and Without:
A Sampling of Trials, Triumphs and Controversies

Although sectarianism had been deeply rooted in Britain for centuries and was transplanted to the American colonies by the first settlers, some members of the Church of England entertained the hope that the Protestant population in the Canadas could be united within a single fold: its own. As late as 1820, Charles James Stewart, then a missionary in the field, still expressed faith in its possibility.

> It is to be regretted that the influence of the Gospel in Canada has by many obstacles been hitherto impeded [he began his report to the SPG]; ...These obstacles arise principally from the want of unity among the people, and the variety of sects into which they are divided; each sect being desirous of a minister, and form of service, agreeable to their own religious persuasion, and, consequently, indisposed to unite in erecting a house of prayer.

Having made this observation—which was certainly well-founded—Stewart urged it as an argument for securing pre-eminence for the Church of England in Canada, presumably by levying church rates:

> Such being the effect of disunion [he continued], it is of primary importance to induce the people to unite in one communion, by contributing to the support of an ecclesiastical establishment, which affords certain provision for the regular performance of public worship, and the best security for peace and prosperity in every community.

Stewart's dreams of unity under the Anglican banner were not to be realized, of course, and the multiplicity of sects continued. In his account of a visit to Melbourne in 1846, for example, G. J. Mountain related that the residence of his missionary, the Rev. C. B. Fleming, stood "upon a line and in close proximity with a row of meeting-houses, belonging to different denominations." Within the limits of this mission alone, "eleven varieties" of sects were to be found. Ever frugal and practical, some communities chose to build a Mission Hall for the use, at need, of any preacher (whether local or just passing through) who could attract an audience (see Window 6).

Malbay G. A. Guides at
Senior Girls Festival, May 1951.
Captain - Mrs. H. I. Apps.

Malbay G. A. Guides.

The Malbay G. A. was organized in November 1945, and were affiliated with the Guides in 1947. The present membership is fourteen.

For the past three years the Malbay G. A. Guides have taken part in the "Gaspé Deanery Senior Girls' Festival". Some of their numbers have also attended camp at "Fort Haldimand."

Mrs. H. I. Apps had been in charge of this group since its formation.

York. G. A. Guides.

The 1st York G. A. Guide Company grew out of a Girls' Club, which was organized by Mrs. J. Comfort. This club became a G. A. Guide Company in 1943. Mrs. Clifford Patterson, who assisted Mrs. Comfort, later became the first Captain. Her 1st Lieutenant up until this year was Mrs. Philip Patterson.   (or Girls' Club)

These G. A. Guides, have attended every festival, since the 1st Festival in Canada was organized by Mrs. Comfort in 1937 or 1938. A good representation of these G. A.

1st York. G. A. Guide Company, at Senior Girls Festival May '51. Captain - Mrs. Clifford Patterson.

Guides have attended every camp, first when the camps were held at Cape Cove, and also since they have been held at Fort "Haldimand" Camp.

Sandy Beach G. A. Guides.

The first Sandy Beach G. A. Guide Company was organized by Miss Nancy Machin and Mrs. Guy Marston in August 1942, with Mrs. Marston as Captain. In 1946 they were taken over by Mrs. E. S. Reed, assisted, by Mrs. Archie Alexander, In Nov. 1947 Mrs. Alexander became Captain, and in spring of 1946 Mrs. Rockejacquelin

---

PLATE 13 *Diocesan G. A. Guides (from the Gaspé Deanery G.A. Scrapbook). Twelve other Diocesan G.A.s are also profiled in the Scrapbook.*

Anglicans, for their part, did not (or at any rate were not supposed to) lend their church facilities to members of other denominations. When it came to Bishop Stewart's attention in 1832 that "one of the Methodist Preachers" in the Eastern Townships had lately made use of an Anglican church "upon occasion of a Funeral," he sent a sharp reprimand to the incumbent responsible for letting this happen:

> Upon the presumption that the information which has reached me is correct [he bristled] ... it becomes my duty to remark that such a proceeding is quite unauthorised and must not be repeated. I could have hoped that the rules and discipline of the Church of England were so well known as to have precluded the necessity of the interposition of my authority in any such matter.... I wish the principles of the Church to be always upheld in a spirit of meekness and charity, but we have no right to compromise them.

This policy of excluding other denominations was neither popular nor equitable, particularly since Anglican clergy were not averse to seeking and receiving accommodation in Dissenting churches whenever convenient. In 1845, Bishop Mountain refused the use of St Anne's Chapel in Griffintown to the Wesleyan Methodists, whose church in the same neighbourhood had lately been destroyed by fire. He was roundly attacked for it in the newspapers.

In a Pastoral Letter to the clergy and laity of his diocese, written soon after the Griffintown affair, Mountain dealt with the question of "Affording the Use of Churches and Chapels ... For the Purposes of Dissenting Worship." The Pastoral Letter alluded to the adverse reaction his ruling had provoked:

> It was easy to foresee [he wrote] that in the exercise of such an act of authority ... the Church and her servant would be exposed to no small share of odium and probably abuse. The attack of the Press ... ready for any opportunity of a new fling at the Governors of the Church of England, was precisely what was to be anticipated, and I was fully prepared for it.

It should be added that, before the Bishop had intervened, the people of St Anne's (residents of a poor working district in Montreal) had spontaneously offered the use of their church to their Methodist neighbours. Mountain's belated injunction had forced his parishioners to go back on their offer, and to turn the homeless victims out. In imposing his decision, the Bishop argued that his hands were tied; yet the criticism he incurred in con-

St. John's Church, Shawinigan Falls

St.
John

The
Evangelist

This city was started about the year 1900 by some people, who decided to make use of the water falls on the St. Maurice river here. They built a dam on the river, other people built a paper-mill and still others a factory to make aluminum. The first Church of England services were held here in 1900 and the Church population was very small. Even then the majority of people were French speaking, although the Industries were all started by English speakers. In the year 1908 our church was still the only Protestant Church and the number of families attached to it was thirty.

To-day there are 35,000 people in Shawinigan Falls and nearly 34,000 of them are French Roman Catholics. There are two Non-Roman Catholic Churches, ours and a United Church and both of them have about 100 families, about 600 people each. We have the same Church that was built originally, but it has been enlarged a little and is covered with stone. Originally it was just a wooden building. It also has a good basement under the whole building with wash rooms and a kitchen. The present Rector is Rev. Sydney W. Williams.

There is a Sunday School with 88 children and 12 teachers. Some of the older boys act as servers. There is a Woman's Guild and a Woman's Auxiliary and an Altar Guild. There are Guides and Brownies and Scouts and Cubs. There is a good school here with grades from Kindergarten to Grade XII.

The largest industry here, employing over 1000 men is Shawinigan Chemicals. It makes Calcium Carbide and acetic Acid and also makes Vynilite Plastic. The Consolidated Paper Corporation is about the same size and makes over 700 tons of paper a day. Canadian Industries Ltd. make all the Cellophane for Canada here and also make Caustic Soda. The Aluminum Company makes Aluminum and Aluminum Wire.

PLATE 14 *Shawinigan Falls (from the Gaspé Deanery G.A. Scrapbook).*

sequence of it stung him nonetheless.

> The disposal of the Church for this purpose or for that, is not among the at-
> tributes of the Vestry; not among the things confided to popular judgment....
> [Not even a bishop] is *at liberty* to sanction or permit the appropriation of any
> Church or Chapel subject to his jurisdiction, for the worship of separatists from
> his own communion.... It is manifest unfairness and injustice to attack the *man*
> for that which his *office* obliges him to do; ...

In other areas of church discipline, Mountain showed remarkable flexibility. The situation in Canada, as he was well aware, was different from that
in Great Britain, and when British-trained clergy wished to adhere strictly
to practices in current use there, the Bishop often counselled moderation.
In 1859, the recently installed A. H. Pearse, SPG Missionary at Bourg Louis,
alerted the Bishop to the fact that there were persons whose marriage fell
within the prohibited degrees in his parish. In this particular case, a parishioner had (some time earlier) married his deceased wife's sister, and Pearse
wished to know whether he should deny the couple the sacraments if they
should present themselves at a Communion Service. Mountain's reply impresses us by its humaneness and moderation. It also suggests that he regarded
the Scriptures (in which he did not find this prohibition upheld) as the final authority.

> Although I hold such marriages in much abhorrence [the Bishop affirmed], I
> have never been able to arrive at a *clear & absolute conclusion* that they consti-
> tute a violation of the Law of God. In this country they are not held to be
> illegal.... In the U. States, although the Bishops & Clergy generally, perhaps
> almost unanimously, disapprove of such marriages, the Church [there] has not
> *pronounced* against them—& there are not infrequent examples of their being
> contracted between parties who continue to be admitted, without any demur
> or remark, to the holy Communion. Such communicants, in different in-
> stances, have passed into Canada &, settling among us, have presented them-
> selves at the table of the Lord, without causing any question to be stirred re-
> specting their title to that privilege. As we lie close alongside of the American
> Church & are constantly liable to the occurrence of such cases, it would breed
> a vast amount of ill feeling & put us in great embarassment, if we were to re-
> pel the parties.

Mountain was well aware, however, that it would be injudicious to make
such a pronouncement publicly, let alone to promulgate it as the policy of
his Church. He therefore urged Pearse to treat his reply as "off the record"

and confidential: "Under all these circumstances I will, if you please, regard your enquiry as strictly private, & I will say *unofficially* that I think it the wisest course to *take no notice* of the irregularity in question.... One thing, known, is very clear, that our Clergy ought not to *solemnize* such marriages."

He underscored the necessity of avoiding open confrontations about such matters by recounting a public incident that had occurred at Quebec over a similar marriage. One of his clergy had "repelled the wife from Communion," and Mountain's authority had been invoked in an effort to reverse his stand. Given the circumstances, however, the Bishop had little choice, whatever his personal feelings:

> Complaints were made to me: & I was obliged to sustain the act of the Clergyman—since he had only complied with the strong & positive decision of the Church in England. A great excitement was caused—the parties seceded from the Church—and the sore has not been healed to this day. Although I ought to be prepared upon such questions, I must frankly confess that this is one which I have found as perplexing as it is painful.

Difficulties of a different order arose when British clergy were sent into outlying regions where their parishioners were unfamiliar with almost every aspect of Church doctrine and usage. Some (like C. J. Stewart) strove patiently to teach their people and to bring them along step by step; others regarded their questions as insolent and beneath their notice. The Rev. Silas Crosse, for example, refused to attend his parish Vestry meetings at Cape Cove, Gaspé, "on the grounds that he has been often grossly insulted." In 1861, George Milne, as Rural Dean, was asked to visit Crosse (who had been posted there on in 1857) to assess the difficulties he was experiencing. Milne reported that

> on speaking with one of the Church wardens, who has been very friendly with Mr Crosse, on this subject, he said he did not know of any [insults] except that Mr Andrew Cass had asked at last Easter meeting whether they were Protestants or Roman Catholics.... The same Church Warden told me that, although Mr C refuses to attend the Vestry meetings to state what he wants, immediately after, numerous notes are sent to the Ch Ws telling them that this or that must be done....There seems to be on Mr C's part ... a sort of complacent self assurance that it is impossible but that he is always in the right. This was apparent in my private conversations with him, when as your Lordship suggested I remarked that a good deal of forbearance & caution was necessary in dealing with people situated like those of Cape Cove ...

Mr Cass, as likely as not, had asked his question in good faith.

Under the circumstances it is not surprising that the first bishops soon saw the advantage of securing clergy of a tractable and adaptable nature, and early entertained the possibility that local people—familiar with the stringencies of pioneer life—might be trained to qualify for Holy Orders. Even so, the demand for missionaries far outstripped the supply (particularly in view of the widely scattered population), so that it was necessary to raise from among the educated laity an unordained itinerant ministry to meet this need.

"For the Purposes of Public Worship": The Ministry of Catechists

From the earliest days of the Diocese of Quebec, the SPG had supported catechists to minister to the Native Peoples, but it was not until Bishop Stewart applied to the Society to extend this provision to the rapidly increasing immigrant population that catechists (with permission to act as lay readers) appeared in significant numbers in the Diocese. After just six years (from 1830 to the end of Stewart's episcopate), at least 33 such persons had been appointed. In return for their services they usually received, "according to their abilities and usefulness," between £10 and £20 per annum—a sum quite inadequate to support themselves and their families. Many were forced to eke out their allowance by taking pupils and teaching school to earn their livelihood.

The duties of catechists included gathering the people for public worship, forming and teaching Sunday schools (which for many children furnished their only opportunity for learning to read or write), visiting the sick, promoting family prayers, and distributing tracts and religious books. Most had to travel extensively to reach their people. In his annual report for 1836, John Eden (catechist at Gaspé Bay) writes particularly of this:

> On reference to my Report, Your Lordship will please observe that I have performed Service at the Church fourteen Sundays during the absence of the Reverend William Arnold, and to shew Your Lordship that I have been diligent in the execution of my duties I have several times after Divine Service in the Morning attended at the Peninsula and Sandy Beach in the afternoon, and [with] the bad state of the Roads during the Winter, it has been as late as ten o'clock at night before I reached my home, and very much fatigued—During the past Year I have travelled about five hundred and seventy-six miles in Boating and Walking on the Sabbath days, exclusive of visiting the Sick; this is on an average of Sixteen miles per day attending on the out-Stations, performing two Services in each day and Catechising and instructing the Chil-

dren during the time of the Services.

Eden served the region as catechist and lay reader for six years, receiving £20 per annum (about one-tenth of a clerical stipend). In the same report he mentioned that the local people had not been able to pay their portion of his salary as local schoolmaster—some were in arrears by "several years"—and that he was consequently experiencing great difficulty in supporting his wife and five children. Despite these hardships and trials, his meticulous reports of attendance at church and in the various Sunday schools reveal that his ministry was crowned with considerable success. He read services and taught Sunday schools at Peninsula, Sandy Beach, and South West Branch, sometimes with congregations of 70, 80, or 90 persons, depending on the weather. In 1835 alone, he prepared 52 candidates for confirmation.

Once persuaded to accept the principle of the widespread employment of catechists, the SPG renewed the annual grant of £500 for the five-year period from 1831 to 1836. When funds fell short, Bishop Stewart advanced money of his own to support them. Indeed, on the settlement of his estate it was found that some £375 was owing to it, partly by the catechists' fund. "The development of this group of lay workers," the Bishop's biographer suggests, "was one of the most effective and practical steps which Stewart took for the welfare of the church throughout his whole episcopate."

Many catechists appear to have been actuated by a real sense of vocation, and some went on to qualify for ordination. At least ten of Bishop Stewart's catechists (Charles Forest being one) took Holy Orders. Others continued year after year, however, without hope of bettering their position. If this seems hardly credible by present standards, it was no less so to Bishop Jacob Mountain:

> Where there is no hope of advancement [he wrote to the Archbishop of Canterbury in 1803], there can be little expectation of engaging the services of men of ability & worth. Respectable & useful Ministers of our Church will not easily be induced to spend their lives in the Wilds of this Country, without any prospect of emerging, to such more convenient & more honorable stations, as their labours & virtues may be found to deserve.—That primitive zeal which could induce men wholly to forgo every comfort of this life, for the sake of propagating the true Religion, I fear is rarely to be found amongst us; at least it has not been my good fortune to find it.

Transfusions and Hæmorrhages: Getting and Spending Diocesan Clergy
Recruiting clergy to serve in the Diocese has consistently posed a major

problem. Many postings continue to be to isolated areas, a situation that has often led to rapid turnover of clergy in the more remote parishes. Between 1914 and 1994, for example, Holy Trinity Church at Grosse Isle on the Magdalen Islands was served by 20 different ministers, 7 of whom remained for no more than a year. Similar examples could be produced for other regions.

In 1970, the Faculty of Divinity at Bishop's University anticipated General Synod's recommendation to confine training for the Ministry "to the three centres" (Halifax, Toronto, and Vancouver), by declaring that "it would no longer be practicable, in view of the paucity of prospective enrolments, for the Faculty to offer, as one of its contributions to education, specific preparation for Holy Orders." Since that time, the Diocese has been entirely dependent on Anglican seminaries outside its borders for the training of its priests and deacons, and it may not be surprising that ordinands presenting themselves to the Bishop of Quebec have generally tended to move on. Of five candidates ordained in 1979, three had left the Diocese by 1984; of fifteen ordained in 1987, only six were still serving there at the close of 1993.

Jacob Mountain's warning that a lack of "more convenient & more honorable stations" would discourage clergy from entering or remaining in the Diocese may well have had its impact, too. The office of bishop aside, the most desirable position in the Diocese is clearly that of Dean of the Cathedral. For Diocesan clergy, however, such a position has almost invariably been out of reach. Although this state of affairs has been due to the exercise of rights vested in the Cathedral congregation and not to diocesan or episcopal policy, the fact remains that of the ten deans collated to the Cathedral since the creation of the Chapter in 1888, all but three have been appointed from outside the Diocese; only one local priest has been called to serve since 1915.

While the early bishops looked to Britain to provide them with clergy, efforts were soon made to prepare local candidates for ordination. The impetus for this appears to have come as much from the citizenry as from the Bishop. As the *Abstract of the Proceedings* of the SPG for 1816 reported:

> The Lord Bishop of Quebec transmits to the Society an application which had been made to him by some of the most respectable characters in the Province, on the propriety of granting an allowance of £50 *per annum* to a certain number of young men from the age of eighteen or nineteen to twenty-three, to enable them to pursue their studies as candidates for Holy Orders, the parents giving security for the repayment of the money should the students relinquish their intention; the Society, duly impressed with the advantages that

may arise from an encouragement of this nature, have agreed to place, for a limited time, the annual sum of £200, at the disposal of the Bishop ...

Until 1828 (the year Bishop Stewart commissioned Joseph Braithwaite to establish a seminary at Chambly in what is today the Diocese of Montreal), "young Canadians desirous of being ordained had to reside in the parsonages of experienced priests of the diocese and learn what they could about theology in the midst of the inevitable interruptions of a clerical household."

Eager as he was to recruit local candidates for the ministry, Stewart was far from uncritical of the abilities and prospects of those who presented themselves to his notice. In a personal memorandum book that noted the names, current occupations, and state of progress of potential students, he recorded that one, a man named Walker, "has poor opportunities" and appeared "weak & dull." Concerning another named Johnson, he remarked that the applicant "w^d be no acquisition"; he "discouraged his expectations & recommended [by letter] his pursuing another line of life." Once accepted for serious consideration, the thoroughness of a candidate's preparation was verified by examinations (both written and oral) set by the Bishop himself and other senior clergy. The first seminary within the boundaries of the present Diocese was established at Trois-Rivières in 1840, with four students, under the direction of the Rev. Samuel Simpson Wood. The project, however, was abandoned three years later with the founding of Bishop's College, Lennoxville. Wood was offered, but declined, the principalship of the College, at a salary of £100 a year.

Henry Roe, one of the original ten who formed the first class at Bishop's in 1845, recalled that, for their first year, Principal Jasper Nicolls "comprised the entire College staff in his own person." Despite its modest beginnings, the College came to exercise "a considerable influence on the development of the Canadian church" by fostering in Nicolls' "old boys" a unanimity of thought and churchmanship that "strengthened the Church in Quebec in the fight against Methodism and also helped to prevent the rise of any appreciable Anglican Evangelical movement in the Province." It remained for Ontario and, in particular, for Wycliffe College (founded in 1877) "to develop the modern Evangelical wing of the Church of England in Canada."

By 1877, over half of the Diocesan clergy (30 out of 53) were "Bishop's men," and more than a quarter of those serving the Diocese of Montreal (23 out of 90) were either graduates or members of the faculty. Of the eight bishops elected since the founding of the College, all but two have had ties with Bishop's. J. W. Williams and Philip Carrington moved to the episcopate directly from faculty positions; Russel Brown and T. J. Matthews prepared for ordination there; while Bruce Stavert (before pursuing theological studies at Trinity College, Toronto) had graduated in Arts from Bishop's and later returned to serve as University Chaplain. Lennox Williams (although he received his university training at Oxford and studied Divinity at Leeds) was born in Lennoxville and graduated as Head Prefect from Bishop's College School.

Fr John G. McCausland, a graduate in Divinity from Bishop's, described the College in 1928 as "one of the last stands of the church-controlled university." He recalled that the Divinity House diploma, given on graduation, "certified that the student had attended retreats, spiritual conferences, the daily meditation, and other spiritual exercises." Dean Jellicoe, in announcing to Synod that the Faculty of Divinity would cease to prepare candidates for Holy Orders, referred to the impossibility of any longer offering that "corporate life of worship, devotional exercises and practical pastoral training" to such small numbers.

> While I am certain that it is God's will [McCausland wrote], I have found it very difficult to accept the closing of the theological faculty at Bishop's University, Lennoxville, Quebec. It is out of date to think of "Anglican colleges and universities," but the relationship between revealed religion and the daily round of community and worship gave us a stability which might be very useful in these present days.

In providing itself with clergy, the Diocese has amassed a considerable debt to other denominations over the years. Indeed, as Strachan did in Upper Canada, Stewart and both Mountains (among others) kept a lookout for local ministers in other communions willing to receive Anglican Orders. Thus they swelled the ranks of their clergy with less recourse to England. Among those serving the Diocese, for example, S. H. Coleman, John Flanagan, and James Thornloe had originally been ordained as Methodists; Jonathan Taylor and A. C. Scarth began their ministries as Presbyterians; and Jean-Baptiste Gauthier had first received Roman Catholic Orders (see Window 13). Besides these reinforcements to the priesthood, a number of converts to Anglicanism from a variety of other denominations have presented themselves as candidates for the ministry. In 1993, this was true of at least six members (about 14 percent) of the Diocesan clergy.

Thus, from the first clergy appointments (by Government) to those of the present day, the Diocese has regularly "broadened the tradition" normally represented in the nurture and training of its priests. What impact this may have had locally is difficult to assess, but the widespread cooperation in ecumenical activities at the grass-roots parish level in this Diocese (as opposed to formal representations between denominations in the national and supranational context) may well bear some relationship to this practice.

"The Question of Christian Reunion"

Although the groundswell for church union of the 1960s—which for a decade seemed to favour a fusion of the Anglican and United Churches of Canada—has largely eclipsed earlier ecumenical discussions, the issue of "Christian Reunion" was then far from new, even in Canadian terms. The startling repercussions of Vatican II, by which Pope John XXIII "brought the [Roman] Catholic Church in a certain sense into the vanguard of ecumenism," was a complicating factor for Anglicans, especially those whose impulse towards unity lay more in the direction of Rome than Geneva.

As it has been pointed out, Confederation was seen by many Protestant leaders as an occasion "for greater consolidation within denominational families." Once this was accomplished, there were soon others who "dared to think beyond these denominational mergers, proposing greater cooperation among denominations."

> It was the Anglicans who actually forwarded the first official proposal for union across denominational lines, spurred on by the discussion of the issue at their 1888 Lambeth Conference. They made important overtures at a Conference on Christian Union held in Toronto in 1889. However, discussions foundered on the issue of apostolic succession, [upon] acceptance of which the Lambeth Conference had insisted.

In the 1890s, the Congregationalists, Methodists, and Presbyterians pursued church union vigorously, and by 1908 "representatives of the three uniting denominations had agreed on a Basis of Union for what became in 1925 the United Church of Canada."

In his 1907 Charge to Synod, Bishop A. H. Dunn made reference to this impulse towards union. Although gently put and mildly phrased, his position was clear. Union among Protestants, where Anglicans were concerned, was of interest only insofar as it would lead to ultimate union with Rome and the Eastern Churches:

> Another matter which I hope is frequently engaging your attention is the ques-

tion of Christian Reunion ... Let us, I would say, whatever our opinion upon the subject may be, let us all be constantly praying for this reunion, leaving the way in which it shall be obtained entirely to our ever Blessed Lord. As members of the Canadian Part or Portion of the Anglican Communion we are not able, even if we would, to ask for less than the Pan-Anglican Quadrilateral, until the Pan-Anglican Conference of all our Bishops at Lambeth calls for less. But by our loving kindness, and by shewing that we have no feeling of superiority and no idea of absorbing other Religious Bodies, we may be able to find a way, in which they will be very glad to receive the Historic Episcopate, as the old plan and the divinely ordered plan for the Consecration and Ordination of Ministers. And we must always remember that we cannot give up this ... without losing the opportunity, ... when all men become more enlightened, ... of re-union with the other Old Historic Portions of the Holy Catholic Church, the Church of Rome and the Churches of the East.

After the fusion of denominations that had produced the United Church of Canada, "Canadian union schemes remained quiescent until 1943, when the Anglican Church of Canada renewed the invitation to discuss union with any Christian body." For the next two decades, "Committees of Ten" from each of three denominations—the Anglican and United Churches of Canada and the continuing Presbyterian Church—"carried on conversations on basic theological principles." In May 1965, agreement was reached by the Committees of the two former bodies on the Principles of Union.

Meanwhile, at the Third Assembly of the World Council of Churches, held in New Delhi in 1961, the Russian Orthodox Church had sought and was given membership in that body for the first time. The Roman Catholic Church, hitherto entirely aloof, had sent official observers. The next year saw the Second Vatican Council (1962-65), and, finally, in the summer of 1963, the Faith and Order IV Conference held in Montreal. "From each of these assemblies there came new initiatives and fresh vision, all interacting, all conducive to a revolution in the ecumenical movement."

Initially, beginning in 1964, a euphoria of ecumenism burst upon the Diocese of Quebec (see Window 39). Numerous interdenominational services were held, and descriptions and photographs of these were prominently featured in the *Diocesan Gazette*. Under the headline "Brotherhood in Action!" the 1965 March issue described ecumenical services held at Trois-Rivières and Thetford Mines; an ecumenical study session at Arvida; and a luncheon, hosted by the Roman Catholic Archbishop of Sherbrooke, at which His Grace addressed a gathering of Anglican, Presbyterian, United Church, and Roman Catholic clergy on the subject of the Vatican Coun-

Saint James, Compton.

The first church, dedicated to St. James, was consecrated in 1827, and was situated off the highway. In 1854, the church was rebuilt on the highway, and was consecrated the following year. The present wooden church was built on the original site off the highway and was consecrated in 1887. Until 1840, this parish was served by the Rector of Hatley (Stewart), who first visited the village in 1810. The first resident Incumbent was the Rev. C.P. Reid in 1874. The second Incumbent was the Rev. Josiah Dinzey, who founded the Compton Ladies' College. In the year 1902, being the year of the Coronation of King Edward VII the school was renamed "King's Hall," in honour of the event. The school has increased in numbers, landed property and in wealth, and in 1925 was in a position to purchase the Parish's property, including the Parsonage, and to pay the major share of the Rector's stipend, who now acts as Religious Instructor and Chaplain to the school.

More recently Compton has received prominence because it is the birthplace of the present, Prime Minister. Rt. Hon. Louis St. Laurent.

The village of Compton first gained its importance as early as 1811 because of the stage-coach service connecting the City of Quebec with Boston. The village was an important stopping place for travellers, because it is at Compton, that the highway crosses the Coaticook River.

KING'S HALL, COMPTON
A Residential Church School for Girls

St. Barnabas', Milby.

St. Barnabas Church, Milby, serves a small congregation and is attached to the parish of Compton. The present Rector is the Rev. H. P. Absalom, M.A.

PLATE 15 *Compton (from the Gaspé Deanery G.A. Scrapbook).*
C.P. Reid actually served here from 1840 to 1853

cil. The historic nature of these happenings was not lost on the participants. It "marked the first occasion that clergymen representing Roman Catholic, United and Anglican denominations had gathered together with their flocks in a joint observance. It was the first time that a Roman Catholic priest had taken part in a service in St James' Church [Trois-Rivières]."

This breakthrough with the Roman Catholic Church was particularly remarkable in the Province of Quebec, where relations between the two communions had been uneasy for many years. Pope Leo XIII's Encyclical *Apostolicæ Curæ* (which denied the validity of Anglican Orders) had led to an angry exchange in the press and provoked an attack on the Roman Catholic position by Archdeacon Henry Roe in 1897. In the 1920s and thereafter, the Roman Catholic stand on so-called mixed marriages likewise caused much resentment. Bishop Lennox Williams reviewed the elements of the latter issue at Diocesan Synod in 1932:

> Whatever regulations the Church of Rome may see fit to make for her own members in the case of Mixed Marriages, and these regulations have been very prominently broadcasted of late, nevertheless, it ought to be made perfectly clear to our own Church people that a marriage duly solemnized between a Roman Catholic and a member of the Church of England by one of our own Clergy is perfectly valid and cannot legally be annulled. This was definitely decided by implication in the decision of the Judicial Committee of the Privy Council in the case of Malvina Despatie and Napoleon Despatie delivered in February 1921. A copy of this judgment will be found in the Synod Journal of 1922. Moreover, in the case of a Mixed Marriage there is no obligation whatever that the ceremony must be performed by a Priest of the Church of Rome, and no promise should ever be made by a member of our own Church in the case of Mixed Marriage that the children, issue of the marriage, should be baptized and brought up in the Roman Catholic Church.

After so many years of conscious separateness and distrust, this new openness and friendship initiated by the Roman Catholic Church was a call to renovated thinking.

Conversely, in the 1970s the prospect of a strictly Protestant church union, such as that going forward with the United Church, seemed to arouse little enthusiasm (particularly at the episcopal level) in the Diocese of Quebec. In 1968, for example, the *Diocesan Gazette* carried a correction in the form of a letter from Bishop R. F. Brown to the editor of the *Canadian Churchman*. On 22 September of that year, the Bishop and Dr C. Campbell Wadsworth of the United Church had inducted the Rev. Phyllis Smyth to minister jointly to the Anglican and United Church congregations housed in Trinity Church, Riverbend, in the Lac St-Jean district. The *Churchman* had subsequently reported on the event in an article which spoke of "intercommunion at Riverbend, Que."

> It is incorrect to state that "I advised" our Anglican people to receive their Communion from the United Church minister [the Bishop affirmed]. This seems to imply that I encouraged them to do so. Such is not the case. What I did say, was that our people must be guided by their conscience in the matter of Communion and that arrangements were being made by which the Sacrament, in our tradition, would be available to them at the hands of our nearby priest in Kenogami. I am glad some reference to this point was made in the article.

Trinity, it should be noted, had been from the first vested in both the United and Anglican Churches "to serve both communions." At the time of its dedication in 1950 by Archbishop Carrington and the Rev. J. MacKay of the United Church, each congregation held services on alternate Sundays.

The General Commission on Union continued its work, however, and in 1972 produced a Plan of Union for final ratification by both churches. Two years before this, at the Diocesan Synod held at Quebec Lodge in 1970, Canon Ralph Latimer and Dr Robert Craig, two Commissioners on Union, were present to report on the progress being made and to answer questions. It was noted by the Anglican Commissioner that, throughout the whole Diocese, only the Gaspé Deanery had made its views known to the General Commission, and he "again urged involvement from this Synod." The summary in the *Synod Journal* of the question period that followed their presentation conveys a negative attitude among those in attendance.

In his Charge to Synod of 1970, the theme of which was "Unity," the Bishop had set the tone:

> As you will have seen from the agenda, the subject of Church Union will be before us first thing to-morrow morning....
>
> There are those who remind us that "Unity" and "Union" are not necessarily the same thing, and I think there is a distinction. Unions of separated Christian churches are only valid if they contribute to the ultimate unity of the whole Church of God. This is a thought to keep in mind as we continue our discussions with our brethren of the United Church.

"The seemingly increasing contrary reaction to union" noted in question period the following day was borne out in a Memorial to Synod on the same occasion, presented by the clergy of the Cookshire Deanery. In it, the four priests comprising the Deanery set out five points on which they differed from the principles underlying the proposed union. Far from endorsing any aspect of the General Commission's work, the Memorial stated that "the general trend of the Church Union Reports is away from the Principles of Union agreed upon by this Church."

The ultimate decision on the Plan of Union was to be made during the episcopate of T. J. Matthews who, on Bishop Brown's resignation, succeeded as ninth Lord Bishop in 1971. That this new Bishop had a very different (and much more inclusive) idea of the Church and its ministry was clear from the outset:

> If Jesus is the Man for Others [began his first Charge to Synod], so His Church is the Church for Others. We need constantly to remind ourselves that the Church is His, not ours. The Sacraments are not ours, they are His. The Word we proclaim is not our Word, but His. We do not confirm, ordain or consecrate each other: He confirms us, He Makes deacons, Ordains priests and Ordains bishops.

Faced with the problem of supplying a resident priest to small outlying congregations (which would otherwise languish for weeks without a full service), Matthews had no qualms about entrusting an Anglican congregation to the care of a minister of the United Church, or, similarly, about permitting one of his own priests to perform services in the United Church tradition. Thus, what appeared to be a truly joint ministry—which included the administration of the sacraments—was instituted under special licence where the need warranted. "Although," as a spokesman for the Diocese has said, "the *theology* of this arrangement has never been thoroughly thought out, the practice persisted under Bishop Goodings and continues to the present day." The first of these special licences (in this case for the Saguenay region) was granted in 1971 to the Rev. Phyllis Smyth.

In 1975, the 1972 Plan of Union between the Anglican and United Churches fell through. Regardless of their Bishop's stand on the issue, the clergy of the Diocese of Quebec had not come around to favour union. As was the case in other dioceses across the country, the stumbling block had been (as the Memorial by the clergy of the Cookshire Deanery had put it) the Plan's "complete denial of our belief in the catholic ministry." Under consideration that same year was another issue over which there was, if anything, still sharper division between the clergy and their Diocesan: namely, the ordination of women.

"The Subject of the Priesthood for Women"

Given the slowness with which women in the Diocese of Quebec had gained the right to be elected as delegates to Synod, it is not surprising that, in the early years of the ordination debate, the strength of the movement lay elsewhere.

Discussion about "the admission of women to share in the ministry of the Church" had begun much earlier. It was mentioned, for example, in the "Encyclical" issued by the Lambeth Conference of 1920. At that time, the Archbishop of Canterbury announced his intention to revive the Order of Deaconesses that had been instituted in the primitive Church. Earlier that same year, an article had appeared in the *Diocesan Gazette* outlining a view of female ordination:

> A good deal is being both said and written to-day on the subject of the priesthood for women and of the right of women to preach in church....

> Now, when we come to the subject of the priesthood for women we are at once aware that we are dealing with a matter much graver than the above.* To put it bluntly, such a proceeding is not to be contemplated. From the point of view of tradition, and from many others, priestesses cannot be suffered. To ordain women to-day would be a catastrophe in Christendom ... [I]t would be a desperate, if not a fatal, blow at the possibility of unity in the Catholic Church....

> ... Some years ago [the article concluded] there appeared a picture by a well-known American artist in which was shown a beautiful woman, vested, and in a pulpit. Underneath the figure was the legend, "Our churches will be fuller then." The illustration holds equally for the altar. Now why did the artist employ those particular words?... Surely because of the presence of a beautiful face, or, in other words, because of considerations of sex?... And I would contend that the very thought of such an element as this present at the Holy Mysteries is horrible. The risk of it would be undeniable; it could not be excluded. Finally, I do not believe that any balanced and sane mind would care to contemplate such a risk being taken. It is an unpleasant task to say this— yet it needs to be said.

---

* The author had just discussed the prospect of women being permitted to preach to mixed congregations in the open church.

An item printed in the *Diocesan Gazette,* describing the gathering of clerical and lay delegates for the Special Synod of 1960, suggests that attitudes towards women's place in the church had not changed much in 40 years. The patronizing, somewhat bantering, tone of the article barely makes an attempt to conceal its misogynic tenor.

> At 10.30 a.m. in the Cathedral, it was noted that the body of the church was filled with men. What a joy to hear 150 male voices, raised in singing to God. The setting for the Office of Holy Communion was Marbecke; this too has added beauty when sung by all male voices.
>
> Many clergy wives were present, some mothers and even a mother-in-law.

Judging from the *Diocesan Gazette,* the first hint that women seriously aspired to anything beyond sewing, cooking, and raising funds for the Church appeared in an item following the worldwide Anglican Congress held in Toronto in August 1963. It gave coverage to a meeting of more than two hundred "wives of delegates, visitors to the Congress and local women" at which a panel was to discuss the general subject: "Women and Church-women—East and West."

> When the discussion was opened to the meeting, a woman who described herself as the "daughter of a United Church Manse and wife of an Anglican priest" suggested that the question of the ordination of women be discussed by the meeting. The chairman said that ... she did not think there was time to go into it at the meeting.
>
> In spite of this ruling, the subject was mentioned again by Mrs. J. G. Barnish, wife of the clerical delegate from the Diocese of Worcester, who said one reason for difficulty in recruiting women for professional church work was that women must always look forward to being subordinates.
>
> It was not unChristian, Mrs. Barnish suggested, for women to have some a[m]bition, and yet there was no room for advancement when they knew that they could never have the charge of a parish.

Ten years later, the 26th session of General Synod held in Regina "accepted the principle of the Ordination of Women to the Priesthood." This decision was not popular with delegates to the Quebec Diocesan Synod, which also met that year. As was the case with intercommunion, once again Bishop Matthews found himself at odds with the majority of his clergy. In his observations on the General Synod resolution, he reassured them in his Charge that "there was no intention of imposing anything on anybody":

I realize that some of you are deeply disturbed about the Ordination of women to the Priesthood. Joy in Ministry and the peace of mind of every one of you means very much to me. I am saddened therefore when I reflect upon your anxiety and distress.... Here in Quebec most of you know what I think about it. But be assured that I have neither the intention, nor desire to impose my feelings upon you. When I was a Priest, I laboured hard to persuade Synod to accept women delegates. We did this less than 10 years ago!

Diocesan Synod held a debate on the ordination issue in 1974. At the request of the clergy, the vote that followed was taken by orders, and the Bishop called for a standing vote. The result in the House of the Clergy was 9 in favour, 14 against, and the Resolution was therefore declared lost. A vote was taken in the House of the Laity, nonetheless; it was 34 in favour to 20 against. The Bishop announced that he would "advise the House of Bishops of the result of the debate."

In the final analysis, however, the issue was to be decided by General Synod, where, unless its implementation was to be indefinitely delayed, female ordination would require ratification at two successive synods. Bishop Matthews extended an invitation on behalf of his diocese to hold the 27th session of General Synod in Quebec. This was the first time since the 4th General Synod of 1905 that the city had hosted the national body.

It proved to be a memorable occasion. Bishop Matthews conducted the Opening Devotions; they included "two musical selections offered by a group of young people from the Diocese of Quebec who invited the members of Synod to sing with them, and the Bishop read a poem entitled 'Dancing on the Water,' which he had written." The hospitality offered by the whole Quebec community was, perhaps, its most striking feature:

> The open arms with which our Roman Catholic friends welcomed delegates into their homes and family life and Churches was a new and precious experience which will be treasured as long as we live [wrote the retired bishop of the Diocese of Huron].
>
> As one of the Bishops who ... enjoyed the hospitality ... Cardinal Roy extended to the Bishops and their wives at Château Bellevue, I think of it as one of the most memorable occasions in the whole course of my ministry.... It could be that the cause of Church Union was moved forward further by the Cardinal's affectionate outreach to us than it was by all that was done in the name of reunion in the business sessions of Synod.

This open and welcoming atmosphere, together with the spirit of innovation of the host-Diocesan, no doubt played a part in securing decisive and final ratification of the ordination issue. It had clearly been the Bishop's hope that it would.

On 6 March 1977, Bishop Matthews installed Ruth H. Matthews* (then a deacon) as Rector of the parish of St Francis of Assisi, and, on 5 June of that year, ordained her to the priesthood. Since that time there has been a fairly steady stream of women presenting themselves for ordination in the Diocese. Their placement, once ordained, has been a different matter. Generally speaking, if they have been given parishes at all, it has been in outlying areas—on the Gaspé coast or the Lower North Shore. Two chaplaincies in colleges and schools are presently held by women, but these appointments are not necessarily indicative of diocesan policy, as they are both within the power of the institutions themselves, and not of the Diocese, to make.

After more than 15 years, female ministry has continued to meet with resistance in the Diocese, particularly among the priesthood. This is thanks to the conscience clause, which (until 1986) enabled clergy to act as if there simply were no women priests. Thus when Ruth Matthews, as an ordinand, was put forward for the usual examination, the Bishop's Examining Chaplain refused point blank to have anything to do with the proceedings. The Archdeacon who, under ordinary circumstances, would have presented her at the ordination ceremony likewise declined to do so. True to his word, the Bishop did not try to compel either of these men to act. Another examiner was found, and the candidate was presented by the Rev. David Whitehouse, Rector of Trinity Church, Ste-Foy, where she had worshipped as a child.

It has become customary at the Cathedral of the Holy Trinity for one woman at least to assist at services calling for several priests, but there continue to be clergy in the Diocese who will not attend any religious ceremony in which a woman priest takes part. Similarly, there are parishes where no woman (unless equipped with a flower vase or a vacuum cleaner) is permitted to set foot within the sanctuary. Had the decision depended on the clergy instead of the Bishop, it seems that the ordination of women in this diocese might well have been delayed, perhaps for as long as a decade or more.

As the third centenary of the Diocese opens, the appointment of the first woman as a canon of the Cathedral—in the person of the Rev. Heather Thomson—will doubtless be perceived as a further opening of the way to responsibilities and honours that have hitherto been denied to women in the Diocese of Quebec.

---

* No relation to the Bishop.

In the "World-wide Anglican Communion"
In August 1963, the city of Toronto welcomed some 657 official delegates from 350 Anglican dioceses around the globe to the second Anglican Congress. Under the general theme "The Church's Mission in the World," participants from nations ranging from Argentina to Zululand met to consider "the Church's future on the religious, political and cultural frontiers, the challenges they present and the organization required to meet them."

One of the official reporters at the event summarized the proceedings for the *Diocesan Gazette*:

> Briefly, the Congress came to the conclusion that "the pictures which we have of one another and of our common life in Christ are utterly obsolete and irrelevant and that our great need is to understand how God has led us through the sometimes painful history of our time to see the gifts of freedom and communion in their great terms and to live up to them."

At the conclusion of the Congress, many of the delegates were invited to visit one of the Canadian dioceses "to promote mutual fellowship, to interchange information and to interpret their work." It had been announced earlier in the summer that the Diocese of Quebec could look forward to receiving four such dignitaries: the Bishop of Barrackpore was to go to the Gaspé, the Bishop of Korea to Quebec, the Bishop of North Nigeria to North Hatley, and the Archdeacon of the New Hebrides to Trois-Rivières. As it turned out, however, it was a delegate not included in this list who would bring home the message of the Congress and be directly responsible for establishing a lasting link between his own diocese and that of Quebec.

As the Bishop of Korea was unable to visit Quebec, his place was taken by the Reverend David Rakale, Rector of Holy Cross, Orlando, in the Diocese of Johannesburg. Besides visiting Quebec City, Father Rakale spent time in the Eastern Townships and even in the northern regions of the Diocese, meeting people, preaching, and talking about the Church in South Africa. He took part in the opening ceremonies of the Indian Residential School at La Tuque and was interested in seeing what facilities were being provided for "the natives of this country whose homeland in northern Quebec was now producing so much wealth in the form of pulp wood and minerals." Through arrangements with Father Rakale's home diocese, his visit was extended to six months; Bishop Brown issued a special licence empowering Father Rakale to officiate locally.

Far from uncritical of what he had seen in Quebec, or indeed of the

Anglican Communion itself, the African priest seems in turn to have provoked reflection in all who met him. Here is a sampling of some of his views
excerpted from an interview with *The Sherbrooke Daily Record* shortly before
his return home:

> If English and French [in Canada] lived a Christian life their problems would
> disappear just as there would be no question of apartheid in South Africa if both
> races were fully Christian.

> Many Africans equate Christianity with Western civilization, which is a pity....
> The time is rapidly approaching ... when my people will have to choose be-
> tween nationalism and religion. I hope it will be religion.

> When some of my people study the Bible they find that circumcision was
> practised; polygamy was normal. They ask me why they should not be allowed
> to practice these customs, which they had been doing until the white man
> came and which is common practice in the Bible. They ask me if it is not better
> to have a number of wives and to support them rather than the "strange"
> Western custom of marriage, divorce; marriage, divorce; marriage, divorce.

> We are sometimes inclined to believe all other religions are superstition. It just
> might be that what they had was religion and what we have is superstition.

By the time Father Rakale returned to South Africa, the Diocese of
Quebec had set in motion a process whereby the funds it contributed to the
Diocesan World Mission Appeal could be earmarked for special projects in
the Diocese of Johannesburg. A variety of articles on South Africa began to
appear in the *Diocesan Gazette*. Bishop Leslie Stradling of Johannesburg sent
a message "to the People of the Quebec Diocese," expressing his delight
about the forthcoming relationship between their two Sees. "But if this relationship is to grow into a truly living partnership," he added, "it will involve a good deal of work on both sides. Preliminary arrangements for a
fellowship in intercession have already been made.... We must share information and plans."

It was decided that, as a beginning, the Diocese of Quebec would fi-
nance one of the African Church building projects. In a letter to Bishop
Brown, Stradling mentioned six country churches in urgent need of replacement—each at a cost of £8,000 to £9,000, or about $11,000 to $12,000:

> The one I would particularly suggest for you is Sannieshof, where the Rec-
> tor is the Rev. J[ohannes] K[hathole] Rakale ... who is a nephew of Father
> [David] Rakale.

PLATE 16A *The Mission to Seamen, Port of Quebec.* (Photo credit: Lynn C. Ross)

PLATE 16B *Forty-five different A.C.W.s from across the Diocese of Quebec designed and contributed a square to complete this unique bi-centennial quilt.* (Photo credit: Audrey Frost)

> Sannieshof is a country town in the centre of a large agricultural district. The Church is old, constructed of very cheap materials and dilapidated beyond the hope of repair. It is also totally inadequate in size for the steadily growing congregation. The people are nearly all agricultural labourers working for very low wages. They cannot possibly afford to build a new Church, but once the Church is up they will be well able to support it.

This suggestion was promptly acted upon, and very shortly thereafter a letter from the younger Father Rakale, describing his parish and people, appeared in the *Diocesan Gazette*. Of the seven churches under his care, he wrote, five were in African reserves. Because of the size of the parish, most of them were "looked after by faithful old untrained Catechists." As for Father Rakale himself, he reported clocking some twelve hundred miles monthly in what he referred to as "the Diocesan Volkswagen." His people, he added, were mostly sharecroppers. They "hire themselves out for ploughing, etc., and get a few bags after reaping as a reward for their labours. It is out of these that one has to feed, clothe and rear a family. The Church gets very little from these people financially." In the February 1964 issue, a further letter from Sannieshof announced that construction of the new church had been slated to commence in March.

> I thank you again for the amount which has come. The building of the church had seemed to be a remote thing to me, but now I am certain we will have a fit place to worship in this very year. I've already seen the Architect, and he is at present busy with the plans....
> News of the great gift to this Parish is received with tremendous joy by all the parishioners and I can assure you that in their hearts they're thanking the good Lord who had shown such great love to them through you. I'm hoping, as soon as I can get a good photographer, to send to you the picture of the old building we've been using as a church and also, as requested, a photograph of the new church when it is completed.

In the course of what would be a six-year relationship, Bishop Brown was the guest of the Diocese of Johannesburg and Bishop Stradling visited Quebec. But far more important to the Dioceses themselves were the relationships established between individual parishes in the two jurisdictions. Sunday schools and A.C.W.s corresponded. Photographs were exchanged. In 1966, when the Rev. Richard Blyth came, on loan, to the Diocese of Quebec, he was struck by the amount of material each parish had received from its South African counterpart and by the sense of personal involvement in the project on both sides.

By the time the partnership was brought to a close in 1970, three churches had been constructed in the Diocese of Johannesburg out of funds raised in the Diocese of Quebec: St Justin's, Sannieshof; St George's, Fochville; and All Saints, Stilfontein. Ties and contacts between the two dioceses were to persist for some time. In 1972, the Very Rev. Gonville ffrench-Beytagh, exiled Dean of Johannesburg, was a guest of the Synod (held at Trois-Rivières), where he spoke of the South African government's apartheid policy, as well as of his own arrest and imprisonment.

In 1991, the Diocese of Quebec again entered into a special relationship, this time with the Diocese of the Southern Philippines. That September, Bishop Bruce Stavert welcomed the Rt Rev. Narciso Ticobay to Quebec; under the ægis of the Companion Diocese Program, the bishops signed a "Solemn Covenant" at a ceremony in St George's Church, Lennoxville. For all the conspicuous differences between them, the two dioceses were united in fact by a number of common experiences, as a reporter of Bishop Ticobay's visit was quick to point out:

> We share in common being an English and Anglican minority in the midst of a majority Roman Catholic non-English speaking population. They also maintain ministry to native peoples which requires translations into indigenous tongues. Their territory is very large and their diocesan population sparsely settled as is our own.

"A Review of Capital Funds and Endowments": Investment and Disinvestment
As a means of bringing economic pressure to bear on regimes guilty of human rights violations, many corporations and institutions—the national Church included—divested themselves of financial instruments with such associations during the 1970s and 1980s. Such action was prompted particularly in the case of South African investments. According to the current treasurer of the Diocese of Quebec, although there was a single attempt through Diocesan Synod to implement such a policy here, it made no headway.

More radical in tendency was a notice of motion brought before the 1970 Diocesan Synod to the effect that the Church Society in conjunction with the Executive Committee be requested to appoint a committee of seven to make a review of the capital funds and endowments, both of the Diocese and individual parishes, "with a view to their liquidation and disbursement" and to bring "concrete recommendations to this end to the next meeting of Synod." In support of his motion the mover argued that "the content of the motion would renew the diocese. The diocese at present was bolstered by three and a half million dollars, the product of a bygone age, and with such wealth, it could not claim to be a Christian institution."

Both the Chancellor (H. E. Grundy, Q.C.) and the Diocesan Financial Consultant (John McGreevy, C.A.) were quick to point out that the retention of endowment funds was a legal matter and that most of the capital was held in trust. An amendment called for a committee of seven "to make a review of the capital funds and endowments ... and to examine the Christian principles and implications involved in the augmentation and/or retention of Church endowments." The mover "agreed to withdraw his motion as long as the principle was retained," whereupon (in something of a departure from normal parliamentary practice) the amendment to the motion was put to the vote and carried. Despite the boldness of this initiative, there matters appear to have rested. The Synod Journals for the years following make mention neither of a "committee of seven" nor of any report filed on the subject of financial divestment. It appears that no particular policy was ever put forward, rejected, or confirmed as a result of this Resolution. Indeed, the management of Diocesan funds, it would be fair to conclude, has been guided more by economic considerations than by so-called questions of conscience.

"Revision, Enrichment and Adaptation": the Diocese and Liturgical Reform
Since the first Resolution (in 1902) to adapt the Book of Common Prayer (BCP) to Canadian use, the Diocese of Quebec has played a significant part in the ongoing process to reform the liturgy. Although at first it was thought that an appendix to the old Prayer Book would be sufficient to meet the need for updating the services of the Church, that idea (in Archbishop Carrington's words) "was knocked flat and rejected" at the next General Synod—held in Quebec City—in 1905. The Joint Committee to tackle the task of a complete revision was chaired by the Bishop of Quebec, Andrew Hunter Dunn, with his Chancellor, Dr Robert Campbell, acting as secretary. In the matter of Prayer Book revision, the Bishop "deprecated any attempt to have a separate Canadian Prayer Book until the results of revision in the Mother Country should be known"; he preferred to introduce flexibility into the service by issuing "special forms" for use. The Chancellor, for his part, argued that Provincial Synod rather than General Synod had jurisdiction and was alone responsible. In 1909, the members of the Committee "took up their task in an intensely conservative spirit." Two years later, the Diocese of Quebec presented a Memorial to General Synod asking that, in the matter of Prayer Book revision, "no steps in the direction of change be taken at the present time."

Although Bishop Dunn retired in 1914, other voices from the Diocese continued to be raised in opposition to the projected revisions. General Synod accepted a draft revision presented in 1915, and the book was sent to the Provincial Synods "for study and suggestions." In response, the Synod of the Diocese of Quebec presented a Memorial to its governing provincial body arguing that the new Book of Common Prayer be rejected outright. As a result, alone in the ranks of the Canadian Church, the Ecclesiastical Province of Canada "decline[d] to give its approval to the revision ... in its entirety ... other than as the accepted basis for further revision and enrichment." A further revision was completed and given final ratification by General Synod in 1921.

Despite what might be viewed as a policy of obstructionism by the Diocese, Quebec contributed materially to the new Prayer Book. Particularly noteworthy were the parts played by Canon F. G. Scott ("with an ear ever attuned to the concord of sweet sounds," who "left no stone unturned in his effort to have the views he held prevail"), and the Rev. Dr F.J.B. Allnatt (who "ranked high in scholarship in the Canadian Church").

The 15th General Synod, which met in Toronto in 1943, called for the appointment of a second Prayer Book revision committee, as well as of a Committee on Christian Reunion. The latter movement, as we have seen, was to have run its course by the mid 70s. The Prayer Book Committee, however, was to see the fruit of its labours fully authorized for use in 1962. The new Prayer Book was printed and bound just in time for it to appear in the historic display "of every Prayer Book used anywhere in the Anglican Communion today" staged at the Anglican Congress in 1963.

Like Dunn before him, Archbishop Carrington would assume chairmanship of the Revision Committee, but unlike Dunn, Carrington was to be the driving force to complete the project. Dean Robert Seaborn and his successor at the Cathedral, the Very Rev. A. E. Coleman, were among those serving on the Committee from the Diocese. On two separate occasions, in addition to its many other meetings, the Committee spent a week "together in work and prayer" at Quebec Lodge, the Anglican Church camp for boys and girls, on the shore of Lake Massawippi in the Eastern Townships.

> Nothing was done [in Carrington's view] to illustrate any special liturgical theory; the aim was to simplify and adapt the book for the benefit of the average church and the average churchman. Certain major changes were introduced ... [T]he structure of the Communion Service was remodelled in accordance with scholarly advice; ... the Calendar of Commemorations was enriched ... [T]he whole book was made more flexible in its application, and adjusted in many more ways to modern Canadian life; but it was fundamen-

tally the old Prayer Book.

A draft version of the new book was given approval in principle in 1955 by General Synod and, once the various corrections had been incorporated, was presented for first ratification in three years time.

> The aim [of the revision] was to preserve the essential beauty and splendour of the English prose of 1662 though a few voices were raised to question some "up-dating" in the psalter where it appeared to sacrifice poetic rhythm in an attempt to achieve a more precise and literal rendering of the Hebrew text. But for the most part, the changes were fairly conservative. And considering the wide spectrum of churchmanship covered by the working party, it pulled together very well.

Carrington had been responsible for the revision of the Collects, Epistles, and Gospels. He had been a champion of the whole project. At the critical meeting of General Synod, held at Ste-Anne-de-Bellevue in the autumn of 1959, it was Carrington, then acting Primate, who chaired the session that would endorse or decline the new book. With an unerring sense of the dramatic moment, Carrington announced that

> the following day, 3 September, was the commemoration of Robert Wolfall, the presbyter who celebrated the first Anglican Eucharist in Canada in 1578. [He] reminded the Synod that Robert would have used the 1559 Prayer Book of Elizabeth I. The Synod would be using the 1959 Prayer Book of Elizabeth II. If it were finally ratified in 1962, the Prayer Book would become the successor of the 1662 Prayer Book.

In 1983, with the qualified approval of General Synod, yet another volume was placed in the hands of Canadian Anglicans on an experimental basis: the Book of Alternative Services (BAS). In contrast to previous ventures of the same kind, the Diocese of Quebec does not seem to have played any significant part in the preparation of this work. One of the Diocesan clergy, a New Testament scholar at Bishop's University, served for some five years on the committee, ostensibly as the "token Evangelical presence."

As regards the use of the BCP or the BAS, a spirit of tolerance has hitherto prevailed in the Diocese of Quebec; no episcopal pronouncements have sought to enforce exclusive use of the latter volume here. Given the scattered, isolated character of the Diocese, this is undoubtedly all to the good. As one parish priest in an outlying area has privately remarked, there was a noticeable drop in attendance by the most faithful churchgoers soon after the BAS was introduced. Tactful enquiry revealed that these parishioners were keeping away because of their embarrassment at not being able to read the responses; years of familiarity with the words of the BCP—even with the phrases at which the pages should be turned—had made these parishioners indistinguishable from the literate members of the congregation. In such parishes, the minister remarked, use of the new liturgy, so far from giving the people greater access to divine worship, only served as a hindrance to the spiritual well-being of many communicants.

"A Deafening Silence": the Diocese and Homosexuality

As a glance at the national newspaper of the Anglican Church of Canada will amply demonstrate, the status of homosexuals and lesbians as parishioners or priests has received an increasing amount of attention over the past two decades. In contrast to numerous articles, news items, and letters centred on this issue, the *Quebec Diocesan Gazette* (which is distributed to parishioners with the national *Journal*) has taken little part in the discussions.

The *Gazette's* apparent indifference to the issue ought not to be put down to a lack of courage. It does not appear that the Diocesan paper has been unwilling to tackle controversial issues squarely. During the 1980s, a number of well-prepared articles on the Church and unemployment, capital punishment, and family violence were featured prominently among its pages. During the same period, however, the subject of homosexuality was characterized by what one former Diocesan priest has described as a "deafening silence." In the early 80s, he recalled, the subject was never brought up, "there was no policy spoken of, no resources mentioned, no speakers or discussions at clergy conferences. For the laity ... a lesgay person in the pew would have found support varying by congregation, but there was certainly no overall supportive atmosphere for anyone having to deal with issues surrounding sexual orientation."

At Diocesan Synod in 1987, notice of motion was given that a statement on Acquired Immune Deficiency Syndrome (AIDS) "be referred to the Provincial Synod of Canada and General Synod for consideration with a view to General Synod setting up a task force and making an in-depth Christian statement on the subject of AIDS."

> If this epidemic were similar to other epidemics of the past, there is no doubt that all of us would reach out to its victims with compassion and understanding. Unfortunately, AIDS is not just another epidemic in that many contract this disease by means of behaviour some of us might find unacceptable.
>
> As a result, many persons with AIDS as well as their friends and families are

shunned by our society and, in this time of dire need, find themselves suffering alone.

The situation is unacceptable.

Although obviously not directed exclusively at homosexuals, the motion appears to have had the gay community in mind, and sought to ensure "meaningful pastoral care" for its members. When the motion was finally voted upon, it had been amended for referral to the Diocesan Executive Committee (DEC). A second motion was also adopted to the effect that "the Bishop be asked to form a Diocesan Task Force to produce a statement on AIDS ... without delay, for the benefit of our Members, our Diocese, and our Quebec Society." After approval by the DEC, copies of the statement were to be "referred to Provincial Synod and General Synod for consideration and action." Unfortunately, the DEC Reports, presented at the next two Synods, make mention neither of AIDS nor of any submission on the subject.

Integrity, a national organization for "Gay and Lesbian Anglicans and Friends," with offices in Toronto and Vancouver, offers a support structure, organizes chapter meetings, and publishes a newsletter for its members. According to a spokesperson for this organization, there has never been a branch of Integrity in Quebec or its hinterland, although occasional postal requests for information are received from the Diocese by the Toronto office.

According to an article covering a three-part lecture series entitled "Homosexuality: Challenged and Challenging," published in *Integrator* (the newsletter of Integrity, Toronto), some Anglican bishops have shown particular sensitivity to the needs of homosexual clergy. One particular bishop, it was mentioned, "never moved them from one parish to another without ensuring that [the] partner's career was going to be OK with the move." This observation was made in an exchange between Phyllis Creighton (General Synod member and co-author of the 1986 *Human Sexuality Study Guide*) and Ted Scott, former Primate of the Anglican Church of Canada. Creighton stated unequivocally that Bishop T. J. Matthews himself had told her that this was his practice in such cases. Officially, the House of Bishops of the Anglican Church of Canada framed its policy on the ordination of homosexual clergy in 1979. It drew a distinction between "homosexual orientation" and "homosexual activity," tolerating the one, rejecting the other. Subsequent legal proceedings have not altered this stand.

The Diocese of Quebec has hitherto been spared the media attention which, in other parts of the country, has so often brought the question of sexual orientation into the public eye. For the future, in line with a Resolution of the 1992 General Synod, Bishop Stavert has proposed that the matter be brought forward for widespread discussion, both at the Diocesan and at the parish level. Confronting an issue long avoided will be something of a departure for a diocese—and a community—that has all too readily tended to become preoccupied with problems of its own survival.

CHAPTER V

Meeting the Challenge

'P'eople brought ashore opposite church cry for water," he wrote. "Old man crawling, in his filthy shirt, out of bed on hands and knees, with his pot to get water out of a dirty ditch." Bishop G. J. Mountain scrawled these notes as if to fix more firmly in his mind the misery he had witnessed during his second tour of duty at Grosse Ile, in the horror-filled summer of 1847 (see Window 11):

> Bedless persons in tents [his jottings continue]; saw two lying on wet ground in rain, one a woman very ill, with head covered up in her cloak, on a bed of rank wet weeds. Bundle of rags lying on floor of tent; orphan covered up within, dying, and covered with vermin from head to foot, unowned, and no connection to be traced (this the case with other orphans also); gave his name in sharper voice than could have been looked for from the little exhausted object, without uncovering himself; voice came out of the rags. Inmates of one tent, three widows and one widower, with remnants of their families, all bereft of their partners on the passage. Filth of person, accumulated in cases of diarrhœa. Three orphans in one little bed in corner of tent full of baggage and boxes, one of the three dead, lying by his sick sister. Dead boy under the tree, who passed on foot, in a division of sick, from east end [of the island], and sat down to die on his road.

Until that fateful summer, the Church Society had supplied a chaplain to minister to the needs of the Protestant immigrants at the Quarantine Station. Then, within a week of the arrival of the first immigrant ships, it became obvious that no one man could perform such duty. Charles Forest, the Missionary on the spot (and only a deacon), appealed to his Bishop for relief.

The situation presented Bishop Mountain with a dilemma of Solomonic proportions. What (if anything) was to be done for these wretched people? Although the means by which "Ship's Fever" was communicated was not then understood, he knew that close contact with the typhus-riddled immigrants endangered the lives of all who ministered to them. The Diocese had no clergy to spare for duty on the island without depriving congregations

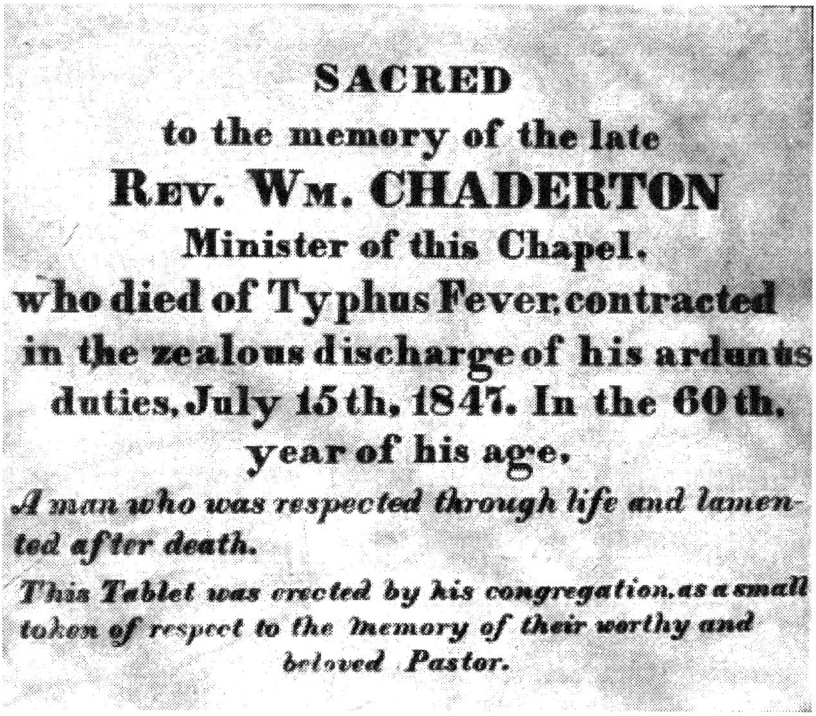

PLATE 17 *Memorial wall-tablet erected by the parishioners of St Peter's Chapel, Quebec, in tribute to their Minister, who fell victim to ship's fever while serving his turn at the Quarantine Station, Grosse Ile, during the terrible summer of 1847.* (Photo credit: James H. Lambert)

of their ministers and indeed risking their permanent loss. He could have invoked Canon Law whereby the clergy need not risk contagion in the course of duty. Yet to fail to send clergy to the sufferers would have been to deny them the spiritual comfort of their Church in their time of greatest need.

The Bishop met the challenge by seeking for volunteers among his clergy, and dividing the burden among as many as possible. Although this policy spread the risk of disease among a larger number of missionaries, it also reduced the time of exposure to infection for each of them. Individuals were approached, but no one was ordered for duty: the Bishop "suggested it to such of the clergy of the Diocese as seemed to be most able for the work, to offer themselves for the service, each taking a week. He took the first in the turn himself." For Mountain, the decision must have been agonizingly difficult, and the cost was a heavy one. Of the 17 clergy who served on the island during the course of that summer, seven (including the original chaplain) contracted typhus, but recovered. Three others died.

In his Charge to the clergy delivered at Montreal in July 1848, the continuing burden of this crisis shows itself in the Bishop's allusion to the events of the previous summer:

> Deeply as we must deplore the loss of so many valuable lives, and severely as it must tell upon the interests committed to us, there can, I think, be but one sentiment, when the case is fairly and fully considered, respecting the plain duty lying upon the Church to supply the service in question. It would have been monstrous, it would have been outrageous, to leave the protestant sufferers at Grosse Isle, after our chaplain became disabled, untended by the ministry of the Gospel; and no means existed to supply this want, but in the succession of visits from clergymen at a distance.

Besides the personal cost of losses among the clergy under his care, the Bishop had been troubled by criticism (particularly among the laity) of the course he had pursued. His Charge refers to this lack of support and goes on to pay tribute to the devotion of the Roman Catholic priests who served on Grosse Ile:

> I have been prompted to make these observations, because among the laity of the diocese, who lament the loss of their clergy, and who have not personally witnessed the exigencies which called them into scenes of danger, there have been questions raised, here and there, respecting the expediency or even justifiableness of their being so employed; and reference, as I suspect, has in some instances been made to a Canon (the 67th) which exempts a clergyman from any compulsory attendance upon persons in his parish labouring under mala-

dies which are known or probably suspected to be infectious. The rubrics, however, in the Office of the Visitation of the Sick, which I conceive to be decidedly the preferable authority of the two, plainly suppose the attendance of the clergy, even in the deadliest prevalence of plague. Would it not have been a reproach—a disgrace ... to have left all the sick and dying protestants at the Quarantine Island to the care ... of priests of the Church of Rome, never slackening in their labours, never shrinking from their task, ... would it not have been an indelible, an everlasting stain in the pages of our history, ... if, while physicians and magistrates and nurses and policemen and grave-diggers were found capable of braving the danger, ... the clergy of the Church of England had turned their backs upon the scene of death and sorrow, and had shut their ears against the cry of the sick for their ministry, and the wail of the widow, needing to hear the words of life and peace?

Although the Diocese has been called to face other ordeals in its history (see Window 9), few have been as harrowing or extreme. Most challenges, in fact, have been chronic or recurring. A summary of the fourth Annual Clergy Workshop (gatherings subsequently to be named Bishop's Conferences), held at Sherbrooke in September 1978, highlights a number of problems that have plagued the Diocese for many years:

> As the reports were heard and discussed it became apparent that, although each area had its own particular problems, there were many common ones: distance, isolation of clergy; lack of real commitment; competition between parishes; smaller congregations; lack of leadership; break-up of family life; an older population and a changed social order.

Shortly after the re-enactment of Bishop Jacob Mountain's landing at Quebec, which marked the culmination of bicentennial celebrations in the Diocese in 1993, the clergy and representatives of the laity gathered in Sherbrooke for the 73rd Ordinary Session of Synod, the first in this 11th episcopate. In his Episcopal Charge, Bishop Bruce Stavert addressed himself to the urgent request, pressed on him by his clergy at the previous Bishop's Conference, for a vision of the Diocese in light of the needs and resources of the present day. "Reduced population and the consequent reduction in resources, both human and fiscal," he warned, would require "some important modifications ... in the various structures of the Diocese"; it was also time to reassess the means by which the mission of the Church could best be served. Referring to the consultative process that preceded the Visioning Committee's recommendations, the Bishop remarked on a number of adaptations made in recent years:

We heard consistently about the heavy financial burden ... of clergy remuneration as well as the enormous strain on clergy in the big cluster parishes of the Diocese. We heard ... that combining more and more small congregations into greater parishes is not necessarily an effective answer everywhere. There are other options: closing churches, stronger lay ministry, non-stipendiary ordained ministry, shared ministry with other denominations. We have some experience with all of these, and need to build on our experience of innovation of various kinds.

It was mentioned in passing that, "just within the last year," three churches had been "deconsecrated and sold or placed on the market or otherwise disposed of": St Albans' (Scotstown), St Peter's (Limoilou), and Christ Church (East Angus). A new "greater parish" had been formed in the St Maurice Valley, which combined the two "shared ministries" of Trois-Rivières and Shawinigan / Grand'Mère with St Andrew's, La Tuque.

The plan itself was to take effect immediately. It called for further realignment of parish boundaries "to reduce the financial load of clergy stipends on individual congregations" and

a move towards a greater reliance on lay-based volunteer ministry, with an important emphasis on effective training of lay people in the parishes. The move ... would mean that some of the ministerial positions now filled by paid clergy would cease to exist when those clergy moved or retired. Some of the finances saved as a result would be available for the training and support of lay ministry.

"Competent, Committed and Faithful": Lay-Ministry in the Diocese

Far from being a recent phenomenon, dependence on a lay-based ministry has long been a part of Diocesan tradition. In the early years of the Diocese, the laity played an important role in keeping alive a spirit of devotion among the people in hopes that a travelling missionary would pass through the isolated settlements now and then, performing those duties exclusive to the priesthood. Keenly aware of the scarcity of clergy and the needs of a scattered people, Charles James Stewart (while serving as Travelling Missionary under Bishop Jacob Mountain in the early 1820s) made the following observations about the Quebec City hinterland and the role he saw the laity fulfilling there:

Frampton, Broughton, Ireland, Inverness—(these are townships on the South side of the St Lawrence)—Port Neuf, Ste Anne, & other places in the French Parishes, all lying within a distance of from 35 to 60 m[iles] from Quebec, contain a number of scattered Protestants to whom the Word & Ordinances have been administered occasionally, at wide intervals, by different Clergymen whose fixed duties are in or about Quebec. They would form an ample field for the labours of a sort of circuit Preacher who sh^d take them in rotation— making his head-quarters at some central point. In some of these places the people contemplate already the creation of churches or chapels; & frequently solicit the services of a Minister ... At Port Neuf a Congregation of 60 Protestants may be collected. They meet among themselves & read the Liturgy & a printed Sermon.

By 1910, the population had increased and the discomfort of travel had eased. Yet the size of the parishes and the difficulties of reaching the congregations within them still persisted. In that year Philip Callis (who had begun his ministry in the Diocese as Travelling Missionary in the District of Quebec) requested that his bishop licence a particularly useful layman, recently come into his parish, as a lay reader to help with the extensive mission field at Thetford Mines and Black Lake.

I spend every Tuesday in Black Lake & I find myself booked for lunch one or two weeks ahead; the people seemingly glad to see me ...

... In Thetford I am getting on my feet & finding or hearing of new people every day.... A Mr & Mrs Lanham came here last November: thorough English gentlefolk. He is accountant for one of the big companies & an enthusiastic Churchman. Is taking charge of choir & will be Sunday School superintendent. His [wife] will also take a class.* I am sending his layreader's licence. You will see it only authorises him to take duty in unconsecrated buildings. I will be very glad if you will licence him as a lay reader in this diocese. He will be a very great help ... I only hope he will remain in Thetford; this seems on[e] of our great drawbacks, the constant change.

Half a century later, in 1963, a similar note is struck in an item featuring All Saints', Hereford, printed in the *Diocesan Gazette*. Under "Parish Notes," allusion is made to the role of "lay readers formally commissioned," and "lay readers called from the congregation to the occasion by the interference of snow or mud with the travel plans of distant clergy" in sustaining the "border ministry" there.

Far from serving as substitutes and stopgaps, however, laymen in the Diocese have shown real leadership in ministry. In 1984, Bishop Matthews paid tribute to the devotion of one such, Herbert A. Simons, a former parishioner and warden at St George's, Lennoxville:

---

* Mr Callis *actually* wrote, "His will will also take a class."

During the years we worked together one aspect of ministry consumed more and more of his time, ... namely the role of the lay reader. Seldom did an occasion pass without Herb making reference to this ministry. At one point he gathered around him at St George's seven layreaders. He arranged for them to meet regularly with the Rector. At each meeting one of them gave a paper on a selected biblical subject followed by a discussion. Once a year he organized a Lay Readers' Conference for the diocese or district to which he invited a special speaker. Members of the group were given instruction in preaching and taking services. In this he was assisted by Howard Woollerton. A meal was taken together and there was always Holy Communion. The layreaders became so competent, committed and faithful that it was a proud boast of the Archdeacon that because of them no church was ever closed on Sunday for lack of a minister.

It had been taken for granted from the first that parishioners serving as lay readers in the Diocese did so without expectation of any remuneration or compensation for their ministry. The odd exception met with stern rebuke. A certain Mr Lindon seems to have put in for expenses to Charles James Stewart (then serving at Hatley). Stewart, who was clearly shocked and angered by the request, made no effort to conceal his feelings.

> Be so good as to tell Mr Lindon [he instructed a third party] that in compliance with his request in his Letter I wrote to the Lord Bishop respecting him, and that his Lordship says he has no more claim for compensation for his service as a lay reader than would perhaps extend to fifty others. "Dr Strachan," says his Lordship, "and Mr Stewart expressed their wish, when I was in England, for permission from me, that serious persons of good character, who were disposed to do so, might read the Liturgy to their neighbours (where there is no Clergyman) on Sundays. I consented to this: no more. Are such persons entitled to be paid, for their voluntary exertion? Clearly not. It was an indulgence, not an appointment, that was asked." I shall be obliged to you if you will read the above to Mr Lindon, and write to me as soon as it will be convenient ...

"We Form But a Very Small Flock": The Efforts of Anglican Church Women

The laity have been involved in the ministry of the Church in many ways. The contribution of laywomen, while frequently lauded in general terms, has yet to be properly documented. Prior the formation of Anglican Church Women (A.C.W.) or its earlier counterpart, the Woman's Auxiliary (W.A.), women's groups were formed to serve specific local parish needs, building up parish finances as well procuring necessary church furnishings.

Sewing Circles and Guilds arose to supply and repair altar linen and hangings. They also produced goods for sale, such as the "useful and fancy articles" offered by the ladies of North Hatley in 1894 "towards pecuniary obligations in connection with the Church of St Barnabas." Most groups appealed to the local community to attend their fund-raising events or to purchase the items they had made, but others had the enterprise to canvass for subscribers far afield. In Trois-Rivières, for example, the ladies of the Sewing Society of St James' Church addressed a letter "to the Christian Ladies of England," and another to those of Scotland, to enlist their aid in raising an Endowment Fund.

> In number we form but a very small flock [both letters stated,] contending with many adverse circumstances, and in the midst of an overwhelming majority of Romanists.... The Clergy Reserves of Canada, when originally bestowed by the Crown, and until perverted by misapplication, gave promise of some support for the Ministry; but the withdrawal of this fund, and also of resources once afforded by the Imperial Government, has greatly tended to increase our difficulties. In addition to the above, we mention the recent devastation of our town by fire, and the heavy loss thus inflicted on some members of our congregation.... [N]evertheless the strenuous exertions of our Sewing Society have not been abated, but rather stimulated by the feeling of our exigencies, so that we have realized upwards of one hundred pounds as a commencement to our Endowment Fund.
>
> We now earnestly entreat you to assist us in increasing this fund, without which we cannot hope our zealous Missionary will be maintained.

In 1858, Rosina Ogden, President of the Sewing Society and acting as Trustee on behalf of "certain charitable ladies of the City of Three Rivers, members of the United Church of England and Ireland," made over to the Bishop of Quebec as President of the Church Society the sum of £150. This sum was "to be held in trust and to form part of an Endowment Fund in aid of the aforesaid Church at Three Rivers, to be called the 'Three Rivers Rectory Endowment Fund.'"

Besides raising funds to meet the basic needs of their incumbents, parish women's groups furnished the capital with which to complete and maintain church buildings. The first undertaking of the Ladies' Guild of St John's, Brookbury (formed in 1898), was "to raise money to cover the cost of sheathing and other materials to finish the inside of the Church." In the "Treasurer's Book" of the Ladies' Guild of St Peter's-by-the-Sea, at Old Harry on the Magdalen Islands, is the record of an order, paid for by the Guild, of paint, shingle stain, and trim to maintain the church building: ivory for the walls, brown for the roof, medium green for the trim, and black for the window sashes. In 1935, their order, which was filled by the T. Eaton

Co., came to $45.44, including four brushes. Because the little white church has long served as a landmark for fishermen, the Guild's contribution was doubly important to the Island community.

Though seldom widely publicized, many parish organizations, usually consisting of a small core of workers, have contended with setbacks and losses. In the 1960 Summer issue of the *Diocesan Gazette,* a one-and-a-half inch item reported that "fire attributed to the act of vandals [had] destroyed the community hall at Barachois West, Gaspé," and that members of the St Paul's Ladies' Guild had "launched a fund" to rebuild it. A year later, the letters to the editor included one from W.M.H. Thomas, Priest in Charge of the Malbay Mission:

> I hope you will print this letter in the next issue of the *Diocesan Gazette* [it begins]. A small notice in your paper last summer told of the burning of the Ladies' Guild Hall here, with all its contents, which included dishes, linen, silver, prizes, and a host of other things, and also over three hundred ($300.00) dollars worth of chairs and tables ... [T]hese were mostly memorials to loved ones ... A dedication service was being planned when ... the hall was burned down. This hall represented the work of half a dozen women who had put much effort into raising money to buy the building and renovate it, the final payment being paid only a month before.
>
> Since then the Guild has struggled to raise funds for rebuilding, but it is difficult to do so without a working centre.
>
> We are hoping that this letter will act as an appeal to everyone who reads it to send the Guild a donation, either in cash or "kind."
>
> All donations will be gratefully received and carefully recorded ...

Although the cost of construction and maintenance of church buildings has often been borne by parish Guilds, the care of linens and vestments, as well as the charge of "beautifying" the church for service, seems to have fallen exclusively to women. A Chancel Guild (later called The Guild of Service) was formed at St Michael's, Sillery, in 1911. The Guild's funds (at various times) purchased a new surplice for the Rector, renewed the paint in the main aisle of the church, procured a fence to enclose the church property, and provided "shrubs and evergreens ... to be planted near the church." At Grosse Isle on the Magdalen Islands, women formed a Cemetery Committee (active until 1974), which raised funds to care for, clear, and fence the burial ground. An extract from the 1891 Vestry Minutes of St Barnabas Church, Lake Megantic (mimeographed for the church's 100th Anniversary celebrations in 1991) informs readers that "the reredos behind the altar was *carved by hand* by the ladies of the Guild."

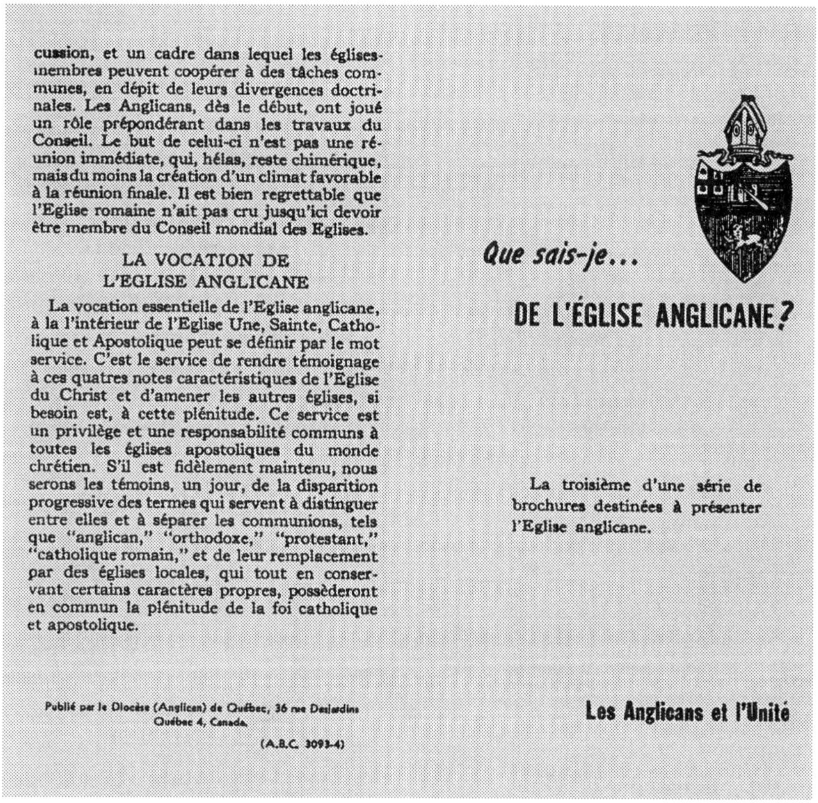

cussion, et un cadre dans lequel les églises-membres peuvent coopérer à des tâches communes, en dépit de leurs divergences doctrinales. Les Anglicans, dès le début, ont joué un rôle prépondérant dans les travaux du Conseil. Le but de celui-ci n'est pas une réunion immédiate, qui, hélas, reste chimérique, mais du moins la création d'un climat favorable à la réunion finale. Il est bien regrettable que l'Eglise romaine n'ait pas cru jusqu'ici devoir être membre du Conseil mondial des Eglises.

LA VOCATION DE
L'EGLISE ANGLICANE

La vocation essentielle de l'Eglise anglicane, à la l'intérieur de l'Eglise Une, Sainte, Catholique et Apostolique peut se définir par le mot service. C'est le service de rendre témoignage à ces quatres notes caractéristiques de l'Eglise du Christ et d'amener les autres églises, si besoin est, à cette plénitude. Ce service est un privilège et une responsabilité communs à toutes les églises apostoliques du monde chrétien. S'il est fidèlement maintenu, nous serons les témoins, un jour, de la disparition progressive des termes qui servent à distinguer entre elles et à séparer les communions, tels que "anglican," "orthodoxe," "protestant," "catholique romain," et de leur remplacement par des églises locales, qui tout en conservant certains caractères propres, possèderont en commun la plénitude de la foi catholique et apostolique.

Que sais-je...

DE L'ÉGLISE ANGLICANE?

La troisième d'une série de brochures destinées à présenter l'Eglise anglicane.

Publié par le Diocèse (Anglican) de Québec, 36 rue Desjardins Québec 4, Canada.

(A.B.C. 3093-4)

Les Anglicans et l'Unité

PLATE 18 *One in a series of pamphlets published in French by the Diocese of Quebec in the 1960s, each designed to acquaint the local French-speaking community with a particular aspect of Anglican beliefs and practices.*

Cumulatively, the effect of such labour is well illustrated by the accomplishments over the years of St Stephen's Ladies' Guild, Coaticook. This Guild (according to an item printed in the *Diocesan Gazette* in 1962) had provided their church with its "hall, kitchen, vestry extension, [and] pipe organ, as well as contributing to the cost of repairs and improvements to all church property."

As Alyson Barnett-Cowan (who was ordained to the priesthood by Bishop Goodings in 1978) has asserted, it is to the Woman's Auxiliary that "women's ministry" in the Anglican Church of Canada owes its beginnings:

> The initials "W.A." [she suggests] conjure up, for a younger generation, images of bales, prayer partners, knit baby clothes, and gracious white-haired ladies writing messages by hand to missionaries "in foreign parts." But the packers of bales and the writers of letters were women consciously engaged in a movement for change in the church and in society ...

Through involvement in the W.A., women in the Diocese played an important role in missionary activities. They contributed to the support of missionaries in the field and helped defray the cost of educating their children; they supplied clothing for distribution in the missions and eagerly awaited news (either directly or through the W.A.'s *Monthly Leaflet*) from the missionary who received their bales and bundles (see Window 26). They learned about missionary work throughout the world and strove to publicize it in their communities by organizing lectures and inviting speakers.

W.A. Branches throughout the Diocese met to sew "outfits" for Native children in residential schools and to prepare other suitable clothing for shipment. At monthly gatherings, members read original or printed descriptions of missionary work, or heard speakers knowledgeable in the mission field. At a meeting of the St Matthew's Branch of the W.A. (Quebec), held on 8 December 1887, three papers were read, one by Mrs Von Iffland (the Rev. A. A. Von Iffland was Rector of neighbouring St Michael's), one from the *Mission News*, and one by "a lady in Ottawa"; more than 50 members were present. At a subsequent meeting held on the evening of 20 March 1888, "the Rev. Thomas Richardson ... read a paper on British Guiana Missionary work ... so full of information as to deserve a far larger audience than that which owing to the inclemency of the weather were able to attend." In nearby Sillery, on 11 November 1896, the St Michael's Branch met at Bishop Mountain School to hear Miss Rose, the Secretary of the Zenana Society of Liverpool, England, deliver "a most graphic & delightful address on the work of women missionaries in India, illustrated by Magic Lantern slides. She held her audience spell-bound until the last word. Mr Dunn [incumbent at St Paul's, Quebec] kindly undertook the management of the lantern."

The W.A. not only enlisted the support of women in the home; it also sent women as missionaries into the field. The first woman to be ordained priest in the Diocese of Quebec, Ruth H. Matthews, had previously worked for six years in the Yukon as a W.A. missionary and, in her capacity as Bishop's Messenger (under Bishop Greenwood), had taken charge of several parishes in the North. In 1977, 23 years later, she became "the first woman to take complete charge of a parish in the diocese of Quebec."

For more than 50 years, another women's group—the Association of Church Helpers—fulfilled a particular need at the Diocesan level. Founded in 1891 by Anna Maria Williams (Bishop J. W. Williams' wife), and with Mrs H. G. Joly de Lotbinière as its first President, it was an organization "dedicated exclusively to the help of Clergymen and their families, particularly in the poorer missions and country parishes ... to which ... they could apply in cases of illness of themselves or their families, or when repairs were needed for their churches or parsonages and they could not undertake the repairs for lack of funds."

The Association's subscriptions were initially raised in Quebec City and Bergerville (Sillery), but in 1935, "owing to the hard times," the members appealed to the Diocese as a whole for support. Besides the many grants made every year, the Association (between 1926 and 1928) had collected "a little over $2,800 for the Mutton Bay Nursing Home in the Canadian Labrador." Some time in the late 50s, the Association disappears from the record. One of its last published Annual Reports, dating from the War years, reads as follows:

> The fifty-first Annual Meeting ... was held on January 14th, 1942.... In November the Treasurer purchased a $500.00 Victory Loan Bond with part of our balance in the bank. The work of the Association has gone on steadily in the past year though fewer grants were made in 1942 than in the preceeding year, sixteen grants being made in 1941 and only twelve in 1942. Of these grants one for $35.00 was made in a case of illness; $100.00 was given for repairs for two parsonages; $125.00 for stoves for two parsonages; $40.00 for a bath for a parsonage; $50.00 towards repainting a Church; $42.00 for a set of Communion Vessels; $17.72 for two sets of Altar Linen; $28.00 for a cassock; $50.00 for Bibles, Prayer and Hymn books for a Sunday School and a Mission Church. During the year many letters of thanks were received from those who had been helped by the Association. We hope that our subscribers will still continue to give us their support in the coming year.

A variety of Anglican men's groups have attracted laymen to church work over the years, but they appear to be of a later date and a briefer duration than those for women. Judging from its Minute Book, the St Michael's Branch of the Church of England Men's Society of Sillery, founded in 1913, was little more than a social club where members (who had been proposed, seconded, and elected by ballot on a two-thirds majority) gathered in the evening for conversation. Their records show (among other details) that the Chairman of the School Board had objected to Bishop Mountain School— their usual place of meeting—"being used at night for smoking."

The Eastern Townships Churchman's Association, founded in 1928, was more of a service organization involving men in work for the community. The Anglican Men's Club of Coaticook (which was formed three years earlier) raised funds "by means of plays, social evenings, lectures and subscriptions," and, according to a report filed in the 1930s, devoted "a large proportion of its income to Parochial objects." A declining English-speaking population has made the survival of such denominationally-based service groups difficult. Judging from the reports filed annually by each parish with Church House, in 1994 only one men's group was to be found among the various parochial organizations throughout the Diocese: that of St Barnabas' Church, North Hatley.

From time to time, *ad hoc* groups have arisen to meet particular needs. In 1963, responding to an alarming decline in the number of candidates presenting themselves for ordination, a group of laymen (under the chairmanship of H. H. Gibaut) established a Diocesan Layman's Ordination Fund. Their aim was to attract students to the ministry by giving added assistance to Divinity students. In that first year alone, $36,820 was subscribed, which had increased to $71,750 by 1969. In 1961, prior to the laymen's initiative, the Diocese had not one student in training. Eight years later, 11 candidates had been ordained, and annual bursaries of $800 each had been made available to assist them from the Layman's Ordination Fund.

Attracting men to involve themselves in particular fields of parish life has, at times, been fostered by promises of exclusivity. The three-day Stewardship Conference of the Diocese of Quebec, held at Maison Montmorency (formerly Kent House) in September 1964, was advertised as "For Men Only" in the *Diocesan Gazette*.

Initially open only to boys, the Diocesan Order of Servers admitted girls to its ranks in 1972. The first of its kind in Canada, and "a new thing in the Anglican Communion when he founded it," the Order had been launched by Archbishop Carrington on Dominion Day, 1951, and set in motion at a five-day Servers' Camp, held at the first Quebec Lodge, on the north shore of Lake Massawippi.

"At the Chapel Service on Sunday evening, July 1st, sixteen Campers made the promise and subscribed to the rules which all had helped to draw up.... They were [then] admitted to the Diocesan Order of Servers by His Grace, the Archbishop," who had taken a prominent part, and, as one participant recorded, "kept clearly before us all the aims and ideals of Christian living, service and adventure." Communities represented at the camp included Asbestos, Danville, Drummondville, Kenogami, Magog, North Hatley, Quebec, Richmond, Sandy Beach (Gaspé), and Sherbrooke.

In 1977, the Rev. Harold Church, who had been involved in its activities from the beginning and had served as its registrar three times, reported that in its first 25 years of operations, 601 boys and 15 girls had been admitted and that "clergy from most of the parishes of the Diocese have had Servers join the Order." The organization still continues to attract both boys and girls as members.

A special form of lay ministry has been performed by the Native People of the Diocese, supplying lay readers, interpreters, and catechists within their own congregations, and providing services, partly or exclusively, in Cree (see Window 25). In his Charge to Synod in 1943, Archbishop Carrington stressed the dependence of the Diocese on Native lay ministry—in some regions for as much as 11 months of the year:

> Little publicity [he pointed out] has been given to our missions to the Indians which are held during the month of July when they come down the rivers to sell their furs at the Hudson Bay posts. This year the Mission at Pointe Bleue will be under the Rev. John Ford; the lay reader is Johnny Meanscum. The Mission at Oskelaneo River will be under Canon Bown assisted by Mr. Ellwood Patterson of Bishop's University; the lay readers are Joseph Gunner and Mark Saccapio. These lay readers are essential to the working of the Mission as we have no clergy who can take services in Cree.

Fifteen years later, Carrington provided an admiring description of several services he had just taken among the Naskapi at John Lake which, in their blend of Anglican and Native tradition, lent added meaning to these ceremonies:

> It was a wonderful thing to see that chapel of St. John filled with the members of the band to take part in the confirmation of twenty-five of their boys and girls, and on the next day for the Holy Communion and the baptism of a little baby. We could learn many lessons from them. The whole band was

there for the baptism, and the whole council took responsibility for the child as sponsors. There was baptism as it should be ... It gave great significance to the words "We receive this child into the congregation of Christ's flock."

The Archbishop was assisted by two interpreters among the Council and by lay reader Joseph Sandy, who conducted the greater part of the service in Cree.

The conditions in which the Native People have come to live have been difficult and destabilizing. In 1963 (the same year in which he dedicated the chapel of the Indian Residential School at LaTuque), Bishop Brown summarized the changes to which the Naskapi have had to adjust in the wake of industrial development and the exploitation of natural resources:

> The Naskapis [he pointed out] ... were brought from Fort Chimo near Ungava Bay by the Government a few years ago in order that the men might secure employment in the mines of the Iron Ore Company at near-by Schefferville. The change from a nomadic tent-dwelling existence to that of a settled village life close to a mammoth industrial enterprise has been a tremendous one for them in countless ways ...

Just ten years later the people moved again, from John Lake to the new village of Matimekosh, where a new church was erected during the summer of 1974. "Although the Naskapi people have for many years had a mission Church and resident Priest where they have lived," the Bishop continued, "the life of regular worship, preaching and other spiritual ministration could not have been carried on [during this period of upheaval] without the presence and leadership of Joseph Sandy."

Sandy served successively as lay reader, catechist (after attending training sessions at Moose Factory), and finally as deacon. His ordination, the first among the Naskapi, was performed in Schefferville by Bishop Matthews in 1976. Tragically, two years later Joseph Sandy, his wife Elizabeth, and their 12-year-old son Jimmy met their deaths in a fire that destroyed their home.

During the 1970s, the Diocese, and indeed the national Church, focused attention on the plight of the Native People and made representations on their behalf (see Window 40). Unfortunately, the social problems confronting them have persisted. In 1989, Chief Joe Guanish and translator Joseph Peastitude travelled to Sherbrooke to address Diocesan Synod and to ask the Church for help:

> I appreciate the invitation to speak to this Synod about the social problems within my Community and the opportunity to be part of this faith commu-

nity and to ask for your support in dealing with our problems concerning drug and alcohol abuse....

We, the Naskapi Band Council passed a By-Law banning alcohol from our Community. The Quebec Judge overruled the By-Law. We had hoped that the passing of this By-Law was the first step in overcoming these problems. I ask for your Prayers for my people.

I ask for your help in obtaining materials to educate them and in sending to visit us people who can help us fight alcoholism and drug abuse by deepening our faith in God and Jesus.

On another matter, we would like our Priest to be able to live at Kawawa with us, but due to the law a house cannot be assigned to a non-Naskapi, so we request help in raising money to build it.

Thank you for listening.

"In Time of War and Tumult"

The first Anglican clergy who served in the Diocese were, as we have seen, military chaplains accompanying their regiments in time of war. During the extended period of hostilities between France and Great Britain, which coincided with the early years of his episcopate, it was Jacob Mountain's duty to conduct special services to invoke divine assistance or to give thanks for victory (see Window 3). The Cathedral was furthermore for many years the repository of some of the proudest relics of the British Army, and bore a distinctly military air. As a guide book (published in 1947) explained to visitors,

> The War-torn Flags that hang in the Sanctuary are the colours of the South Lincolnshire Regiment, the "69th." They were deposited here in the presence of Prince Arthur, afterwards Duke of Connaught, on June 22nd, 1870.
>
> The Regiment was stationed in Quebec at the time.... This famous Regiment was raised in 1756, and served with distinction at Cape St. Vincent in 1797, being on board the same ship as Lord Nelson. It took part in the attack on the Isle of Bourdon. It served in Java and in India at the time of the Mutiny, and it was at the battles of Quatre Bras and Waterloo.

The blessing of the new Regimental Colours, performed by Bishop J. W. Williams, took place on the Parade Ground. No less impressive was the ceremony in which the old Colours were deposited in the Cathedral. The following Order of Service describes the occasion in all its drama:

> The doors of the Cathedral are closed. The Clergy are assembled at the Communion Table.
>
> The Captain of the Escort, on arriving at the West door, knocks three times.

The Rector desires the Church-Wardens to enquire who knocks.

The Church-Wardens ... inform the Rector that it is Captain Thomas Henry Charleton, of the 69th Regiment, who craves speech of the Authorities of this Cathedral.

The Rector desires Captain Charleton to be admitted.

Captain Charleton, on reaching the Communion rails, addresses the Rector: "I have been commanded by Lieutenant Col. George Bagot to repair with the old colours of the 69th Regiment, under a sufficient escort, to this Cathedral, in the hope that its authorities will permit these venerated emblems of loyalty, Christianity, and civilization, to find a fitting resting place within the walls of this sacred building, in the midst of a loyal and God-fearing population."

The Rector replies: "Inform Lieut.-Colonel Bagot that we receive these colours as a sacred trust, not only as emblems of loyalty, Christianity and civilization, but in remembrance of a Regiment which has been conspicuous in repelling a recent invasion of this Province ..."*

The Clergy in procession, advance to the West door, and return, followed by the escort and colours.

When the Clergy have assumed their places within the Communion rails the colours are given to the Rector, the escort presenting arms, the organ playing the National Anthem.

There in the sanctuary the Colours hung for more than 120 years, forming part of the impression carried away by generations of visitors to the Cathedral (see Window 16). In 1993, following its restoration, a splendidly refurbished Cathedral was rededicated and reopened for public worship. Sadly, the tattered Colours of the 69th Regiment, so long a feature of its interior, have not been reinstalled.

Although the clergy and laity of the Church of England in Canada could be counted on to support the Mother Country (even in her more dubious military ventures), Bishop Dunn was led to conclude that the majority of those living within his diocese felt neither enthusiasm nor sympathy for the colonial wars of the Imperial Government.

I think it right to name to your Grace [Dunn wrote, in 1900, to the Archbishop of Canterbury], that I have received several communications from clergymen & others, looking for a "Day of Prayer & Humiliation" in connection with the Transvaal War.

Here, where we are but a small minority compared with the large population of French Canadian Roman Catholics, even a Proclamation from the Queen w^d probably not lead *them* to take much part, altho' in the first Canadian Contingent there are about sixty French Canadians out of a thousand

* The Rector refers to the Fenian Raids.

men.

For certain this war has revealed some anti-English feeling among the lower classes at any rate—& perhaps it reaches up to some of the better educated people also, altho' they are to our faces quite friendly & pleasant.

The disaffection Bishop Dunn had remarked on would intensify and grow in the Province during the two World Wars which followed.

On 3 January 1915 (the National Day of Intercession), British subjects throughout the world were called upon to pray "for the cause on behalf of which our Empire and our allies are fighting." One of the sermons preached on that occasion was printed in the *Diocesan Gazette*. The April issue contained some stirring verses entitled "Your King and Distant Countries Need You," and a "Letter from a Chaplain with Our Soldiers at the Front":

> To-day is Sunday, Feb. 28th, and I am writing after our Church Parade. We left the little village where we were first billetted and marched here, the distance was about 12 miles or a little over. At one point of the road we skirted Belgian soil....
>
> ...At night our men, who had been in for 24 hours, moved out and another company came in. I went then to the next trenches belonging to the Queen's Westminsters where some of our men were. That night I slept in an upper bunk, a young Officer being below me and his servant on the floor.... When we woke in the morning it was very foggy and the Major would not let us have the Public Service. A fog hides the sound as well as the sight of the approaching enemy. However, in a little hut we had Holy Communion and six received. Officers as well as men. We were so crowded I could not stand up straight. The table was covered with an illustrated paper ... and only two could kneel at once to receive, but it was most impressive. Such fine young fellows. Later on in the morning we had two casualties.... Our men are behaving splendidly and are trusted implicitly by the people of the villages through which they pass. This is a great opportunity for work, and the hearts of our men are wide open.

At the 1916 session of Synod, Bishop Lennox Williams announced that—at the request of Sir William Price, Commanding Officer of the 171st Regiment, Quebec Rifles—the Rev. Lieutenant J.F.B. Belford would address the members on the subject of the recruiting movement. After "his patriotic and admirable speech," a committee was struck to frame a Resolution incorporating "the suggestions contained in it." It read (in part) as follows:

> —That the members of the Synod of the Diocese of Quebec, in view of the grave peril that is threatening the life and liberties of the Church of England, and the whole British Empire at the present time ... with a view to the speedy

and successful termination of the conflict, desire to respectfully impress upon the Government of the Dominion, the imperative need of a systematic registration of all men of age and fitness for military service, as well as of all others that are available for other departments of national work; and at the same time, the pressing call for the conservation of all the resources of the Dominion to secure an early accomplishment of the same great result; and, further, the members of the Synod do hereby pledge themselves individually and collectively, to do all in their power to further such measures as may be adopted along the lines indicated; and that a copy of this resolution be sent to the Prime Minister of the Province of Quebec.

Reviewing his episcopal Acts since his consecration as Bishop in January 1915, Williams reported to the Synod that he had confirmed 817 individuals and ordained one priest: "I have ordained no one else, as *all* the men who were reading for Holy Orders have joined the Canadian Overseas Expeditionary Forces and have gone to the war and one of them, Eustace, has made the supreme sacrifice." Anglicans, it was noted, had been foremost in volunteering for the Armed Services, and "from the school and university of Lennoxville more men have gone in proportion to their numbers than from any other educational institution in Canada."

Williams paid tribute to four Diocesan clergy on Leave of Absence who were serving as Chaplains in the Canadian Expeditionary Forces, and to another (the Rev. Vere E. Hobart) who had left the Diocese to take a Commission as an Officer in the 148th Battalion. On the subject of members of the clergy enlisting for combat duty, however, the Bishop's position was unequivocal:

> Some of you I know, feeling a strong desire to do your utmost for your King and Empire ... have questioned whether it would be right for you to volunteer as combatants and have asked my advice in the matter. I admire your patriotism, but I want to make it quite clear: that I do not think it right for the Clergy to enlist as combatants.

In June 1918, the Bishop impressed on the members of Synod the need for personal sacrifices at home to aid the troops overseas:

> At this moment our thoughts are continually with our brave men who together with our Allies out there on the Western front are facing overwhelming numbers of the enemy, unafraid, undismayed, fighting on with the utmost bravery, standing between us and a flood of barbarism....
>
> We must uphold them by every means in our power ... One small thing we can at least do at the present time is to deny ourselves those articles of food

which are so greatly needed overseas. We can all go on reducing to a minimum the consumption of wheat, beef and bacon in our respective households, and doing our utmost to encourage the production of food. Let our rule be: *Save much, waste nothing, produce as much food as possible.*

We shall be called upon to subscribe to another War Loan this year. The Red Cross and other Patriotic Funds must be maintained.... All this comes at a time when the cost of living is very high and not likely to be lower for a long time. To do our duty at a time like this entails real downright self-sacrifice; it means giving up a great deal that we were accustomed to look upon as a necessity. But do it we must.

Williams urged the clergy, "in addition to the observance of the Day of National Prayer and Humiliation," to hold frequent Services of Intercession and, at least in summertime, to keep open, every day, *all* the churches in the Diocese for private prayer. The war had taken a heavy toll on his people. In 1918, as the Bishop informed the Synod, 45 percent of the Canadian troops in active service were "members of our Church"; yet, according to the census of 1911, Anglicans ranked only fourth among the religious denominations. Losses were correspondingly heavy. The Bishop's own son James was killed in action on 18 November 1916, one of the many Canadians to die in France.

By 1918 the number of Diocesan clergy "serving with the colours" overseas had increased to 10. Foremost among them was F. G. Scott, Senior Chaplain, first Canadian Division (see Window 29), described as "one of the strongest spiritual forces in the Army." At home, the shortage of ministers had made it necessary "to unite two missions under one priest," but, as the Bishop noted in his Charge to Synod, "owing to the self-sacrifice on the part of the clergy who have undertaken double work ... little or no loss has been suffered."

When the war was over, the Diocese joined fervently in the hopes for a better future. As Bishop Williams told the Synod in 1920, "We must get a really new and better world. The Church has her part to play.... She dare not merely drift back into her old ways, but must set her house in order, correct her mistakes and go forward with renewed zeal and earnestness to help to win the world for Christ."

Through the "Bishop's Letter," instituted in 1924 as a regular feature of the *Diocesan Gazette,* Williams probably reached more of his people and played a greater part in shaping Anglican opinion in the Diocese than did any of his predecessors. These communications show him as a man of conscience, deeply perturbed that, only 10 years after the Armistice and despite the League of Nations and the Kellogg Pact, "the big nations are spending more money preparing for war than ever before in peace-time history." Until his resignation in 1935, the Bishop continued as a tireless critic of rearmament, the arms trade, and "selfish Nationalism" (see Window 32). Of one mind with him in this matter was C. R. Eardley-Wilmot, editor of the *Diocesan Gazette*:

> The present generation [Eardley-Wilmot maintained in 1934] has no illusions about the glory of war; it has seen that there is even no such thing as the spoils of victory. Can it be possible that there is any considerable number of people in any country that would be willing to engage in war?
>
> Undoubtedly there is a strong feeling in almost every nation against war, but the pathetic thing is that at any moment a country may find itself in a position where war seems to be the only honourable way out. However true it may be that man is master of his own destiny, it is only in a very limited sense true of nations.

On Sunday, 10 September 1939—the fateful day on which Canada entered the Second World War—Bishop Carrington preached in the Cathedral. The sermon was printed in the *Diocesan Gazette*:

> War is hateful to the Christian soul; it blindly destroys mankind and all his works; it creates nothing that is either permanent or good. Yet we have reached the stage where circumstances offer no alternative, except to allow the triumph of the evil mind armed with force undreamed-of in the world before. The next few weeks or months will show how the nations will align themselves in the contest. I do not see how we can escape from it any more than from an earthquake or plague.

With a detachment quite untypical of the moment, Carrington spoke, too, of the "years of agony and confusion the German nation suffered before it came to trust itself to this one man," and mused on the "wild and twisted sense of justice" of some of Hitler's utterances, and the "injustices in the Treaty of Versailles."

In the same issue, Canon Eardley-Wilmot's editorial (for he was to continue as editor of the *Diocesan Gazette* until ill-health forced his retirement) was deeply pessimistic:

> Twice within a quarter of a century [he wrote] those nations of Europe which claim to be the most enlightened and the most advanced in civilization have decided ... that the only way to settle their differences is war. We find ourselves once again the helpless victims of the tragic failure of human wisdom and the defeat for the time being of the forces which make for peace and goodwill. Yet at the same time we have to recognise that no nation and no individual can

rightly disclaim responsibility for the state in which the world is to-day. It is the result of human blindness and selfishness and sin.

Such a view of world events harks back directly to those Jacob Mountain held in the eighteenth century: namely, that war is a judgement sent by God (see Window 3).

Once again, the loss to families and communities throughout the Diocese was very great. The tiny Anglican community of Entry Island, comprising fewer than 150 people, lists 38 names on the Roll of Honour for World War II, 14 of whom served in Hong Kong with the Royal Rifles of Canada. More than half of them died in the prison camps there. The municipality of Bury in the Eastern Townships supplied the largest number of service personnel per capita "of any Town in Canada." One hundred and thirty of its men and women were on Active Service; ten would not survive. The Rev. A. E. Tulk and Mrs Tulk of St Luke's, Magog, lost two sons, both junior officers: Arthur Raymond of the Royal Engineers and Waldo Eugene of the 8th Princess Louise New Brunswick Hussars. Both died in the Italian campaign, the first in 1944, the second in 1945. This handful of examples hardly suffices to convey a sense of the suffering and loss experienced by the people of this Diocese in consequence of the War.

With the end of hostilities in 1945 came the need to reintegrate former servicemen and women into civilian life. According to the Rev. W. W. Davis, who had shared in the responsibility of assisting this process, some 859 Anglicans discharged from the Army, Navy, and Air Force returned to the Diocese. In addition to these, numerous war brides entered the Diocese from overseas, 72 of whom were Anglicans. In a remarkably frank article entitled "The Church and Discharged Men and Women from the Forces," the Rev. A. V. Ottiwell, who had himself served overseas, spoke of the ambivalent impact the war had had on the spirituality of its participants:

> One of the expectations which has never been realized [he wrote] is that a war will make people, not only men but women also, more sensible of the need for religion. It has always been hoped that they would turn to God in their distress and seek by prayer to plead their cause, confident that it was a righteous one....
>
> What was actually the case? While it is true that some, perhaps many, were more sensible of the need for religion, and did become more regular in their church attendance and did pray for our cause ... yet we know that there was not that seeking after God which had been expected at a time when the world was confronted with the greatest crisis in all history....
>
> It is not to be supposed that army or service life would quicken men's in-

terest in religion any more than that a world crisis should bring civilians to a deeper awareness of God.

This viewpoint may seem to be at odds with what has been regarded as a golden period of growth and expansion in the churches immediately following the War. Yet it is in line with Stackhouse's recent assessment of the reality underlying the seeming renascence of religious feeling in Canada at that time:

> The United and Anglican Churches, for instance, saw their memberships rise by about 25% between 1951 and 1961. This increase represented an understandable post-war desire to "get things back to normal."... It also reflected, however, the many social and service opportunities available in churches. Society had been fragmented by war-induced separations and made more conscientious, perhaps, by experiences of wartime suffering at home and abroad. Men's and women's church groups flourished ...

However, Stackhouse concludes that "it seems that there was less of a revival of genuine and lasting spirituality in the post-war boom than of a revival of general cultural conservatism and consumerism of which church involvement was a component."

Since World War II, the Diocese has from time to time released temporarily a parish priest from his duties to serve as chaplain to Canadian contingents on United Nations peace-keeping missions deployed in various parts of the world. In 1993, the Rev. Capt. Jacques Cloutier of the Greater Parish of St Francis of Assisi was posted for duty in Croatia.

"The Least of These My Brethren": A Ministry to Strangers
The Diocese of Quebec has had a long history of ministering to transient populations, among them notably to the seamen passing through the Port of Quebec. St. Paul's, the Mariner's Chapel, was consecrated by Stewart in 1832, and St Luke's, the chapel in the Marine Hospital, by G. J. Mountain in 1859. Both institutions have long since disappeared, but the service continues.

In the early days this ministry was confined to the summer months, and the hospitals in Quebec were often crowded with sailors during that season. However, with year-round navigation the demands on the mission multiplied and the needs of the transients changed. The Fall/Winter issue of the Missions to Seamen *Newsletter* for 1992 (in calling for donations of "used men's clothing such as sweaters, coats, mitts, scarves, or wool socks") pointed out that "many of the seafarers who come to the port during the winter are not adequately clothed for our climate":

> Last February [the *Newsletter* reported] the Missions to Seamen came to the
> rescue of one seafarer who had frostbite in one toe. Port Chaplain, the Rev.
> Glenn Stone, took him to hospital to receive the medical attention he required.
> This seafarer, Sotero by name, had the miserable job of chipping ice on the
> deck with only spring-like shoes. Sotero was returned to the Philippines where
> he could receive the ongoing medical attention that he needed.
> Before his ship left port, his shipmates were properly clothed for the win-
> ter.

Although the Diocese presently appoints the Chaplain, volunteers for the
Mission represent a variety of religious affiliations (both Christian and Jew-
ish) and are drawn from the French- as well as English-speaking communities.

Such cooperation in the ministry surrounding the Port of Quebec has
not always been evident. In 1888, for example, a major altercation was reported in detail in the local press when a Presbyterian minister, the Rev. Mr.
Love, applied for and was appointed to the chaplaincy of the Marine Hospital. As the post had apparently been supplied by the Diocese since the
founding of the hospital and was regarded as its preserve, Bishop J. W.
Williams objected that the Government, for the first time and without any
prior notice of its intention to do so, had made this appointment on the
strength of an application from an individual for the position. Unfortunately,
the reply to his letter (directed to the Hon. Charles Tupper, Minister of
Marine in Ottawa, and responsible for the appointment) arrived after the
Bishop had departed on a visit to England. The Bishop's Commissary, the
Ven. Henry Roe, thereupon entered into an irate correspondence with
Tupper which he proceeded to transmit to the press. When Tupper proved
to be immovable, Roe demanded "an acknowledgement of the claims of the
Church of England to the gratitude of the country for her past services, and
her claims as being by far the largest Protestant body in Quebec [city], as well
as that body to which the very large majority of the Protestant patients in
the hospital have always belonged." Tupper, equally peppery, maintained that
the consecration of the chapel conveyed no rights over it, and expressed his
amazement "at the importance this action has assumed." When news of the
unfortunate affair reached Williams, he expressed regret that it had been
thought necessary to publish the correspondence. Despite this discomfiture,
the Rev. T. W. Fyles, the Emigration Chaplain, who was aided in his ministry by a grant from the SPCK, continued to provide Anglican services at

the Port of Quebec at this period and until his retirement in 1908.

In the 1980s and 1990s, support for the various projects of the Mission to Seamen (such as "Operation Shoebox," which provides gifts for seamen at Quebec or at sea for Christmas) has become ecumenical, with participation from Baptist, Presbyterian, Roman Catholic, and United Church congregations, as well as from all the deaneries within the Diocese. In 1992, almost 800 shoeboxes were filled and distributed.

In 1981, Bishop Allen Goodings was asked to take responsibility for the Missions to Seamen. Since that time, three Anglican priests have succeeded each other as chaplains. In 1993, Port Chaplain Glenn Stone was appointed as the Missions to Seamen representative to the Board of Directors of the North American Maritime Ministries Association (a branch of the International Christian Maritime Association) "linking all port agencies and individuals welcoming merchant seafarers into their ports."

Another type of mission to transients in the Diocese took clergy landward, into the newly-opened wilderness. The Rev. G. R. Fothergill, missionary to the labourers constructing the Transcontinental Railway in 1908, has left a vivid description of life in the camps near LaTuque:

> From the beginning of August the Church has provided a missionary to work among the engineers and men who are constructing the Quebec part of the new line. It is his work to visit the camps, which lie at intervals along the line generally by the side of lake or river, and to become acquainted with the men in them, and to hold services.
>
> The work on the grade, at which most of the men are employed, is rough and hard,—filling trucks with earth and sand or dragging stones to build up the dump, ... working with pick and shovel in the cuts, or where the grade passes over streams, wheeling concrete for the culverts,—and some of the men have become rough and hard too....
>
> They sleep in long log shacks, with two broad shelves, one above the other ... divided into partitions, in each of which sleep generally, two, sometimes three, men.... Down the centre is a more or less open space, partly occupied by the stove and pipe, and on each side ... is a seat formed by planks....The general thing in a shack is a game of poker, at which five or six play with a few looking on, a few reading by a fading light, and a good many smoking, and a great many doing nothing....The times when the men are working are so hard, and the times when the men are not working are so dull, that in the majority of cases the life is only endured till such time as enough money has been earned to be spent ... in an incredibly short space of time in Quebec, or more generally in Montreal.There is no drink in the camps except where it is smuggled in, but whether because it is much thought about or talked about, there is always the feeling that the demon of drink is hovering around.
>
> As nearly all nations are represented, so are nearly all religions, but almost

all who understand English, whether Church of England, Church of Rome, Presbyterian, Lutheran, Baptist, Methodist and others, seem to come readily to an occasional service and listen attentively. These services are necessarily of an informal character—generally an address followed by a few prayers—and are held ... more generally in the sleeping shacks.... No celebration of Holy Communion has yet been held in any of the camps.

The need for another type of mission to transients made itself felt during the Depression. One of the six Unemployment Camps, nationwide, was located in the Diocese of Quebec at Valcartier. Although relief workers were provided jointly by the Missionary Society of the Church of England in Canada and the Council for Social Service, the local Church population was called upon to meet this challenge, too.

One of the most striking examples of ministry to the transients and the destitute in the Diocese was that taken on by a number of "Ladies' Committees," formed in the early years of the nineteenth century by groups of remarkable laywomen in the Quebec City region.

The duty of Protestant poor relief in the city fell to the churchwardens of the Cathedral, who paid out occasional sums (duly noted in the parish accounts) to widows, orphans, and those too ill or infirm to be able to support themselves. In the case of orphans, the practice was, at first, to pay some poor but respectable person to board individual children until such time as they could be expected to fend for themselves.

Realizing how unsatisfactory an arrangement this was, and in the absence of any local institution for Protestant orphans, a group of 12 women (largely attached to the Cathedral congregation) determined to establish a home for orphan girls where shelter, food, and clothing could be adequately seen to, a proper Christian upbringing assured, and provision made for preparing the children for some respectable service or trade. In the first year, the ladies hoped to accommodate a dozen girls and to increase the number to 20 as soon as possible, resources permitting. On 5 March 1829, the day on which the Protestant Female Orphan Asylum (as it was first called) was officially opened, there were five children in residence. At the end of five years of operations, the Asylum's Register bore the names of 53 children.

Funds to support this venture were raised by the women themselves at an annual bazaar of fancywork and other donated items held in the City. Far from being primarily concerned with fund-raising, however, the Ladies' Committee set up a roster of duty requiring each of their number to oversee the home for a particular month annually, visiting almost daily, checking the accounts, ordering supplies, inspecting the linen, instructing the matron, and monitoring the children's progress and well-being.

Although the Asylum was intended for children with no living parent, sometimes circumstances required bending this rule a little. Thus, shortly after the Asylum opened, the Secretary of the Ladies' Committee was informed by Archdeacon G. J. Mountain of a particularly pressing case:

> Madam,
>
> I am apprehensive that the Ladies who superintend the affairs of the Orphan Asylum will think that the cases brought under their notice by myself are multiplying rather fast, yet I cannot forbear from stating to them the situation of Mary Anne Newman, elder sister of Anne Newman admitted a month ago. The mother of these children has become deranged & has burnt almost all the articles of furniture of which she [was] possessed as well as part of her children's clothes. I have made the case known to the Physician of the General Hospital & I believe it will be found necessary to convey the woman to the *Moral Cells* in the Establishment. The little girl still with her has no place to go to, & altho I should endeavour, of course, to do my best to provide for her, it would be impossible for me to do so in any way which could be compared, in point of advantage, with her being admitted, for the present, into the Asylum.... The child states herself to have been 12 years old on the 15th of last month; but the Ladies will perceive that in appearance she is younger.

Mary Anne's six-year-old sister (whose name appears as Fanny Newman in the Register) had been admitted on 16 March. At the April meeting of the Committee it was resolved that Mary Anne should indeed be admitted for a month in hopes that, after that time, she would be found suitable as assistant to the Matron (for she was marginally older than the girls regularly admitted). Mary Anne must have been capable for her years, for the May Minutes record that a place in service had already been found for her and that she had left the Asylum. Fanny Newman remained until she was 14, at which time she was taken into the Mountain household. Mary Mountain, as her private correspondence amply shows, was a kind employer and took a great interest in her servants. She saw to it that they were well treated and not overworked. When the girls married, it was not unusual for her to buy their "Wedding and other dresses" lest they should do without.

Although most of the orphans were proposed for admission by one or another of the local clergy, this was not invariably so. Thomas Trigge of Nicolet informed the Committee of the case of four-year-old Jane Hughes, whose family had been sent to that place from Quebec "as paupers, by the Emigrant Society." A memorandum records, laconically enough, that the child was born at Nicolet about 13 or 14 January 1825. Her mother died on the 15th of same month. The Father left the Place the ensuing Spring & has not since been heard of. The child has been maintained since her Birth at the Expence of Mary Chandler who placed her with a neighbouring settler, but she is now of an age to benefit from instruction which there is not the means of affording her there.

Each child was considered individually and her admissibility decided upon by vote. As Jane Hughes came from outside the region, there was some discussion about her eligibility for acceptance into the Asylum. Two of the members, unable to be present at the meeting that would decide the case, took care to send their votes by letter. In the event, it was resolved to admit the child, and she arrived there on 17 November 1829. She died, while still an inmate, three years later.

The orphans of soldiers attached to regiments stationed at Quebec were urged upon the Committee as well. Technically, these children should have been cared for by the Military, but, as their spokesman pointed out, "the Military Asylum is necessarily open to adults and temporary Inmates, and the Committee have not the means of giving that undivided attention to the Interests of the Children, which the [Orphan Asylum] offers." Accordingly, in 1843, the ladies undertook to admit five military orphans: Maria and Sarah Davis, aged seven and three, whose parents had both died of Yellow Fever on their passage to Quebec; Mary and Ann Collins, aged eleven and six, who had travelled with the 56th Regiment of Foot from Port Royal, Jamaica, where both their parents had died in 1839; and Susan Langley, "about 7," whose father had deserted his regiment at Laprairie in 1842 and had abandoned her.

Such was the challenge of caring for the homeless and friendless taken up by these laywomen. A further Ladies' Committee (comprised of many of the same women) undertook to establish a Male Orphan Asylum on a similar plan in 1832. When the Finlay Asylum for "the needy and helpless" (caring for homeless old men as well as accommodating the boys from the Male Orphan Asylum) was opened by Bishop G. J. Mountain in 1862, it was yet again a Ladies' Committee that took charge of its management. Eventually, with ever greater involvement in the realm of social service by the state, the need for such institutions declined. The Female Orphan Asylum (more recently known as Bishop Mountain Hall) closed its doors in 1968; the Finlay Home, in 1970.

On looking over the records of the Asylum so many years after the events that cast these unfortunate children onto the charity of the public, one is struck above all by the unflagging and unstinting care of those who met the challenge, steadily and in all seasons. Despite the numbers of orphans being cared for, no inmate appears ever to have been treated as a mere nameless statistic. The records of the institution are brimful of instances of the caregivers' personal interest in and familiarity with their individual charges. One example will suffice. In 1838, Miss Pike of the Ladies' Committee took December as her month of duty at the Female Orphan Asylum. As was the custom of the establishment, she recorded the accounts, together with her personal observations, faithfully in the "Visitor's Book" provided:

> 20th [Dec.] Visited. And was pleased to hear the improvement in reading and writing, also particularly the eldest Paterson. Murray has been much longer, therefore I spoke of Paterson, as having been very diligent and desirous of improving, but Murray reads by far the best and seems a steady good Girl.*
>
> 21st. Visited; all very busy, some taking up Wood, others shoveling snow from the steps and making a path to the Asylum, others working at their Needle; only the 3 little ones Idle....
>
> [24th] I went at six o'clock in the evening of Christmas Eve, heard their evening devotions, the elder Girls read: they all sang the evening Hymn, and Miss Goode [the Matron] pray'd. They then walked of[f] to Bed; they do this every night; it was a very pleasing sight. I ought not to have omitted 3 very little creatures, one 2, 3, [and] 3½,† repeated some verses very perfectly on Christmas and sang by themselves wonderfully well.

The entry for the following day is the briefest and most eloquent:

> 25th. All at Church and well.

---

* Elizabeth Paterson and her sister Matilda were admitted to the Asylum on 21 September 1837 at the age of 13 and 11 years, respectively. Mary Anne Murray, a much younger child, had been admitted on 4 November 1835 at the age of 7.
† Probably Caroline Hatton, Frances Woodward and Sarah Lynam, whose ages (as indicated in the Register) seem closest to those given.

Afterword

The theme of "pilgrimage," chosen for the bicentenary of the Diocese, is a particularly appropriate one. As Bishop Stavert pointed out in his Charge to the 1993 Synod, both the word and the concept "suggest a sense of the past, an activity in the present and a movement towards the future."

The path the people of the Diocese have followed over the past two centuries (and indeed from 1759) has been challenging and circuitous, with varying fare and provender along the way. Many individuals, both clerics and laypeople, have contributed to setting the pace and even to choosing the byways, and the character of the whole cavalcade has set its stamp on each of the pilgrims. The features of the countryside have played their part, too, and a rich fund of stories—some funny, some sad— has lightened the spirits of the travellers on their way.

As the Diocese enters its third century, the ground seems once again strangely familiar. Small resources, scattered numbers, an uncertain future, and an increasing dependence on the commitment of the laity were familiar to those who first planted their staffs here. Their story, with all its difficulties and disappointments—as well as its successes and triumphs— serves as a signpost, a warning and an invitation.

Some 40 years ago, in 1955, the Diocese published a guide to its work and a statement of its mission. "It has been our claim throughout the years," the preface reads, "wherever there is a group that needs our ministrations, however small they may be, that we will be there, some-how, sometime, with the Gospel and the ministrations of the Church. The burden on our small resources and our scattered Clergy is a heavy one, but God has enabled us to stick to our post."

In light of the current revaluation by the national Church of what it can reasonably seek to accomplish with shrinking congregations and dwindling resources, the continuing commitment of *this* Diocese to its mission will call for singular devotion and resolve.

Meanwhile, the pilgrimage continues.

WINDOWS
An Anthology of Diocesan Vignettes
1765-1993

Lord, how can man preach thy eternal word?
He is a brittle crazie glasse:
Yet in thy temple thou dost him afford
This glorious and transcendent place,
To be a window, through thy grace.

George Herbert (1593–1633)

Clergy Wives: Frances Brooke, Grace Marston and Gwendolyn Carrington
1765, 1960 and 1984

Among *the numerous Anglican clergy wives to take their places within the territory of the present-day Diocese of Quebec, the earliest was probably Frances Moore, the Lincolnshire-born wife of the Rev. Dr John Brooke, chaplain to His Majesty's forces. Arriving in 1763, Mrs Brooke lived in Quebec or neighbouring Sillery for nearly five years, moving in the society of the military establishment which, in due course, would form the background of her novel* The History of Emily Montague, *published in London in 1769.*

That she was a bright woman with a sharp eye there can be no doubt. A letter of hers to the Bishop of London, preserved in Lambeth Palace Archives, outlines the religious climate in Quebec in 1765 as she had observed it.

 M. Morisseau, Curé of Charlebourg, near Quebec, teaches his people to obey the King & enter into his Service ...
The Seminary priests are a Branch of those of St Sulpice at Paris, to whom part of their Revenues are remitted, all French, very rich & bigotted & active in making Converts. One of them lately went to a Fr. Protestant merchant on his Death Bed & threatened him with Damnation. Mr Brooke & Capt. Holland, Surveyor Gen[era]l went to tell the Governor this, but he would not hear them.

The Jesuits also are native French, more learned & less violent than the Seminary, perhaps less attached to France since their Expulsion.

The Recollects are inoffensive, have no property but their House, church & Gardens, live on the Alms of the Engl & Fr, lend us their Ch w^n they can spare it: they & the parish priests almost all Canadians.

M. Récher, Curé of Quebec, the most bigoted priest in Canada, let the part of the Cath[olic] Ch[urch] Yard in wch alone the English are buried to build Houses on; & suffered their Bodies, 25 at a time, to be dug up, & exposed. After doing it thrice, he denied that he knew it, ag[ains]t the oaths of the workmen that he commanded it. The Judge ... hath endeavoured to stop this: but the Contempt of the French for us, on suffering it so long, is inconceivable.

Although few today would think of Frances Brooke as a clergy wife, her very presence in Quebec was due to her husband's position. By drawing the attention of the authorities "at Home" to the local situation, she was clearly trying to serve the interests of her husband's flock. A woman of education and attainments, she was well equipped to fill the social role traditionally demanded of a clergyman's wife.

Almost two hundred years after Frances Brooke's arrival, Grace Marston, herself a professional librarian, was to take a serious look at the clergy wife's role at a gathering of women like herself.

The following excerpt is drawn from an item entitled "The Role Of The Clergy Wife In The Parish" published in the 1962 May issue of the Quebec Diocesan Gazette.

This contribution appears to have been prompted by an increasing need among the wives of clergymen in the Diocese for "frank discussion" and mutual support. The bulk of the article came from "a paper … read at the initial gathering" of Eastern Townships Clergy Wives, organized "some time ago" by Mrs Thomas Hardy, wife of the incumbent at East Angus.

As a contemporary account of the occasion shows, the initial meeting was of clergy wives in the District of St Francis. The programme consisted of a Communion Service at Christ Church (with the Rev. Guy Marston, Rector of St Peter's, Sherbrooke, as celebrant), followed by a luncheon at the rectory served by members of the East Angus Girl Guide Company. During the afternoon Mrs. Marston read "a very interesting and well-planned paper on the duties, problems and privileges of the clergyman's wife" which was followed by "a stimulating discussion." The text gives remarkable insight into the position occupied by the female members of a clergyman's family well past the middle of the twentieth century:

One of the characteristics of the average Anglican parish [the paper begins] is that it normally prefers a married clergyman as its rector. This fact is clear and evident proof of the significance parishes place upon the function of a rector's wife. I suppose when most of us reached the momentous decision to marry our husbands we didn't hesitate because they were to be clergymen. Rather, we were glad of their high calling. I am sure we did much serious thinking about our roles as parsons' wives. Our husbands had been trained for their service to the Church. The wives they chose had been trained in various other professions, prepared as other girls to care for their husbands, their children and their homes, but seldom trained in any specific way to be the wives of clergymen. Here the daughters of the rectory have had the great advantage. They have had the most realistic preparation of all … But to many of us, our participation in church and parish life had been that of a woman in the pew. Then suddenly we were placed in a rectory, given great responsibilities, not only in caring for our families but in playing the new, significant, indeed, the unique role of a parson's wife.

What then are some of the qualities such wives should strive to possess in order to help their husbands and make their own contributions to parish life? First, I think, is *awareness*. This is the basic quality in living the Christian life. Awareness is opening the eyes of one's soul and one's mind to the physical, mental and spiritual needs of the people one has to deal with. One has to become aware in order to help....

Another quality of importance is *teachability*. We must be able to be taught. We must be able to learn from our own mistakes, from situations, and above all, from people. And the sum total of all this learning along the way becomes a sort of wisdom which is of great value in parish life.

A third quality among the many one could possess is the *ability to be happy*. The parson's wife who can laugh, who can handle situations with a light touch is the one who is going to wear well in a parish, and who is going to save herself a lot of heartache....

Of course the all-encompassing quality we must have to be good parsons' wives is *dedication*. We must want to serve, even as our husbands serve. We must have singleness of purpose and the desire to give of ourselves, our time and our abilities. Then and only then, the frustrations and difficulties will seem of little importance, and parish life will take on its true proportions.

But when we walked over the threshold of our first parsonage, however earnest we were, however full of ideals, we were just beginning the training through experience that we shall continue all the days of our parish life. For as to the life itself, it is by growth we attain any sort of stature as wives of clergymen.... Perhaps we could do no better than take a straight look at ourselves and ask ourselves three questions: What kind of a parson's wife have I been in the past? What kind of a parson's wife am I being in the present, and what kind of a parson's wife am I becoming?

And what of the problems that face us as rectory wives? There are a good many, of course. Let me name just a few: The difficult problem of personal friends—to have or not to have; the problem of being regarded as different, perhaps not quite like others; the problem of rising to situations; the ever-present problem of whether or not to be the parish curate; the problem of not-too-plentiful funds; the constant problem of finding time for reading and personal recreation. Such problems plague us throughout our rectory life. They are real and omnipresent, but we must not forget that the privileges and joys are omnipresent too.... Think of the opportunities to meet and know interesting people; think of a whole parish of friendly people rather than a handful of close friends; though these are not forbidden either. We may not be numbered among the wealthy but a sense of security and certainty pervades parish life. There are opportunities for leadership for those equipped to lead, and opportunities for work, worship, fellowship and service to suit the abilities of practically any type of clergy wife.

Clergymen's wives (and daughters) have been expected to play a prominent part in founding, leading, and supporting parish activities. Even outside the parish setting this has been so. When Philip Carrington as Dean of Divinity took on the organization of the 1935 Diocesan Youth Conference at North Hatley, for example, it was Mrs Carrington who served as Hostess, was leader of the Girls' Conferences, and held a Mission Study Class.

On her husband's election to the episcopate that same year, "Gwen Quebec" (as she was somewhat irreverently dubbed) gained full scope for her exceptional gifts and became, in the context of the modern diocese at least, the ultimate clergy wife. Although she could and did strike terror in the hearts of some, her many contributions—often of a most practical and useful nature—to the life of the Church and to the lives of individuals have won for her a special place in the affections of Quebec Anglicans. The following is an excerpt from Canon W.H.M. Church's brief tribute to her memory, printed in the Diocesan Gazette:

As Quebec's First Lady, Gwen Carrington found outlet for her great energies, her ever active mind and innumerable humanitarian interests. She began with kindly help and understanding to the wives and families of clergy in the mission areas. Through quick initiative, rectories were improved, children's health and education given special attention, plumbing renewed, and new rectories made more practical from a housewife's point of view.

In 1940 Gwen was elected President of the Diocesan W.A. Due to her vision ... the work of that invaluable auxiliary to the National Missionary Society (MSCC) ... was extended to embrace every aspect of Women's work in the Church. The logical outcome, long after her retirement to England, came about with the transformation of the W.A. to the A.C.W....

... Everyone knew her charm and tireless drive. Few knew how tenuous was her real health. All saw her human insight and eye for potential in the hundreds of girls she discovered, sponsored and sustained at camps like Quebec Lodge and Fort Haldimand, through the J.A. and G.A.,* Schools, Special Courses, and Universities. Her system of self-perpetuating leadership training, remains to this day [1984], and is the reason that the Staff and Counsellors at Quebec Lodge are a model for all.

... [I]n spite of being possibly too awe-inspiring to some, those who came close to her would well understand one little girl's heartfelt tribute— "you are such a doll." This one Gwen never forgot.

The position of the clergy wife in the Diocese of Quebec has changed a good deal from that described by Grace Marston in the 1960s. With growing tendencies to consolidate parishes, close churches, and reduce the number of clergy in the field, no longer is "that sense of security and certainty" pervasive in parish life. While there has been little improvement in the purchasing power of clergy stipends, community respect for the clergyman and his family, clergy wives attest, may no longer be taken for granted.

Since the ordination of women to the priesthood in the 1970s, the whole concept of "the clergy spouse" has been rethought, particularly because it is not unusual for both husband and wife in a clergy-family to have received ordination. By 1995, five such couples had ministered on a regular basis within the Diocese of Quebec although the wife had not invariably filled a stipendiary position.

Meanwhile, what began as a modest day-excursion to East Angus—the initiative of the clergy wives of the St Francis District—has become a regularly scheduled, weekend event organized for the Diocese as a whole, encouraging all the clergy spouses who wish to do so to gather annually for "frank discussion" and "mutual support."

---

* J.A. = Junior Auxiliary and G.A. = Girls' Auxiliary, patterned on the W.A. or Woman's Auxiliary.

Relations with Other Communions: Trois-Rivières 1794

O*n 2 June 1972, Bishop T. J. Matthews and Mrs Matthews, together with Canon and Mrs Gourley, visited the Ursuline Convent at Trois-Rivières at the invitation of the Mother Superior. Diocesan Synod was meeting in the city at that time, and the visit took place on the afternoon of the first day. "This was the first such visit by a Bishop of the Diocese to this Convent," the Journal of Synod records, "since the time of Bishop Jacob Mountain in the late 1700's." Jacob Mountain's visit had taken place in July 1794 during the course of his first Visitation of the Diocese, within a year of his arrival in the Canadas. The following account is taken from a family letter to England, dated at Masquinongé on 15 July 1794.*

The Bishop had set off on the 11 July, accompanied by his brother Jehoshaphat in "my own travelling calèche" and his nephew Salter with a servant in a post calèche. Two days before, he had sent off a bateau under the care of another servant and five bateaux-men to rendezvous with them at Trois-Rivières, carrying the "travelling apparatus" they would need under the primitive conditions they expected to endure on their journey beyond Montreal and in the Upper Province.

They spent the first night at Portneuf—disturbed throughout by "millions" of flies; when protective curtains were removed, these settled so quickly on hands and faces "as to make it impossible to brush them away." They reached Trois-Rivières on Saturday, the 12th, where they "found a hotel, and comfortable accommodation—such as might have made us fancy ourselves again in England" and settled in for three days. Salter preached on the Sunday, but it was the following day that proved to be the memorable one.

On the Monday [the Bishop recorded] I held a Confirmation, and afterwards received a message from the Ursuline Convent in the town, in consequence of which, I went with my brother, Salter Mountain, and a gentleman of the place, to visit their nunnery. They are almost all of them, people of family, and are, notwithstanding their seclusion from the world, extremely cheerful, conversable and well bred. The Supérieure, La Révérende Mère Thérèse de Jésus, conducted me through every part of the Convent, which is very spacious, handsome and airy, followed by the other gentlemen, and the whole train of nuns. The beautiful neatness of everything about them is both pleasing and surprising. Their chapel is of course highly ornamented. Their refectory is very handsome; and a large room which they appropriate to conversation for an hour or two in the day, when there is a pause from their religious and other exercises, is of noble dimensions, and commands an extensive view of the town, river and country.

In this apartment (at the upper end), I found a large crimson damask chair, in which I was desired to repose myself. The Supérieure placed herself at my right hand, in a common chair, and all the nuns ranged themselves, but at some little distance, in a sort of half moon, on benches, on one side of the room. On the other side chairs were placed, but at some little distance also, for the gentlemen. Our conversation then began, and was supported for some time in a manner very agreeable to me. We then proceeded to view their hospital, schools, offices, and botanic garden, and physician's and apothecary's apartments. They have one hospital (for so they call it), consisting of one spacious room for the sick of their own community. Two other large rooms, separated from the other apartments are for the sick who may choose to avail themselves of their charity, and for whom, while they remain there, everything is provided by the nuns. In both these hospitals everything is done by the nuns themselves: ... [t]he nun-physician, and the nun-apothecary, are bred from their youth to their respective studies. The latter has a large room, very completely and handsomely fitted with cases full of bottles, drugs, etc, etc, and the former has all the gravity of conversation of a male-physician ... One of their schools consists of the young ladies who are taken entirely into the Convent for education, upon pensions, and reside there till their education is finished. The other, which is separated from the Convent, though within the walls, is a charity-school for the young girls of the town and neighbourhood, of whom, I believe there were not less than a hundred.... I must not omit to mention that the Supérieure assured me that while I was ill last winter at Quebec, *les sœurs* said mass for my recovery!—an instance of charity for a heretic, for which you may be assured, I felt myself greatly indebted. Before we came away, the Supérieure and some of the chief nuns put on the robes in which they perform their religious ceremonies, to gratify our curiosity.

When we left them (as when they received us), they all drew themselves up in a half circle, with the Supérieure at their head, and bowed very low, letting their arms fall forward (for they never bend the knee except in prayer), and I assure you, made a very graceful appearance.

On 30 December of that year, the Supérieure addressed a letter to Bishop Mountain in which she recalled this visit and offered him the continued good wishes of the Community:

Monseigneur,

J'ose me flatter d'après les témoignages sensibles de votre estime dont notre monastère, qu'elle voudra bien agréer l'honorable et gracieuse liberté que nous donne le renouvellement d'année pour nous procurer l'indicible satisfaction de lui présenter nos très humbles hommages et assurances des vœux que nous adresserons au ciel pour sa précieuse conservation et prospérité de son illustre famille. C'est avec ces vifs sentimens que nous avons l'honneur d'être, avec le plus profond respect, monseigneur, de votre seigneurie les très humbles et très obéissantes servantes.

Sr Thérèse de Jésus,
Sup. aux Ursulines de Trois Rivières

"A Sermon Preached at Quebec," A General Thanksgiving 1799

On 1 August 1798, Nelson won a re-*sounding victory at the Battle of the Nile and the fleet assembled by Napoleon was destroyed. By Royal Proclamation, Thursday, 10 January 1799, was declared a day of General Thanksgiving to celebrate "the late unexampled and most important Victory obtained by His Majesty's Arms, over the Fleet and Forces of the Enemy." A Special Form of Prayer was drawn up for the occasion. By request, the sermon preached at Quebec by Bishop Jacob Mountain at the Service on that day was later published.*

The Bishop, who long before his rise to the episcopate had acquired a reputation for his preaching, was well aware that a sermon designed for delivery was handled differently from one meant merely to be read. In a letter, printed as the preface to the published sermon, he asks the reader to make allowance for any liberties he has taken with "the refinements of exact composition" to strengthen the impact of his meaning on the listener.

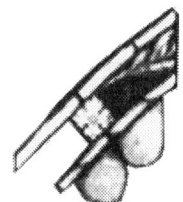

The Hearers of Sermons, and the Readers of them are, for the most part, different classes of people [the Bishop remarked]. It is the business of the Preacher to go as directly as he can to the understandings and the hearts of his Congregation;—and in attempting to do this, he will often find it not only safe, but expedient, to neglect the refinements of exact composition. Studious of perspicuity and force, he will be little solicitous about the structure of a sentence, or the rounding of a period. It will be his object not to fix the attention of his auditors upon his own rhetoric, but to turn their thoughts inward upon themselves. But in printed Sermons a greater regard to the established Rules of Composition, and to the graces of a correct and elegant diction, is justly expected ...

The Form of Prayer set out was that of Morning Prayer with readings from Psalms 33 ("Rejoice in the Lord, O ye righteous: for praise is comely for the upright"), 46 ("God is our refuge and strength, a very present help in trouble"), and 98 ("O sing unto the Lord a new song; ... his right hand, and his holy arm, hath gotten him the victory"). The Proper Lessons were I Chron. 16: 8-37 and Luke 12: 4-10. The use of the Prayer in Time of War and Tumults stipulated for the special service gives emphasis to the ongoing nature of hostilities.

Nations [the sermon continued] undergo chastisement by various means, arising out of their own misconduct; by the irregular ambition, the factious intrigues, the seditious turbulence of their members—by civil commotion, civil insurrection and civil war—by the annihilation of order, and the subversion of government—by the destruction of their fleets and armies—by the failure of their resources—by the growing power of their enemies, and by the diminution of their own power, and the loss of their independence: these various calamities are the result, and, under Providence, the punishment of public vices. Nations prosper by the concurrence of events which are the reverse of these: and their prosperity is the fruit, and the reward, of their public virtue.

Using examples drawn from the Old Testament and Ancient History—Canaan, Israel, Assyria, Persia, Greece, and Rome—Mountain equates the fall of nations with their moral decay:

The attentive observer will not fail to remark, that the successive subversion of these great and powerful empires, as they respectively became notoriously wicked, strongly confirms the doctrine of a National Providence—they shew that communities change their fortune with their manners—that empire is uniformly transferred to the more virtuous and worthy, from the vicious and abandoned. "Corruption is never far remote from dissolution" and the invariable end of great National Depravity, is National Destruction.

Mountain's Sermon reflects the widely held view, both in Britain and the Canadas, that the excesses and irreligiousness of Revolutionary France had called down Divine punishment. Those nations that opposed her were regarded as the instruments of Providence.

We are *now*, happily for ourselves, and for the world, made the instruments of chastizing the arrogance, and of humbling the power of France.—But amidst our triumphs, it certainly behooves us to consider, the danger which we may incur of suffering in our turn, if we do not resolutely resist the growing spirit of *Irreligion*, which has so remarkably spread itself amongst us!...

    Instead, therefore, of indulging in the sanguine imaginations of self-confidence, and self-applause,—instead of dwelling upon the weakness, and wickedness of other nations, with secret exultation in our own superiority, it will become us to meditate seriously upon the causes of their misfortunes; and to reflect that the same causes, wherever they are suffered to exist, will not fail, in the end, to produce similar effects.

In 1814, Mountain's son George entered into the responsibilities of his first parish (at Fredericton), and the Bishop, anxious to offer guidance and help, included the following observations on the importance of the manner and spirit in which a minister should approach his duties:

Be very watchful over yourself, that no degree of languor or indifference creep by degrees into your manner of performing divine service. Impress upon your mind the fixed recollection, that when you open your lips in the church, it is to address yourself to the Almighty Lord of heaven and earth, in behalf of yourself and of all who are assembled with you.... In the pulpit, always keep it in mind, that the eternal condition of all, or of many at least, who hear you may depend upon and date from the doctrine and the exhortations that you deliver, ... and keep the same things in mind in the composition of your sermons, never addressing yourself to this part of your duty without prayer to God for His blessing upon your labours.

Mountain's own preaching is said to have been commanding and impressive. The following contemporary description allows the reader to picture the Bishop in the act of delivering his address:

In the pulpit, ... the advantage of his fine and venerable aspect—the grace, the force, the solemn fervor of his delivery,—the power and happy regulation of his tones,—the chaste expressiveness and natural significance of his action, ... and that piety, ... which was, and showed itself to be, pregnant with the importance of its subject, and intent upon conveying the same feeling to others,—made him altogether a preacher, who has never, in modern times, been surpassed.

A Family Excursion, Lac Beauport
1804

Although the state of English-language educational institutions in the Canadas made it necessary for Bishop Jacob Mountain to send his sons to England for all but their elementary education, he was well aware that there were opportunities not to be missed by them to learn about their new home and its people before their enforced departure.

"As my boys will leave Canada next summer," he recounted in a personal letter written 31 October 1804, "I have taken every occasion of leisure to shew them as much of the Country as I can. With this in view, we have made many family excursions—taking with us a cold dinner, & sitting down to eat it under trees, or in a farmhouse, as the distance, or chance, or whim, or the state of the weather, might happen to direct.—Even little Charlotte [then aged only three] has not been excluded from these parties; and has made no inconsiderable part of the pleasure of them. ... & never in a single instance has she been in the smallest degree troublesome, or betrayed even a momentary wish to do any thing, but what she saw us disposed to do: Which, if I don't mistake, is a great deal to say for so young a Lady, or, indeed, for a Lady of any age whatever.—" He goes on to describe two specific expeditions, too strenuous to include "the ladies and younger part of the family," one to Lac Beauport and the other to the summit of Mont Ste-Anne.

The adventurers on the first of these excursions were the Bishop (then 55 years old), his three elder sons—Jacob, George and Robert, aged 16, 15 and 14, respectively—and the Rev. Matthew Fielde, their tutor.

... we set off early in the morning, & breakfasted at the house of a Gentleman on our road who accompanied us to the foot of the mountain, & there delivered us over to the care of a Canadian, his tenant, whom he had provided for our guide. We were all on horseback, but a servant in a *very* light cart with us, to carry our provision. The cart was able to follow us up about a league, this road cut for the purpose of bringing down wood on slays in winter. We were able to go upon horseback about a league further. We then tied all our horses to the trees, & began to proceed on foot; after crossing, with a good deal of labour & difficulty, over the summits of two mountains, & having descended a little, we came to the Lake. It would be vain to think of describing it. I shall only say that we congratulated each other upon having made the attempt to see it; & that, from its form, & the beautiful & sublime mountain scenery that surrounded it, we agreed in thinking it more charming than any thing we had ever seen.—But time w^d not allow us to enjoy it long—we were to look to the labour of returning (for we had again to cross the summets of two mountains) & the danger, if it should become dusk, of being lost in the woods. The most difficult of the obstacles that crossed our way, arose from trees which, having been for ages perhaps accumulating, after being hurled down by the violence of the winds, were deeply covered, & entirely concealed, by an infinite variety of mosses—so soft, that we plunged up to our knees at every step, & were only prevented from going deeper (& perhaps from sinking to a very dangerous depth indeed), by the intertwining of the branches of the upper trees, which tho' entirely covered, were not yet entirely decayed.—Over these immense beds of moss we crept, & tumbled, & rolled, as well as we could, & were sometimes glad to rest upon them—for no bed could be half so soft or downy.—When we had crossed the two mountains, & were fairly got to the foot of the second, it appeared that our guide had entirely lost himself.—After some hesitation, he said that we must reascend the mountain, & then he should be sure of being right. The sound was not a very pleasant one; particularly to me. I was not perfectly well when I left home. The unusual breakfast of Coffee, & the more unusual glass of *liqueur* which our entertainer forced upon us after it, rendered me more indisposed, & consequently more sensible to fatigue: I felt that it w^d be scarcely possible for me to reascend; for, ... we had been much longer without food than usual, & my strength began to desert me. I therefore desired the guide to make a circuit, while I rested at the foot of a tree, & to endeavour to get again within the sphere of his recollection. (He had been accustomed for 20 years to traverse these mountains.)

I must own that my feelings, during his absence, were very painful.—To remain all night in the woods would not have had any thing in it very formidable; even to remain so long without food, after so much fatigue, tho' painful, w^d not have been intolerable: But my uneasiness arose from the sense of what Mrs Mountain & Jane, & the poor children at home must have suffered, if we had not been able to reach home. For it is a very dangerous thing for Europeans to lose themselves in the woods, & they who do are sometimes lost forever—& they w^d certainly have believed that we were lost.—I concealed my anxiety as well as I could from my companions, & they in their turn did every thing they could to cheer me.—We heard our guide shouting at a distance, in hopes of being answered by the servant, & his son, who were left with the horses:—it was a dismal blank, to find that no answer was returned.—He soon however rejoined us, & told us he was now sure of his way, & without reascending the mountain.—He expressed himself with so much feeling respecting his error, which he said, & I believe truly, originated in a desire to shorten the way, from observing that I was much fatigued, & thinking it not possible that by so doing he could bewilder himself,—that he gained upon the good will of us all. In about half an hour ... we came to our horses, & I scarcely recollect a more *comfortable* sensation than [that when] I found myself seated upon mine; except perhaps that which soon after followed, & which was common to us all; when we found ourselves resting *comfortably* under the trees, with each his dinner on his lap.—All fatigue was now forgotten. The boys were in the highest possible glee. I never felt better in my life. There are few situations which touch the heart more, nor more agreeably, than when we have escaped, without injury, from what might have been a serious evil: or that give us a more proper, or a more pleasing sense of the goodness of our all benevolent Protector. We were now secure of getting home about the time we had mentioned: & therefore greatly enjoyed our ride home, & the talking over of what we had seen, & encountered.

Another account of the Lac Beauport expedition has been preserved, written by one of the three boys. It adds a wealth of detail: that their breakfast was had at Mr Duchesnay's, that the name of their guide was Jean-Marie Bélanger. The boy who stayed with the cart was the guide's, not the servant's, son, "a boy of sixteen yet in appearance hardly ten, his growth, as he said, having been interrupted by labour."

The distance from their way when they were lost is given in more detail, too: "by having a little changed our route ... [we] were surprised with a proof that, in a wood, to be lost ten yards is to be lost as certainly as a thousand.... [T]he path ... was certainly not twenty yards distant." On their return, the Bishop's son records, they spied a ruffled grouse "called here the spruce partridge ... a very beautiful creature." Like his father, the boy's account is very positive. "Fully satisfied with our day's expedition," he concludes, "we arrived home after dark."

Jacob Mountain is often portrayed as he appeared in his public persona: dignified, unbending, proud, and autocratic. A glimpse at his family life, his concern for the feelings of those near him, his genuine enjoyment of experiences shared, his gameness at taking risks, serves to humanize an otherwise unduly austere figure.

The Bishop's letter describing the excursion to Lac Beauport—in spite of his momentary anxiety—conveys his delight in the overall adventure and his boys' "highest possible glee." He was well aware, however, that the events themselves might be viewed less positively by others. In concluding his letter he took care to urge that his correspondent be discreet. "I w^d rather you w^d not mention this excursion to our common friends, because, without the necessary explanation, it might appear, on my part, what I think it was not,—an imprudent & improper indulgence."

The SPG and the Search for "Proper Clergymen to Go Abroad" 1811

T*he SPG had been a presence within the Diocese since the arrival of the British troops before the Battle of the Plains of Abraham. Its Missionaries, serving with the army as chaplains or, later, fleeing from dispossession and persecution at the time of the American Revolution, served among the earliest clergy in the new colony.*

When the SPG was entrusted with the administration of the parliamentary grant for clergy in the Canadas in 1813, this merely consolidated a relationship of long standing with the Diocese of Quebec. To entice British clergy for colonial service (admittedly a difficult task), the Society began to publish assurances in its Annual Reports that the interests of missionaries overseas would be well protected, and that the emoluments held out to them were adequate and secure. The following appeared in the Society's Annual Report for 1811:

The Society having of late years found great difficulty in prevailing with proper Clergymen to go abroad in their service, and conceiving that one cause of this disinclination arises from an ignorance of the whole of the Emoluments and Advantages annexed to the situation of a Missionary in the Colonies to which they are sent, think it proper to publish the following more particular account than what appears in the general Annual Abstract of their Proceedings.

The Colonies to which the Society now sends out Missionaries are these following: Newfoundland, Nova Scotia, New Brunswick, Upper and Lower Canada, Cape Breton, and Africa.

It may be useful to notice, that before the Society send out a Clergyman to any new place, the people first petition the Society to do it, and signify that they are able and willing to contribute towards the Missionary's support. In general, it is required that a Church be built, a Glebe secured, a Parsonage House erected, and a subscription entered into by the people themselves, or such Engagements made as may induce the Society to establish a Mission before they are completed; but where the people have failed in the performance, the Missionary has been removed to another station.

Upon the opening of a new Mission, the Society grant a yearly Salary of £50. Afterwards, it is increased or diminished according as circumstances may seem to require, the Glebe lands being in some places of more value than in others. Half a year's Salary is advanced to each Missionary upon his going abroad, and an allowance made towards the charge of the voyage, generally about £30. ...

The Missionaries in Canada have each of them an annual Salary of £100 from Government, and no one has less than £50 from the Society.

In addition to the benefits of entering the Society's service outlined above, there was also a list of "qualifications or considerations in choosing applicants" for Missionaries, and for "presenting them to the notice of the Society." The candidates' fitness was to be determined on the basis of the following information, to be furnished by applicants for appointment:

1. The age of the person.
2. His condition in life, whether single or married.
3. His temper.
4. His prudence.
5. His learning.
6. His sober and pious conversation.
7. His zeal for the Christian religion, and diligence in his holy calling.
8. His affection to the present Government.
9. His conformity to the doctrine and discipline of the Church of England.

The wisdom of the SPG's policies made possible a great increase in the number of new parishes with resident clergy, a trend that, according to Carrington, was well under way in 1819. Before this date, however, it had become clear that there was great advantage to be gained from a native-born and locally-trained clergy to supplement those sent in from abroad. Here, too, the SPG provided help. At the Rev. John Strachan's suggestion, Bishop Mountain "took up the idea of training men for ordination in Canada, and in 1812 the SPG voted £200 to support four students, and continued the grant for many years, thus bringing a number of men into the ministry."

Although the Diocese ceased to receive a regular grant from the SPG in 1900, ties of affection and gratitude persisted for many years. The following is an excerpt from an editorial printed in the July issue of the Quebec Diocesan Gazette, *1932:*

A resolution having as its object the recognition of the great work done by the Society for the Propagation of the Gospel was introduced by the Dean of Quebec [the Very Rev. A. H. Crowfoot, seconded by Canon A. R. Kelley], and passed unanimously at the recent meeting of Synod. The motion was: "That in view of all that the Society for the Propagation of the Gospel has done for this Diocese in its early days, and for many years afterwards, the Lord Bishop be requested to set apart the Feast of St Peter or the Sunday nearest, to be observed in every year as a day on which the Clergy offer special thanksgiving and Prayer for the great work which the Society has done and is doing.

Sadly, this custom has fallen out of use.

6

To Declare for the Church: Stanstead 1816

Shortly after his arrival in the border area of the Eastern Townships, the Hon. and Rev. C. J. Stewart began paying visits to nearby communities and spreading the influence of Anglican worship. He met with great success in persuading the people to build churches, to which he contributed heavily, and to secure the regular services of a minister of their own. In 1815, Stewart temporarily left his mission in the hands of a curate, his protégé (the newly-ordained James Reid). He wrote to the young man continually for news of his congregations and those he hoped eventually to attract to the Church. One such "target congregation" was at Stanstead.

The following excerpt is taken from James Reid's annotated transcript of Stewart's letters to him, prepared in 1850, long after Stewart's death. After quoting directly from the seventh letter in the collection, dated 2 January 1816, Reid describes the events that led to its writing:

 The people of Stanstead, alluded to by Mr. Stewart, ... built a Meeting house the summer and Autumn after he had embarked for England. They were totally unacquainted with the doctrines and usages of our Church, but nevertheless being moved by the recommendation of Mr. Stewart, who had visited them a few weeks before he left, to build a Church and apply for a minister, they did so, without coming to any decision as to the Denomination to which they should connect themselves. They left that an open question to be afterwards determined. In the meantime they proceeded with the building; and, when finished, kept it open for the use of ministers from any or all denominations, as they would come around, until they should make their election. Some years after the House was built, the Bishop of Quebec, at their desire, sent them a gentleman, then recently from England, on trial, that, under his ministry, they might have an opportunity of becoming acquainted with the doctrines and usages of the Church, before they would make their choice of a denomination. The experiment proved a failure. The people did not like the minister, and, as a natural consequence, did not

choose our Church. The Union House has been of no real service to any form of religion, though it cost the people more than 6000 dollars, and has been abandoned for many years to the use of any strolling preachers that chose to hold forth in its Pulpit. The Methodists, Congregationalists and Baptists have since formed Societies in the Townships, and built several good meeting houses. Our Church has obtained no footing in that Township yet, which is to be attributed to the unfortunate choice that was made in the person of the first missionary, placed there on trial to teach the people the doctrines and worship of our Church. Such is the responsibility, resting on the first minister that enters into a locality where the Church is not known. He may open the door for the Church, or shut it against her for ages!

The plan to build a church for the use of several denominations was not at all unusual for the times. As Mrs Day, in her pioneering history of the Eastern Townships, was quick to point out:

The first houses of worship built in the country were small wooden edifices, erected by the united efforts of parties professing different faiths. They were called 'Union meeting houses,' and were occupied as occasion required by each alternately, or by such preacher or lecturer as visited the locality. In process of time, however, the lines of separation between the several sects became more clearly defined; preferences became prejudices; controversies were introduced begetting rivalries, jealousies, and the deplorable spirit of detraction which is so prolific of evil. One of the results of this we may see in the number and variety of sects among us; some of which, however, are but *distinctions* with very little *difference.*

Reid had a special interest in Stanstead and its people as he was to have been sent there on Stewart's return to his parish from England. Stewart, however, had begun to think of allowing Reid, who had a wife and an increasing family, to stay where he was and establish a new mission at Stanstead himself. After visiting the people in January 1818, however, Stewart decided to go instead to Hatley, where "the people were avowedly building for the Church of England, and most anxious to obtain his service and assistance."

The "unfortunate choice" of a clergyman for Stanstead to which Reid had referred was the Rev. Richard Knagg, an SPG Missionary, sent to the community in 1819 by Bishop Jacob Mountain. Stewart seems to have known, or known of, Knagg, for he had written to Reid on 29 October of that year that he did not think that Knagg would suit the people.

What Knagg may have done in Stanstead to turn the people away from the Church is a matter for conjecture, but his activities elsewhere, after the people of the Township had decided against becoming Anglicans, is on record.

By 1821, Knagg was serving on the Gaspé Peninsula. He does not seem to have made much of an effort to win the hearts of his people in this new sphere of activity, however. On 8 December 1823 one of his parishioners, John Gallie, went to Knagg's residence—of which Gallie was the owner. The house still contained, by agreement, some of Gallie's effects, including a supply of potatoes which, Knagg had apparently threatened, "would be let freeze as last winter." When Gallie, with four of his neighbours, arrived at the house to remove the potatoes, they made temporary use of a barrel that Gallie had agreed to lend to Knagg. At this point the clergyman flew into a rage and ordered them off the property. As Gallie's sworn statement asserts:

... the said Richard Knagg came and said that the Barrel was his and ordered it to be emptied immediately whereupon another dispute ensued when the said Richard Knagg ordered the said John Gallie out of the house and said if he did not go out he would blow his brains out and repeated the same expressions several times whereupon he Immediately went into one of the rooms of the House to get a musket and was heard snapping the gun, but his wife Mrs Knagg locked him in the Room to Prevent his coming out— so the said John Gallie continued at his work until he had done and went his way.

Gallie was sufficiently alarmed by this event to go to the local Justice of the Peace at Paspebiac, who advised him "to Inform the Lord Bishop of the whole Circumstance" and that he, no doubt, "would provide a suitable remedy." In his letter to the Bishop, dated 12 February 1824, Gallie wrote: "I do not want to go to Law because you have sent him .... [T]his papear that I have sworen to will show you what he is and I could tell you a good deal more before his face which I hope I will be able to do next summer or else that Mr Nag will be gone for we all wish to have a good and a decent minister that we could take his part and defend and do all we could for him."

There was an investigation, as was usual in the case of serious complaints against members of the clergy. In the opinion of G. J. Mountain, who visited Gaspé in 1824, Knagg's ministry had done the Church considerable harm. As he wrote privately, it had produced "effects which his successor must endeavour to remove. He was unguarded in his demeanour & coarse & rough in his manners, & he was greatly obnoxious to a Party subsisting within the limits of his charge."

Following Archdeacon Mountain's recommendation, Knagg was relieved of his mission and dismissed from the Diocese. The SPG struck his name from their rolls.

Christ Church, Stanstead, while it remembers Richard Knagg, counts its founding from 1858. "A Historical Sketch" of the parish, published one hundred years after that date, quotes the Stanstead Journal *for 9 July 1857 as follows:*

I am pleased to inform you, and the readers of your paper, that an Episcopal Clergyman has at last come to reside among us permanently. Through the zeal and influence of the Rev. Dr. Hellmuth, this very desirable result has been brought about, to whom no doubt the inhabitants of this place feel very much indebted.

The Rev. Mr. Thompson is from England, and a graduate of one of her colleges. He comes with the highest testimonials and the full concurrence and approbation of the Lord Bishop of the diocese, who has been pleased to licence Mr. Thompson to the curacy of the Township of Stanstead. Mr. Thompson is the only Missionary Clergyman of this diocese in connection with the "Colonial Church and School Society."

The people have voluntarily come forward and bound themselves to contribute for five years towards his support, and it is hoped that ere long he will secure a large congregation in Stanstead.

Until further notice there will be church service regularly every Sunday in the brick store belonging to Mr. Judd, Stanstead Plain, morning service at 11 o'clock, evening service at 5.

Thus did the people of Stanstead "declare for the Church." A year later, Christ Church was constructed.

The Church and the Benefits of Education: 1816, 1845, and 1864

Although Bishop Inglis had discussed the need for educational institutions in the Canadas with Lord Dorchester, and Bishop Jacob Mountain had urged the Government to establish grammar schools at strategic points in the Diocese of Quebec, it was often the initiatives of local clergymen that brought functioning schools into being.

The Rev. John Doty, who had arrived from Schenectady in 1777, established a school at Trois-Rivières in 1803. It was not unusual for clergymen to tutor two or three pupils in their homes, but in 1816, Doty's establishment accommodated 37 young people of both sexes, of whom 17 were boarders. Although most of the children were Anglicans, the school represented a wide cross-section of religious backgrounds; in addition to 26 Anglicans, there were five Roman Catholics, five Jews and one Presbyterian. Some of these children, such as the two Slicer boys and the three Gugy girls, had one Protestant and one Roman Catholic parent. The 27 Protestant children, Doty reported, were required to repeat the Church Catechism every Saturday and Sunday but the others were not.

When G. J. Mountain returned to Quebec in 1816 after serving in the parish of Fredericton for two years, he would put to good use the experience he had gained in the neighbouring Diocese of Nova Scotia, which was far in advance of Quebec in the field of education. As a result of his efforts, the system of National Schools for boys and girls and Diocesan Committees of the London-based Society for the Promotion of Christian Knowledge were soon to extend the benefits of widespread education in the Diocese. The Society's Annual Report for 1830 gives some idea of the scope and history of these schools:

The Twelfth Annual Report of the Quebec Diocesan Committee contains the following interesting particulars: ...

... [I]n proceeding to the first branch of their operations, the distribution of Books and Tracts, [they] have to state, that the following Clergymen and Schoolmasters have been supplied with books by the Lord Bishop, since the last report, *viz* ... the Rev. L. Doolittle, *Bay of Chaleurs* ... W. Arnold, *Gaspé Bay*, R. R. Burrage, *Quebec* ... [and] Mr. J. S.

Tuzo, *l'Anse au Beaufils* (Gaspé)....A variety of Books and Tracts have also been gratuitously distributed in small quantities at a time, among the inhabitants of newly formed settlements in the District of *Quebec,* ... in *Frampton, Aubert Gallion, St. Charles, La Belle Alliance, Broughton, Leeds, Inverness, Ireland,* and *St. Giles....*

The Committee now turn to the second object to which their attention is directed,—the education of the children of the labouring classes on the Madras system. They are much gratified in bearing testimony to the regular attendance of the children, which is in general remarkably good; and also to their behaviour, which is characterised by morality and propriety. Since its first establishment in November, 1819, four thousand children have been admitted into the School ... The number of children at present on the list is 142 boys and 90 girls. The annual public examination of the children took place on the 23d December last, in the presence of many respectable persons, who take an interest in the Institution. His Excellency Sir James Kempt, was pleased to honour the Schools by his attendance. The performances were on the whole decidedly satisfactory; and the boys in particular acquitted themselves better than upon any former occasion.—The Legislature has liberally granted £100 to be employed towards the maintenance of the establishment.

As the Government began to interest itself in widespread education, legislation was passed to provide for the election of School Commissioners to oversee local schools. Many members of the clergy served as Commissioners and acted as spokesmen for their communities, dealing with the Government on educational matters. Grants to build schools had to be applied for; payments were slow to arrive. In 1845, the Rev. C. P. Reid, Chairman of the School Commissioners in Compton, wrote to Quebec to inquire when the local allocation of funds could be expected so that the school could pay its teachers:

... if it is in your power will you have the kindness to give me the information? It is now the last day of March 1845, and yet in many instances the teachers of last year are not paid. It appears to us an exceeding hard case that they should be thus compelled to wait for their well earned pittance after it is due. Can there be no remedy? Is it not possible to pay the teachers semi annually? According to the present system a teacher who was engaged to instruct a school during the winter of 1844, for example, is compelled to wait for his pay in full, until after the month of March 1845, or else, if he is unable to wait, he is obliged to take grain &c, at a loss, and so risque his right to the Gv^t allocation in favor of some third party that will advance the money.

In addition to serving as a Commissioner, Reid sat on the Board of Examiners of School Teachers. Although he called these functions "thankless duties," he performed them conscientiously.

Educational facilities expanded, but still there were young people who reached adulthood without adequate schooling. Here, too, the Church attempted to provide encouragement and help. In 1864, Bishop J. W. Williams delivered a lecture entitled Self-Education *to* The Church of England Young Men's Mutual Improvement Association:

... this is a fact which may not be relished, but which cannot be ignored [he warned his audience] that we live in an age of examination—that a literary examination is becoming the door to all appointments. We in this country are not as yet under the influence of the system so much as they are at home; but we feel the movement; and we shall I doubt not, ultimately be carried along with it. Some day we shall find ourselves, in respect of this latest development of our civilization, almost upon a level with the Chinese, with whom this system has been for many years thoroughly carried out ...

Now the kind of education which will enable a man to win in this race, is emphatically the regular education. Scholastic training will always outshine even genius in an examination. Well, but I address those whose chance of scholastic training is gone. What they are likely to get of it, they have had. But they must not sit down therefore in despair. Culture they must have. And I purpose to show this evening, that the very best culture they may have; for after all there is no education, which for its best and highest results, is equal to self education. I say its best and highest results. I here waive of course the question of examinations for appointments, and speak of that mental culture which does not merely supply literary adroitness, and argumentative skill, but which enables a man to reason rather than argue—enables and prompts him to feel nobly, to think bravely, and to act manfully. These I call the best and highest results of education. And this is a part of his education, which, whatever may be his advantages, each man gets for himself....

And here, as I am addressing my juniors, I shall not be thought egotistical, if I speak briefly of my own experience.... I was brought up at a good school, and I took my degree in the University of Oxford; but I honestly think that, in all that is valuable in my small stock of acquirement or faculty, I am a self educated man. And of my studies—my secular studies—I verily believe, that the most influential—the most beneficial to my intellect—were those carried on by myself out of two small volumes, for one of which I gave sixpence, and for the other of which I believe I was so extravagant as to expend ninepence. One was an odd volume of the writings of Dean Swift. The other contained the essays of Lord Bacon. It is many years since I had either of these volumes in my hand, but, at one time, they were hardly ever out of my hands. I carried them in my pocket, and at all times, under hedges, and in lone lanes, I read, and re-read them; till my mind was saturated with their contents. And hardly a day passes in which I do not feel their power.

Thus much of the feasibility of self education, and of its quality. It is not however to be denied that the solitary student labors under some disadvantages, disadvantages which it is the object of such associations as ours in some degree to remove.... A very high place amongst educational influences must ever be occupied by attrition of thought and collision of mind. There are excitements of intellectual activity, and corrective of its vagaries, which we must procure for ourselves as best we may. And even without them we need not despair, where there is a will there will always be found a way. They are stimulants and correctives, but the solid work must still be done within us. If our thought is to be of any value, we must acquire and beget a self-sustained and independent capacity for elaborating thought within the recesses of our own minds....

...You may educate yourself, but you must be in earnest. Nothing comes of trifling. Earnestness is one of the foremost of qualities. It is noble and beautiful in itself and it gives power to the other virtues. Without it there can be no greatness in character, no permanent success in life; a fickle, frivolous, sauntering disposition being contemptible in itself, and generally bringing a man to sorrow.... Take, then, the wise king's advice, and whatsoever thy hand findeth to do, do it with thy might. Keep in mind that old saw "without labour nothing prospers." And (you are a Christian) recollect this too, without Christ nothing prospers. "Whatsoever you do in word or deed, do all in the name of the Lord Jesus."

8

The "Duties of Visitation and Confirmation": the Eastern Townships 1821

In December 1816, Jacob Mountain attempted to resign his bishopric. He was then 66 years old and had served the Diocese for 23 years. During the previous summer and autumn, he had "traversed the two Provinces of Upper & Lower Canada, in the Visitation of my Diocese," and, as he wrote to the Earl of Bathurst, "I returned to Quebec with the entire conviction of my inability to perform that duty any more." He was convinced that, "in the present state of the Protest[ant] Church in the Canadas, the most useful of the Episcopal functions are comprised in the duties of Visitation, & Confirmation" and therefore pressed the Earl to appoint a younger man in his place.

Mountain's request was denied. The following excerpt, a description of his Visitation of 1821, is drawn from a personal letter addressed to his son Jacob, a clergyman serving at Hemel Hampstead in England. It is dated at Belmont, a country house near Quebec, 25 March 1821.

 I can't write much. My business, of late particularly, has accumulated so much, from my Diocese, from Political turnings, which can not be escaped, from my being Principal of two Corporations, of which the affairs are rapidly growing, & from various applications, Letters, &c, &c, that I have far more work than ever I had in my life. And if you could see the masses of Papers now lying round my Desk, which all put in some claim to immediate attention, you would say that I am a good old Gentleman for writing at all.

Between the 7th of February, & the 3d of this month, I completed my Visitation, by going thro' the New Townships near the line 45, & by confirming at every place (ten in number) at which a Clergyman is established. And I preached at each of these places an extempore sermon. There was considerable exertion required to accomplish this. It was necessary previously to fix the time for each Confirmation, and I was impeded, first by a heavy rain, at Sorel, which spoiled the roads as far as St Johns (50 miles), & then by successive falls of snow, which nearly obliterated them, thro' the whole of the Townships. I did, however, accomplish my object, & confirmed at every place upon the day appointed. I went with hired horses, & drivers, & took with me only Paine. When I first determined upon this plan, there was an expectation that George's Mary w^d be confined almost immediately after the time of my departure; & altho' she was safe in bed before I started, I adhered to it; feeling that he could not (after the loss of their two last infants) leave home without a heavy weight of anxiety; & feeling moreover, that in travelling thro' this new country one Gentleman might find accommodation, that could not possibly be extended to two.—I had a cold during the whole journey: but, except for a few hours, I was never ill. The new Churches rising every where, & the neat & handsome manner in which several of them were finished gratified me greatly: & the Country itself, even in winter, is most beautiful. There were scenes, along the sides, & over the tops of the mountains, & along the deep & narrow vallies, which would well have repaid a traveller, who had no other object but to see them. The descending from the mountains to my favourite of all Lakes, Memphramagog, & some scenery afterwards, along the banks of the St Francis (an Ancestor of Fanny's, I suppose,—I well know how his scenery w^d delight her), had an effect I think, as fine, as I ever saw any where in summer.—Amid these beauties, the road was so bad, that I was once overturned three times, in less than an hour: but was very little hurt.—The whole journey was about 600 miles.—

Some of the personal references in the Bishop's letter concern his daughters-in-law Frances and Mary. "Fanny," the lover of scenery whose relationship with St Francis the Bishop playfully suggests, was most likely his son Jacob's wife. Elsewhere in his letter he speaks of her by name: "I have an unspeakable longing at my heart, to see you at H[emel] H[ampstead], with my own Frances, & the lovely, & sweet offspring, with which it has pleased God to bless you.—In his good time, I hope I shall." The Bishop's concern for "George's Mary," his son George Jehoshaphat's wife, was not unfounded. Although Mary Mountain had—in 1815 and 1816—borne her husband two children who had lived, the next child to survive was born in 1823. She must have lost the baby expected during the Bishop's Visitation tour.

If one relies on the Reports of the SPG for accounts of the Church in the Diocese during this period, there is little to be gleaned about Jacob Mountain's confirmation tours, or the impact of his presence— tall and commanding—on local congregations. The Society could only publish the information that was sent to them, and the Bishop seems to have felt that his letters should bring in money and Missionaries rather than tell interesting stories. The Society reported (in 1820) that "The Lord Bishop of Quebec ... was induced to draw the attention of the Society to the peculiar circumstances of Quebec [City], where the labours of the Minister have of late years increased to such an extent as to exceed the powers of any one individual adequately to discharge," to the effect that they "have agreed to appoint an assistant Missionary at Quebec, with a salary of £200." The Report of 1821 concerns the missionary labours of the Hon. and Rev. Dr C. J. Stewart.

Stewart's approach to communications was completely different from Mountain's. His interesting and detailed accounts of his circuits as Travelling Missionary encouraged donors, particularly in England, to see the needs of the Diocese in concrete, human terms. The Society's report for 1821 shows Stewart at Ascot, Sherbrooke, Shipton, and Drummondville. The Bishop's Visitation is not featured.

9

"The Late Awful Visitation of the Cholera Morbus" 1832

T he great epidemics in the Canadas coincided with massive immigration, and the first to strike occurred in 1832. When navigation opened on the St Lawrence that year, the precautions taken to detect and quarantine victims of disease as they entered the country were far from adequate. By the end of the first week of June of that year, about 25,000 immigrants had arrived in 400 ships from the United Kingdom; from the first days of their arrival, the death toll mounted. By 15 June, there were recorded in Quebec City alone over one hundred deaths per day.

The clergy, especially those in the region of Quebec City, were constantly called upon to visit the sick, relieve the destitute, minister to the dying, and bury the dead in great numbers. A sermon of Archdeacon G. J. Mountain's, preached in the Cathedral on 30 December of that year—by which time the season of trial had come to an end—recalled these all-too-recent events in such terms that the horror and weariness of those who worked among the victims is vividly evoked.

 ... the retrospect of time escaped from us presents always the images of change and uncertainty attaching to all below; ... but when did we ever know such a year as this?—when did this city, since its foundation, witness such scenes?—pestilence and horror stalking abroad in her streets—dismay in every countenance—death knocking at every door—none knowing who might next be the victim,—"one taken and another left"...

Mountain then went on to mention the Service of Humiliation and Supplication held at the Cathedral, and the flight from the city of those who could afford to take up quarters elsewhere. He quotes the scriptural account of plague from Exodus 12: 30, in which "there was not a house where there was not one dead," before recalling to the congregation the recent scene as he remembered it:

—the general alarm and consternation which prevailed—the gloom of sudden bereavement thrown over the smiling enjoyments of many domestic circles; the stillness which reigned in scenes of traffic and places of concourse; the suspension of business,—The interruption of labour,—the closing of houses whose inhabitants fled to the country; of shops from the death of the dealer, or the cessation of all demand for his articles of trade:—the undiscriminating strokes of death, which although they fell more thickly in some classes of society, found victims in all,... no prudence could oppose a shield to them, no comforts at command, no habits of life, no temperament of body.—... [D]id we not see new places of interment opened to receive the aggregations of the dead; needy labourers who had been bribed high to dig their graves, sometimes abandoning the task in terror; and the weary Clergy attending at one stated hour, to afford the Christian decencies of burial collectively, unwitnessed for the most part by surviving friends, over all the sad deposits of the day—amounting upon two consecutive occasions, when it fell to my own turn to officiate, to seventy and upwards in a day, of the Church of England alone?

Yes, we saw, within our city, all this and more: we saw in our deserted streets, more signs of death than life—hearses carrying their load, or hurrying back to answer fresh demands—cart after cart piled up with bodies from the hospitals, met by some vehicle conveying ghastly figures to take their places destined soon to return, as corpses, in the same way—the constituted authorities who watched for the public safety, increasingly upon the alert, in token of danger ... Physicians and Ministers of Religion traversing the streets night and day with a hurried pace, and unequal to meet their multiplied calls—the few stragglers besides, who appeared abroad, pressing to their nostrils, as they walked, some corrective of the air which they feared to breathe:—fires before every house, loading the atmosphere with vapour from prepared materials supposed of purifying power—or the official guardians of health with their badges, profusely scattering lime along the range of the more suspected habitations—these were the spectacles exhibited in our city— and images of deeper horror might be added were I to carry you into the precincts of the hospital in the first burst of the calamity ...

Mountain recalled that the Seminary had been closed to enable the Roman Catholic priests to attend their sick and that, one by one, every school had followed suit. The Board of Health had provided covered vehicles to carry the piles of coffins to be buried, but, as there were too few to accommodate the dead, open carts continued to be pressed into service. Rumours were rife of victims sometimes buried alive because of the order that interment take place within a specified number of hours of death.

According to the census of 1831, Quebec City had a population of 28,000 inhabitants. In 1832, there were 2,800 deaths from cholera recorded there. The number of burials recorded by the Church of England for the whole of 1831 "was not far short of that number in the month of June alone."

After Mountain's almost surrealistic description of the disease-ridden city, he concludes with a recollection of its dream-like contrast with the beauty of the season during that particular summer:

It was a remark that I often made during the continuance of the cholera, how little the face of Nature betrayed the sadness of the time, or showed any symptoms of that principle of death which was in such fearful activity ... I was particularly impressed with this kind of feeling upon some of the lovely summer evenings, on which I officiated at the burial-ground, then still unenclosed. The open green, skirted by the remains of a tall avenue of trees, and contiguous to the serpentine windings of the River St. Charles, beyond which you looked across meadows, woods, and fields dotted with rural habitations, to the mountains which bound the prospect, the whole gleaming in the exquisite and varied lights of a Canadian sunset, formed altogether a beautiful and peaceful landscape and seemed a "fit haunt of gods." How melancholy and striking the contrast with all that had been deposited, and which it remained to deposit, in the spot upon which I stood.

Fifteen years later, in 1847, Mountain and his fellow clergy would once again be plunged into tireless activity among the destitute and dying, as immigrant ships, again riddled with disease, deposited their human cargo on the wharves of the city, or left them for mass burial on the shores of Grosse Ile.

10

A Ministry in French:
1835, 1850, 1896, 1986, and 1991

Although *the appointment (in 1768) of
exclusively French-speaking Protestant clergy to serve in the recently-acquired Canadian colony had been ill-advised, a knowledge of the French language—to be able to
"marry and bury in French," as Frances Brooke had noted three years earlier—would
continue to be a valuable asset for ministers intended for the region.*

*Bishop Jacob Mountain, of Huguenot origin and master of several modern lan-
guages, was fully capable of conversing or ministering in French. His son George in
his turn actively sought bilingual clergy for those districts in which French-speaking Protestants had settled. In 1835, Bishop C. J. Stewart's printed* Regulations Respecting Chapels ... in the Parish of Quebec, *stipulated that, on one Sunday in each
month, St Peter's Chapel in the suburb of St Roch should make provision for "all persons whose native tongue is French, desirous of availing themselves of the Service performed in that language." Some 150 years later, Bishop Allen Goodings revived the
practice of offering regular French-language services at St Peter's (then relocated in
Limoilou) under the ministry of the Rev. Terry Blizzard.*

*In 1844, G. J. Mountain (by this time Bishop of Montreal) reported to the SPG
on the situation of the Gaspé mission as he had found it at Cape Cove and Gaspé
Bay that year:*

 The great body of the people just about here [he wrote] are
from the islands of Jersey or Guernsey, with which the fish-
ing establishments of the whole district are much connected.
Most of them understand English very imperfectly—some not at all ... [O]ur
Missionaries within the Bay having been, with one exception in the case of
the Rev. C. Morris, who was there but for a short time, unable to officiate
to them, or to converse with them in a language which they could understand, they have been led to attend upon the preaching of laymen, called local
preachers, among the Methodists, and they have two little unappropriated
wooden chapels[*] in which their meetings are held. At the same time, they

---

[*] They were not consecrated to the use of any one denomination.

profess to be of the communion of the Church ... and most thankfully avail themselves of my own ministrations in my triennial visits,—the more so, however, because I officiate to them principally in French.

Mountain had long since appealed to the Society (in his report of 1826, for example) to send a missionary to the region "who should be qualified to do the same."

The Rev. Henry Christmas, who had newly arrived from Britain in the 1840s, observed of Canada East that "in all this part of Canada one had need to rub up one's French, if one knows any.... Any clergyman ... proposing to apply to the bishop of Montreal for employment, would find a knowledge of French a great acquisition."

Mountain himself recruited a number of French-speaking clergy, particularly for the Gaspé region. Among them were Francis De La Mare, a Jerseyman, and Joseph De Mouilpied of Guernsey. While the former young man was preparing himself for the ministry at Bishop's College, Mountain arranged for him to teach French at Lennoxville at the same time. In 1850, not long after De La Mare (newly ordained Deacon) had been sent to the Gaspé, Mountain received a letter of thanks from the region:

Nous les soussignés habitants de la Côve Au Sauvage [the letter began], nous adressons humblement à Votre Grandeur afin de lui presenter nos remerciements à l'occasion de l'appointement de Monsieur De La Mare à la charge honorable et importante de Ministre de l'Evangile dans le District du Bassin et du Petit Gaspé....

Il était à la verité difficile, pour ne pas dire impossible, de trouver immédiatement un Ministre mieux qualifié pour les besoins de notre Communauté, ne fut-ce que sous le rapport des deux Langues en usage parmi nous.

The chief purpose of the letter, however, was to petition Mountain that De La Mare (himself a former Wesleyan Methodist) might be permitted to conduct services in French for that denomination as well as for his own flock.

Another communication the following year, this time from "Cove St George," made a similar request:

On nous dit que nous sommes Wesleyens. Nous avons tous été baptisés dans l'Église d'Angleterre et avons reçu le sacrement avec le ministre de cette Église. Monsieur Wesley était un ministre de l'Église d'Angleterre.... Si c'est votre plaisir nous desirions que vos ministres nous visiteraient comme par le passé nous administrer les sacrements, et nous prêcher dans toutes les occasions dans nos chapelles ...

Although it was Mountain's habit to jot down a brief summary of his reply on the letter received, neither of these bears any indication of his response. It seems certain, however, that De La Mare and others were given strict instructions to adhere to the services in the Prayer Book and to offer no others.

As for evangelizing the French-speaking Roman Catholics (whether of European or Native origin), Mountain was most hesitant to do so. The Bishop's description of his conversations with the two guides who accompanied him by canoe up the Restigouche and Matapedia Rivers in 1824 gives evidence of this attitude:

They asked many questions about the Indian tribes in the higher parts of the country, some of whom they had heard were "de bons gens *comme nous*," and others reprobates "qui ne croient pas au bon Dieu." I asked them whether they would not desire the advantages of education ... and they heartily acquiesced; but though I encouraged them, as far as occasion could be taken, in every moral and religious feeling of a correct nature, I did not think it my business to endeavour to wean them from any of the errors of the church of Rome.... I made it my object to give the conversation such a turn as might tend in some degree to conciliate their good will to Protestantism, and thus at least I might be instrumental in improving their charity. I know there are some zealous Protestants who would think me wrong. And I should think them so.

Given his attitude of "live and let live," Mountain was consequently opposed to the French Canadian Missionary Society (FCMS), founded in Montreal in 1839; in his Charge of that year he "expressed a hearty desire to avoid altogether the subject of French-Canadian evangelization."

This was a great cause for disappointment in some quarters. In 1859, for example, the Second Annual Report of the Diocesan branch of the Colonial Church and School Society (CCS) lamented that, until very lately "nothing has been done by the Church of England, though Canada has now been for a century a British Colony, to preach in its purity the Gospel of Christ to our fellow subjects, the French Canadian Roman Catholics, who number about 700,000 souls."

The CCS mission to French Canadians and Germans in Quebec City was conducted by the Rev. Jacob Mombert, who was able to officiate to local congregations in both those languages. The tradition of French-language services continued into the 1890s at Trinity Church. At that time, the French-speaking parishioners were under the care of the Rev. L. V. Larivière and the English-speaking members were served by the Rev. S. H. Phillips.

In 1860, through the efforts of the Rev. Dr Isaac Hellmuth, the Lower Town Infant School was opened in Quebec. The teacher, Miss Mattinson, reported that the majority of the 32 children then present were French Canadians.

In addition to the French-speaking Gaspesian Protestants, there were scattered settlers of English origin in the Diocese who had become French-speaking by absorption into the surrounding population, but had retained their religious affiliation with the Church of England. In 1851, the Rev. William Wickes, Travelling Missionary for the Church Society, came face to face with this situation in the vicinity of Chicoutimi:

Oct. 25. Sunday. Gave a full morning service to a congregation of nearly fifty. A desk spread with ample folds of black cloth had been provided, and a small table, covered with a white napkin, placed by its side, on which stood the white bowl that was to serve as a font. I baptized four children after the 2nd Lesson. It was a touching scene.... Two of the children were older than usual, and their sweet and solemn faces, their snow-white dresses, and the Saxon cast of their features, might have reminded one of Gregory the Great's exclamation, *Non Angli, sed angeli.*

After the service, I married two couples. A difficulty occurred in one of the cases, for neither of the parties understood English. However, after some delay, a French translation of our own Prayer Book was found, and with that I solemnized the service.

I may here remark that should (as I hope may soon be the case,) a Clergyman be sent to reside among these people, it will be necessary that he be a French scholar. Many of the Protestants, reared from their infancy among the French Canadians, speak not a word of English.

On 7 October 1901 (as the following report in the Diocesan Gazette *records) Bishop A. H. Dunn consecrated All Saints' Church, Ste-Ursule Falls, in the county of Maskinongé, built and endowed specifically to provide such a population with a ministry in French. The Anglican community had been long established there; an earlier church, which All Saints' replaced, had dated back to 1795.*

The Church, certainly, far exceeded the expectations of the Bishop. It is a most comely structure, surmounted by a Bell Turret, containing a good Bell, and under it are the quarters of the Missionary, most suitable and comfortable in every way.... After the Service, the Bishop was driven back to Louiseville by another of the farmers, who all generally speak French with each other, although they understand English, and are to some extent of English origin. They are, in fact, *our* people, and were never Roman Catholics. But living as they do in entirely French country, they might easily have become Roman Catholics but for the eager interest of the late Mr T. H. Dunn* and his family.

The little community was first served by the Rev. J.-B. Gauthier and later by the Rev. J.-J. Roy. For a period of about 40 years, a small one-room French Protestant school occupied the ground floor of the building with places for about 30 pupils. By 1963, the Anglican population had sharply diminished, and the church was deconsecrated by Bishop R. F. Brown: "Ce dernier "meeting" [the French Press recorded] a pris l'allure d'un pèlerinage, car on remarquait dans l'assistance nombre d'anciens paroissiens de Ste-Ursule venus une dernière fois prier dans ce milieu si cher à leur mémoire. C'est en pleurant que plusieurs quittèrent l'enceinte qui sera démolie d'ici le mois de décembre."

In the 1960s, in an effort to make contact with the French community, the Diocese published a series of three pamphlets in their language. "If you have French-speaking friends and neighbours who have shown an interest in our Church," ran an item in the Diocesan Gazette *in September 1963, "the pamphlets describe our position and will answer their questions in terms they will understand. Ask your Rector about these."*

At the 1979 Synod it was moved that "whereas there is a need for clergy to be leaders within a predominantly French-speaking milieu it is therefore important that the clergy be bilingual." A programme to assist the clergy in second-language training had been in place for some time, but had not produced the desired effect on a wide scale; the Resolution sought to draw attention to the need and to provide a more efficient means to serve it.

In the 1980s there was an effort to establish a modest French-language ministry in the Diocese. Following a 1986 Resolution adopted by the Executive Council of Synod, Bishop Allen Goodings announced that the Rev. Keith Dickerson, incumbent at St. George's, Lennoxville, would be devoting half his time to "a ministry in French in the Eastern Townships area." A year earlier, Church Society had been addressed by a Québécois Anglican of 25 years standing, who urged all Quebec City Anglican churches "to initiate a French liturgy at least once a week (as does the Cathedral) and ... to extend a personal invitation to their co-citizens to attend."

Since the consecration and installation of Bishop Bruce Stavert at a fully bilingual ceremony in 1991, all major services at the Cathedral and all charges to Synod

---

* T.H. Dunn, who was born at Ste-Ursule, was no relation of the Bishop's.

have had a significant French component. By 1993 the Cathedral's French-language congregation, ministered to each Sunday by the Rev. Pierre Voyer, numbered over 30 persons and represented a wide range of traditions, African and European, as well as local Québécois.

In 1992 the Primate, Archbishop Michael Peers, called for a consultation on francophone ministries, attended by representatives of the Dioceses of Montreal, Moosonee, Ottawa and Quebec. Their report recommended that "the Anglican Church … launch an evangilization campaign aimed at francophone Canadians." The Diocese of Quebec now has at least three priests whose mother tongue is French. But for the apparent unwillingness of most Anglicans to evangelize anyone at all (an attitude confirmed by the 1993 Angus Reid "Religion Poll" published in Maclean's*), the Diocese of Quebec has already risen to the challenge.*

Despite a record of substantial effort on the part of the Church in this diocese to minister to French-speaking Canadians in their own tongue, the Anglican Church of Canada, in its statement to the Royal Commission on Bilingualism and Biculturalism in 1965, saw fit to tender what sounds like an apology to the nation at large:

In many parts of Canada [the submission read] Anglicans have concentrated their ministry upon English-speaking citizens, and with the exception of work amongst the Eskimo and Indian population, have had little relationship with those whose mother tongue was not their own. For this failure to communicate the Anglican Church expresses its penitence and is coming to realize that our Church has been impoverished by this kind of isolation.

Whatever the situation may have been in other regions of Canada, it seems that, for once, the Diocese of Quebec had small grounds for such reproaches. Judging from its long-standing tradition of linguistic outreach (including a ministry in Swedish to an immigrant population settled in the vicinity of Waterville), it would seem that this diocese has not failed over the years to respond to the needs of a variety of cultural and linguistic groups within its extensive jurisdiction.

Famine and Quarantine
1847

For six months of the year, ice in the St *Lawrence River cut the Canadas off from European shipping. However, news of events abroad did reach the landlocked colonies, often months after their happening, in the form of newspapers carried overland from such year-round ports as Boston and New York. It was from this source that the people of Quebec learned in the early months of 1847 of the widespread destitution that had fallen upon Ireland and the Highlands of Scotland. Appeals such as that by Dr Charles F. Staunton of the Dublin-based Irish Relief Association for the Destitute Peasantry appeared in various North American papers, including the Quebec Anglican weekly* The Berean. *His letter to the editor of 17 December 1846 was printed in the issue for 4 February 1847.*

 We are now engaged in trying to feed our poor starving countrymen, and I believe, with all that private benevolence ... can do, that tens of thousands will die of starvation.... We are looking for sympathy and assistance in all quarters. The Scotch Greys have given a day's pay. The Press in Canada might take it up—and if local subscriptions were raised, advertisements might be put in your Canada Papers. We feel we cannot spend money in advertisement abroad, trying to spend every penny on the starving multitude. The prospect is fearful.

The response was immediate. At a sermon preached at Trinity Church, Quebec, in aid of the sufferers, the offering raised £24 / 1 / 0 for famine relief. Shortly afterwards, the Mayor—at the request of the clergy and citizenry of Quebec—called a public meeting at City Hall to be held on 12 February "for the purpose of taking into consideration the best means of contributing to the relief of the destitution and distress at present existing in Ireland and the Highlands and the Islands of Scotland." Members of the clergy and laity of all communions seem to have attended. A committee was set up and collectors for the different wards appointed, again representing all denominations. By 25 February, as The Berean *reported, they had raised a total of £2904 / 0 / 2. When one considers that in January of that year the Quebec Market was offering a pound of beef at sixpence or less and a bushel of oats from two shillings to two shillings sixpence, it becomes clear that the sum collected represented considerable*

purchasing power locally.

In an attempt to draw on the benevolence of his diocese as a whole, Bishop G. J. Mountain sent a letter dated 29 March to all his clergy asking that they canvass their parishioners for famine relief. A report printed 17 May in The Quebec Gazette shows the result of this wider appeal. Among others, the Rev. Christopher Jackson of Hatley remitted £15, the Rev. Robert Knight of Frampton, £5 / 10 / 0, and the Rev. William Arnold of Gaspé Bay, £23. Arnold, who was born near Dublin, collected a remarkably large sum considering that his parishioners were far from well-off themselves.

The Diocesan Archives contain letters of thanks from the chaplain of the Archbishop of Dublin for drafts totalling £125 / 9 / 0 "towards the relief of the distress with which Ireland has been visited," and from Edinburgh for £32 / 8 / 0 for the destitute Highlanders. All three are dated in the summer of 1847, by which time the Canadas themselves had been plunged into a crisis precipitated by the arrival of thousands of sick and starving and immigrants.

Since 1832, the year of the cholera epidemic, immigrant ships had been required to stop for inspection at the Quarantine Station established by Government at Grosse Ile, below Quebec on the St Lawrence River. This afforded some protection for the settled population of the colony against incoming disease. From the beginning, the spiritual needs of all Protestant immigrants passing through Grosse Ile had been provided for by an Anglican missionary stationed on the island during the navigation season.

In 1847, the river ice was late in breaking up; not until 7 May did the first trading vessel reach Quebec. In the second week of May, the first immigrant ship, the Syria of Liverpool, arrived at Grosse Ile. Of her 243 passengers, nine had already died and been buried at sea, and a four-year-old child died at the island. Hers was the only death that week, but with many sick on board and the arrival of more ships, there were 16 deaths the following week and 71 the week after that. From then on, the rolls of mortality, regularly printed in the newspapers, grew exponentially.

Wretched conditions on the ships and the malnourished state of many of the passengers made the immigrants easy prey to infection of any sort. Children and infants were especially vulnerable. The Rev. Armine W. Mountain, doing temporary duty at Grosse Ile during this first period, performed 13 burials among the Protestants alone from May 20 to May 24. The short and simple entries in the Register bear silent witness to the end of many a journey to the New World:

Margaret, aged seven months, daughter of Michael Farnen, dairyman, late of County Dublin, "died on board the ship *Wandsworth,* lying at the Quarantine Station" on 20 May.

Ellen, aged one year three days, daughter of Thomas MacPherson, ploughman, of County Armagh, died 21 May.

Sarah Eliza, aged two and a half years, daughter of Matthew Ellison Graham, labourer, of County Down, died 21 May.

Alexander Purcell, aged two, son of Alex^r Purcell, passenger of the Bark *Perseverance* of Dublin, died 21 May; "It was impossible to obtain further particulars [Mountain noted in the entry] the body having been left at the ground, and the father having proceeded to Quebec without seeing the officiating minister."

Eliza Farren, aged 19, of County Donegal "died aboard the Bark *Royalist* of Galloway lying at the Quarantine Station" on 22 May. Her brother signs as witness to the burial with his mark.

George Neil, aged one year, son of Andrew Neil, farmer of County Tyrone, died on board the *Lord Seaton* lying at the Quarantine Station on 22 May.

Thomas Hollinger, aged 30, late of County Antrim, passenger on board the *Lord Seaton*, died on board on 22 May.

Catherine, aged two years, daughter of James Mack of Linlithgow Scotland, died on 22 May.

John Armstrong, aged one year, his father a labourer from County Cavan, died on 23 May.

Prior to 1847, a Travelling Missionary appointed for the whole season served Grosse Ile, using it as "his head-quarters" for the district. It quickly became apparent that no one man could be expected to do so now. That year the task had fallen to The Rev. Charles Forest, who appears to have taken up his duties on or immediately before 25 May. On 9 June, as the pressure of arrivals mounted, he wrote urgently to Bishop Mountain for help:

My Lord,

My Memorandum of yesterday shows an increase in the number of immigrants under hospital treatment which more than justifies me in making formal application to your Lordship for assistance in my arduous duties. When the Revd A. W. Mountain left the station the whole number of sick did not (if I rightly remember) exceed fifteen—and the calls from the ships had hardly commenced. Now there are on the Island:

June 8th (Immigrants) belonging to

the Church of England	111
Presbyterians	33
Prim. Methodists	1
Methodists N. C.	1
Independents	2
Unascertained	22
	170 exclusive of children under 14

And to meet the wants of these it is altogether impossible that any one man can suffice. I do not speak, my Lord, in regards to any personal fatigues—altho I might do so without inconsistency (as 40 tents were, on the evening of the 7th, added to the number in the list of my daily visits) but with reference to the insufficiency of *any* exertions, on my part, to satisfy the honest demand for Clerical attendance and advice. Five out of every eight that die pass into the other world without the possibility, on the part of their clergymen, of ministering to their comfort or relief.

As the Registers show, many immigrants died in harbour before they could disembark. Incredible as it may seem, on 28 May there were 36 vessels at Grosse Ile waiting to be cleared —among them the Perseverance, *the* Royalist, *and the* Lord Seaton, *aboard which A. W. Mountain had recorded deaths a week before. On 28 May the Anglican Register records three more deaths aboard the* Lord Seaton *alone, all of them children aged from three to six. She was still waiting a week later by which time Forest was in the midst of his duties; he recorded the burial of James McIlvain, aged 18 months, from County Antrim, who died aboard this ship on 6 June.*

Once alerted to the situation on Grosse Ile, Bishop Mountain acted swiftly, setting about to supply a succession of clergy to serve a brief term each, thus distributing the duty and decreasing the danger to any one person through prolonged exposure and exhaustion. As his biographer describes it: "The Bishop suggested it to such of the clergy of the diocese as seemed to be most able for the work, to offer themselves for the service, each taking a week." He himself took the first turn at the station, joining Forest within days of the latter's appeal for help. On 12 June the Bishop penned a hasty letter from the island to his son Armine:

There are about 1800 sick on the island, (besides a great & increasing number in the ships) of which about one tenth are Prot!—Many in the ships, & sometimes whole families, sick, who arrived here from home in good health. I spent the greater part of yesterday in going from ship to ship & visited &c,

after which I made partial visits to the hospitals. Mr [Forest] takes the *tents*—I the buildings—the ships & the funerals, just as it happens. There is *full* & hard work for three clergymen—one for the tents—one for the buildings—one for the ships. We witness most deplorable scenes—but the poor people are so glad to receive our ministrations & in not a few instances, in the midst of dirt, sickness, want & affliction, are so resigned & full of faith, that it is soothing to visit them. In fact, if it were not for the sense of one's utter inability to do all that is wanted, I could cheerfully give myself up to this kind of work. I could give many interesting as well as shocking details did time permit.... The Gilmour ha[d] a *ships company* of 25—by sickness, death & the desertion of five men, who got frightened & stole one of her boats to escape, they are reduced to two hands.

He mentions Forest's conscientiousness in his duties and the cooperation he had received from the ships' captains in supplying boats for him to visit their ships. Finding time to eat or drink was almost impossible, he found. "But with such sufferings & such intense wants all round," he added, "it is impossible to care about such trifles as these, & I am very well, thank God, & strong." It is clear from his letter, nevertheless, that the Bishop had undertaken to do his part at the Quarantine Station in the face of opposition. He continues, the handwriting almost illegible: "People may blame me— but I do not care—for I think it is my plain duty to set an example in this matter to the Clergy & to provide for the work & I cannot provide now, except by my own labour. It will be very desirable that somebody should come down immediately when I go. Perhaps you could write a line to Mr Torrance for me."

The danger to those working with the sick and indeed to the population at large was very real. The following letter from Dr G. M. Douglas, Medical Superintendent at Grosse Ile, to A. C. Buchanan, Emigration Agent at Quebec, appeared on 11 June in the Quebec Gazette:

"... out of 4 or 5000 that left this [place] since Sunday, at least two thousand will fall sick somewhere before three weeks are over. They ought to have accommodation for 2000 sick, at least, in Montreal and Quebec, as all the Cork and Liverpool passengers are half dead from starvation and want before embarking ... I never saw people so indifferent to life—they would continue in the same berth with a dead person until the seamen or captain dragged out the corpse with boat-hooks.

Good God, what evil will befall the city wherever they alight! Hot weather will increase the evil.

Now give the authorities of Quebec and Montreal fair warning from me. I have not time to write, or should feel it my duty to do so. Public safety requires it.

Although "the clothes he wore while engaged among [the sick]" had to be destroyed, the Bishop suffered no ill effects from his work on Grosse Ile. Others were not so fortunate. The following report on one of his clergy appeared in The Berean *on 28 October:*

The Rev. C. P. Reid, Missionary of the S.P.G.F.P., at Compton, who had been at Grosse Isle, ministering to the sick, left that station of pestilence and death, on the 21st ultimo, in company with the Rev. Messrs. Morris and Anderson, since dead, and with great difficulty made out to reach his father's house, in Frelighsburgh, on the 25th. There, lingering under the disease, which he carried in his system until the 2nd instant, he was at length taken down in a case of confirmed typhus. For twelve successive days there was hardly any expectation left of his recovery; but on the thirteenth day of his confinement his friends were very much flattered with the hope that his life will be spared, as his fever began to abate. Dr. Chamberlain, his Physician, has been most indefatigable, and, it is to be hoped, very successful, in his attendance upon, and treatment of, him.

There were 17 Anglican clergy (besides the Bishop) who served at the Quarantine Station: Richard Anderson, John Butler, William Chadderton, Charles Forest, Narcisse Guerout, William King, Richard Lonsdell, George Mackie, Charles Morice, Charles J. Morris, Armine W. Mountain, G. J. Mountain, Edward Cullen Parkin, Charles Peter Reid, Charles Rollitt, Edward George Sutton, John S. Torrance, and Andrew Trew Whitten. Of these, the majority "caught the fever." Butler, Forest, King, Lonsdell, Parkin, Reid, and Torrance were to recover, but Anderson (of Upper Ireland), Chadderton (of St Peter's, Quebec), and Morris (of Portneuf) did not. The others who served were unaffected. Of Bishop Mountain's clergy ministering to immigrants who had made their way to Montreal and St John's, Mark Willoughby and William Dawes also perished.

12

The Travelling Missionary:
From Quebec to Dudswell
1849

*W*ith a thinly scattered Anglican population *in many portions of the Diocese and limited funds from which to pay stipends, the Church Society appointed a small number of Travelling Missionaries to make a circuit through a large district. The Missionary would visit the isolated homesteads of settlers on his route and distribute tracts, preach in schoolhouses, marry, bury, and baptize as the occasion presented itself. As this sort of duty was strenuous in the extreme, involving long hours of travel and makeshift accommodations among strangers, it was normally offered to young men who were newly ordained.*

Thomas Shaw Chapman set out as Travelling Missionary of the Church Society within three days of his ordination as a deacon. Thus his first stint of duty was to be the culmination of a gruelling sequence of events that included a two-day journey from Lennoxville, where he had just completed his studies at Bishop's College, and two days of examinations—both written and oral—administered by Bishop G. J. Mountain and his Examining Chaplain Dr Mackie. The ordination itself had taken place the following day during the morning service at the Cathedral on 23 December 1849.

The following passage is an excerpt from Chapman's diary. At the time of the incidents described, he was 25 years old.

Dec. 26th.—[Quebec] Spent this day purchasing things necessary for my outfit as Travelling Missionary.

Dec. 27th.—Bought a harness for my horse and a pair of buffalo robes &c., &c. Mr. Mountain* lent me his sleigh to drive to Lennoxville; got over the river with it and the rest of my luggage during low water. Paid my horse's fare, harnessed and drove down about a mile to Mr. Torrence's [at Levis] where I put up for the night.... [T]hey have three fine promising children. I must say that they appear to be the most happy and hospitable pair that I ever met with. Mr. T. has two churches, one at New Liverpool the other at Point Levi, which is in course of building at

---

* Probably Armine W. Mountain, the Bishop's son.

a cost of £1700.—and both are of stone.

Dec. 28th.—Received a letter of introduction from Mr. T. to Mr. Whitten of Leeds and after receiving his good wishes and "God bless you in your undertaking," I started—put up at St. Nicolas, a distance of 15 miles at the house of Mrs. M. who is the only person belonging to the church in the place—gave her some words of consolation and left some tracts for her perusal—had supper at Richardson's, St. Giles, 16 miles distant, arrived at the house of the Rev. Wm King, formerly of Barry [*i.e.*, Bury] but now of St. Sylvestre. Found both father and mother gone, but Miss King was very kind and hospitable to me on finding out who I was.

Dec. 29th.—Started after taking leave of the family and having renewed pressing invitation to call again if ever I passed that way again. Had advanced a little way when I heard a halloo behind—turned and saw a boy at full speed, stopped till he came up—he was the bearer of a bundle of ginger bread and old cheese with Miss K's compliments. Received them thankfully—sent my thanks in return—called upon Mr. Whitten after travelling 5 miles—He was a nice kind of a man and has rather a fine looking daughter. He performs his duty faithfully as a preacher of the gospel but he is sadly crippled and interfered with by the Baptists and Nothingarians, particularly by the former. Staid overnight with the Rev. S. Simpson in Upper Ireland; he is boarding at the present time at the house of Ira Hall—Spent rather a pleasant time with him recounting the scenes of bygone days.

Dec. 31st. Sunday—However I got the family [of Ira Hall, presumably] together, with two or three others and gave them a familiar lecture on the importance of reading the scriptures, prayers, &c., then made an extemporaneous prayer (which by the way was the first I ever made before others) and made ready for starting. I was well received here although the people were Universalists; they gave me a hearty shake of the hand on parting and wished me Godspeed. In passing through the settlement which consists of eight families I distributed tracts. On nearing one of the houses I saw a man chopping away boldly at a log of wood before the door. When he saw me, guilty conscience prompted him to shrink away into the house out of observation. I happened to have a tract with me upon "The Christian obligation of the Sabbath" upon the back of it written in a plain hand, "attend to this," when I drove opposite to the house and motioned to some persons at the window. The chopper made his appearance with his countenance suffused by a blush of mingled shame and conscious guilt. I handed the tract to him, inquiring his name, bid a kind good morning, and drove on. It no doubt was a timely and forcible rebuke to the offenders. It came so sudden and unexpected upon him, just as if I had foreknowledge of him.

Arrived in Dudswell about three. These roads were bad and my sleigh was not suited to the double roads, which kept me four hours going seven miles. Preached to a congregation of about thirty-five. It was small on account of the short notice.

This area was to be Chapman's first and only parish. He was appointed to Dudswell, Ham, and parts adjacent in 1850, and remained there until his death in 1912. When he took charge, this large area was "without churches or Protestant services of any kind except on funeral occasions" when a clergyman from Cookshire, Hatley, or Huntingville was called in. Chapman established six different centres in his parish, two or three of which he visited every Sunday.

As a student, Chapman had been versatile and hardworking, financing his university education "by making tables and chairs, teaching school in Sherbrooke and acting as barber to his fellow students." As a priest, he was a simple Prayer Book churchman.

13

"Pilgrims & Proselytes":
Conversion and the Priesthood
1855

T he Anglican Church in the Diocese of
Quebec has had a long history of drawing clergy from various denominations. In 1803,
Jacob Mountain ordained such a redoubtable churchman in the person of John Strachan,
later Bishop of Toronto, who had been raised as a Presbyterian and, before emigrating to Canada, had enrolled himself briefly at St Andrew's College with a view to
becoming a minister in the Church of Scotland. Charles James Stewart, even before
he became Bishop, was constantly on the lookout for likely candidates for the ministry. Of his two assistants in the parish of St Armand, one a Methodist, the other a
Congregationalist Missionary, both would be ordained, first as deacons in 1815, and
the following year as priests by Jacob Mountain.

Charles Roy, three of whose sons became Anglican clergymen, was received from
the Roman Catholic Church into the Anglican communion by G. J. Mountain in
1846. Isaac Hellmuth, a converted Jew—later to become Bishop of Huron—was ordained both Deacon and Priest by Mountain that same year.

Many other clergy could be mentioned, some who served the Diocese for many
years, others who moved on: George Milne, a former Presbyterian, who served as Rural
Dean in the District of Gaspé; Archibald Campbell Scarth, also a Presbyterian, Rector
of Lennoxville and a Canon of the Cathedral; Charles Henry Brooks, a former
Congregationalist Minister at Constantinople, who, after his ordination by Bishop
Dunn, served briefly in Barnston and was then lost to view.

Of those who entered the Church in this manner, many paid a penalty in their
estrangement from family and friends. Hellmuth, in the midst of difficulties over his
appointment to Bishop's College, lamented to G. J. Mountain, who had been sympathetic to him, that "severed from my own kindred & nation, on account of my faith
in Christ 'I am become a stranger unto my Brethren, & an alien unto my Mother's
children,' [and] I feel the more every & any act of kindness from my Gentile Brethren ..." Roy, on telling his father of his intention to be received into the Anglican
Church, was told that he would be disinherited. Scarth, who described himself as "an
outcast and renegade" in the eyes of those closest to him, has left an account of how,
nonetheless, he came to join the Church. The following is an extract from his Memoir:

I came down to Lower Canada (as it was then called) from Toronto in May, 1855, where I had been a student for the Presbyterian ministry for three years previously, and had completed my first year in the Divinity Hall, having delivered a homily (as my certificate states) "with much acceptability"—and was employed as a catechist in the neighborhood of Chateauguay under the direction of the Rev. Donald Fraser, then the leading minister of the Free Kirk in Montreal ... Here I became known to, and was honored by the friendship of Dr. Leach, Rector of St. George's Church and Vice-Principal and Prof. of Ethics and Moral Philosophy, of McGill College. Through his instrumentality, I was lead to study the questions at issue between the Church of England and the various denominations, more especially the Presbyterians, with the result that I offered myself, after some months of careful study, and many anxious days and sleepless nights, to the Bishop of Montreal* as a candidate for Confirmation.

William Turnbull Leach, "who had himself gone through the same burning fiery furnace," as Archdeacon Henry Roe put it, had been educated at Sterling and Edinburgh and licensed to the Ministry of the Church of Scotland before emigrating to Upper Canada in the early 1830s. In 1835, he was called to St Andrew's Kirk, Toronto. He was actively involved in establishing Presbyterian College at Kingston and was a Trustee of Queen's College when it was granted its charter in 1841. In 1842, however, because of growing doubts about the doctrine of predestination, he resigned from St Andrew's and was tried for heresy by the presbytery of Toronto. Early in 1843, he was received into the Anglican Church. That year he was ordained by G. J. Mountain. It is not surprising that Leach took such pains with young Scarth.

I cannot look back to that period of my life even now after the lapse of so many years without the most profound emotion [wrote Scarth in 1902]. It is hard to understand in these days of liberal thought the bitterness of feeling which prevailed against the Church in the minds of those belonging to the straitest sect of Presbyterians.

I was confirmed by Bishop Fulford in the autumn at Lachine: walking in to Montreal from that service. From that time for many years I was regarded as an outcast and renegade by my own kith and kin, as much so as if I had renounced Christianity altogether and become a Mohammedan or

---

* Francis Fulford, First Lord Bishop of Montreal.

a Hindoo.

Through the influence of Leach and Fulford, Scarth spent two years studying at Bishop's College. He was ordained Deacon on Trinity Sunday, 1857, and Priest in the following year. After starting his ministry in the Diocese of Montreal, Scarth was invited in 1859 to assist the incumbent at Lennoxville. He was to remain there as Rector until 1904, the year of his death.

It was his sincerity that was remembered. "His tenderness of heart was conspicuous," Roe wrote of his old friend. "He could not read the more pathetic passages of Scripture or of our own poets without tears. But after all, it was his sincerity and simplicity which gave his words the convincing power they had.... Even the careless and irreligious, who boasted that they could live without Mr. Scarth's religion, found that they could not die without it, and almost invariably sent for him to baptize them on their death beds."

14

A Second Chance in a New World
1858 and 1902

To many immigrants from the British Isles, the Canadas offered the opportunity for a new life. To the peasantry, who often had little choice in leaving their native place, it was an opportunity to break out of a punishing cycle of poverty and degradation. "Shure we'll all be jintlemen!" shouted a fellow "of gigantic proportions, whose long, tattered great-coat just reached below the middle of his bare red legs," reports a horrified Susanna Moodie of a new arrival as he leapt onto the rocky shore of Grosse Ile. It was 1832. The Moodies, whose ship had been given a clean bill of health and leave to go on to Quebec, were ashore only to visit an acquaintance at the garrison. They had emigrated to take up land offered to officers in the military and, like many other emigrants of their class, hoped that what income they had would go farther in the New World. This was a hope, as Mrs Moodie put it, "of escaping from the vulgar sarcasms too often hurled at the less wealthy by the purse-proud, commonplace people of the world." Others, like the Rev. William Gore Lyster, left their homeland to escape from the rigidity of the social system.

Lyster was a young man of some property, son of an Irish gentleman and nephew of Sir Edward Cusack, the eminent Dublin surgeon. He had graduated from a good university and had been newly ordained Deacon. Although only an assistant curate, Lyster as the former ward of the Rector of Tallaght, whose parish included the summer Palace of the Archbishops of Dublin, seemed destined for advancement in the Church. Then he made an unpardonable social blunder. He contracted an unsuitable marriage.

Having compromised his position in society, Lyster lost all hope of preferment in Britain and, together with his wife, emigrated to the United States. He first intended to acquire land and proceeded to Cincinnati, Ohio, thinking of engaging in farming there. His vocation, however, soon reasserted itself. On 30 March 1858, he wrote to Bishop G. J. Mountain explaining his circumstances and begging for employment:

May it please Your Lordship,
I am a Deacon of the United Church of England and Ireland.
Having received the Divinity Testimonium from Trinity College Dublin, and having passed an examination conducted by the Archbishop

of Dublin and his Grace's Chaplains, I received letters dimissory from his Grace, and was ordained by the Bishop of Down and Connor on the 30th of November 1856.

On the 15th of January 1857 I entered upon the duties of assistant Curate of the Parish of Kilskeery, Diocese of Clogher—I remained there eight months.

During the latter part of my stay in the Parish, I became attached to a Girl who was so much my inferior in station, that I could not marry her without disgrace and loss of social position. I became so much blinded however by my unhappy passion that I at length yielded to the infatuation, resigned my curacy and crossed over to England where I was soon afterwards joined by the Girl, whom I married.

I hardly need tell your Lordship that but a short time elapsed ere I became painfully aware of my error—My eyes soon opened to the reality of my position—The sense of neglected duty, of post deserted, of prospects for ever blighted and of friends and relations alienated perhaps for ever by my act continually haunted me and made me miserable. No small addition to my unhappiness was the reflection that I had abandoned my sacred calling and that my Wife's social position and want of education were such as to make me despair of ever returning to it. God alone knows how much I repented my rashness and want of earnestness in His service—On the 18th of November, having been delayed by difficulties in the sale of some property, I sailed for America. A fellow voyager, an inhabitant of this City [Cincinnati, Ohio] induced me to come here, by holding out advantageous prospects in case I turned my attention to agriculture. At the suggestion of a valued friend who wrote to me before I sailed and who earnestly exhorted me not to despair of readmission to the ministry, I wrote to my late Rector, the Rev. J. G. Porter for a testimonial—of that as well as of a certificate from Rev. A. Irvine, Senr Curate. I take the liberty to enclose Your Lordship copies.

I have been here now more than three months during which period the hope and the wish that I may again be employed in the ministry have continually increased. I have made my case known to only one Clergyman here, the Rev. W. R. Nicholson who has given me his advice and much encouragement. I may be permitted to inform your Lordship that I have lately attended sedulously to the education of my Wife. The disparity between us is I believe daily lessening and will, I trust, gradually become imperceptible.

I propose, My Lord, previously to engaging in the active duties of the Ministry in Your Lordship's, or in any other Diocese, should I be fortunate enough to obtain the employment I humbly and earnestly seek, to devote a year to the education and improvement of my Wife. I beseech you My Lord consider my case as that of one who is sincerely anxious to engage in the work of the ministry and to prove by earnestness and increased diligence a zeal, I pray God, renewed and redoubled in the service of his Lord and Master.

Should Your Lordship permit me, I shall without delay on receipt of your Lordship's favor, present myself with my papers and certificates with the original also of those I enclose [to] Your Lordship now....

I have thus, My Lord, laid before you my case to which I earnestly entreat your Lordship's favorable consideration,

> And anxiously awaiting your Lordship's reply,
> Beg to subscribe myself
> Your Lordship's humble ob^t serv^t
> William Gore Lyster

Mountain seems to have responded in not very positive terms on 12 April. On 21 April, Lyster replied with pathetic eagerness, as the following excerpt from his letter attests. He even pledged to support himself on what personal resources he possessed—£500—if Mountain would only give him a parish:

Tho' your Lordship's letter affords me little encouragement, I have decided upon once more addressing your Lordship rather than applying for employment in another Diocese ...

I am quite ready and willing to undergo the trouble and expense necessary to be incurred in making a journey to Quebec ... I will willingly labor in Your Lordship's Diocese with no other remuneration than the sense of duty being performed and of position having been regained.... Let me assure your Lordship that considerations of advantage or emolument do not influence me in my wish to obtain employment in the ministry. Did not nobler motives urge me in the course I now pursue I would be tempted to forgo the pain of telling my story to a stranger, the anxiety as to the result and perhaps the mortification of disappointment.

To this letter Mountain appears to have replied that, as long as it was clearly understood that he had made no commitment to employ him, Lyster might present himself at Quebec. On 10 May, Lyster wrote to inform the Bishop that he was setting out the next day.

Mountain was sufficiently persuaded of the young man's worth to propose that he undertake a further journey to visit the Rev. George Milne of New Carlisle, Rural

Dean in the District of Gaspé. Mountain trusted Milne's judgement and continued to rely on him to assess and resolve a variety of delicate situations. In December of that year, Lyster was appointed to Hopetown and Port Daniel in Milne's jurisdiction.

By the end of his first year, Lyster was able to report his progress with his three congregations. A church had been started at Port Daniel and the materials for the frame for another at Hopetown had been procured. "The third, that of Shigouac," had only recently been formed. His Report to the Church Society for 1859 concludes:

I am glad to be able to testify to the gratifying earnestness about religion evinced by many in the Mission, as well as to the feeling of gratitude with which the Society, that has done so much towards supplying their wants, is regarded. I may be permitted, too, to give expression to my own thankfulness to the Almighty for the encouragement thus far received; and to my own earnest hope that he who hath begun this good work in us will perform it even unto the end.

Perhaps he intended this final paragraph as a pledge to merit the confidence he had received; in July of that year his Bishop had raised him to the priesthood.

The young man and his family were kindly received by laity and clergy alike. On 27 June 1859, in respose to a request that he sign Lyster's testimonials prior to his proposed ordination, the Rev. Robert Short of Leeds congratulated him, agreed readily to support his candidacy and—what was more, perhaps—concluded with an invitation: "You must endeavour to visit me this summer;" Short wrote, "bring Mrs Lyster & child—Remember however, you are coming to Bachelor's quarters therefore do not anticipate many comforts & Luxuries."

Jane Thompson, Lyster's wife, was to bear him 13 children of whom 6 died young. An affectionate father, the loss of each child was a great blow to him. "From the unexpected death of my brother Louis," wrote one of his sons many years later, "my father never rallied."

Lyster was to remain serving the people of the Gaspé, first at Port Daniel and, from 1863, at Cape Cove, until his death in 1902. On Milne's retirement in 1875, he became Rural Dean, and somewhat later, he was appointed Government Inspector of Schools for the District of Gaspé. He was a man of wide interests, "well-read in English Literature and every department of Belles-Lettres as well as in the literature and learning of his own profession." Science, too, attracted him: the natural sciences, geology, astronomy and botany, "and from his attainments," wrote a former professor of Theology at Bishop's College, "was in a position to advise his brother Clergy how best to meet the difficulties felt by some as to the relations of science and theology." As a friend observed of him:

A man of Mr. Lyster's ability and attainments, many have thought, was very much thrown away upon an obscure Mission on the Gaspé Coast. This was not altogether the fault of others. No one appreciated Mr. Lyster more justly than did Bishop [J. W.] Williams who tried more than once to draw him out to the front. The writer is in a position to say that some twenty or more years ago on the occurrence of a vacancy in one of our most important Parishes, Bishop Williams asked Mr. Lyster's permission to nominate him to it. This, however, Mr. Lyster declined. He felt himself too much rooted in the soil to change.

Lyster died at the age of 71. Still apparently in good health, he had set out by sleigh from his home in Cape Cove on 17 January to visit a friend at Gaspé Basin some 50 miles away. There, he suddenly fell ill and, although "two doctors were with him immediately, ... the remedies used were to no avail." He called for his son Ralph "who had [to] come to him from Cape Cove, and gave him his last instructions, and sent him back to prepare his mother for the bereavement then evidently close at hand." The "tender and loving provision of one to comfort his partner of a long life," his obitu-ary notes, "can escape no one." He died within two hours of his son's departure, just three days after being stricken.

In preparing Lyster's obituary, the Ven. Henry Roe was able to draw on accounts of his brief illness and his death as reported by friends and family members, but it was from many years' personal acquaintance that he paid tribute to the character and merits of an old friend.

Such [Roe concludes] is a short and very imperfect notice of this true-hearted servant of God, who, like many another son of our Mother, the Church of England, gave his whole Ministerial life to an obscure mission on the Gaspé Coast. He was modest, quiet, never given to push his own way, lived for his people, and was everything to them; doctor, friend, teacher, preacher, adviser, example, to whom they all went, when in trouble, sorrow, need, sickness, or any other adversity. When the tidings that he was gone ran along the coast all men mourned ... The whole coast, all its inhabitants, of whatever race, of whatever religion, turned out to honour his Remnants, as he was carried home, so that his return to Cape Cove, from Gaspé Basin, was more like a triumphal procession than anything else.

A Difficult Birth: Quebec's First Synod 1859

*I*n *July of 1851, Bishop G. J. Mountain held his triennial visitation of the clergy at the Cathedral, at which 36 of the 40 then serving in the Diocese were present. Following the visitation,*

 a meeting of clergy and of lay delegates, whom the Bishop had invited the different congregations of the diocese to send, was held to consider the steps necessary to be taken with reference to the threatened spoliation of the Clergy Reserves. All the parishes and missions of the diocese had elected delegates, except the distant places in the district of Gaspé, and three others; and forty-one delegates were present out of fifty-seven who had been chosen, many of whom attended at great inconvenience to themselves. The proceedings were unanimous and conducted with great spirit ...

Later that same year, on 23 September, the Bishops of Toronto, Newfoundland, Fredericton, and Montreal gathered at Quebec "for the purpose of consulting together on the steps which it might be possible to take" to secure for the Colonial Church the "inherent privilege, indulged to every other religious body under the whole circle of the heavens [as Mountain had phrased it in his recent Charge to the clergy], of holding her own formal and deliberative conventions for the regulation of her internal affairs."

Without at all touching the question of the revival of Convocation at home [Mountain observed in a Pastoral Letter], I am not aware of the existence of any opposition in the minds of Churchmen within this Diocese, clerical or lay, to the exercise of synodical action within the Colonial Church: I am very sure that the want of it is experimentally felt and generally acknowledged among us; and I cannot possibly fail to see that the proximity of the United States, in which the triennial Conventions of the whole Church and the annual Conventions of each Diocese ... have been long seen to work efficiently and advantageously for the Church and to provide for many points at which we are at a loss ...

The initiative of the British North American bishops (after a number of legal hurdles had been surmounted) was to lead eventually to the institution of synodical government in the Canadian Church. Judging from the initial cooperative spirit that Mountain had seen manifested among his own clergy and lay representatives in July 1851, as well as among the conferring bishops two months later, one might suppose that all would have flowed smoothly for "the synodical movement" in the Diocese of Quebec. As events would show, this was not to be the case.

Bishop Strachan in the Diocese of Toronto had proceeded immediately to form a synod, "the first with lay delegates to be held in the British colonies," some four years before the requisite legislation was secured, but Bishop Mountain had waited. On 28 May 1857, "An Act to Enable the Members of the United Church of England and Ireland to meet in Synod," was proclaimed in the Canada Gazette. *The Act stipulated that each diocese wishing to regulate its own affairs must formally "adopt" the legislation and frame a constitution. To accomplish this end, Mountain convoked a meeting of the clergy and laity of the Diocese to take place on 24 June 1858 at the National School House in Quebec. He did not at that time provide for the number of the laity who might attend or for their adequately representing the people of the Diocese at large. As a local newspaper, the* Quebec Mercury *reported, "the greater portion, though not all, of the Church of England Clergy of the Diocese" were present, together with about 150 lay members, "of whom not more than ten had come in from the country parishes."*

The Bishop, who was in the chair, informed the meeting that

they had met for the purpose of considering and adopting the Act of Parliament by which synodical powers had been conferred on the bishop, clergy and laity of the church of England, and framing a constitution and regulations for the government of the church.... His Lordship said that the present meeting was not a synod, but simply a meeting to prepare the way for the formation of a synod; and in the furtherance of this object, he had availed himself of the assistance of several gentlemen to draw up certain resolutions, which would be submitted to the consideration of the meeting. The first resolution had merely reference to the adoption by this meeting of the Act of Parliament; the second was for the purpose of establishing the principle of representation in the synod when formed, and it was open to all persons, members of the church,[*] to propose such alterations therein, and amendments thereto, as were consistent with the general principles of the church.

---

[*] This applied exclusively, of course, to Anglican men; women were not legal persons.

The adoption of the Act passed unanimously, but the second Resolution, that the Synod be composed of the Bishop of the diocese, the clergy of the same in Priests Orders ("to include Professors of Divinity and headmasters of schools under the jurisdiction of the Bishop and not under ecclesiastical censure,") and of lay representatives "as hereafter to be provided" ran into difficulties. It had obviously been the Bishop's intention that the constitution of the proposed Synod would be prepared at a later date, and under his eye, to be presented to a subsequent assembly for ratification. He had, apparently, no inkling of the intention of the "Low Church Party" to turn out in force and seize the initiative on so-called democratic principles.

Mr Jeffery Hale asserted that he did not believe that "this meeting could delegate its power of forming a constitution to any other parties," and proposed an amendment to the Resolution providing for a committee of twelve, to be appointed by ballot, to draft a constitution for the regulation of the Church of England in the Diocese. When the Rev. Samuel Simpson Wood, who had proposed the Resolution, asked the chairman "whether it was understood that the voting was to be by orders," the "enquiry created a decided manifestation of opposition among the lay members present, from which moment [as the Quebec Mercury *observed]:*

the discussion became irregular, and our reporter was unable to note the proceedings with any thing like accuracy.

The question was repeatedly raised whether the meeting did not already constitute a synod.

Mr. James Bell Forsyth [of the Cathedral congregation] maintained that such was the case from the moment that the first Resolution had been passed, and that, this point established, the right of the clergy to vote by orders could not be denied them.

The Revd Mr Parkin [who had seconded the Resolution under discussion] could not conceal his surprise that, constituted as the assemblage was in the proportion of twenty laity to one clergyman,—a feeling should exist against the right of the clergy to vote as they considered they had the right of doing.

Mr Hall [acting mayor] expressed his surprise that the clergy should wish to set themselves in a position adverse to the will of the laity.

Mr Parkin maintained in reply, that the present meeting, constituted as it was, could not by any means be looked upon as a representation of the laity....

The Bishop stated that it was his conviction, the clergy having with one voice decided against the motion of Mr Hale, the amendment was rejected.

The cry of "question," on Mr Hale's motion, being raised by Colonel

Fitzgerald and other gentlemen, the Bishop again stated that he was under the impression that the clergy had declared their view on the subject....

From this point in the discussion of the subject, an animated and by no means orderly system of debate prevailed ...

Here the Rev. E. W. Sewell of Trinity Church, Quebec, intervened on behalf of Hale* and urged the clergy "to throw aside any claim they might have to vote by orders." Captain Rhodes of St Michael's, Sillery, pointing out that he was the only member of his own congregation present, declared that the assembly "was only a representation of a party of the city of Quebec." His parish, he was convinced, "would be most reluctant to accept the decision of the present assemblage on any point. He therefore proposed an adjournment to this day two months," but it appears that there was not sufficient order at this point to vote on anything. The Bishop several times left the chair "as he saw no possibility of proceeding without the principle being acknowledged of the clergy having the right to vote as a separate body":

Among the speakers who evinced warmth, the Revd Mr Roe declared against admitting any promiscuous assemblage to assume the rights of legislative action, that [there was] no precedent in the history of the world, in any instance, save during the French Revolution.

During the height of the discussion, it is deeply to be lamented that any portion of the lay element should have so far forgotten themselves as to have taunted the clergy with such gross language as "Church-emptiers," "Beavens,"** and "Fish-eaters." Repeatedly also, to the manifest disrespect of the same class towards the chair, it could not but be noticed that much needless loud conversation and shuffling, or moving about, was kept up, whenever his Lordship addressed the assemblage.

It was clear that the only thing to do under these circumstances was to secure an adjournment. After several attempts, one such motion, "which was carried to the first Wednesday in September," was finally put through, after which "his Lordship with much emotion pronounced the benediction."

---

* Both Hale and Fitzgerald were prominent Quebecers and members of Sewell's congregation. Hale was to found a hospital on St Olivier Street for the Protestant poor of the city in 1865, and had already established a Sunday school.

** Dr James Beaven, Professor of Divinity at King's College, Toronto, was associated with the Tractarian Movement.

Following this unpleasant encounter, Mountain set about immediately to secure further legislation "to explain and amend" the earlier Act, ensuring that future lay participation would be truly representative of the parishes, missions, and cures throughout the Diocese. On 18 August, the Bishop issued a circular to inform his diocese that the Bill to remedy "the evils of the first act" had become law, and that the adjourned meeting called for 1 September "of necessity falls through."

The experience had no doubt shaken him, however: "I cannot close this Circular," he wrote, "without expressing my warm and thankful appreciation of the unanimous assurance, communicated to me after the scene of the 24th June, in the shape of a resolution passed by a large meeting of Clergymen, of their attachment to my person, and their confidence in my administration of the Diocese. It was indeed a comfort to my heart—"

Mountain's sense of relief, as it turned out, was premature. His difficulties were far from over. A Lay Association was formed, which denounced the Bishop's action and issued a pamphlet "warning the laity that their rights are being invaded and that they must come forward in defense of their religious freedom." On 6 January 1859, the Sherbrooke Times *alluded to the Lay Association's charges:*

To us, resident at a distance from the scene of trouble, the conduct of the Bishop in securing the rights of the Church in the Diocese in general, by allowing representation in fair proportion by delegates from every parish, seems the most liberal policy.... The extremest reformer could not call for more, for the choice of delegates is left entirely in the hands of the laity themselves.

We have felt it our duty thus to allude to this pamphlet, and we earnestly hope that the good sense of the people in the townships, to whom we more particularly address ourselves, will lead them to avoid joining any exclusive party in the Church ...

On Wednesday, 6 July 1859, Bishop Mountain greeted the members of the clergy and laity gathered at the National School House for his first Synod. This time, each of the 158 laymen present took his place as the chosen delegate of a particular parish in the Diocese; each parish could send at least one, and no parish more than three, delegates. The first day's proceedings were taken up with the election of two secretaries, one by the clergy, the other by the laity, to examine the certificates of election which the Lay Delegates were expected to produce. The Rev. E. C. Parkin and George Short Carter, Esq., were duly elected and, at the evening session, reported that all the certificates were in order except for the chapelry of St Peter's, Quebec, "where two elections appear to have taken place and certificates thereof presented respectively."

The actual business of the synod was to commence on the afternoon of the second day, preceded by an address to those assembled in which the Bishop endeavoured to put the trials leading up to this convocation into perspective:

Of the interruptions of Christian peace and the ill-omened appearance of any separation of the interests of the Laity from those of their pastors, I wish to say but little. It is impossible, however, to refrain from saying that we might have indulged the hope of doing our work without disturbance [he remarked]....We have precedents and patterns all ready before our eyes and all uniform, in their essential characteristics, throughout the empire. We are now following in the wake of sixteen Colonial Dioceses, being the whole number in which Synodical action has taken place, and in every one of them, without a single exception, that particular principle has been embodied and recognized as an indispensable feature of Church of England Episcopacy, which is conceived in some quarters here, to be a special grievance and which constitutes a main object of active and organised assault. But this opposition, we may well hope, will die away.... And it cannot be doubted that gentlemen who have been found hand to hand opposed to each other, in the conflict of opposition upon points of the constitution, will afterwards cordially co-operate in all which they shall be alike persuaded to tend to the common good. In the meantime, we may challenge all parties to shew what special and local grounds have existed for attempting to make a difference in this point between the diocese of Quebec and all the other dioceses of the empire. Yes—the day will come when the excitement of the occasion having passed off and the clouds of some prevailing prejudice having cleared away, the objects upon which we fix our regards will be seen as they really are,—leaving it only a subject for wonder that any such agitations should have existed at all, and a ground for true thankfulness of heart that all differences upon the subject may be forgotten.

Following this earnest address in which Mountain defended Episcopacy and the episcopal veto, it was moved by the Rev. Dr Falloon and seconded by G. O. Stuart, Esq., that "[w]e, the Bishop, Clergy, and Lay Delegates now assembled, do hereby accept the said Acts, and declare ourselves a Synod for the Diocese of Quebec, and will proceed to the consideration of the Constitution and Regulations to be adopted for the due ordering of the same." The first of these was that every "rule, canon, law or regulation to be in force in this Diocese as the Act of this Synod" must have first received "the concurrent assent of the Bishop, the Clergy, and the Lay Delegates; the assent of the Clergy and the Lay Delegates to be determined by a majority of votes ... taken separately, in each order, whenever it shall be so required."

An amendment was moved by Mr H. S. Scott and seconded by Mr G. Lanigan that adoption of any rule, canon, law, or regulation require "a majority of the Clergy and of the Lay delegates" only, and that "if any measure so passed be objected to by the Bishop, such measure shall stand reserved for reconsideration," to become law if adopted in like manner at the following session of Synod. The amendment was put to the meeting and lost by a majority of 105. Among the clergy, three supported it: the Revs. E. W. Sewell and Isaac Hellmuth of Trinity Church, Quebec, and W. L. Thompson of Stanstead. Voting against it were the remaining 36 members of the clergy and 106 Lay Delegates. There was a further attempt to add to the wording of the original motion that the episcopal veto should only extend to the life of the present Bishop. That too was defeated. The original motion was then put and carried by a large majority.

To be absolutely certain that there was no misunderstanding about the previous Resolution, it was then moved by J. B. Forsyth, Esq., and seconded by the Hon. H. Black, that "the Synod shall consist of the Bishop of the Diocese, of the Clergy of the same, and of Lay representatives to be elected as hereinafter provided; and no act or resolution of the Synod shall be valid unless it shall receive the concurrence of the Bishop and of the majority of the Clergy and Laity present and voting at the meeting."

The motion was carried, supported by 37 clerical and 109 lay votes; 3 of the clergy and 34 of the laity voted against. The evening session that day had reassembled at 2 o'clock and was adjourned at 9 p.m. The next day's session opened with Divine Service at All Saints' Chapel (adjoining the Rectory) at 10 a.m. and continued (with a break for lunch) until 10 p.m. at night when the business of this first Synod was finally concluded.

At the close of the Synod [Armine Mountain recounted], a member who had taken a very active part in all the proceedings ... of a body styled "The Lay Association" [G. Hall], proposed a vote of thanks [to the Bishop] for the address which he had delivered at its opening, and for his able and impartial conduct, of which he suggested that all present should mark their sense by escorting him in a body to the rectory.* He declined the honour, and after dismissing the synod with the benediction, rode four miles on horseback, with a lightened and thankful heart, to his home. It was nearly midnight when he reached it.

---

* Mountain had moved from the Rectory (the present 'Bishopthorpe' in the Cathedral Close) in the spring of the previous year "on the recommendation of his medical advisors," and was then residing at Bardfield, near Quebec.

Waiting for the Minister to Call
1861, 1952, and 1963–1980

A visit *"from the Minister"* is a special *event, especially in remote places, out of reach of any parish church. On the Lower North Shore, where the people are widely scattered in settlements accessible only by boat or dog sled—or more recently by plane or snowmobile—such visits have often led to lasting ties of affection and commitment between the minister and individual members of his (or her) flock.*

In September 1861, the Rev. John P. Richmond was sent to "the Canadian Labrador"* as the Mission's first priest. Earlier that summer, Bishop G. J. Mountain had fulfilled a long-standing ambition in paying a visit to the coast to ascertain first-hand the needs of its scattered Protestant population, by then a few hundred in number. The first Bishop of Quebec to make the trip, Mountain (then 72) travelled much of the way under the most difficult circumstances, often on foot or by open boat. "Eleven services were held in the Canadian part of the coast, and several children baptized," reported the Bishop's son Armine. "Everywhere the people manifested a kind and thankful spirit."

In the spring of the year following his appointment, Richmond reported his progress in a closely-written 13-page letter to the Bishop. He described his travels and the various means of transportation used, the need for Church schools, and the competition he was having from Mr Carpenter, a Dissenter, who was away from the Coast that winter but slated to return.

 In my own mission [his account reads, in part], I paid five visits to the people situated as far as Bradore Bay, and in March immediately after my return from Red Bay, I started from Forteau with the intention of proceeding Westward as far as circumstances would permit me to go. I was fortunately able to hire

---

* In Richmond's day, and until Confederation, the 200-mile stretch of coast from Natashquan to Blanc Sablon (thought of as a part of Labrador, but lying within Canada) was referred to in this way; after World War II it became the "Quebec Labrador," or the Lower North Shore.

a kammutik [komatik, *i.e.,* a dog sled] and driver—and am thankful to be able to say that I visited about 150 miles of Coast ... and saw 230 persons belonging to the Anglican Church. During an absence of nearly eight weeks on this journey I had much disagreeable weather, but only <u>one</u> day when travelling was impossible. The ice on the Bay gave way before my return to Forteau and I had a rather troublesome journey homeward. It is now my intention (DV) [*i.e.,* 'God willing'] to start tomorrow to pay a farewell visit to the Eastern people ...

It appears that Richmond's appointment was only for a year, and Mountain soon informed him that in all likelihood he would be succeeded in the Mission by Frederick Cookesley, newly sent by the SPG from England (see Window 18). It seems, however, that Richmond's attachment to the people—even in so short a space of time— had become such that he wrote to the Bishop offering to stay, should the plan fall through. "In case your Lordship has not been able to provide for the Labrador [he ventured], I shall be willing with your Lordship's approval to remain the coming winter. I should be sorry to leave the people to be misled by dissent."

In July 1955 Robert A. Bryan, then a Divinity student at Yale, and his wife, Faith, paid a visit to Quebec that would have far-reaching consequences—both for themselves and for the people of the Lower North Shore.

The Anglican Cathedral in Quebec City [he was to recall in 1992] seemed dreary as my wife, Faith, and I tiptoed down the aisle toward the chancel. Tattered and torn historic flags hung from the balcony. Everything in the building reflected the timeless feeling we had while visiting the old walled city of Quebec.

On a table near the church entrance was a pamphlet describing the work of the Anglican Diocese of Quebec. My eyes fixed upon words that have stayed with me and have been an inspiration throughout my lifetime: "It makes no difference how few and far between they are; we will be there somehow, sometime ..." The words referred to the families in the 250,000-square-mile diocese ...

... Leaving the church, we encountered an elderly gentleman walking through the churchyard and asked where we might obtain more specific information about the diocese. He directed us to Bishopthorpe on d'Auteuil Avenue, the residence of Archbishop Philip Carrington, whom I knew to be a world-renowned New Testament scholar.

After a few long rings on the bell, the door opened a crack and a severe-looking elderly housekeeper dressed in grey and white peered out at us.... My three-week beard and scruffy clothes, which had made sense during the canoe trip Faith and I had just taken 250 miles north of Quebec City, now made a poor impression on the housekeeper ... At that moment, Archbishop Carrington appeared. He looked out and saw Faith with a red kerchief on her head and a small knapsack on her back. I blurted out my mission: I was a student at Yale Divinity School involved in a summer project conducting a survey among the people of north central Quebec.

The Archbishop welcomed us in and soon we were sitting in front of a silver tea service. When I told him about my love of the outdoors and remote areas, he began to tell us of the work of the Anglican Church on the Quebec North Shore.

During their visit at Bishopthorpe, the Bryans viewed a film (by means of an ancient Bell and Howell silent projector) of the Archbishop's latest visit to the easternmost section of the Diocese. They took their leave "fully determined," as he describes it, "to return some day and work in an area where it made no difference 'how few and far between they are ...'"

In the 1960 Summer issue, the Quebec Diocesan Gazette *printed a modest 14-line item announcing that the Rev. Robert A. Bryan, Chaplain of Choate School, Wallingford, Connecticut, would be "working as a missionary on the Labrador Coast during the summer months, using his own plane.... Mr Bryan is giving his services without cost to the Diocese, and we are most grateful for his interest and the contribution he is making to the work." In 1961, he founded the Quebec-Labrador Foundation (QLF), whose initial goal was to help promote local or indigenous leadership through educational programmes, and scholarship grants and bursaries to promising young people.*

In the "Chairman's Message" of the QLF's 1992 Annual Report, Bryan alludes to the 37 years that had elapsed since his visit with Carrington, and to the opportunities afforded him "to share my life with families on the Quebec North Shore," but it is in such reminiscences as the following unpublished one (titled "Aunt Lizzy") that the nature of that special relationship is evoked. Here even the landsman and suburbanite can catch a glimpse of what a "visit from the Minister" can really mean in remote areas—and to those who anticipate his coming.

When I first met "Aunt Lizzy" Anderson* she was losing her sight. A person of great character and strength, Aunt Lizzy had outlived three husbands.

---

* Residents of the Quebec North Shore who are 65 years of age are commonly referred to as "Aunt" or "Uncle."

During the summers of 1960, 1961 and 1962, I had not been able to visit her on Shag Island. It was impossible to get into a house-to-house visiting schedule during a six-week summer period. However, in 1963 when I became a Harrington Harbour resident for 16 months, Aunt Lizzy expected I would soon visit. My work and official duties began in June and by mid-July I had not yet seen Aunt Lizzy.

One afternoon at a wedding supper, Aunt Lizzy confronted me. She told me she did not think I was "much of a minister" because I had not been to see her. She told me she had been brought up as an Anglican, but if she did not receive better care and concern from the Anglican Church, she was going to turn and become a Roman Catholic. I apologized for not having been to her house, but she was not mollified. I tried to think of how I would win her friendship.

The Sunday after the wedding, a northeast storm hit Harrington Harbour; the wind blew 35 to 45 mph. The rough seas in the harbour made it difficult to take a small boat from island to island. Nonetheless, I decided I was going out to see Aunt Lizzy on Shag Island. It was not a life-threatening trip, but I was soaked through when I reached the house where Aunt Lizzy lived with her daughter, Jane, and her son-in-law, Victor Cox. Grandchildren in the house told Aunt Lizzy they thought they could see the minister coming. It was a terrible day and she immediately became concerned for my safety. When I came inside she gave me a hard time for going out in such bad weather and taking chances, but I could see she was delighted I'd made the effort to come to see her.

We talked a long time and then had prayers together. That day started a friendship that lasted until her death 17 years later. Aunt Lizzy's sight continued to fail rapidly and within a few months of my first visit, she was only able to distinguish between light and dark. When I went to visit, I sat down next to her to talk. She recognized my voice, but put out her hands and touched my face, my forehead and my eyes and said, "I know it's you."

I tried to see Aunt Lizzy on Shag Island or in Aylmer Sound, where she lived in the winter, at least once a month. The Bryan family would call bad weather "Aunt Lizzy days" as I tried my best to see her in the worst weather. This was a source of amusement for both the Cox family and Aunt Lizzy, who would admonish me and say, "You should not have come out on such a dirty day." (On the Quebec North Shore, "dirty" is the word they use for bad weather.)

On good days if I passed over Aylmer Sound, I flew as low as possible over Aunt Lizzy's house. Occasionally I passed no more than 20 feet over the chimney. Just a few seconds before I flew over, I turned the propeller pitch up to make a tremendous roar that, according to the Cox family, shook the house and sometimes rattled dishes on the shelves. The closer the better for Aunt Lizzy. She said to all in earshot, "That's my minister!" A flyby of that sort was as good as a visit. She told all those who came to the house about how I had flown by and often said, "I seen him come" or "I saw him go by." She could not see, but she heard the noise and knew I was making the pass over the house just for her.

The visits to Aunt Lizzy continued through the years. Through the grace of God, I was on my way to the Quebec North Shore at the time of her death and was able to conduct her funeral service. This meant a great deal to me because she was a special friend. I so enjoyed her honesty and direct-ness. She was quick to give me a hard time if she felt I had been away too long, but she had a way of teasing and chiding that reflected the special friendship we had.

Aunt Lizzy's spirited frankness caused problems with some of her other friends who missed coming to visit with her when they were in Aylmer Sound. When they stopped in at Aunt Lizzy's on a subsequent visit offering an apology, such as "I am sorry I missed you the last time. I had to get to Harrington for my dinner," or gave some other reasonable excuse, Aunt Lizzy would give them the most severe dressing down, reminding them that her minister, Mr Bryan, came to see her in spite of the fiercest weather condi-tions. This amused the Cox family and Aunt Lizzy's neighbors who were used to her ways, but was not always appreciated by the one who took the tongue-lashing.

During the last ten years of her life when she was almost totally blind and confined to a chair by the stove all day, her complaining at times became difficult for Jane, Victor and their children. Nonetheless, they cared for her, carrying on the remarkable tradition of concern for the elderly that is such a unique part of life on the Quebec North Shore.

In 1952, shortly after the Rev. Hollis H. A. Corey had retired from mission work in Japan and Hawaii, he heard that Archbishop Carrington "was looking for a vol-unteer to undertake the summer Labrador Mission." Thirty-three years earlier, Fr Corey and his wife had served on the Coast* and so, as he recounted in the Dioc-

---

* In 1962, the last of the Mission Boats was to be named the *Hollis Corey* in his honour. He was 69 years old at the time of the visit described; he died in the United States, aged 71.

esan Gazette, *he volunteered. With Leonard Buffit as boatman, he set out from Mutton Bay on 23 June, aboard the* Glad Tidings III.

The task the Lord Archbishop had assigned to me, was to visit every Anglican family on the 250 miles of coast-line belonging to St. Clement's Mission, and to see to it that every person had the opportunity to receive the Blessed Sacrament. This I think I accomplished. At least, I did not consciously miss a family nor an individual.

St. Clement's Mission ends at Blanc Sablon. But I felt I must renew acquaintance with our two Anglican strongholds just across the border, in territory belonging to the Diocese of Newfoundland. I therefore had a day and a night in L'Anse au Clair, and another day and night in Forteau, holding a full round of services in each place. L'Anse au Clair is 100% Anglican; and it is a joy to minister there. The people come in waves to Church, until nobody is left in the village. They begin to ring the bell thirty minutes before Service time, and ring it steadily till the Service begins.

Serving the people from one diocese or the other is a venerable tradition in this part of the world, and before the Rev. John P. Richmond's arrival, the people of St Clement's had been served, when possible, by the Rev. Edward Botwood of Newfoundland. When Richmond arrived at Blanc Sablon in October 1861, he and Botwood just missed each other. Botwood was on his way to Quebec "in one of LeBoutelliers vessels." In 1864, Frances Monck, sister-in-law of Viscount Monck, Governor-General of British North America, met Botwood (then doing duty at St Michael's, Sillery, and briefly to be curate there). She was fascinated by his tales of life on the Coast and recounted several in breezy, colloquial style.

Once winter sets in [she wrote], the people there are really dead to the world, for they never hear anything of any one till spring, and then only by chance. Letters are sometimes thrown on the shore from ships, and if any one picks them up they get them; if not, they don't ever get them. Mr. B's sister in London once wrote to him, and the letter did not reach him for sixteen months! He did not laud himself at all; our incessant questions found out all these facts. The G.G.* said it would be pleasant to him to look back on his Labrador life. He said, "Oh yes, I liked it; the hard work was pleasant!"... I fancy it was because of his wife that he gave it up; it was so terrible for her, he said.

---

* Governor General

Catherine Julia Botwood, a young lady from Quebec City, was a member of the prominent Hall family. She had married and had gone to the Coast during her husband's five-year stint of service there. "When he used to go out visiting," Monck recounted, "he said his wife was so nervous about him, as the sea rushes up in such a curious way, people are often suddenly drowned. The snow-storms are so violent that he had seen a sleigh ... with a team of twelve strong dogs, and with four men on it, overturned by the violence of the hurricane." Two of their children died, aged 2 months, 20 days, and 7 months, within a year and a half of each other. Finally, Mrs Botwood had returned to her father's house, and it was 18 months before her husband could rejoin her. Yet, in spite of these hardships and privations, Botwood undoubtedly longed to resume the Coastal ministry, if only for a visit.

On a later occasion, Frances Monck again reported having seen the Missionary. "Mr. B. is going to run down to Labrador some summer to see his people again [she wrote]. He loves them so, and they are very fond of him. He says the people are so hearty and hospitable down there."

PLATE 19 *Sketch map of the 250-mile coastline of St Clement's Mission, drawn by the Rev. H. H. Corey, for several years the incumbent at Mutton Bay.*

17

Selling the Pews: Bury
1862

R*aising funds to build, furnish, and maintain a church was usually a difficult undertaking, especially in the country districts where money was scarce. Most of the early churches followed the practice of renting pews to members of the congregation, the pews often being allocated by auction. Although there were usually some "free sittings" to accommodate those who wished to attend but could not or would not pay, some churches were entirely proprietary.*

Pew sale, with an ongoing yearly rental to maintain possession, was sanctioned in the Diocese well past the middle of the nineteenth century, and was often pressed upon a would-be parish. Under the Church Temporalities Act of 1843, Vestries (the governing bodies of churches) were to be formed by all the pew holders "whether holding the same by purchase or lease." It was also stipulated that the "absolute purchase" of any pew "shall be construed as a Freehold of Inheritance, not subject to forfeiture by change of residence, or by discontinuing to frequent the same." To those imbued with the democratic spirit—particularly common among settlers close to the American border—such practices seemed wrong. The following letter to Bishop G. J. Mountain, dated 5 July 1862 and signed by the churchwardens at Bury, voices their objection to transactions of this kind.

My Lord,

It is with the greatest diffidence that we venture to occupy your Lordship's attention for a few minutes.

After much trouble & great difficulties, with the liberal assistance of kind friends, we have, thank God, our New Church almost ready for Divine Service & our great regret is that it will not in the first instance be dedicated by your Lordship to the Author & giver of all good things.

When the subscription list was first opened it was understood that the Pews would be sold by auction subject to an upset price to be fixed by the Vestry—We have an objection to selling seats in God's House; we do not think it becoming reverence to Him to Whom they will belong. We cannot look upon it as right, even if legal, thus to alienate His property, neither do we consider that many persons would be willing to give the value of the pews.

We propose that a List of all paid subscriptions shall be submitted to a public meeting & that after setting apart a pew for the use of the Minister's family each subscriber shall choose a seat in order of his subscript^n beginning with those of the largest amount—each choice to be subject to the following conditions, to an Annual Rent to be fixed either by the Vestry or Minister & Churchwardens—that any person allowing the said seat to be in arrear, say for six months, shall forfeit the right to the seat.

That any person ceasing to occupy the said pew, whether by reason of removal from the Township or otherwise shall forfeit all right to the said Pew.

That all forfeited pews shall be disposed of as the Vestry or Minister & Churchwardens shall see fit.

That the Churchwardens shall have the right to put persons for that service into any sitting not occupied at the commencement of the First Lesson. We cannot willing[ly] be parties to any proceeding that will give any person real estate in what is called & should be *God's* House & we therefore respectfully request your Lordship's advice on these or any other points it may be necessary for us to know …

P.S. We forward this through Mr Kemp who will be able to give your Lordship any further information.

The Rev. John Kemp had been one of the original class of 10 students admitted to Bishop's College in its first year of operations, described by a classmate as "an untiring student, an omnivorous reader and a very able speaker." According to the Diocesan Clergy file, he was born in England and raised as a Methodist, emigrating with his family to Quebec in the 1840s. Bury was his first parish, to which he was appointed while still a deacon, in 1847.

In his mission of Bury and Tingwick, Kemp was responsible for three churches: St John's, St Thomas's, and the congregation at Robinson—the subject of the above letter. Although the records of this church date back to 1838 and the building was begun in 1844, its consecration as St Paul's did not take place until 3 July 1864. On 18 January 1903, St Paul's burned down. Rebuilding took only a year. During that period services were held in the old Methodist church.

It is worth noting that the system of rented pews was retained at the Cathedral of the Holy Trinity until the very end of the century. Having been pressed by some members of the Cathedral congregation to abandon or modify the proprietary nature of Cathedral sittings, Dean Norman, who was not in favour of the proposal, prepared a pamphlet "Printed for the Information of the Congregation," and on 29 Novem-

ber 1890 read it before the Select Vestry.

"To imperil our income, in order to offer free and unappropriated seats to our people would be a very questionable policy," Norman reasoned. "There remains also this problem, whether it be wise to abolish a system which has been in vogue, and not unsuccessfully on the whole, for many years, and introduce one diametrically and essentially opposed to it." After a long discussion of the question he concludes:

Public opinion is becoming more and more in favour of free seats in Churches. There are not a few, as we are told, who would gladly contribute their quota towards the maintenance of the Church, but who cannot afford to pay pew rent. They are very reluctant to avail themselves, as a frequency, of any vacant seats, and feel themselves as interlopers in a building where others enjoy vested rights. Such persons merit all kindly consideration, but the only way of meeting their needs that is perceptible to myself is to arrange that a certain number of pews in the Church, in good positions, should be free to all comers. The precise location of such pews might be left to the discretion of the Churchwardens, or decided by the select Vestry. This might be tried as an experiment, without interfering with the present arrangements of the Church.

The Dean resigned in 1899. Bishop A. H. Dunn, who had been unhappy about the managing of his Cathedral since his arrival in Quebec in 1892, approached Lennox W. Williams, then Rector of St Matthew's, Quebec, to be Norman's successor. Williams agreed to accept the appointment only on condition that pew rents in the Cathedral would be abolished and that the envelope system would be adopted to offset the loss of church revenue once all the seats were free.

Dissatisfaction with proprietary churches and the practice of pew rental as voiced by the people of Bury was also manifesting itself in the countryside to the north of Quebec City in the 1860s.

The parishioners of Christ Church, Valcartier, had initially adopted pew rental when their new church was built in 1864, and the rate for each pew had been determined by auction. The Vestry Book for that year gives the charges arrived at for 18 pews; £1-8-9 was the highest figure, paid by Col. Wolff, a member of the community's leading family, with amounts descending to ten shillings, which was the "upset price."* The Churchwardens' Reports filed for the parish show, however, that between 1865 and 1866 pew rental was abandoned at Christ Church. In that period the parish reported having gone from 26 pews rented and no free sittings to "all free sittings

---

* Lowest acceptable bid.

for 135."

On the subject of selling pews, Bishop Mountain had placed his views on record at least as early as 1851 in a circular to the clergy on the subject of church furnishings: "I do not at all hesitate to profess myself opposed, in principle, to the system of leased as well as of proprietary pews, which I believe will gradually disappear in Christian Churches—but it is a system recognized by law in this country and must be tolerated while it lasts."

18

An "Augustinian" Ordinand:
Labrador and Bourg Louis
1862-1863

W*hen men set out from England to be Anglican missionaries, if they went with the sponsorship of one of the great mission-ary societies—such as the SPG—they did so strictly at the request of a colonial bishop. As emigrant populations swelled, however, the demand was increasingly difficult to meet. Relatively few experienced British clergy could be persuaded to transplant them-selves and their families to the rugged conditions of a backwoods mission. Great ef-forts were made to attract ministers already in the colony (even to the extent of "raid-ing" other denominations to do so) or to train men on the spot, but local ordinands were few and far between. In 1844, St Augustine's Missionary College, Canterbury, was founded, better to meet the need for priests.*

The graduates of St Augustine's were prepared especially for missionary work but, although they underwent thorough examinations in theology, they were sent out unordained. This allowed each local bishop to examine his candidate before ordaining him, thereby taking responsibility for his qualifications. It also guaranteed that these graduates would not attempt to serve in England, as ordination by a colonial bishop was not held valid for the Church in the mother country.

The writer of the following excerpt, Frederick Cookesley, was "an Augustinian." According to Cookesley's father, himself a clergyman, the boy had set his heart on becoming a missionary at age five. It must have been a particular disappointment to him that, after successfully completing his training at St Augustine's and being adopted by the SPG as their Missionary for service in Natal, he found himself in the service of a bishop who neglected to ordain him.

After a year as a teacher and lay chaplain employed by Bishop Colenso, whose churchmanship seemed lax and whose views were later to be judged heretical, Cookesley secured permission to return home. There the SPG redirected him to missionary work in Canada. He sailed from Liverpool for Quebec on 4 September 1862. His diary recounts his reception, examination, and ordination by Bishop G. J. Mountain, all within four days of his arrival at Quebec.

18th [Sept. 1862]—Got up very early; found we were anchored at Point Louis [Point Lévi, presumably], opposite Quebec. Great confusion about luggage; after much trouble and bother got my things safely conveyed to the other side of the river, in a ferry-boat; drove to the house of Mr. Housman, the Bishop's examining chaplain. He gave me a paper on the Articles to answer, and desired me to write an essay on Isaiah liii. 12. I rode out to the Bishop's in a most shaky conveyance, called a calèche. The Bishop's palace is called Bardfield, about three miles from Quebec. Felt rather unhappy, but struggled prayerfully against my feelings, and received comfort. The Bishop conversed with me: he is a most loveable old man, and kindly welcomed me. In the evening he gave me the eleventh Article to put into Latin.

19th—Drove into Quebec with the Bishop. Attended Litany service in the private chapel attached to the Bishop's rooms. Mr. Housman gave me a paper to do on the Prayer-book, and another on the Old and New Testament. After waiting awhile, he told me my papers were "very satisfactorily done." I returned to Bardfield. In the evening the Bishop gave me a vivâ voce examination in the Greek Testament, and then told me that my examination was over, and that I had passed it most creditably. Give God the glory, who has thus far prospered my undertakings!

20th, Saturday—Dined with Mr. Hamilton; returned to the Bishop's in a carriage, which he had kindly sent for me; received pleasant consolation from the Bishop. Oh, blessed Lord, strengthen me for the solemn ordinance of to-morrow!

21st, Sunday—Rode into town with the Bishop and the Rev. Mr. Kennedy, from Toronto. Went to the Cathedral; the Rev. Dr. Adamson and the Revs. Messrs. Housman, Ward, and Kennedy assisted at the ordination. Was much impressed with the solemn service and the Bishop's sermon. May I ever fight as an officer in the army of the Lord of Sabaoth, and finally attain unto life eternal! Read the lessons in St. Michael's church, in the evening. Thus has passed the most eventful day of my life. May I never regret it! but look back upon it as the turning point of my life,—the seal of mine Apostleship. Oh, Lord, correct me, but in mercy: not in anger, lest thou bring me to nothing.

On September 23rd, Cookesley was aboard the schooner Marie Louise, *bound for Labrador, his first mission. He had been sent to Natal because of delicate health. Now his small frame was to be subjected to one of the harshest climates in the Diocese. His diary records his efforts to reach his parishioners in summer and winter along the 150-odd miles of coast for which he was responsible, distributing tracts and Bibles, doing what he could. He soon learned to use snowshoes and a komatik or dog-sled (which he calls a kommakik), and to signal by putting up a flag "on the hill near my house, in order to let the people know when I have service." As a mere deacon, however, he could not as yet administer the Sacraments.*

On 12 July 1863, Cookesley returned to Quebec to receive priest's orders and was examined together with another candidate, Anthony Aaron Von Iffland, who had been serving in Portneuf. Since Cookesley's last visit, Bishop Mountain had died. It was to Bishop J. W. Williams that he presented himself. "Went to the Bishop's to be examined," his diary records on 1 August. "Dr. Nicholls gave us a general paper; and then a severe vivâ voce examination on the Greek Testament and Scripture history. Thanks to the Great Disposer of all things, we passed. Lunched and dined at the Bishop's." On the following day, a Sunday, he was ordained at the Cathedral. The diary gives no details of the ceremony, but a letter written 28 August to the Warden of his old College does so, and also describes his new appointment nearer to Quebec.

On the 2nd of August I was admitted to Priest's orders, in the Cathedral at Quebec. Two others, graduates of Lennoxville, were ordained with me. It was Bishop Williams' first ordination. I need hardly tell you that it was a solemn and impressive time for all of us. I am sure you will not forget to pray that we may be kept in the right path, and be good stewards of the mysteries of the kingdom of heaven.

The Bishop did not wish me to return to Labrador this winter, because several missions in the diocese are vacant. He has therefore appointed me to take charge of the mission of Bourg Louis [in the parish of St Raymond], which has been vacant since Mr. Roberts was compelled by ill health to leave the diocese last winter. It is a mission of considerable extent, containing about eighty families, all engaged in farming.

The church is a very neat little wooden building, with a steeple surmounted by a plain cross. I came in a steamer part of the way, up the beautiful St. Lawrence, and was landed at a place called Port Neuf,—about four miles from which lives the missionary of the place, who was one of the candidates ordained with me. I staid at his house for three or four days, and then he very kindly drove me to Bourg Louis, about seventy [he means seventeen] miles distant. Immediately on my arrival I set out visiting all the people, which occupied me some days.... The Bishop came over last Sunday, and preached in the afternoon: the church was, I am happy to say, quite full. Our Synod passed off very satisfactorily: you will be able to see the proceedings in the Journal I am now sending you.... The hot weather is almost over in this country: we have had a most lovely summer: in two months' time we must look out for winter again.

Men are sadly wanted in this diocese: there are two or three missions now vacant, and no men to occupy them. I wish another Augustinian was coming to join us this autumn.

From the account left in his diary, Cookesley worked devotedly to build up his mission at Bourg Louis. His health, however, had been broken. By early January of the next year he was "unable to preach a sermon, and could scarcely get through the service." On 19 January he called on the Bishop, and it was decided that he should relinquish his charge. On 29 January 1865, having travelled to an ice-free port in the United States, Cookesley sailed for England, where he died in 1867.

In a letter to G. J. Mountain, dated 2 November 1862, a correspondent from St Augustine's (the writer's name is cut off by the binding) thanks the Bishop for news of their graduates. "It is most satisfactory to have the intelligence that our men are fulfilling the work for which they went out," he writes, and adds that Cookesley is "a single-hearted little fellow, with tolerable ability." The young ordinand, who was then on the Coast, seems to have made a lasting impression on the Bishop. "Poor little Cookesley," he said, as he lay on his deathbed, "God bless him in his work, and open the way for us there." Mountain's final utterance, "before he turned to bless his children and dependents," was the single word, "Labrador."

19

Questions of Ritual:
Bishops College, Lennoxville
1868

J asper Hume Nicolls, appointed in 1845 *as the first Principal of Bishop's College, was a graduate of Oriel College, Oxford, and had been an undergraduate when John Henry Newman was tutor and junior treasurer there. Not surprisingly, his churchmanship "was to some extent influenced by the Tractarians." G. J. Mountain, his Diocesan, uncle, and (since 1847) his father-in-law as well, was to remark privately that, although Nicolls was "a sound believer & a thoroughly & entirely conscientious & high-principled man & uncompromising Churchman," he saw in him "some leanings in Religion ... acquired at Oxford, which are not in perfect accordance with my own views upon those points."*

The following letter, dated at Bishop's College, 21 January 1868, from Nicolls to J. W. Williams, who had succeeded Mountain as Bishop in 1863, asks for clarification on what ritual he should sanction in light of the practices being introduced into services held in the College Chapel.

My dear Lord

I wish to ask your Lordship's advice upon certain changes in the celebration of Divine service which are creeping in amongst us here, which I have hitherto simply forborne from interfering with.

1. Turning towards (1) the East (or what should be the East) End of the Chapel or Church, or towards (2) the Altar during the repetition of the Creed.

2. A like position during the doxologies after the psalms.

3. A like posture during the singing of hymns.

Some turn on all these occasions, some on the two last, some on the first only.

4. The repetition of the responses and Amens to a musical note, when the service is merely read.

5. Bowing at the name of Jesus throughout the service (I am aware, of course, of the authority for this).

6. Standing up while the offertory collection is making.

7. The joining aloud in the words of the [word illegible] only in the Holy Communion Office, allowing the Priest to repeat by himself the words which precede "Therefore with Angels—saying."

I do not myself attach the importance, pro or con, to these little matters which some do, and hitherto I have not interfered with them (either as regards Chapel or Church) so as to give any directions about them: tho' I have once or twice expressed opinions upon some of them. But I cannot but feel that the beauty & solemnity of the services are marred and disturbed by this variety of practice, and that in our Chapel, if anywhere in the Diocese, we ought to have uniformity.

However I see no way of dealing with them, either one way or other, effectually with any authority that I understand myself to be invested with at present. Nor am I clear that I can do better (unseemly as the thing may be) than "let them alone"—

I write therefore to have the benefit of your Lordship's advice, or order, upon the subject whether I should do anything, and if so, what?

I should also wish to know whether it would be desirable that I should meet the wishes of a great many of the pupils of the Institution, as well as of some of the Officers of it, by having the service intoned either (1) regularly or (2) occasionally.

Believe me, my dear Lord

Faithfully & respectfully yours

Jasper H. Nicolls

In the early days of the Tractarian Movement, such leading men as Newman and Pusey had not been sympathetic to changes "of trivial detail which might offend" or to "unnecessary provocation in ceremony." By the 1860s, however, cauterized by riots and disruption in British churches, the older Puseyite austerity and fear of ceremonial began to vanish; for, as Chadwick suggests, restraint was now associated with cowardice and lack of principle.

Anglo-Catholics had become "a party of fighters," and with the organization of the English Church Union in 1859-60, the "ritual troubles" began in earnest. Nicolls, more Catholic in his sympathies than Mountain had been, was himself separated by a generation from the practices of the Anglo-Catholics that appear to have been surfacing at the College under his care.

Williams seems to have taken particular interest in the churchmanship of the clergy in the Diocese as well as of those proposing to enter it. He asked for specific information on the subject of anyone applying to him for a parish from outside his jurisdiction. The answer to one such enquiry, by a young Gloucestershire clergyman who had been serving for a short time in Cleveland, Ohio, shows some discomfiture over such questions. The applicant probably assumed that, if he embraced the wrong party, his application would be refused. After describing himself as a moderate High-Churchman he concluded as follows: "I am sorry, My Lord, that I cannot better define my views, but it is one of those things that are most difficult to do by letter ... Perhaps if I state that I shall consider myself bound by the direction & wishes of my Bishop, both in points of Doctrine & Ritual, so long as I am in his Diocese, whether they are agreeable or the reverse to myself—I shall better answer your question." Such an attitude to doctrine and ritual was the very opposite of that associated with the Anglo-Catholicism surfacing at Bishop's College.

20

Parish Endowments: Nicolet
1868

The objects of the Church Society of the *Diocese of Quebec as outlined in the Constitution adopted 21 July 1842 were five in number: missionary labour; education; assistance to those preparing for the ministry; circulation of the Holy Scriptures, the Book of Common Prayer and other religious books; aid towards the erection of churches and parsonages, "and the management of all matters relating to endowment of the same."*

It was hoped that through the formation of District Associations "all the members of the Church, rich and poor," would be drawn into "the free and full exercise of enlarged Christian beneficence." Influential members of the laity, many of whom contributed generously to the Society, were encouraged to show their concern for their community in giving and earmarking special funds to form local endowments for the church.

Such was the case in Nicolet. Of the 18 designated contributions recorded in the first Annual Report of the Church Society, two were put towards "building a Parsonage House at Nicolet": the subscribers were listed as R. C. Chandler and F. (probably a misprint for T.) Trigge. By 1845, there had been established in conjunction with the Church Society a Nicolet Endowment Fund that amounted to £100 / 2 / 6.* T. Trigge is named as paying into it a life subscription of £12 / 10 / 0.

Nicolet, which fell into the District of Three Rivers, did not attract English settlement. The Protestant population was consequently small and tended to decline. By 1868 it was decided that the region did not merit a resident clergyman and would best be served by the visits of a Travelling Missionary. The following is part of a letter to Bishop J. W. Williams from H. W. Trigge, dated at Nicolet, 31 March 1868:

My dear Lord Bishop,

I have to acknowledge the receipt of Your Lordship's letter of the 23[d] instant, in which you inform me that at a meeting of the Central Board of the Church Society, held on the 19th instant, it was moved that a

---

* In the 1840s many of the Diocesan clergy were expected to live on £100 a year; Nicolet's endowment was a large one for the period.

sum not exceeding $200 should be paid from the revenues of the Nicolet Endowment fund to provide the services of a clergyman. Your Lordship adds that you had mentioned what I had stated in my letter of the 5th instant, viz., that the fund could not be touched for any but a resident minister; that this had been denied; that it was maintained that the fund is held in trust by the Church Society without any condition of the kind; that the Board, moved by others than your Lordship, and in the exercise of its right & in the discharge of its responsibility, had decided that the disbursement ought to be made; and that the vote had been passed accordingly. Your Lordship is good enough to intimate further that you have authorized the Revd O. Fortin to visit among the people and to celebrate Divine Service in Nicolet Church on every alternate Sunday—assigning him $140 out of the sum voted by the Central Board.

I regret the action thus taken by the Central Board, considering it to have been precipitate, and calculated to lead to results other than desirable. Had the Board before coming to a decision, afforded me the opportunity which it is usual to grant in such cases, of explaining the grounds upon which I had advanced the objection contained in my letter to your Lordship, it would, I think, have been in a position better enabling it to have rendered justice in the premises.

I shall now endeavor to show Your Lordship that it was not wholly without cause that I advanced the statement "that the Nicolet Endowment fund was established for the special purpose of maintaining a *resident* clergyman here, and that any payment out of its revenues towards other purposes could not properly be authorized."

Your Lordship is probably aware that this fund owes its origin to my late father, who started it five & twenty years ago, when, unless I am mistaken, there was not such a thing as a local Endowment fund in connection with the Church within the Diocese. From the date of its inception in 1843 up to the date of his death in 1863 he did not cease to watch over it, contributing continually to its development, and that without stint, both his time and his substance. In evidence of this, if evidence be wanting, I may refer to the Church Society's own recognition of the fact, as it stands recorded in the published reports, for example at p. 16 of the report for 1852 & at pp. 32 & 38 of that for 1863. Now, I wish to shew what his understanding of the object of the fund was. That he told me repeatedly that it was established especially for the maintenance of a resident minister here, may possibly be objected to as hearsay evidence. Happily he has left behind him something to which this objection cannot be made. I have the original subscription list before me. Its heading is in my father's handwriting, and commences as follows: "Nicolet 6 January 1843. Subscriptions to the Church Society. To be appropriated to the special purposes of forming a fund toward the support of a resident clergyman at Nicolet"... *[Trigge goes on to quote from his father's list of Rules to govern the Fund, stipulating the reinvestment of interest not used to pay a resident minister and finally a relevant passage from a legacy to the fund in his father's Will.]*

There are of course other considerations connected with a question of this kind which ought not to be lost sight of, such as the legal right of every contribution to a special fund to demand the absolute fulfilment of the conditions upon which the money is subscribed, and the impolicy of the Church Society sanctioning any course likely to weaken, even in the smallest degree, public confidence in the strict impartiality of its administration of the local funds committed to its keeping. But I refrain from dwelling upon these points now.

Trigge's father, besides supporting this local endowment, had served for many years as a Treasurer of the Church Society, there being one for Montreal (Mr T. B. Anderson) and one for Quebec.

The name of the Rev. Mr Fortin came up in Trigge's earlier letter to the Bishop. Rather than have the clergyman's expenses paid out of the Endowment Fund, Trigge had initially offered to assume them himself: "On this point I expressed myself distinctly to Mr Fortin when he broached the subject during his last visit here. I told him … I would undertake to send for him & to send him back, free of charge, and that he should be welcome to such accommodation as the Manor House could offer during his stay."

Fortin also wrote to the Bishop. His letter was full of complaints and centred entirely on the cost and difficulty of travel to Nicolet.

In the first place I have to pay a Carter two and a half dollars each trip besides the ferries which amount to twenty-five cents—my hotel bill also amounts to one dollar and more each trip—then the people are very much scattered, some of them living at a distance of fifteen miles from Nicolet. To visit there I must hire Carters all which will very materially diminish the thirty-five pounds which your Lordship gives me for my services there—I therefore pray your Lordship to give me the remaining fifteen pounds which were accorded by the Board. I think I need say nothing more to show that fifty pounds are not too much for what I am doing—Besides I must say that during the fall and spring I shall not be able to get carters under three dollars a trip, the roads being very bad in this part of the country.

In 1869, the Rev. Joseph de Mouilpied was appointed to Nicolet as resident minister. A Channel Islander trained at St Bee's, de Mouilpied's testimonials to the Bishop (presented with his application to enter the Diocese in 1855) had stressed that, "from his knowledge of the French language," he "hopes to become a useful minister." He had previously served in the Gaspé, at Malbaie.

De Mouilpied's Annual Reports to the Church Society tell the story of the Anglican population at Nicolet, most of whom had moved on, died out, or been absorbed. "There are only three church families in this once prosperous congregation of Nicolet, while there are 6 Protestants distributed in so many families at St Monique and at Chatillon, a distance of 8 and 15 miles from Nicolet," he wrote in 1870. "At the request of a member of the church we had a funeral service conducted in French. Some 30 or 40 Canadians* assisted, who sat composedly for a half hour or so, while I addressed our own people, who all understand the French Language."

His attempts to visit among the local Roman Catholics "at their own request, for religious conversation" seem to have been "misunderstood by those very parties who had suggested them" and were apparently discontinued. "I have visited, at stated intervals, the scattered members belonging to us," he wrote. "I have administered the Lord's Supper to an old member, 14 miles from Nicolet, and my presence at his house is always welcomed."

---

* "Canadian," at this period, almost invariably meant French Canadian.

21

Expanding the Church:
From Cookshire to Randboro
1884

Arthur Horner Judge was ordained by J. W. Williams to the diaconate in 1882 and to the priesthood in 1883. Judge's first charge was Cookshire, a large district centred in the village of that name, with a parish church dating back to about 1815 and a second church some miles distant.

One would assume that by the 1880s the Anglican population within such a parish would have been identified and incorporated somehow into the circuit of visiting performed by the incumbent. However, as the following letter, directed to the SPCK, makes clear, this was not the case. Because the writer hoped to gain the Society's aid, he took pains to introduce himself and the circumstances surrounding his appeal. The result is a vivid and engaging account of missionary activity in the late nineteenth century.

 My parish of Cookshire, to which I was inducted on the 1st of July 1882, is of very large extent, covering some 300 square miles of country. I had been regularly ministering to my people at the village of Cookshire and Island Brook, some eight miles apart, but as I grew to know my cure better, I discovered in a most obscure corner of it a small colony of English Church-people, at a little hamlet called Randboro. If you will permit I will tell their story plainly and shortly.

Hearing of this small village, I harnessed my horse and set out one morning to find it. After driving some nine and a half miles I came to the place, and, stopping at the house of one of the settlers, who proved to be a Churchman, I remained only long enough to make myself known and appointed a day when I would come again to see them, and also baptize his little infant daughter; then I hastened homewards to fulfil an engagement for the evening at Cookshire, my headquarters.

On the day set I again sought my new-found friends, and when about noon I came to the log house, there were a number of waggons drawn up in the farmyard, and on entering the house, to my surprise I found some 15 people there, all gathered to welcome me, and having with them all the unbaptized Church children of the neighbourhood. In conversation with these people I learned that for *thirteen years* they have been absolutely without the ministrations of their Church. Isolated here on the very border of the forest, they had, owing to a combination of circumstances, been without spiritual blessings. The nearest place of worship to them was a Methodist chapel three miles distant, and beyond that a Congregationalist chapel six miles away. In spite of the influence of Dissent, they remained firm to the good old Church, though, I was told, some had fallen away. Before I left them that day all the children were received into the Church, and the promise of a monthly service made. One month later the first Church of England service was held in the school-house at Randboro, and that night I preached to over 100 people, crowded together within the narrow limits of a country school-house. So enthusiastically was the service received that a monthly service was firmly established, and since then I have had every reason to be thankful for the zeal, the delight, and the deep interest shown in the work. The body of Churchmen have been most staunch, and many Dissenters have been attracted to us. So great was the encouragement that three months ago a meeting was called, which resulted in the resolution to build a church. An excellent site was settled upon and given to us, and plans of a correct and pretty church adopted, and also my proposition gladly accepted. The latter was this: that if they would give $500 in money and build a foundation—at least $100 worth—I would be responsible for the other $500 necessary to the church's completion. If you could have seen the joy of these men when what I have just told you was settled, and the happy delighted way in which they talked it all over in perfect accord, each yielding any little private desire for the general good, your sympathy would be with them in this effort.

I have only now to say that the people have, with great self-denial, made up their $500, and I do not think they can do more. They are a small band among a much larger Dissenting population, and from these latter no help has been obtained ... So earnestly did my people beg that a church might be built, that I felt that I must become responsible for $500, seeing that they had made so great an effort on their part ... Of the $500 (£100 sterling) I undertook to collect for them, I have acquired $125, and shall receive $100 from the Church Society of Quebec. If then, you can grant us any sum either above or below the £20 I have ventured to suggest, we shall be deeply grateful ...

The church, to be of wood on a foundation of stone, was to furnish 135 "kneelings."
Judge described the congregation as "farmers, generally well-to-do, but without ready

money."

The SPCK required all applications for funds to be forwarded with an endorsement by the Bishop. Williams' accompanying support for the project placed due emphasis on the personal qualities and initiative of the applicant. "Mr Judge is one of our most efficient missionaries recently ordained," he wrote, " and I have no doubt that his faithfulness, energy, and attractiveness will build up and establish a congregation in the settlement at Randboro. I shall be very glad, therefore, if the Society can grant the aid he asks for." The Minute Book of the SPCK records that the Standing Committee recommended a grant of £20, the maximum requested. This sum was duly voted.

It was not unusual for a clergyman to assume personal responsibility for the construction of a church in his parish and literally to go begging for the necessary funds. The accounts, dated 1849, of the Rev. William King for building the Dudswell Road Church, Bury, offer another excellent example of the frequent risk of personal indebtedness assumed by clergy in the rural districts (see Window 25).

The Randboro church, dedicated to St Matthew, was built in 1884 and consecrated by Williams on 7 July 1886. Judge, who did not remain in the parish of Cookshire beyond 1888, is listed in the Diocesan clergy file as "still living in U.S. ... our oldest surviving priest" in 1942.

22

A Parish Complaint:
Grindstone
1886

Joseph William Norwood's first parish in the Diocese was the Magdalen Islands, to which he was licensed in September 1885. He does not seem to have actually arrived on the Islands until 1886; his son, Joseph R. Norwood, took up residence immediately, however, and served as Lay Reader until his father came. Shortly thereafter, Bishop Williams received a Memorandum bearing 17 signatures complaining about Norwood's ministry on the Islands.

The Bishop responded on 19 May that his regret at the reception of this communication was equalled only by his surprise, in light of the testimony he had received of Mr Norwood's "character, efficiency, and soundness in the faith," from the clergyman's previous Diocesan and former congregations. Since, as the Bishop pointed out, the protest did not state "any specific offence with which he is charged," he had sent Norwood a copy of the document for comment. The following, dated Grindstone Island, 26 May 1886, is part of Norwood's reply:

My Lord,

Receive my thanks for the copy of the petition & also for the kindly manner in which you mention my name in answer to the Petition.

With reference to the petition I can say that the names attached are all that could be obtained after many weeks of labor.

Three of the signers are Baptists & one a Presbyterian. Only one name could be obtained from Gross Isle ... None could be obtained from Entry, from Amherst or from the other outlying districts.

There has been no ritual used by me in any of the Churches but what is in strict conformity with the plainest teaching of the Prayer Book. It is true that I have visited some of the Clergy of the Church of Rome, but every visit was made in the capacity of a doctor & I have had the pleasure of restoring to almost perfect health one of these gentlemen who was very near death's door & for this I have received their grateful thanks. I can with pleasure refer your lordship to these gentlemen as to the character of my visits to them & to their congregations. Those who have lost the benefits of our Holy

Church this Winter are those only of the petitioners who were habitual in their neglect of the Church during incumbency of former pastors.... I have visited Gross Isle seven times, holding services there each time. Once I sent my son who read the services & one of my sermons. Amherst I have visited three times, each time making the circuit of the island in response to the call of the sick. I have visited Entry Island five times, holding services every day during my stay. The wife of one of the petitioners was visited by me during a time when she was very ill. I not only provided medicine for her but food also when she was destitute. I gave her husband wood off the land enough to build a house. I gave him glass, window boxes & sashes. I procured for him employment when he was out of food & money. With this man the great mass of the people are indignant at what they call his meanness. Others of the petitioners I have helped in their sickness. From their own report keeping away from the Church the petitioners are unable to judge the character of the services held.... And now my Lord in conclusion I believe, was a petition to be gotten up, as has been suggested, praying that I should remain here, that nearly every one on these Islands, French & English; Roman & Anglican with the exception of those whose names are on the petition which your lordship has received [would sign it.]

   With sincere regret that there should be any disturbance ...
   Joseph W. Norwood

P.S. I am happy to state to your lordship that in the face of the opposition made by the petitioners the amount due the Diocesan Board of Missions ($18.) was very readily & cheerfully made up by the parishioners & forwarded last week.

Norwood's account of the service he had rendered in his parish is independently borne out by a letter from James Cassidy, Lighthouse Keeper and member of the congregation on Entry Island. "I was highly astonished when I heard [of] the petition ... signed by some of the people of Grindstone Island," he wrote to the Bishop on 24 June 1886; "I can conscientiously say that there has never yet been one that was so much fitted for the work on these Islands."

   From Cassidy's letter it becomes clear that, far from exaggerating his contribution to the health and well-being of the Islanders, Norwood had neglected to mention that his services had been offered without charge. "During the long winter months," the letter continues, "he has been attending to the wants of the sick and suffering, in the doctoring both of French and English, free gratis.... All the inhabitants of the other Isles— with the majority of that [on]Grindstone speak of him in the highest terms of praise."

Despite widespread support for his ministry, Norwood's initial request for a transfer, made during the unpleasantness surrounding the petition, was accepted. "The Missionary on these Islands," he wrote to the Church Society; "must bear the qualifications of a doctor, a sailor, and a preacher." The duty, with its "many journeys by day and by night" subject to "storm, wet and delay" and "the tender mercies of frozen fields of broken ice" had been difficult to sustain. "I have been a Missionary among the Savages of Africa, and also among the Indians and Cow-boys of the 'Far West,'" Norwood's Report continued, "and I am compelled to believe that this field is the very hardest one that I have ever labored in...." The next year found him in Shigawake, where he described himself as "very much encouraged by the kindly attitude and devotion of the people" of his three congregations, but by 1891, his name no longer appeared among those of the Diocesan clergy.

23

A Parish Complaint:
Drummondville
1887

Frederick George Scott's first parish in the Diocese was Drummondville. He had studied at Bishop's College and was ordained deacon by Bishop J. W. Williams in 1884, but did not take up duties in the Diocese of Quebec until 1887, having assisted prior to this in Montreal and later in England, where he was ordained priest.

It seems that Scott had arrived in his new parish on 10 February and, by Easter, had got into difficulties with some members of his congregation at St George's Church, including the influential Watts family. The bone of contention was Scott's preaching, notably his sermons on the nature of the Eucharist. A complaint to the Bishop had been filed. Most of the parishioners seem to have stood behind their rector, however. Others had forwarded a counter-protest to the Bishop, together with a copy of a Resolution in support of Scott, passed on 11 April 1887 at the Easter Monday Vestry Meeting.

Before dealing with Scott, Williams appears to have consulted with the previous rector, the Rev. F.J.B. Allnatt, who had left St George's in 1885 for St Matthew's, Quebec, but had since been appointed Professor of Pastoral Theology at Bishop's College. Each then wrote to the young man. The Bishop instructed Scott to read his letter to the assembled congregation in an effort to rectify the situation and clear the air.

When a second protest from the same quarter reached the Bishop, Williams once again addressed himself to the problem and wrote to Scott, questioning him on the specific charges laid. Were people staying away from church? Was there talk of establishing another place of worship? What was he actually preaching about the Eucharist, and what changes in ritual had he introduced? The following excerpt comes from Scott's letter, dated 4 November 1887, replying to the Bishop's enquiries about this second complaint. As was characteristic of Scott throughout his ministry, he expressed himself boldly on matters of conscience and paid little heed to how his views might be received.

After admitting that "some did abstain from coming to church after Easter" and affirming that "the movement towards the establishment of another place of worship here is not new," Scott came to the question of doctrine and ritual:

3. As to this point, I question Mr. Watts' capacity to judge of doctrine. I need only say, there has been nothing said in the church but what was in accord with church of England doctrine, & I am quite ready to forward ye my sermons which are written in full, for your inspection.

Mr Watts *falsely* states that I have acted against your letter on the doctrine of the Holy Eucharist. What I told the people, on reading your letter publicly to them, was exactly what ye & Mr Allnatt said in your respective letters. One may hold the doctrine of the objective Presence of our Blessed Lord's Body & Blood (I did not tell them of course in these words) as a *private* opinion in the church of England, & that I did so, but that it could not be distinctly enforced upon the people as an article of her teaching, but I added that we ALL had to believe the *fact that in some way or other,* left open to us, in the Eucharist *we became partakers of Christ's Body & Blood,* & that should such an expression as this "We who have received our Lord's blessed Body & Blood," recur, as it would probably in my sermons, the manner in which we have thus received them it was to be understood was left to the congregation as individuals. I said, "I held my view on the subject & that I was not alone in holding it, as it was also the opinion of some of our Bishops & great Divines," but as the Bp of Quebec says I have gone beyond the distinct statements of the formularies of our Church, I am sorry. It was only because of the trouble that I touched upon the subject.

As to ritual all that I do is to bow to the Altar on entering & leaving the church, not at other times now (Mr Scarth at Lennoxville does as much), and I take the Holy Communion, I fancy, in the same manner as they do at St Matthews, or as Mr Allnatt did here. We have ordinary bread on every 1st Sunday in the month. As to modification your Lordship knows enough of human nature to know that compromise for the sake of pleasing people in the congregation never works well. At the time of the trouble, my only course was to stand firm.

When Allnatt was preparing to leave Drummondville to take up new duties, he had written to the Bishop as follows on 31 March 1885: "I feel somewhat anxious, of course, as to the future of Drummondville. During the short time that remains, I intend to strive with might & main to get the parish on its legs as regards its financial position.... It is certainly an easy parish—only one church & the whole congregation within reach of it—at least ⅔ of the people within 3 miles of the church. At the same time it is a parish that needs a careful hand,—or the Dissenters will soon be making

attempts upon it." Before Scott had arrived at St George's, there had been two cler-
gymen serving the parish in the interval between himself and Allnatt. The finances of
the church had deteriorated and the endowment had been dipped into. At first some
of the disapproving members of Scott's congregation tried to bring him to heel "by simply
starving him out," as he had affirmed to the Bishop.

Scott was to remain in Drummondville throughout the remainder of J. W.
Williams' episcopate. In 1896, he resigned, and in September left the parish to be-
come curate to Lennox Williams at St Matthew's, Quebec. In his last report to the
Church Society for Drummondville (1896), which shows the greatly improved financial
position of the parish, Scott writes:

The Services this year. have been carried on as usual, and the attendance at
them has been as in previous years. The plan of taking the late celebration
of the Holy Communion on the first Sunday of each month, without making a pause after the prayer for the Church Militant in which the non-communicants should retire, has been found to be most beneficial. Hardly any
one ever leaves the Church; and thus young and old, communicants and
non-communicants, are present at the offering of the Great Memorial Sacrifice, and I trust are beginning to realize the joy of Eucharistic worship.

24

"Visitation by Land & Sea"
1887

I*n the summer of 1887, Bishop J. W. Williams visited Gaspé, Labrador, and the Magdalen Islands, all in the same year— the first time that he, or any previous bishop, had managed to do so. This was accomplished because Dr Wakeham, Commander of the Government steamer* La Canadienne, *had offered to give the Bishop and his chaplain passage in his ship from Gaspé Bay to Grindstone Island, with stops along the coast of Labrador.*

According to an account of the Visitation written by the Rev. Albert Stevens of Hatley, who accompanied the Bishop and acted as his chaplain, the eight days prior to their departure aboard La Canadienne *had been spent "in a tour around the Gaspé Bay," where the Bishop "had confirmed 300 candidates, delivered 26 addresses, and travelled over 300 miles, by boat, steam and carriage."*

They had begun at Gaspé Basin, where the Rev. J. P. Richmond had welcomed them at the wharf. Other clergy mentioned along their way were the Rev. Joseph Eames of Sandy Beach, Sydney Radley-Walters of Point St Peter, William Gore Lyster of Cape Cove, W. V. Lloyd of Shigawake, and Thomas Blaylock of New Carlisle.

On Monday, 11 July, the Bishop and his Chaplain left the Admiral, *by which they had reached the Gaspé, and boarded* La Canadienne. *On the 13th they entered the harbour at Natashquan (which Stevens calls Natasquin). Here follows a passage from the Chaplain's account of their visit to the various stations on the Coast:*

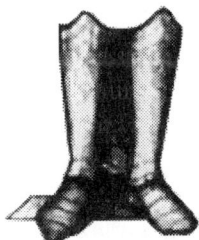

Here [at Natashquan] is a large fishing house, but it was closed and there was only one man who was left in charge. This has all the characteristics of the Labrador country, bare granite rocks without vegetation of any kind. Not a tree or a shrub is visible, and in some parts there is not soil enough upon many acres to grow one blade of grass. We found here several bags full of papers and letters for the people along the coast, which was taken in charge by Commander Wakeham.

Thursday morning we went to Wolf Bay, and the Commander took us in his boat to the house of Mr. Gilbert Jones, about five miles from where the steamer anchored. We had Service and the Bishop preached. There were seven present, among them an English gentleman, who had been spending some time on the coast in hunting. It would be impossible to imagine a more lonely life than these people lead, but they seem to prefer it to any other. We returned to the ship in the evening, taking with us some fresh codfish for dinner.

The next day we went on to Harrington and found there letters from the missionary, the Rev. Josiah Ball. He had been here and spent three or four weeks and had prepared a class for Confirmation. There are fourteen families in the place. We went ashore and visited some of the people, and in the evening had Service in the house of Mr. Daniel Bobbit.

The next day we went on to Mutton Bay, a village with fourteen families, calling at two houses to give notice of the Sunday Service. The Service ... on Sunday morning was held in the Mission House—the lower part being used for a dwelling and a school room, and the upper room for a Church. A large congregation assembled, and six were confirmed. We intended to hold Service in the evening, but as the Commander had finished his business and the day was fine he felt compelled to hurry on. Sometimes fogs come on and they are detained for several days ... Immediately after the Service we bade the People "good-bye" and proceeded on our journey. The day was fine, the sea calm, and it was just cool enough to be comfortable on deck without an overcoat.

Nothing could be more delightful than our journey that Sunday afternoon. The hundreds of islands, the narrow passages and rigolettes, through which we steered, the various forms of the red granite rocks of the coast devoid of trees or verdure, the numerous birds swimming or flying, now and then an iceberg in the distance, here and there the hut of some solitary fisherman ...

At six o'clock we anchored off the mouth of the St. Augustine river, near the house of Mr. Kennedy. The Bishop intended to have had Service here, but we found a young man in the house sick with a fever and quite delirious. So we had prayers with the family and for the sick man, and after Dr. Wakeham had prescribed for him, we left for the ship.

Monday morning we proceeded to Old Fort Bay, and met Captain Tripp, a Gaspé whaler. We boarded his ship and gave him letters from home. A few days before our arrival they had harpooned a large whale of the variety known as the "Sulphur," drawn him to the shore and tried out the blubber, from which they took seventy-two barrels of oil. The Commander took us over to see the skeleton, and an immense one it was. We found an

Esquimaux and a Frenchman picking the bones for dog food.

That afternoon we went in to Stick Point. Mr Ball had been there just two weeks beforehand and had prepared several candidates for Confirmation. Here there were more signs of life and business. Just across the Bay was a large fish guano manufactory. Several schooners were in sight, and small boats were continually passing laden with salt and fish offal, and fishermen were going to and from visiting their traps and nets. Tuesday evening we had Service and Confirmation in Mr Goddard's house.

In the passages that follow, Stevens continues to intersperse his description of the "business of the Visitation" with the passing scene. Accounts of recreation are not lacking. When the Ship's Engineer "wished to clean the boilers," for example, a fishing party was organized up the river. "The Bishop hooked a fine salmon, and landed him safely, and his chaplain, as was right, caught a smaller one."

The ship then proceeded to the Magdalen Islands where candidates prepared by the Rev. Joseph Norwood were confirmed at Grindstone and Entry Islands, and visits paid to Grosse Isle and Amherst Island as well.

Before leaving for the Magdalens, they had hoped to meet Ball, who was himself visiting the Coast, but they missed each other at Blanc Sablon, which Ball had left for Forteau, in the Diocese of Newfoundland.

Ball's report to the Church Society reveals that this was his first season on the Coast. He had arrived not much more than a month before the Bishop's visit, and the tradition of the place was full of interest for him:

The great difference in numbers attending the services now and formerly [Ball wrote of Mutton Bay] was frequently the subject of remark by the older members of the little community. During Rev. Mr. Hepburn's incumbency the Mission House was filled ... But those were the palmy days of the fishing interests, and the additional attendants were supplied by the schooners' crews from Newfoundland and Nova Scotia, who came annually to the coast to fish. As many as fifty and sixty vessels have been anchored at one time in Mutton Bay, and each having a crew of from eight to twenty men aboard. Now not more than two or four schooners are seen at any one time, having Protestant crews, and these remain only a week or two.

Ball had come to the coast prepared for river travel, but with the added warning that the present Mission Boat was "unseaworthy." He found on his arrival, however, that the old North Star "had been repaired and treated to a new coat of paint" and so set off on his first voyage in her.

My cruise was rather a rough one. We had to beach the boat at Esquimo Island, during a fog, on the eastern trip, and returning came very nearly being wrecked in attempting to round Point Geroux during a gale; much of the inconvenience was occasioned in consequence of my pilot's inexperience with the coast. He was unacquainted with the inner run, so, in order to avoid rocks and shoals, kept out to the open sea. Since the old pilot left, no one is willing to go for the same wages ...

I arrived back at Mutton Bay, just seven weeks from starting.

On Stevens' return home to Hatley, "having been absent just seven weeks," he calculated that he had travelled 3,000 miles, "half by land and half by sea." Before breaking off his narrative, he cast his mind back over the travel arrangements he and the Bishop had enjoyed. "In other years," he observed, "the Bishop has had to go the whole distance along the coast in an open boat without conveniences of any kind, and exposed to all kinds of weather.... I trust that in the years to come he may be able to make his Visitation in the same comfortable manner as this year."

25

A Ministry to the Native People:
Pointe Bleue
1889 and 1932

I*n the Quebec Diocesan Archives is a hard-cover exercise book, titled on its spine* Pointe Bleue. *Its first 27 pages are written in the crisp, clear hand of the Rev. H. C. Stuart, Rector of Trois-Rivières. Several darkened newspaper clippings, carefully dated and identified, are pasted in here and there among the later passages. A second narrative on four separate sheets—each stuck across a double page—written in a smaller, more tightly-spaced but still legible scrawl, is preceded by a letter in yet another hand.*

This book, minutely and devotedly recorded, gives the history of the Church of Saint John the Divine, serving the small summer population of Cree "on the Montagnais Reserve, Lake St. John, P.Q." It was begun by Stuart, whose initiative had also started the mission. Sometime after Stuart's death—of typhoid fever, in 1909—Bishop Lennox W. Williams, as his addition to the narrative explains, asked the Rev. Phillip Callis to pick up the story where it had broken off. "This he has done," the Bishop remarks, "in a most interesting way. The whole account will be of great historical value."

The following excerpt is drawn from Stuart's account. After an interval of more than one hundred years, some of the expressions used may grate on the modern ear, but the interest and importance of the record is undeniable nonetheless.

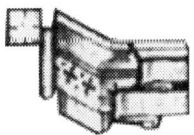

In the spring of 1889 [the narrative begins] I received a letter from Mrs. John Cummins, wife of the Agent of the Hudson Bay Company, stationed at Pointe Bleue, on the Montagnais Reserve, Lake St. John, requesting me to go there for the purpose of baptising her little boy. She stated that there were on the Reserve several families of Church Indians, for whom she had been in the habit of reading prayers every Sunday during their Summer stay at the Post, for the past eight years.

I at once acceded to her request, and visited the Hudson Bay post, where I was astonished to find several Indians, members of the Church of England, who had taken to farming, and still more astonished to find that quite a large number of Indians of the same faith, who were then absent on their trapping expedition, had made their headquarters at Lake St. John for some thirty or forty years.

The French half-breeds, or Montagnais Indians, outnumbered our Indians by seven to one, perhaps ten to one. During all these years, clever Oblate missionaries had conducted missions at the post every Summer, and done their best to make converts of our Indians, but without success. The only clergymen of their own church our Indians ever saw were the missionaries who preached missions annually at Lake Mistassini. There their children were baptized. Some of the children, however, were taken to Rupert's House for this purpose. The Indians specially mentioned Bishop Horden, and Archdeacon Vincent. The Missions north of Lake St. John are in the Diocese of Moosonee. When the Hudson Bay Company first opened its posts on the shores of Hudson Bay, the Company's agents at the various posts read service on Sundays, and through their agency the bulk of the Indians in that region at any rate became Christians. The families of our Indians have been Christians several generations.

Having had service among these people, I was deeply interested in them, and made arrangements to visit them every month.

During the Summer of 1889 I preached a 12-day's mission among them, and I doubt if any mission was ever better attended.... [It] was brought to a fitting close by the Confirmation of some eighteen Indians. The Company's store was utilized as a church, but for the Confirmation we put some timbers across two buildings and covered them with grey cotton, carpeting the ground with green sapin boughs. This place was cool and delightful in the clear Summer weather ... The Bishop consecrated the little Indian cemetery at this period.

At this point Stuart breaks off his own narrative to quote from Bishop J. W. Williams' 1890 Annual Report to the SPG, an account which adds considerable detail.

A missionary field, not large, but of great interest, has developed itself within the last few years. The Rev. H. C. Stuart, then the Society's Missionary at Bourg Louis, having heard that among the Indians—mostly Roman Catholics—who in the Summer frequent the reservation at Lake St. John (about 200 miles from the mouth of the Saguenay, and about the same distance from Quebec), were some who belong to our Church, went up to see them. There he found some forty Indians, who had been baptized and instructed by the Bishop of Moosonee, but who had been living and hunting around Hudson's Bay, out of the reach of any clergyman, for 20 or 30 years. They could read; and they possessed and *used* the Bible, or parts of it, and the Prayer-book, in their own language. They received Mr. Stuart with welcome, ... and at Mr. Stuart's request I visited the reservation, when 17 were confirmed and Holy Communion was celebrated, which was, indeed, a Eucharistic Feast.

I was obliged to speak to the Indians through an interpreter, as many of them do not understand English, though some do.

Their burial ground was also consecrated, when the earnest looks of the Indians and their dark faces and bright costumes lighted up in the rich glow of the afternoon sun, made the service a scene as beautiful as solemn.

A site has been given by an Indian, and money has been raised for the building of a small church, which I hope to consecrate in July next.

Mr. Stuart is now rector of Three Rivers, but he retains his charge of the Indian Mission, and receives a small grant from the Diocesan Board to defray the expense (which is considerable) of his visits.

Stuart could ill afford to shoulder the bulk of the expense of these journeys. His parish of Three Rivers, in the face of "the gradual depletion of its congregation by removal and death," was struggling to subsist. Moreover, his salary was frequently in arrears. In spite of these difficulties, he set about virtually single-handed to raise the money for the Pointe Bleue church.

The task was a difficult one; some of the pledges, despite the best will of the subscribers, could not be honoured. There was a serious fire at the Company Store, and Mr Cummins was unable to give the $100 he had pledged. The Indians themselves, who wished to raise an equal amount, were disappointed by reason of a bad hunt. An architect, Mr Harry Staveley of Quebec, donated "a beautiful plan," however. And a contractor, Edmund T. Nesbitt of Quebec, was found to undertake the construction. Stuart personally bound himself to pay $1020 "in separate payments as the work progresses, upon the certificate of Mr. B. A. Scott of Roberval, who shall at intervals of two weeks establish the value of the work done and materials delivered."

The projected cost of the church to begin with was $800, but the final expense, "including everything needed to fit it for Divine Service," was $1495.47. As Stuart had not been able to raise this amount, the church, although completed, could not be consecrated. Once again he set out collecting. The entire subscription list, totalling $1437.71—from Senator Price's donation of $275 to Annie Walford's 25¢—is carefully noted in Stuart's record. At last, on 12 July 1893, the church, now free of debt, was consecrated by Bishop A. H. Dunn.

That anyone should have undertaken and carried through a project of such magnitude (albeit a modest structure in a remote region) is remarkable enough, but that someone of Stuart's gifts and temperament should have done so is noteworthy indeed. He is described by A. R. Kelley (himself a scholar) as a typical Oxonian, an English gentleman, and a theological scholar of the highest order, "lacking in that indefinable quality of clerical aggressiveness, which brings men to high places in the Church."

In 1900, after a variety of clergy had succeeded Stuart in the mission, the Rev. Philip Callis took charge, returning to the congregation every summer for almost 40 years. His addition to Stuart's narrative, quite different in style, is discursive and anecdotal. The following is drawn from his "memo," as he calls it, written in 1932. The most interesting part of it contains his recollections of individual parishioners, men and women, who had enhanced the life of the Church over the years:

The old Indians of Mr Stuart's days have nearly all passed away. I think Joseph Gunner, our old lay reader, is the sole survivor; perhaps we may include Sandy Mistassini and Jim Robertson.

"Old Charlie," as we called Charles Robertson, the first of our interpreters, died quite unexpectedly in January 1904. He was ... most distinguished looking ... and a fine interpreter. May I recount an amusing anecdote. A visiting priest was preaching on temperance and the evils of drink. After the service Charlie told the Clergyman he had preached on the right subject, it was just what the Indians needed, only he had not given it to them half hard enough. "Oh!" said the clergyman, "I will preach again on the subject." "Well, Sir," said Charlie, "You need not trouble. I put in all you left out."

His place was taken by ... Maggie Robertson. She had been a resident on the Reserve for many years. She was always addressed by the Indians as "My Grandmother." Greatly loved and respected, she was a very mother-in-God to the Indians.... [H]er devotion to her Church and the numerous ways she unselfishly served [were] an inspiration to all who knew her....

She was succeeded by a young man, Charles Downing, who had been adopted & brought up by "Old Charlie," and he with Joseph Gunner received the Bishop's licence, one as interpreter and the other as lay-reader. I believe Joseph has read the service in Cree at the little Church ever since it was consecrated, and even in the year 1931, after the missionary had him fitted with new glasses, he was still able to do so, although ... he must be at least ninety years of age....

During all these years the Lord Bishop of the Diocese has regularly visited the Mission. You will not find a young Indian lad or girl unconfirmed unless it is from lack of opportunity; nor do we find any lapsed communicants.

One cannot help paying tribute to the love the Indians have for their Church, their reverence, the devout way in which they come to their communion. It is very striking & impresses one greatly. The Bishop's visits are looked forward to with great anticipation & preparation. Generally a big feast is held in the Bishop's honour. The Church is carefully decorated & salutes are fired when the Bishop arrives & leaves the Church....

Generous contributions are made by the Indians to the Church. It frequently happens that when an Indian family is unable to come to the mission, a fur skin is sent to the Church. Fur is really the Indian money: they know the value of fur much more so than the various denominations of money bills. Consequently they place fur in the alms basin as their offering. Some of the Indians make a practice that the first fur trapped during the hunt is laid aside for an offering to God.

Despite his obvious pride in the achievements of his congregation, their faithfulness and loyalty, Callis concludes on a note of apprehension: "Now the Indians are passing a very critical period. The price of fur has fallen to a very low figure. The continual opening of Canada farther & farther north, has made the hunting very difficult by reason of fur-bearing animals becoming more scarce every year. It is a great problem what is to happen to these people and indeed to the mission at Pointe Bleue."

26

"The Missionary Work of
All Church Women"
1890

"**O**n 16 April 1885, the Board of Missions was in session in Ottawa, the Lord Bishop of Ontario presiding, when a deputation of ladies waited upon them," begins the Report of the Provisional Committee authorized to organize a Woman's Auxiliary to the Board of Foreign and Domestic Missions of the Church of England in Canada.*

In an effort to secure the Board's "consideration of women's work," one of their number spoke as follows:

There are in the Church to-day Marys who have chosen the better part; there are the restless serving Marthas, who only want the opportunity to do something for Jesus; the Magdalens, who tell the story of our blessed Lord's resurrection; the Phoebes, who convey messages of love and Christian greeting; the Tryphenas and Tryphosas, Dorcases, who are never weary in well doing; Priscillas, who are occupied in shewing the way of the Lord more perfectly; yes, in the Church of Canada—from Victoria to Sydney—there are women longing to labor more abundantly, to consecrate all their talents to the Lord's work. And, knowing this, we ask that as the Apostles of old recognized the women of their day, as laborers with them, you, our beloved Fathers in Christ, may recognize the women of the Church in Canada, and give your hearty and earnest consent that there should be established, in connection with your Board, a Woman's Auxiliary.

Anna Maria Williams, wife of the fourth Lord Bishop of Quebec, had already shown a keen interest in missions, and it was she who would compose the original Woman's Auxiliary (W.A.) prayer for use throughout Canada. Her election as chairman of the meeting held in Montreal on September 9th and 10th, 1886, where a Constitution for the W.A. was adopted, was a happy choice. Some months before, on 11 February, a meeting had been called at the Williams' residence for the purpose of organizing a Diocesan Branch of the W.A. At this meeting, the formation of ten Branches was announced: at the Cathedral, St Matthew's, St Michael's, St Peter's, St Paul's and

Trinity (all in and around Quebec City), as well as at Lennoxville, Windsor Mills, Cookshire, Richmond and Melbourne (in the Eastern Townships).

To draw the members together and exchange news of the projects and accomplishments of the various Branches, a Monthly Letter Leaflet *was begun in Toronto. The following excerpt is drawn from the April 1890 issue, and gives a good idea of the activities of the Quebec Diocesan Branch.*

A quarterly meeting of the Quebec Diocesan Branch of the Woman's Auxiliary, was held in St. Matthew's Parish room on Friday, 17th January, at 3 p.m. The President, Mrs. Von Iffland, in the chair. After the usual prayers, and business ... quarterly reports from the Parochial Branches were read, giving an account of the work done since the last meeting. Part of the report from St. Matthew's Branch was very interesting, giving the following account of the Industrial Home, Winnipeg. "At the last Annual Meeting this Branch undertook to provide outfits for six little Indian girls in the Industrial Home in St. Paul's Parish, about six miles from Winnipeg ... This school will accommodate eighty pupils, boys and girls, from the various reserves in Manitoba.... Friends of Missions should look upon it as a privilege to help in the maintenance of such schools. The cost of each pupil is about $50 a year. The six outfits have been sent, valued at $150."

Notice was given of new Branches formed at St. George's, St. Sylvester; also at Campbell's Corners, Inverness, and one to be formed at Point Levis shortly. The Secretary read a circular from the Bishop of Algoma, giving the names of several children of missionaries needing education ... Representatives were present from Sherbrooke, Inverness, Richmond, Melbourne and St. George's ... The doxology was sung, and the meeting then adjourned.

Then follows a list of what each Branch had produced. Here is a sample: The Cathedral sent "two barrels of clothing, valued at $135," on 27 November and a third a month later valued at $50, to "missionaries in the Saskatchewan District." St. Peter's "sent off this autumn to the Bishop of Saskatchewan, a barrel and box of warm clothing and a few books, the whole valued at $50.36." St Paul's, described as a "small parish ... struggling to take its part in missionary work," dispatched "a barrel of clothing to the Wawanosh Home (value not given)." New Liverpool sent "to Rev. E. F. Wilson, Shingwauk Home, a barrel of clothing for general distribution, value $46. Also $6, contents of Mission Box of the children of the Sunday School, towards presents for children of the Homes." Sherbrooke remitted $50 "to Rev. R. Renison, of Nepigon, for rebuilding the Mission House, destroyed by fire. Also proceeds of children's bazaar, $45.26, to Zenana Missions...." At Compton "owing to scarlet fe-

*ver breaking out at the rectory, work has not been resumed this winter, and not any
sent off."*

    *At the founding meeting of the W.A. in Montreal, one of the speakers was a Miss
Emery of New York, Chairman of the parallel body of the Protestant Episcopal Church
in the United States. She had some very sensible advice for the Founding Mothers of
the organization: "Always try and employ those who seem to be interested.... Never
let your officers be figure heads.... [I]n order to keep up interest, ... have constant
communications with the points to which effort is being directed." In line with this last
directive, the* Monthly Letter Leaflet *printed communications to the specific benefactors
of mission work. The following is part of a letter, from the Mission House, Sarcee
Reserve, Calgary, to Mrs Chambers, "Pres. Ladies' Aux., St Peter's Church, Quebec." It is dated 27 January 1890 and printed in the May issue of the 1890* Leaflet:

My Dear Madam,—Bishop Pinkham very kindly handed to me, for the
benefit of my poor Sarcee, the clothing which you so kindly sent to him, and
he has since given me your letter to him that I might thank you personally
for the gifts. If you could have been present and have seen the pleasure
manifested by the Indians on the receipt of the clothing, I believe you would
have felt amply rewarded for all your labor and expenditure on their behalf.
The feast took place on Friday, the 3rd inst., at half-past two in the afternoon,
and lasted for nearly three hours. It was a bitterly cold day, but it made no
difference in the attendance. I had visited each house and visited each Indian personally, and with the exception of two or three sick ones, all came.
Very many also came from the Upper Camp, five miles distant. The school-
room, which is a good sized one, was "packed." The women sat three and
four deep on the floor, and the men and boys two deep. We were obliged
to use our little chancel for the men whose mothers-in-law were present, for
the Indian son-in-law must never look his mother-in-law in the face, and
he would sooner have stayed away from the feast ... The little chancel is shut
off from the school during the week by means of folding doors. The sons-
in-law therefore sat inside the chancel which I arranged for the occasion.
Through the liberality of friends in Calgary we were enabled to prepare a
very excellent dinner for our people. We first distributed small presents of
tobacco to each adult. Then came the huge tins of fresh beef, about 120 lbs,
some of which was boiled and some baked. I cannot say how many loaves
of bread there were. There were buns too, and cake in abundance. An almost
unlimited supply of tea also was to be had nicely sweetened; each ate and
drank until satisfied, and took home besides more than they consumed in the

school. This was followed by the distribution of candies and nuts. Then came the clothing. Each soul was given something—some two or more things. We allowed each to say what kind of article they would prefer; and without much noise and without any disturbance, we were able to satisfy all. My dear wife, and also the wife of the Indian Agent, worked very hard to make things a success, and felt not a little cheered by the results. Before leaving, each adult had about a quarter of a pound of tea given to him or her. Then I addressed them, telling them who the donors were of the good things which had gladdened their hearts, and it was not difficult to discern a mixture of surprise and pleasure upon their countenances. In the names, therefore, of these poor Sarcees, let me express ... to the ladies of St. Peter's Church, our most hearty thanks for all your kindness. I trust you may feel sufficiently encouraged to help another year. May God abundantly bless you whose hearts He has disposed to do this kindness for His name's sake.

With all heartiness, believe me, my dear madam, yours very sincerely,
H. W. Gibbon Stocken, Missionary to Sarcee Indians.

Ideas on the appropriate means of ministering to Native People have changed since 1890. Indeed, they have changed since 1963, when Bishop Brown was advocating the placement of Native children in non-Native foster homes. However, there is no doubt that the members of the W.A. thought that they were heeding "the pressing call on all sides for aid in missionary work." As Miss Jane M. Price of the Quebec Diocesan Branch wrote in a contribution to the Leaflet: "'Charity begins at home,' but it must not end there. It must overflow and embrace every good cause that comes within its reach."

27

"The Quebec Cathedral Imbroglio" 1894

*I*n *a period of circumspection, when the fear of being sued for libel or slander has made the press cautious, it is difficult to imagine the acrimonious nature of the pamphlet wars of the nineteenth century. The following passages are drawn from a series of attacks and ripostes over innovations Bishop A. H. Dunn had introduced at the Cathedral and in the Diocese at large, shortly after his arrival.*

As his biographer points out, when Dunn came to take possession of his Cathedral, the services—as he first experienced them—were to him "a cause of regret and disappointment." He found that the congregation took practically no part in the responses during service. The choir consisted of an unsurpliced collection of men and women stationed in the western gallery, and the choral service had been discontinued.

 The Altar had but one frontal, which had been at one time very handsome, but its gold ornamentation was now black with age. There was no credence table in the Sanctuary, no Cross upon the Altar, and no other ornaments, save the solid silver candlesticks (part of the plate given by George III), which were placed on the Altar on Sundays, but were put away in the safe during the week.... The pulpit, which was on wheels, occupied the centre, completely blocking out the view of the Altar.

Dunn, who had been elected Bishop in absentia, had first reached Quebec a few months before the centenary of the Diocese, and was determined that this occasion should be celebrated in befitting style. It was also an excellent opportunity to deal with the sorry state into which the Cathedral had fallen.

When the congregation turned out on 1 June 1893 for the Service of Thanksgiving on the occasion of the Centennial Celebration of the Diocese, four visiting bishops were in attendance. The music, under the superintendence of an organist in full sympathy with the bishop's plans, was suitable to the occasion and beautifully performed. There was a surpliced choir—no longer in the gallery, but brought down into the body of the Cathedral—and the Altar, with "an exquisitely worked Altar cloth, frontal and superfrontal" of "rich gold embroidery upon a white satin foundation," was decked with flowers. A large number of fragrant narcissi had been beautifully arranged around the base of the pulpit, "from the desk of which depended a festival banner hanging, in white and gold." On the retable there stood "a magnificent floral Cross and vases of beautiful flowers, and on each end two large candle-sticks ..."

The service was choral throughout. Morning Prayer was sung by the Rev. A. G. Hamilton Dicker, Incumbent of St Barnabas, Acton Vale, London, and formerly Dunn's Curate, who had crossed the Atlantic in order to assist at the service. "Mr. Dicker possesses an admirable tenor voice," a contemporary newspaper reported, "and sung the service very beautifully and with considerable feeling and expression."

While such a celebration was occasioned by a special event and not intended for repetition, the attitudes towards modes of worship that had shaped the Service continued to be felt at the Cathedral. Some parishioners, however, found so great a departure from their usual practices more than they were prepared to accept. There were objections of a most outspoken kind. Other voices, equally strident—from outside the congregation—joined in.

The "Quebec Cathedral Imbroglio," as it was called, was even made the subject of the seventh circular of The Protestant Churchmen's Union and Tract Society, based in Toronto. "What is taking place in the Parish Church of the Holy Trinity in the City of Quebec," claimed S. H. Blake, President of the Society, "furnishes a seasonable illustration of the aims of these innovators and their mode of action."

The Bishop had issued a circular the previous November enjoining several kinds of changes. Some, the Protestant Churchmen's Union thought, were reasonable, such as "placing the pulpit, choir seats, and lectern in more convenient places, arranging the pews, and the seating of worshippers at a certain period of the service." Others, however, were pronounced to be "of doubtful expediency," or "alien to our Church and intended to build up a Sacerdotal Ritualism." These latter included asking the people to stand on the entrance of the Clergy, furnishing the Altar with a Cross and two candlesticks, having the choir face eastward for the creed, and providing a surpliced choir for Cathedral services. Following this list is a quotation from "the late High Church Bishop Wilberforce," who is said to have regarded these observances as "truly alien to the Church of England," incorporating "fidgety desires to have everything non-Anglican. This is not a grand development, as some seem to think," Wilberforce continues. "It is decrepitude. It is not something very sublime and impressive, but something very feeble and contemptible."

Closer to home, a protest on behalf of "a majority of pew-holders of the Cathedral and Parish Church," signed by T. H. Norris and G. Veasey, was published in June 1894. It begins:

All who are familiar with the membership of the Cathedral Congregation are well aware that we have ever been loyally attached to the doctrine and discipline of the Church of our fathers, and the distinguished Bishops and Clergymen who have had rule over us in the past, taught us the value of and practiced themselves that form of service to which for several generations we have been accustomed.

It is quite unnecessary to proclaim a fact unfortunately too well known, that the doctrine taught and the ritual practiced by such distinguished Prelates as Bishop Mountain, Bishop Williams, and hardly less distinguished Clergymen such as Drs. Hatch, Mackie, Adamson, Percy, Hellmuth, our late Rector, and others ... are directly antagonized by Bishop Dunn, so that, had we no weightier reason than respect for the memories of the Bishops and Clergymen who have taught us loyalty to the Church of England as a Protestant and Reformed Church, we should still feel bound to resist the innovations that are being thrust upon us to the great detriment of our Congregation and to the scandal to religion in this city and diocese....

As an illustration of this tendency, we give the following quotation from a booklet called "Our Church Manual" issued by the Bishop of Quebec, and recently introduced here:

> "It is a great and precious opportunity on every Sunday and Holy Day, whether we have received the Holy Communion at an early service or not, to be present at the later celebration without receiving, with a view to adoring our Blessed Saviour, who comes at THE WORDS OF CONSECRATION into our very midst, etc."

Comment on the above quotation is unnecessary....

It is of course a matter of deep regret that in a city where we have had every opportunity of becoming familiar with the ornate service of the Roman Catholic Church, the adoption of a ritual which wholly or in part finds its embodiment and exposition in the Latin Church should be introduced.

Apart from the manifest disloyalty to our own convictions in lending our sanction to such innovations, we are well aware of the incalculable injury that is being done to the English Church in this country by the introduction of forms and ceremonies that have little to commend them beyond their novelty; while negatively they are not productive of any spiritual life in the participants ...

Much less polite than the foregoing were the numerous pamphlets put out by the Rev. William Noble of Trinity Church who had waded early into the fray. The following sample of his remarks is taken from "A Remonstrance: An Open Letter to the Lord Bishop of Quebec," published 26 January 1894:

My Lord Bishop:

Your reckless aggression, as a leader of the Romish propaganda in the Church of England, imposes on me a very unpleasant duty; but God, as well as England, expects every man to do his duty. The unparalleled audacity with which you are unprotestantizing the Church of England, and assimilating her to that of Rome, and the dishonorable methods by which you seek to crush all opposition, demand a plain and fearless exposure. You have tried by a mean form of tyranny, and by bribery, to gag my mouth and fetter my pen. You have tried by dishonorable means to antagonize my congregation against me, and to create discord amongst them.

It is difficult, at this distance from the case, to trace the circumstances behind such charges. In view of Dunn's well-known tolerance for a wide spectrum of churchmanship, regardless of his personal views, it is hard to credit Noble's accusations as they stand. One thing is clear, however. Dunn did distribute a little book of his own composition entitled "Our Only Hope" as a gift to each of Noble's candidates for confirmation. His sermon at the confirmation, which strove to focus the candidates' thoughts on the rite just performed, did centre on the importance of the Eucharist. Noble describes the event as follows:

You came to a confirmation in my church last March, and, laying aside all considerable courtesy, you taught from my pulpit apostolical succession, baptismal regeneration, and transubstantiation; and by garbled quotations and gross perversion of the Word of God, you claimed for yourself the power of giving the Holy Ghost in confirmation. Such blasphemous claims belong to the priests of heathendom and their servile imitators, but shock the feelings of all loyal and intelligent members of a Protestant Church.

In addition to assailing the Bishop's activities at Trinity, Noble launches an attack against a "Circular" and "Questionnaire" received from his Diocesan the previous December, enquiring about what ornaments each church possessed, "including bells, organs, covering for the Lord's table, altar linen, painted windows, crosses, flowers, vases, candlesticks, etc., if any."

Such a question [Noble fulminates] is a gross insult to a loyal clergyman of the Protestant Church of England ... My Lord Bishop, what a prostitution of your episcopal office! thus to occupy your time and attention with such bric-a-brac as "crosses, flowers, vases, and candlesticks"—things which, you ought to know, were swept from the Church of England at the Reformation, as subversive of divine worship....The reason assigned for making these inquiries is: "That you may be able to draw attention to any deficiencies"; and then you add: "In this way every church and parish will be sure, in process of time, to be supplied with all needful items."

Understandably, Bishop Dunn was not pleased by Noble's "Remonstrance" and attempted to discipline him. When Noble refused, demanding to be brought before "the proper tribunal" to determine any guilt on his part, the Bishop cancelled his engagement to confirm Noble's candidates until such time as he should comply. Noble, who saw this as an "attempt to punish the innocent candidates" rather than himself, threatened to appeal to the Metropolitan and, in fact, did so.

The Metropolitan—the Archbishop of Ontario—supported Dunn; in a letter dated 16 December 1895, he advised that Noble withdraw the "Open Letter" and tender an apology. Noble responded with what seems to be his final word in the debate in a pamphlet called "An 'Open Letter' to the Archbishop of Ontario: With Appendix," dated Quebec, March 1896. He appears to have left his parish—and the Diocese—that same year.

When Noble's initial pamphlet was published, it was boldly refuted by another, entitled "A Lay Reply to Rev. W. T. Noble's Open Letter to the Lord Bishop of Quebec," dated 1 May 1894 and signed by R. J. Hewton and C. R. Jones, both of Hatley.

Rev. Sir—Your reckless disregard for authority and the courtesy which is supposed to govern a controversy between Churchmen, who differ in opinion, together with a knowledge of the evil your unwarranted statements are calculated to produce among uninformed churchmen, induce us as laymen to reply to your recent open letter to your Chief Pastor....

You accuse the Bishop of Quebec of Romanising the church, of dishonorable conduct, of bribery and tyranny, and you advance in proof of this the statement that in Trinity Church he taught "Apostolic succession, baptismal regeneration and transubstantiation." In regard to the latter we are compelled to state that having heard the Lord Bishop preach on the Holy Communion, ... his Lordship must reserve such teaching for Trinity Church ...

If our church does not believe in apostolic succession, what means she by using the term "priest," ... and what by putting an absolution into his mouth again and again?...

In the baptismal office we find the following in the second prayer: "That he coming to thy holy baptism, may receive remission of sins by spiritual regeneration," ... and [later] "We yield Thee hearty thanks ... that it hath pleased Thee to regenerate this person."

Can the English language be made stronger? Can a priest of the church who remembers his vows teach any other doctrine?...

...We will not attempt to follow you in your wanderings among the symbols of ancient paganism, such wanderings are evidently hurtful to the mental balance. We do not need to do so for you have failed ... to connect the T of the Greek alphabet with the cross of Calvary, the cross of Christianity, the cross of England's flag, the cross of England's church—of God's church, which was signed on your forehead at your baptism in token that you should not be ashamed to confess Christ crucified, but manfully to fight under His banner....

...Vituperation and abuse only prove you devoid of argument and lead us strongly to suspect you of adopting this method of stabbing our dear old church in the back, lest she should do that which the signs of the times seem to indicate as likely, viz., to win back to Christ's fold the erring factions among English speaking Christianity, which have torn his church ... into so many bleeding fragments.

28

Church Lighting:
St. Peter's, Sherbrooke
1897

L ighting was both awkward and expen-
sive in the early nineteenth century. Service times, especially in country churches, were
usually adapted to take advantage of available natural light, but if a clergyman had
several churches to visit each Sunday, it was not possible to circumvent the need of providing lighting for some of them.

At first, candles were used. Members of the congregation brought their own, and
lighted their way home with them after the service. An instance of this practice can be
found in Bishop G. J. Mountain's account of his Visitation of the Eastern Townships
in the winter of 1837: "Divine Service was held in the school-house in the evening,
and I preached to a good congregation. They brought their own candles, and as they
walked home through the snow with lighted candles in their hands, they had very much
the appearance of some procession."

Later, many churches, such as the Church of the Epiphany, Way's Mills, installed
oil lamps, but they required constant cleaning to remain effective. If hung from above,
they needed to be let down to be filled and trimmed. With the advent of electricity in
the late nineteenth century—much later in many parts of the Diocese—it seemed as
if problems with lighting were at an end.

The following selection suggests that the early subscribers to electrical services had
great faith in their suppliers' ability to provide them with uninterrupted power. It is
the complete text of a letter, dated 27 December 1897, addressed to "The Superintendent of the Electric Light Co^y" from the Rector of St Peter's Church, Sherbrooke.

Dear Sir,
I beg to draw your very serious attention to the interruptions in our Church Services caused by the Electric
lights going out. On the morning of Christmas Day
when the Church was nearly full of people and in the very middle of the
Service at 7.30 a.m. all the lights went out and it became impossible to see
at all. Yesterday, Sunday, the same thing happened a few minutes before 8 a.m.
just as Service was beginning. This early Service is the one at which it is
specially important to have light, which will be needed throughout the win-

ter; and I trust I shall have an assurance from you that these unseemly inter-ruptions will not take place again.

　　Yours faithfully

　　Geo W. Dumbell, Rector

From the perspective of a technologically more sophisticated age, and after almost one hundred years of pannes d'electricité, Dr Dumbell's demand for such "assurances" from the Powers-that-be seems touchingly naïve!

29

The Church at War:
A Chaplain to the Forces in Europe
1915

I*f the items printed in the* Quebec Diocesan Gazette *in the early months of 1914 are any indication, the danger of schism in the Anglican Church by the formation of internal party factions constituted greater cause for alarm than any issue of international proportions. Then, like a bolt from the blue, the September issue recorded that "Friday, August 21st, was observed throughout the Diocese as a Day of Prayer and Intercession on behalf of our Nation and her allies in the present distress of war and for the Blessing of Peace." On 4 August, Britain had declared war on Germany, and Canada was at war.*

In his reminiscences, The Great War as I Saw It, *Canon Frederick George Scott—initially Chaplain to the 8th Royal Rifles, later Senior Chaplain, First Canadian Division—says he first knew that he had "to go to the war" on 31 July.*

 It was a queer sensation [he wrote] because I had never been to war before and I did not know how I should be able to stand the shell fire. I had read in books of people whose minds were keen and brave, but whose hind legs persisted in running away under the sound of guns. Now I knew that an ordinary officer on running away under fire would get the sympathy of a large number of people, who would say, "The poor fellow has got shell shock," and they would make allowance for him. But if a chaplain ran away, about six hundred men would say at once, "We have no more use for religion." So it was with very mingled feelings that I contemplated an expedition to the battle-fields of France, and I trusted that the difficulties of Europe would be settled without our intervention.

On 15 February 1915, after months on Salisbury Plain, Scott arrived in France. On the following Sunday, he had his first Church Parade in the war zone. "After a brief stay in Caestre the whole brigade marched off to Armentières.... I went with the 15th Battalion, and, as I told the men, being a Canon, marched with the machine gun section." It must have been in these early days that he wrote a personal version of "O Canada," which, as he mentions in a note on the text, was "written in Armentières,

France, 1915, and sung by the Soldiers in the YMCA Hut on the Neuve Eglise road, near Ploegsteert" in Belgium:

O Canada, my country and my love,
O Canada, with cloudless skies above,
    Where e'er I roam,
    Where e'er my home.
My heart goes back to thee,
    Thy lakes and streams,
    Thy boundless dreams,
Thy rivers running free.
    O Canada, O Canada,
God pour His blessings on thee from above,
O Canada, my country and my love.

Writing of the interval at Ploegsteert, from July to December, he describes taking Services:

I used to arrange a Communion Service for the men every morning....The box I used as an altar was placed under the green trees, and covered with the dear old flag, which now hangs in the chancel of my church in Quebec.* On top was a white altar cloth, two candles and a small crucifix. At these services only about ten or a dozen men attended, but it was inspiring to minister to them. I used to hear from time to time that so and so had been killed, and I knew he had made his last Communion at one of such services. It was an evidence of the changed attitude towards religion that the men in general did not count it strange that soldiers should thus come to Holy Communion in public. No one was ever laughed at or teased for doing so.

In 1941, Scott published a small volume of his war poems, together with some new ones, entitled Lift Up Your Hearts; *the royalties were to be donated "to the Queen's Fund, London, England, for the relief of civilian war victims." Among the more recent compositions is a sonnet entitled "Should Freedom Fall," dated 12 September 1940. It concludes:*

---

* St Matthew's Church on rue St-Jean. The church, now a public library, retains a number of its memorials, including those set into the walls or inscribed in the windows.

When young and old were slaughtered day and night,
And pity, love and mercy cast aside,
When monster hordes, in their satanic might,
Were tearing down the cross on which Christ died,
If I had held aloof and gone my way,
Hell's worm and fire would gnaw me night and day.

In the life at the front [Scott wrote] no doubt there was much evil thinking, evil talking and evil doing, but there was, underlying all this, the splendid manifestation in human nature of that image of God in which man is made. As one looks back upon it, the surface things of that life have drifted away, and the great things that one remembers are the self-sacrifice, the living comradeship, and the unquestioning faith in the eternal rightness of right and duty which characterized those who were striving to the death for the salvation of the world.

30

The *Glad Tidings*
1927, 1944, and 1951

F*or generations, the people in the isolated communities of the Lower North Shore relied on "the Mission Boat" to receive the services of the Church. The auxiliary schooner* The Faith, *for example, was built by public subscription at a cost of about $2,000 for the use of the St Clement's Mission and formally handed over to Bishop A. H. Dunn in 1913.*

In 1920, the Rev. F. G. LeGallais, priest-in-charge of the coastal mission, spoke proudly of the Good Hope—*the gift of Sir William Price—as "the most serviceable boat, the coast people say, that the Mission has ever had ... [She] fills a long-felt want in the work of the Mission." She was a "dory type, light draft, capable of entering the smallest harbours, and tying up at any stage head." Unfortunately the ship suffered severe damage when, returning from Sunday Services at La Tabatière and Old Poste, the engine broke down and she was driven onto the rocks during a storm.*

Much later, in 1962, Bishop R. F. Brown commissioned the Mercedes-Benz diesel-powered M.V. Hollis Corey. *She was built locally, by Roderick Jones of Wolf Bay. The incumbent, the Rev. D. Percy Graham, publicized the estimated cost of the fittings "Cruiser Steerer, Bulkhead type, $187.80," "Bow Lights $30.90 per pair or $9.35 (cheaper set)," "Fog Bell (to double as a Mission bell at outstations) $32.40," "Search Light $43.50 ($38.40 to $195.25)," "Log Book, $5.75"—and gifts for particular items poured in. The* Diocesan Gazette *reports that $32.40 for the fog bell and $100.00 for "Searchlight and installation" had been received before the next issue of the paper had come out. A gift of $300.00 from the Bishop Kemper Missionary Society, Nashota House, Wisconsin, paid for the anchors and cruiser steerer. Unknown to most people, the Rev. Robert A. Bryan (see Window 16) quietly rallied friends in the United States and Canada who added $8,000.00 to the funds for construction and the necessary fittings.*

Of all the vessels serving Anglicans on the Coast, however, it seems to have been the Glad Tidings, I, II, *and* III, *that come to mind when mention of the Mission Boat is made. In 1927, W. G. Horwood, a life insurance agent from Newfoundland, accompanied a fellow-countryman, Max Young, to St Augustine River, where the latter was a clerk of the Hudson's Bay Company. Horwood has left a vivid description of this journey, including a leg aboard the Mission Boat:*

Not before my last day at Harrington did I meet the Reverend George Harrington, priest in charge—the name is merely coincidence. He had come up from his Mutton Bay headquarters to marry a young couple and we were invited to the wedding and spent a very social evening. My next move was to Mutton Bay, so next morning after bidding farewell to Uncle Will [Bobbitt, his host] and his family, the good priest took me on board his boat the "Glad Tidings" and five hours later I was enjoying a good snooze in Sam Wilton's parlour at Mutton Bay....

I could see no opportunity of getting East again for a fortnight and was indeed glad to hear the Rev. Harrington at Divine service announce that he was making his last tour that way in a few days. Immediately after service was over I booked passage with him. A kindly, genial sailor-priest is Harrington; one cannot help admiring this combination of mariner and divine.... With only a small motorboat—she lives up to her name too—manned by himself as captain and a boatman, this intrepid sailor travels the coast as long as ice conditions will permit....

We left Mutton Bay early Friday morning, and passed many picturesque villages. In trying to pass through a certain place known as the Rapids, the tide had fallen so low that our boat grounded and on pulling her off we discovered that the propeller had become unlocked from the shaft, which necessitated our putting her ashore and trying to make repairs. Our boatman was equal to the task. After we had piled our ballast in the bow in order to raise our propeller as near as possible to the surface, we pulled her in by the shore where our boatman plunged in and after a long while made a splendid job. He worked nearly all the time under the water actually doing the work of a diver ... Had the task been a few minutes longer I'm sure that the skeletons of three stalwarts would have remained on a certain rock near the Rapids, victims of that terrible Labrador pest the mosquito ...

Our intentions were to make Old Fort by nightfall, but as it was now past three o'clock and the early part of the night being moonless, we decided to make for Rocky Bay and call it a day.

The wind had veered to the south east (dead ahead) and a nasty chop was making itself felt aboard the boat. We were making good headway and just before it was completely dark we rounded the point of an island and hauled her in for what we supposed was Rocky Bay point; our engine stalled and there we were in a not too enviable position—about two hundred yards to drive and the good ship "Glad Tidings" would soon have been drift wood.

I am a bit of a sailor myself, so I suggested to the Captain that we get the jib on our boat, let her fall off a bit, get the mainsail up, jibe it and see if we couldn't clear the point we had just formerly rounded. We did ...

We ran back before the wind about half a mile and discovered an opening into which we poked our frail little craft and mighty glad I was too.... I will say though that friend Harrington didn't worry; I suppose these things are commonplace with him.

After getting our engine going again we steamed on up the creek and finally discovered that this was Rocky Bay and that we had passed in the growing dusk of the evening.

Our good priest was ashore the next morning before myself and the boatman were astir. He held a Communion Service which I believe every confirmed Anglican attended.

On 4 August 1944, the Rev. Sydney Meade was preparing for his departure for another parish. He wrote a long letter to Archbishop Carrington headed "Impressions & Views of St. Clement's Mission: Canadian Labrador" in which he spoke at some length of the needs and care of the Glad Tidings.

A subject dear to my heart, though an inlander [he writes] is the Mission Boat. The present "Glad Tidings" has now given us sixteen summers of service. There will be need of a new one rather soon. In one way or another she has been subject to quite a bit of strain and stress. One of the main mistakes, I think, was the repeated hauling up and launching on her side. This has weakened the planks and started some of the nails.

I strongly urge that a cradle be made for the boat so that she can be launched upright. A simple "slip" could also be made easily here, and this would be a great joy at hawling-up and launching time, as well as saving much strain and wear.... If a new boat cannot be built soon, then a thorough check-over should be made next spring—new caulking, and perhaps new nailing. It is noticed that plank nails begin to show signs of "jumping" when under strain.

If and when a new boat is built, I'd like to go on record as recommending one of much the same general plan and dimentions [sic] as the present "Glad Tidings"—she's a fine sea-boat, with good lines. An improvement would be a bit of flange in the hull forward—so that she would not "throw water" against a wind-lop as much as the present one does. And a real acquisition to aim for would be a four-cycle engine—a "Grey" or a "Kermath"—about 20 h.p., complete with clutch and self-starter. The cost of such a motor should be much less after the war. It's my opinion that the initial higher cost of a four-cycle engine would soon be more than compensated by smaller consumption of fuel, general ease of operation and better service.

"Joe" Gallichon continues to be a jolly good boatman, and faithful Mission servant.

During the annual Summer and Fall Boat Trips the priest-in-charge would cover considerable distances, often performing several services a day, frequently at different stations. The following represents a segment of the Rev. John Anido's 1948 "Fall Western Boat Trip," which extended that year from September 10th to 26th in the Glad Tidings. *An Oxford graduate with "a good degree," Anido had come to the Diocese from a parish in Surrey, England, in 1947 and had been sent straight to Labrador; the* Glad Tidings III *("a 36' ketch, Marconi rigged, [with] 12 hp auxiliary engine") had also begun her service in that year. The Mission Boat—as usual—set out from her home port of Mutton Bay. Old Fort Bay was her first port-of-call. The following is taken from the Outstations Register 1939-49, and records the dates, times, and types of services held, as well as their locations and the numbers present in each case:*

Sept. 13 (Mon.)	7.00 p.m.	Evensong	21 present	Old Fort Bay School
Sept. 14 (Tues.)	7.30 a.m.	HC*	10	Old Fort Bay
Sept. 15 (Weds.)	7.00 a.m.	HC	4	St Paul's River Church
	8.00 a.m.	HC	3	St Paul's River PC†
	8.00 p.m.	HC	15	Bradore Basin
Sept. 16 (Thurs.)	7.00 a.m.	HC	12	Bradore Basin
	8.45	HC	2	Bradore Plains
	4.00 p.m.	HC	14	Blanc Sablon
Sept. 17 (Fri.)	11.30 a.m.	HC	12	Salmon Bay
	3.00 p.m.	HC	8	Stick Point
	8.00 p.m.	Evensong	6	Old Fort Island
Sept. 19 (Sun.)	11.30 a.m.	HC	10	Shekatika Island
	1.30 p.m.	HC	9	Canso Island
	4.00 p.m.	Holy Bapt.	5	Spoon Cove

---

* HC = Holy Communion
† PC = Parish Church. Spelling of place names (such as St Augustine River) follows that in Anido's record.

Sept. 20 (Mon.)	7.00 a.m.	HC	9	St Augustine's River School
	4.00 p.m.	HC	5	St Augustine's River PC
	7.00 p.m.	Evensong	61	St Augustine's River School
Sept. 21 (Tues.)	7.00 a.m.	HC	11	St Augustine's River School
Sept. 23 (Thurs.)	2.30 p.m.	H. Matrim.	30	Old Post
	4.00 p.m.	Evensong	14	La Tabatière School
Sept. 24 (Fri.)	7.30 p.m.	HC	6	La Tabatière School
Sept. 25 (Sat.)	11.00 a.m.	HC	8	Whale Head

In July 1951, the Very Rev. Robert Seaborn accompanied Archbishop Carrington on his Visitation of the Labrador coast. He and Carrington had left Quebec on the North Pioneer *on 6 July on which they sailed as far as Mutton Bay. There they met the Rev. John Anido and transferred to the* Glad Tidings. *The following is a selection from Seaborn's diary:*

Wednesday July 18 / 51

Up for breakfast in leisurely fashion and a walk to the Church & to Buffit's Landing where the Mission Boat was tied up ... Tried the water, but too cold for a swim! Left in slight fog about 1.30 p.m., smooth sea, mostly grey, with fog lifting & then down. Stopped briefly at Meccatina Island to tell of Confirmation about 5 p.m. in sunlight.... Into Harrington Harbour at 6.30 p.m. To the Parsonage for supper with Mr & Mrs Ray Batten (lay reader) & Miss Wheeler of the Grenfell Mission. Confirmation (5 boys & one girl) at 8 p.m. with congregation of 110. Lovely church inside with fine oak altar & cross & candle-sticks & panelling in the sanctuary. To Dr. & Mrs Hodd's for tea ... and talk: then bath & bed.

Thursday, July 19 / 51

Up for HC at 7 a.m. (30 [present]), followed by breakfast at the Hodd's and left H.H. at 9.35 in sea as "sooth as oil" & overcast sky. Coffee & talk at 11 a.m.... Arrived at Wolf Bay at 2.55 p.m. after a perfect run: 2 flags flying in little cove with 4 or 5 houses, at end of a point jutting out 6 miles: completely isolated community. Watched terns hovering & diving as we lay at anchor & took pictures. Came ashore & visited the 3 Jones families: Archbp to stay at Henry Jones. A[nido] & I at Fred Jones. Supper at Henry

Jones: the 3 of us eating alone (as is the Coast custom) in the dining room: fresh fried fish (i.e. cod) was delicious, with peas & pears, cake & tea. Confirmation at Fred Jones' at 6.30: 2 candidates ... & congregation of 20....

Friday, July 20 / 51

Strong wind (S.W. to S.) & overcast sky, so no move. After breakfast went out to boat, lop increasing. H.C. at 10 a.m. in Fred Jones' living room. Wind was followed by rain and a great sea developed, with spray flying over the rocks....

Saturday, July 21 / 51

Sea subsiding, but fog thick at 5 a.m.; after breakfast sun began to break through and we set out again at 11 a.m. with Frank Jones on board as pilot....

Set off on 40-50 mile Westward run with bright sun, freshening west wind and white caps. Glad Tidings is a good ship in a sea! On an inside passage, sheltered by islands, from 12-1.30 when we had a good meal. Past Romaine around 3 p.m. and kept on going with great pitching & tossing and spray and waves breaking over the bow & port quarter. Slept for an hour (2.30-3.30) but for the rest outside in raincoat & rubber boots & sou' wester. Saw quite a few eider ducks & one gannett. Finally reached Kegaska at 7.30, i.e. in 8 hours & 20 minutes, instead of about 6 hrs. Engine stopped once, well out from any rocks! Glad to be ashore and supper at Dave King's....

Sunday, July 22 / 51

Celebrated H.C. in School House at 7 a.m., with Anido assisting, and 22 present. Henry Dumeresque, lay-reader & school teacher of 42 years standing, had school fully decorated with sea shells ... "Welcome to our Archbishop of Quebec" above the altar & very nice red dossal curtain & cross & candlesticks. At 10.30 a.m. we had Mattins & Confirmation with 50 present and 5 confirmed & Henry playing the organ.... Evensong at 6.30: 52 present and [I] preached. Went looking for sea shells and found a few as darkness fell. Some conversation with the menfolk & tea, before bed at 10.30 p.m.

Monday, July 23 / 51

Up at 3.30 a.m. and underway soon after 4 as the sun rose in a cloudless sky. Had a cup of tea, an orange & a slice of bread to keep going. Still quite a heavy swell, but lots of birds rising from every rock & shore ... Got to Romaine soon after 8 a.m. & Frank Jones rowed ashore for a parcel and we tucked into a proper breakfast with eggs & coffee. Washed up & underway again by 9: wind freshening, so when we got to the Bluff at 10, the sail was hoisted to help us along the inside passage. Just passed a seal sleep-

ing on a rock. Engine now functioning 100%! Arrived at Wolf Bay in a rolling sea at noon ... On our way again by 12.30 ... to Harrington Harbour at
5.30 p.m. & to Dr & Mrs Hodd's for a supper with the Grenfell Staff. Meeting of Church building committee at 8 p.m. in Parsonage went well....

Tuesday, July 24 / 51

After breakfast inspected Grenfell Mission Hospital with Dr Hodd: very
fine, light & well-laid out, with patients all on 2nd floor. Climbed up to see
Reservoir. Held Confirmation ... with congregation of patients. A quick
"mug up" at Dr Hodd's & set sail at 12.10 p.m. with sail up & following
wind: boat still rolling, but sea less. Landed at stage at 3.50 p.m. Evensong
and Confirmation at 7 p.m. with 75 present and 3 boys & 2 girls confirmed.
The Eve of St James and so Archbishop spoke of his Consecration 10 years
ago the next day and of the work of a bishop. It was dark in the Church
before we finished.

The Glad Tidings *served as the Mission Boat until the close of the 1961 season; her
last boatman was Chesley Yarn. On 7 July of that year she carried Bishop Brown,
John Burke and D. Percy Graham to Bradore from where they "travel[led] by car over
the newly-made road that connects [Bradore Plains] with Newfoundland Labrador"
in order to visit Forteau. Their purpose was to commemorate the 100th anniversary
of the fortuitous meeting of G. J. Mountain and Edward Feild, where the two bishops had concelebrated "in a pretty and well-appointed little church," St Peter's. Arriving
at Forteau, Brown met Seaborn, by this time Bishop of Newfoundland—"just arrived in order to consecrate a church in nearby Lanse au Loup"—and history repeated
itself.*

In the Summer issue of the Diocesan Gazette, *Bishop Brown announced that
the Ladies Guild of the Church of St Andrew and St George at Baie Comeau had
given $1,000 towards the construction and fitting-out of a new Mission Boat, and that
she would be named the* Hollis Corey *"in memory of [one of] our greatly loved Labrador missionaries."*

The final entry in the log book of the last Glad Tidings *reads as follows: "1961
Sept 26, Time 1805, Harrington Harbour: The Glad Tidings III will now return
to Mutton Bay and be retired from her career as the Mission Boat on the Quebec
Labrador. Ave atque Vale!"*

31

Faith of Our Fathers (and Mothers): Defining the Church 1932

A *lthough the* Quebec Diocesan Ga-
*zette, founded by Bishop A. H. Dunn, gave regular account of "The Lord Bishop's
Engagements," it was not until his successor's episcopate that the "Bishop's Letter"
became a feature of the paper. Unlike his successors, Bishop L. W. Williams did not
open his remarks with any salutation, such as "My Dear People," used by Bishops
Carrington and Goodings, or "My Dear Friends," by Bishops Brown and Matthews.
The tone, nonetheless, was personal and immediate.*

*The "Bishop's Letter" for May 1932 examines what was still known as the
Church of England and traces the Bishop's vision of strengths and shortcomings—its
unique characteristics as he saw and hoped to see them—in the Church at large and
in his own diocese in particular:*

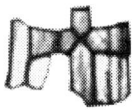 There are certain characteristics about the Church of England,
and about the whole Anglican Communion [he begins], which
are to be found, so far as I can see in no other body of Christians. One of these characteristics I wish to speak about in this Letter, namely,
its Comprehensiveness. The very Comprehensiveness has its advantages and
its disadvantages; in fact, Comprehensiveness may be said to be both the
Glory and the Danger of our Church.

The Church of England which is both Catholic and Reformed, includes
within its bounds men and women of widely differing views. There are High
Churchmen, Low Churchmen and Broad Churchmen, which we may perhaps better designate as Catholic, Evangelical and Liberal. If we can hold
together in genuine fellowship these differing types of Churchmanship, each
of which stands for some important element of truth, then Comprehensiveness has great advantages and constitutes our Glory. This very Comprehensiveness may, some day, prove to be a very important factor in the solution
of a great problem as our characteristic contribution to the cause of Christian Unity.

In the report on the Unity of the Church at the last Lambeth Conference, referring to the part which our Church has to play in the whole Church of God, there occurred this passage:

> Our special Character and, we believe, our peculiar contribution to the Universal Church arise from the fact that, owing to historic circumstances, we have been enabled to combine in our one fellowship the traditional Faith and Order of the Catholic Church with that immediacy of approach to God through Christ to which the Evangelical Churches especially bear witness, and freedom of intellectual enquiry whereby the correlation of the Christian revelation and advancing knowledge is constantly effected.

On the other hand, we are bound to admit that in this Comprehensiveness, unless it is safe-guarded, there are disadvantages which constitute a real danger.

The very fact that we have these differences, sometimes makes it difficult for our Church to speak with one voice on any topic of the moment and creates an impression of indecision which others are able to avoid. Then, again, there is the danger of "party spirit" leading to bitter controversy and complete absence of that charity which is or ought to be the essential characteristic of the Christian. There is no reason whatever why there should be any lack of friendliness and good will between people who do not see truth exactly from the same angle, or between people, some of whom like a simple mode of public worship and others who prefer more elaborate services. Men's minds have always differed and will always differ. What is helpful to one is not helpful to another. These difficulties, however, are merely incidental to our mode of corporate life which I believe to be the best for our branch of the Holy Catholic Church.

The present Archbishop of York in one of his recent books, writing about this subject says, "To my mind it is entirely desirable that there should be what are sometimes called 'Schools of Thought' and sometimes 'Parties.' What is altogether undesirable is, that through the existence of 'Parties,' there should arise the spirit of Partizanship, in which members of the different groups in the one fellowship tend to regard each other as opponents instead of colleagues—not comrade regiments in the one army, as they truly are, but in some way opposing armies."

Whether or not we agree with the Archbishop that it is desirable that there should be "Schools of Thought" or "Parties" in the Church, one thing I am profoundly thankful for, and that is that in our Diocese there exists very little, if any, of that extreme partizanship which is contrary to the spirit of Christ, certain to hinder the cause of true religion and apt to bring the

Church into contempt in the eyes of the World.

There has existed amongst us, in the Quebec Diocese for many years, a spirit of harmony and good will which, I take it, is not due to any lack of zeal but rather to a spirit of reasonableness, fair play and a willingness to give to others what we claim for ourselves, viz: credit for acting conscientiously according to our convictions.

That this may always be recognized characteristic of our Diocese is my earnest wish and prayer.

Lennox Quebec

32

The Voice of Conscience:
the *Quebec Diocesan Gazette*
1934

S *ince it was founded in 1894, the* Que-
bec Diocesan Gazette *has, from time to time, been a forum for the major issues of
the day, whether social, political, or religious, national or international, in scope. This
was particularly true in the mid-1920s and 1930s when the editorship of the Rev.
Charles Revell Eardley-Wilmot coincided with the episcopate of Lennox W. Williams.
The temper of the paper was serious and outspoken, and it did not shrink from controversy.*

*In 1934, the economic climate was still a matter for much concern, and the edi-
torial in the January issue sounded a cautious note of optimism in national affairs:*

 1934 opens with a new spirit of hopefulness. There are
definite signs that conditions are improving. The number
in employment is greater than it has been at any time during the last two years and is increasing month by month.
The Christmas trade showed a decided improvement and in business in general the outlook is better. There is a general feeling that the worst of the
depression is over. On the other hand, the world is still full of unrest and
anxiety.... Confidence is increasing in national life, but fear and suspicion still
hold sway in international affairs.

*After voicing grave concern about the failure of the Disarmament Conference and the
future of the League of Nations, the editorial then turned to the subject of war. With
a mixture of horror and anger that the world could be precipitated into yet another
conflict equal in magnitude to that begun just twenty years earlier, the editor lashed
out at the forces he saw as responsible:*

There has been a great deal of talk lately about war. Men in the highest
positions have stated that the danger of another war is a very real one. The
world is drifting back into the state that existed previous to 1914. It is a bad
thing when people begin to talk about the possibility of war. We must not
allow ourselves to even think that war is inevitable. Peace will never be se-

cure until nations give up the idea that war is a normal factor in international policy and that therefore they must be prepared to fight. Appalling revelations have been made recently of the part played by private manufacturers of armaments in fostering this idea. That there should be great and powerful organizations which for the sake of increasing their dividends wish to keep alive a spirit of fear and distrust among the nations, is a crying scandal.... It is a matter that should be dealt with by the League of Nations, but the League can do nothing until it has behind it a far stronger force of public opinion than it has at present. Many people ridicule the League of Nations and ask what good it is, but the League stands for the ideal that disputes between nations can be settled by more civilised methods than an appeal to brute force, and if the League is powerless it means that there are not enough people yet who really believe that war is unnecessary and useless....

The ultimate factor in international relationships, as in all social matters, is public opinion—what the mass of the people think, the standards and ideals which prevail. The root of all our difficulties (as we have been repeatedly told) is moral and spiritual. "The work of righteousness shall be peace," wrote Isaiah, "and the effect of righteousness, quietness and confidence for ever."

The Diocese did its best to speak out for peace. Synod passed a resolution denouncing "the unrestricted manufacture and sale of armaments and munitions of war by private firms," and Bishop Williams forwarded a copy of it to Arthur Henderson, President of the Conference in Geneva. Henderson's courteous reply was duly received and printed in the January 1935 issue of the Diocesan Gazette.

Williams, like Eardley-Wilmot, held strong views on war. He had begun his episcopate when, as he mentioned in his Charge to Synod in July 1934, "the Great War had begun to rage in all its fury." Now it looked as if the cycle was beginning again as he entered his 21st year as Bishop. His Pastoral Letter, issued in Lent 1935, echoed this dark thought. It began:

After the Nations had been in the grip of the Great War, that terrible crisis of incalculable issues, I believe that God was then calling to the World to awake and realize its condition, its moral and spiritual condition, to turn from sin to righteousness, from selfishness to God.

Did the World, after the War, answer and obey that call? Did we, as Christian people, turn to God in deep sincerity and determination to enthrone Jesus Christ in our hearts and live our lives in strict accordance with His Life and teaching? No, we did not.

The reason that things are not right with the World at the present time is largely due to the unheeding carelessness with which we went back to the old selfish ways and were not "renewed in the spirit of our minds."

There was a call of God, at the time of the Great War, but it was unheeded. God is calling to us again now. He has been very merciful to us for although the times are hard and there is much suffering, yet God has spared us hitherto from a greater catastrophe. If the World turns a deaf ear again to His call and the nations clash together once more in deadly conflict, who can tell but that our so-called civilization may be blotted out altogether.

Following a plea to his people as individuals that they live "close to God" in their own personal religious lives, Williams announced that this would be his last Lenten Pastoral Letter. His resignation took effect 30 April 1935. When "the inevitable" happened four years later, it fell to Philip Carrington to see the Diocese through World War II.

33

Vestry Books: Paspebiac
1937–1942

A mong the duties of the priest-in-charge of each parish is the keeping of a Vestry Book to record the acts of the parish: the types and number of services taken, on what dates, by whom, the number of communicants, and the amount of the offertory.

Long before books of printed forms for this purpose came into general use, incumbents kept personal records from which to make up their notitia parochialis—the number of births, deaths, and marriages performed—to be filed with the Bishop at the year's end. Minutes of Vestry meetings and financial statements often found their way into the record as well.

Many nineteenth-century so-called Vestry Books (and some of those were kept well into the twentieth century) have less to do with the services of the church than with the material history of the parish. They may contain accounts, records of pew rental, or purchases of materials for the Sunday school, copies of letters sent or received or notices of particular interest to the parish or the community at large.

Some of the oldest Anglican communities in the Diocese of Quebec are found on the Gaspé Peninsula. The church at Paspebiac, the subject of the following excerpt, was nearing completion in 1824 when Archdeacon G. J. Mountain made his first Visitation to the Gaspé. More than 20 years later, it was he who consecrated it as St Peter's when at last (as was required by Church Society regulations) the title to the land was clear and the building free of debt.

Gaspesians have a strong sense of history, and the clergy have played their part in that record-keeping tradition. On the fly leaf of the Paspebiac Vestry Book for 1933–1954 is the following memorandum, written during the incumbency of the Rev. A. S. LeMoignan, neatly penned and filling the whole page:

1937 A Memorial Year
1st The Coronation of our Beloved King George VI and Queen Elizabeth on May the 12th.
2 *Two* Memorial Windows.
   1. From the Bouillon family in loving memory of their daughter Leila Grace.

2. From Miss Ella Hamon in loving memory of her brother William, for many years a keen supporter of St Peter's Church, Paspebiac.

3 A picture of Major Rev. Buckland, for many years Rector of the Parish, presented by his son Archie.

4 Xmas Day, 3.30 to 4.30, a special Service broadcasted from St Peter's Church, Paspebiac for the benefit of the Church people isolated on the Canadian Labrador.

On the verso of the fly leaf, the high points of three additional years are given, all on the one page.

1939
A gift of £100 from Miss Hamon for the St Peter's Endowment Fund Paspebiac.
Credence Table (Cloth) in memory of Mrs Le Couture.

1941
Mr & Mrs E. A. Bouillon celebrate their 50th Wedding Anniversary—Special service of Thanksgiving was held—the Congregation presented them two Prayer Books with suitable inscriptions.

1942
On Sunday afternoon December the 20th 1942 St Peter's Church was complete[ly] destroyed by fire—Held service at 10.30 a.m. and at 3.30 p.m. the Church was gone—Saved the two Communion Cups & Paten presented by the Gallie family in 1846.

From the style of their varying script, these last three entries were added to the Vestry Book one by one. The record, brief as it is, captures the painstaking manner in which church furnishings are assembled in small, rural parishes. Its testimony to the church's centrality in the life of the community makes this simple chronicle all the more poignant.

34

Parish Traditions and Church Ceremonial: Trinity Church, Quebec, and Christ Church, Harrington Harbour 1881, 1939, and 1991

S*ome parishes in the Diocese have a strong tradition of churchmanship. Others will take on whatever practices are favoured by the incumbent, whether Evangelical or Catholic, High or Low Church. Taking into consideration the degree of church ceremonial to which a congregation is accustomed has become, for most priests, either a question of tact or a matter of will.*

Trinity Church, Quebec, is unique in the Diocese in that the form of its ritual is protected by an Act of the Provincial Legislature, passed 30 June 1881, incorporating the congregation. The preface to the by-laws defining the position of Trinity Church states:

> With the view of preventing, as far as possible, all misapprehension as to our objects or the principles upon which we desire to proceed, the congregation in its corporate capacity, puts on record in permanent form its firm determination that "Trinity Church" shall forever remain as a Free, Evangelical Church of the Church of England, and that the services therein held shall always be conducted with Christian simplicity; avoiding all those unjustifiable practices, calculated in their symbolism or otherwise to teach errors discarded by the Reformers: and which are either in the spirit or the letter, opposed alike to Holy Scripture and the principles of the Church of England, as explicitly declared in the XXXIX articles.

Thus, when candlesticks first appeared on the altar of Trinity in about 1991, it was the decision of the congregation to adopt this innovation.

Other congregations with a tradition of simple ceremonial have sometimes found themselves at the mercy of an incumbent determined to change their ways. The following excerpt, taken from a list of suggestions drawn up by a departing priest for the benefit of his successor at Harrington Harbour, shows how such innovations were contemplated (in some parishes at least).

You will be wise to talk over any new idea you have and gradually push it home before you introduce it. Even then you will not get everyone with you.... Don't be afraid to be firm and decided on the <u>first</u> occasion when such a course is necessary. They will respect you after that. I tried to be gentle, and was at once put down as "soft" (as you will sometime probably be told!! ...) I suggest that you take your own course quietly but decidedly and not worry when you are told that Mr. Dicker or Mr. Barnett did not do that! Each new minister is told such things about the one before him. (See if I'm not right?)

My own way of introducing a change of policy or custom has been to talk about it in conversation steadily whenever the chance to do so occurs to prepare their minds for it and make them see its advantages. Although this slow process will take you a year, or years, to produce the fruit you want, I believe that it is the best and most effective method.

The next section deals entirely with how to cope with local churchmanship and is headed "CHURCH CEREMONIAL":

Be careful what method you use in changing any of the ancient customs here!

I see two methods.

One is to make your changes boldly RIGHT AT THE BEGINNING OF YOUR TIME, stick to them, take the cracks and arguments and all the hullabaloo that it will cause, and live them down, letting the qualities in you that they like gradually take their effect and gradually overcome the opposition.

Without having tried this method I cannot recommend it from experience, but as I look back on my time here I am under the impression that I ought to have been tough enough to do it.

The other method is the one I have tried. I have talked of my ideas at every opportunity, and gradually pushed them forward, but I have still found opposition and sometimes hostility, even after trying for some years. I have thought this the best plan and have tried to work *with* the people rather than enforcing my views at once. For this they have considered me "weak."...

My advice to you is to make up your mind just what you want to do and do it irrespective of results—but you will have to fight for it for *two or three years.*

If you are strong-willed enough you will be able to stand the strain, and gradually they will come round and back you. If not, try my method and wait and get experience and see what you can do gradually.

They are scared stiff of the Roman Church. Anything you suggest that is different from what "Grandpa" said in 1880 is put down as Roman Catholic....

Mr. Barnett put the two candles on the altar in 1932. Three families promptly left the Church. Perhaps he was unwise, and yet any change will be received like that....

The compromise reached was to light the candles at the early H.C. Service, and leave them "out" for the other services. I started and have stuck solidly to lighting them always for the Baptism Service.... If you back me in this you will gradually win them over. I have done this all my five years here, so it is not a new idea—or a R.C. idea—as they will still tell you.

At St. Paul's River and at Kegashka the candles are lit at every service in the normal Christian manner.

Reading these comments, probably written about 1939 although they are unsigned and undated, one wonders why it was so important to impose candles on a congregation despite their opposition. When, some nine years later, the Rev. C. S. Brett-Perring wrote his impressions of the various congregations along the Coast then under his care, he remarked, apparently without prejudice or consternation, that at this particular station "any of our ancient Catholic practices" were regarded with suspicion and hostility. "Candles are anathema," he wrote, "and their would-be use some years ago caused a grave commotion."

35

Youth Work in the Diocese:
Camping at Leeds, Quebec Lodge,
Fort Haldimand, and Brion Island

C*amping for both boys and girls has long formed a leading part of the Diocesan tradition. Summer Schools for young people, held in the 1930s, were precursors to camping here, particularly when Dean Carrington, a keen organizer of such events, added elements from Scouting to the programmes.*

Then, in the summer of 1942, a Boys' Camp was held at Leeds as an experiment. It was announced from the start as "a training camp for war-service and other kinds of service," meant to be "hard work," not a "hotel in the woods." Twenty-five boys, representing 10 parishes, took part in this first camp. It was staffed by Bishop Carrington and T. J. Matthews, John Comfort and H. I. Apps. The success of the venture led to the appointment of "a permanent Boys' Work Committee" consisting of six clergy, three of whom had taken part in the Leeds experiment, for the purpose of organizing Week-Ends and rallies for boys of 14 years and older.

Forty-seven boys attended a Week-End at Cookshire, opening on 21 November 1942, with "ten more from Coaticook ... on the afternoon of the 22nd in the form of a 'Commando Raid' adding to their number." A second Week-End for 30 boys was staged at Shawinigan Falls in early December. In both, the programme of training was in the hands of the Bishop and of the Rev. Colin Cuttell, assisted by members of the local clergy. The boys' "enthusiastic support" determined the organizers to extend the plans of the Work Committee to allow for further Camps.

An Anglican Girls' Camp, also focused on war-service, was held at Cedar Lodge, Memphremagog, that same summer. Twenty-seven girls took part. Activities involved "drilling, marching, and military discipline" and included "First Aid, Air Raid precautions, Artificial Respiration and Physical Training." One former camper recalls being one of a troop of hikers, ready at an instant to dive for shelter in a road-side ditch at a wave of the Chaplain's arm! A highlight of the week's programme was the visit to the campsite of the Chief Commissioner of the Girl Guides in Canada.

In 1943, the Diocese ventured formally into the camping business with the purchase of its own campsite at North Hatley. The August issue of the Diocesan Gazette *described the property as follows:*

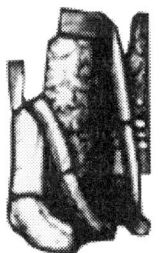

It would be hard to find a more beautiful and suitable site for a camp than the one that has recently been bought by the Diocese on the lake at North Hatley.

Standing high above the water level are two cottages within a few yards of each other. Both have a wide Verandah on two sides of the building, which would accommodate 15-20 cots for any campers wishing to sleep out of doors. In the one cottage there is a dining room and kitchen, with bedrooms and bathrooms overhead; in the other a sitting room with a fireplace, 8 or 9 bedrooms and four bathrooms. These cottages are fully furnished and equipped.

A little below the cottages is the boat house built over the water; this is in excellent condition and in the process of time might well be furnished as a Chapel—at present it contains two boats which look to be ready for service.

The cottages are fitted with electric lighting, and water is laid on from the lake; there is a pump house at the back of the property.

The beach below the cottages is excellent, and the bathing good; there is a large field adjoining the property, which is available and can be rented for games and other camp activities.

A Camp site such as this could well be used for a variety of purposes, such as Conferences and Retreats ... [I]t has every chance of fulfilling a great need and of being a strong asset in our work for boys and girls and young people.

This was the first site of Quebec Lodge; the property occupied by the present camp (on the other side of Lake Massawippi) was purchased by the Diocese in 1954.

Camping activities, although vividly recalled by the participants, are seldom recorded in any lasting form. A happy exception to this is provided by Fort Haldimand Camp on Gaspé Bay. In 1948, this historic site was acquired as a second Diocesan campsite. From the first, the early organizers set out to document the day-to-day activities of each camp, and kept it up faithfully from 1948 to 1954 at least. Their records are bound in a large, plywood-encased volume, measuring 33 by 48 centimetres, fastened by three leather straps, and stabilized by two large bolts. In it may be found the names of campers and staff for most of the camps held during this period, as well as timetables, duty charts, patrol rosters, and daily camp and chapel logs. At the back are a number of snap-shots.

The daily logs for the Boys' Camps, whether junior or senior, seem to have been kept by the clergy, either in their capacities of Chaplain or Camp Director. However, the girls—judging from the handwriting—appear to have been allowed to keep their logs themselves. The following is taken from the Junior Girls' Camp log, 6 to 13 July 1949:

July 6
Campfire and wiener roast on the beach.
July 7
Evening programme consisted of games, singing and folk dancing.
July 8
New girl, Eva Bowes, arrived in camp from Anticosti. Played volley ball & horseshoes. Games very much enjoyed.
July 9
Another new girl, Denise Fortier. Wiener roast & stunt night.
July 10
Visitors' Day. Sing song, games, sang hymns till bedtime. Picnic supper. Girls from tent moved into house due to rain storm.
July 11
Went on hike. Did handicrafts, swimming, cooked supper outdoors. Had movies for evening entertainment. All are tired but happy. Movies shown were "Care of Pets" & "Beach & Sea Animals."
July 12
Banquet. Campers had a good time. Movies shown "Windsor Castle" & "Wind from the West."
July 13
Camp breaks up. Shirley Ross first to leave.

The daily schedule, which appears with the log, shows that reveille was at 7.30 a.m. Flag raising took place at 8 and breakfast at 8.15; then followed patrol duties, chapel, and inspection. An hour of swimming and another of handicrafts preceded dinner at 12.15. In the afternoon was tuck, rest period, and swimming, then half an hour of Guiding and an hour and a half of sports before supper at 5.30. Preparation for evening programme was followed by sing song and chapel; then evening programme. Taps was at 8.45, and bedtime, 9 p.m.

The list of participants—elsewhere in the volume—shows that there was a staff of eight women: a Programme Director (Anna Apps, wife of the Rev. H. I. Apps of Malbay), a "Swimming Instructress," two Guide Leaders, one Counsellor, a Nurse, and two Cooks.

With the exception of two leaders from the Montreal area, all the staff members came from the region. The 31 campers who attended came from Hopetown, Sunny Bank, Malbay, Wakeham, York, Sandy Beach, L'Anse aux Cousins, Belle Anse,

Haldimand, Gaspé, and Anticosti.

Each girl was assigned to one of four patrols: the Dandelions, the Caraways, the Busy Beavers, and the Forget-Me-Nots. The name of the camper who was first to leave may have been particularly noted because she had been one of the leaders—Patrol Leader of the Dandelions.

Another log, although not complete, is worth quoting. It, too, was written by a camper, this time at the Junior Girls' Camp of July 1951:

Wednesday, July 18: Campers started arriving at 9.30 a.m. New Carlisle, Paspebiac, and Port Daniel girls arrived in time for lunch. Everybody made their beds in the house or tents, then wrote home to say that they had arrived safely. After this went to the beach for walk and then had supper. After having chapel, patrols were formed and named. Games followed and hot chocolate was served. Then a story was read by Miss Fish and lights out.

Thursday, July 19: Schedule started. Swimming charts were made consisting of three groups: tadpoles, frogs, fish. Only one fish was caught in the whole camp. She was Helen Agnes. Rain prevented a wiener roast on the beach so wieners and drinks were served at supper, followed by a campfire and songs in the Hall. The two tents moved beds and luggage into the Hall because of rain and strong winds. So ended the first full day in camp.

Another, shorter-lived venture, but of lasting impact on the participants, were two Brion Island camps held in 1962 and 1963 on the Magdalen Islands. In previous years some Magdalen Islanders had ventured to Fort Haldimand for summer camp, but for most of the children Brion Island provided their first opportunity for such an experience. The camps were the brain-child of the Rev. J. L. Young (incumbent on the Islands and a "Padre" at Quebec Lodge), who was assisted in the first year by Barbara Gibaut, the Diocesan Youth Worker. The October 1962 issue of the Diocesan Gazette *carried a description of the initial camp, which had accommodated 19 boys and 15 girls in two separate sessions of nine days each:*

Brion Island [the report explained] is ... about six miles long and up to two miles wide lying about nine miles north of Grosse Isle, the headquarters of the Magdalen Islands Mission. There are no permanent inhabitants ... as a site for a camp [however], it can have few parallels. There are large level playing fields, areas of pasture, very large wooded areas, sand beaches, safe and sheltered swimming areas—none of them used by any others and all available and handy to the campsite.

The actual site was ... at an abandoned farm homestead ... The house

... still has floors, outside walls and a watertight roof and was used as a head-quarters for the camps, for a dining room and kitchen, for indoor activities in wet weather ...

The price which had to be paid for this ideal camp site was in the problems which nine miles of sometimes rough water between it and civilization at Grosse Isle provided. A daily boat service ably run by Mr Ralph Goodwin of Grosse Isle (weather permitting!) solved most of the transport problems, however. And the isolation of the site in rough weather did not work entirely to the detriment of the campers—although a plea from the boys as their nine days camp grew to a close that they be allowed to stay longer was sternly denied, the weather dictated terms and the camp lasted an extra three days!...

Camping everywhere is dependent on leadership, funding, and, in most cases, the willingness of those in authority to tie up money in real estate and equipment. In 1993 (its 50th anniversary) Quebec Lodge narrowly escaped being closed and the site put up for sale. Thanks to the determined efforts of campers (past and present), parents, and the general public, the survival of Quebec Lodge—for the immediate future at least—seems now to be assured. Oblivious to such material considerations, however, generations of campers variously situated in the Diocese of Quebec have continued to place their hopes in the prospect of "next year."

"Will there be another Brion Island adventure next year? This question asked anxiously by everyone who was at this year's camps is not yet decided," the account of this first camp concludes, "but if those who ask questions were responsible for the answer, it would be a resounding YES!"

Mission to Industry: Sept-Isles
1951 and 1985

After World War II, and especially in the 1950s, there was a sense of expansion in the Diocese of Quebec. The following extract from an account by the Ven. William Wallace Davis of his visit (in the autumn of 1951) to Sept-Iles and Knob Lake (now Schefferville) is marked by some of the spirit of momentum inherent in the times, the urge to move with the projects of industry, and to form a part of the rising communities in what, just months before, had been little more than wilderness.

 On Wednesday evening, October 3rd, I arrived in Comeau Bay and spent the night and the following day with the Rev. Leslie Gourley and Mrs. Gourley in the hospitable parsonage beside the beautiful twelve-year-old Church of St. Andrew and St. George. Mr. Gourley and I visited the new power development nearby on the Manicouagan River—one [of] the many pastoral responsibilities which keep our priest at Comeau Bay constantly on the go. The others include services at Mont-Joli, Forestville, Shelter Bay, Trinity Bay, Seven Islands and Clarke City.

Thursday evening, armed with information supplied by my host, I arrived in Seven Islands going directly to the new Seven Islands Hotel which was to be my home until the following Monday morning.

Friday morning I looked out of my window [at] this 300 year old north shore village which has sprung into sudden prominence through the development of the iron ore mines at Knob Lake over 300 miles north. At present the North Shore and Labrador Railway Company and the Cartier, MacNamara, Mannix and Knudson Construction Company are engaged in a joint project for the construction and operation of a Railway. The Hollinger Iron Ore Company is engaged in extensive preparations at Knob Lake ... for the moment when this railway will be completed and the iron ore will move down to Seven Islands at the rate of 40,000 tons per day.

Seven Islands, as one might expect, is a combination of the new and the old. The gigantic work afoot is echoed in the two modern hotels opened since 1951 began—the modern theatre owned by Mr. Jack Leyden, Mayor of the Town, and the appearance of stores and restaurants where a steadily growing volume of business is being carried on. During the morning I met a number of Church folk—some in Seven Islands—some at Three Mile Camp, and perhaps the largest number at the Air Port.... That evening there was a large party with dancing at the Hotel where I was introduced to a goodly number of the English-speaking community.... Seven Islands already has the open-hearted hospitality typical of new settlements where the very newness of everyone present forms a common bond.

At 1.30 a.m. Saturday morning, through the kindness of Mr. Leyden and the Hollinger Ungava Transport, I climbed into a transport plane and flew northward to Knob Lake.

I stepped out of the plane into what seemed like a new snow-covered world, and was informed that, for Knob Lake, winter had now begun. After a few hours sleep in the comfortable staff house, I visited the ten family homes in Burnt Creek (Hollinger Headquarters) and enjoyed a drive around the minefields [sic] in the companionship of Mr. Harold Gardiner, the Assistant Manager. It is hoped that the new townsite will be erected and occupied by some 3,000 people in 1954....

Sunday morning at 9.45 a.m. we had a celebration of Holy Communion in the [Lido] Theatre placed at our disposal by Mr. Leyden. At 10.30 the regular service attended by Anglicans, United Church people, Presbyterians, Lutherans and Baptists was held in the side aisle of the theatre ... Sunday afternoon ... I was taken by a boyhood friend, Jack Serson, now one of the Hollinger foremen, along the new railway to Twelve Mile Camp. Here a tunnel, half a mile long, has been cut through the mountain on the approach to the Moysee River Canyon, and a great steel bridge is nearing completion....

Sunday evening I conducted a service in the little Chapel in Clarke City in the Office building of the Gulf Paper Company where I was entertained by the Manager and his wife, Mr. and Mrs. Overstrom. Everywhere I visited I heard of the fine work carried on by the summer students, Mr. [Harry] Seeley and Mr [John] Mayoh, of Rev. Leslie Gourley's faithful visits, and of the visit of Archbishop Carrington and Dean Seaborn on their way to the Labrador.

Monday morning I returned by plane to Quebec. My last impression was formed by seeing the seven islands which give this growing town its name—a striking sight surrounding the harbour where, in a few years, ships will come to carry off the ore to make steel for our modern multiple forms of construction. Seven Islands is the ideal location, too, for the centre of a new North Shore Mission—a home for our missionary who will care for Church people in Knob Lake, Havre St. Pierre, Clarke City and other points in this area which reflects the rapid industrialization of our Province.

The Seven Islands Community Church would serve both Anglicans and members of the United Church. Their respective clergy, C.H.S. Cheesman and Robert Shorten, worked together to provide a place of worship to accommodate both congregations. On 20 May 1956, the church was dedicated and consecrated in a joint ceremony by the Ven. T. J. Matthews, Archdeacon of the Gaspé, and the Rev. T. D. Everett, President of the Montreal-Ottawa Conference of the United Church of Canada.

In 1985, T. J. Matthews, then a retired bishop, presented congratulations to the Anglican congregation of All Saints, Sept-Iles, which had by this time acquired a separate church of its own, an all-new building. Although it was the occasion of the "25th Anniversary of Services" for All Saints, Matthews chose to recall in some detail the old Community Church as it had evolved during the heady interval of rapid expansion—the days of co-operation and making do:

There was an abandoned, one-room, small school house near the village which was made available to us. This we hauled to the site and remodelled into a Community church for the use of Anglican and United Church people. I remember drawing up a form of service which I hoped would be acceptable to the members of the congregation, which of course represented more than one denomination. For source material, I used the Anglican Prayer Book and hymnal and the United Church Book of Praise. I shall always remember how surprised and delighted I was to discover so much material common to both denominations ...

In due course, the congregation grew too large for the school house to accommodate and we enlarged it. It had always been my hope that we could continue as one congregation in one church, using one church building. However, changing personnel, both clerical and lay, felt it to be more expedient that there be two autonomous congregations, Anglican and United, instead of one. Naturally, this led to two church buildings. The same thing happened at Knob Lake and in Murdochville. As I look back on it now, I realize that these, what I felt to be retrograde, developments were the result of [the] policy of the establishment in Toronto and Quebec more than expressing the will of the people involved at the grass roots. I was in no position in those days to tell the establishment what to do, so it was their view which prevailed. All they said to me was, in effect, "Oh Tim, you are before your time!"

After 1985 the Protestant population of Sept-Iles suffered a sharp decline. Consequently, by 1990, the Anglican and United Church congregations once again found it expedient to share their resources, in this case the services of a single minister: the Rev. Paul Derry of the United Church of Canada, also licensed by the Bishop of Quebec. Derry officiated for both denominations according to the rites and forms of each tradition until his transfer from the Diocese in 1993.

37

Bringing the Gospel Home:
Theology and Experience
1961

P*hilip Carrington, whether in the role of scholar, priest or teacher, possessed the gift of captivating an audience and infusing with life the topic under discussion. When, during his tenure as Dean of Divinity at Bishop's, it was known that Carrington was to preach, "the Chapel was full, with not a few faculty of Science men and a coterie of self-styled agnostics in the pews."*

Depending on the setting or the occasion, the Dean would make use of his considerable theatrical skills of voice and gesture: his "curious thin-lipped, slightly snarling voice reserved for … a withering moment," for example, or his "instinctive awareness of the dignity and greatness of the priestly office." He even resorted to "Maori tribal yells learnt … in his youth in New Zealand."

Similarly, in his writing, a lively style rendered his arguments convincing through his use of concrete illustration. The following, an excerpt from a review (printed in the Quebec Diocesan Gazette*) of a recently published theological treatise, shows how he could provide examples from his ministry to clarify a New Testament text.*

This book [*According to Mark*], as the sub-title indicates, is a "Running Commentary on the Oldest Gospel," the latest book by Archbishop Carrington, retired last year from the Diocese of Quebec …

The Archbishop writes as he converses—interestingly, challengingly, often provocatively. The reader can approve, admire, disagree, but seldom be bored or unmoved! His style almost has an element of drama, so that the material, at the same time erudite and dramatic, seems to come alive before the mind's eye as in a play.

There is bound to be critical comment by certain specialists on some controversial points, but usually warm praise of this book has been forthcoming … witness this report from Colin Wood, editor of the Braille Theological Times …

This second reviewer, Colin Wood, observed that Carrington's book, although aimed

*at "the theologian and preacher," was equally attractive to "the interested layman"
because of the work's down-to-earth quality. He continued as follows:*

To his task, the Archbishop brings not only scholarship of the highest order,
but also a magnificent and robust common sense that enables him to burst
so delightfully some of the bubbles of absurdities of certain biblical scholarship. Here is one example, and particularly appealing since it is drawn from
our Labrador Coast. "The disciples had set out for Bethsaida, but doubtless
the storm had driven them back. They limped into harbour at Gennesareth,
and moored there. The material which Mark is handling now is full of local colour and local names. It has been severely criticised and found inconsistent and inaccurate, but I can only say that after twelve missionary journeys in a small boat on the Labrador Coast, I am more than satisfied with
it. I have had many encounters with contrary winds and with strange place-
names which fail to appear in a consistent form. The 'Kegashka' of the postal
authorities (and the Anglican Mission) is often called 'Casca' or 'Casco'* by
those who live there. The 'Passage Saint Germain' (as it appears on the charts)
is 'Passerjammer' in the language of the coast fishermen, and I take it to be
a corruption of 'Passage à Mer.' So I am not worried about Khersa or Gerasa
or Gergesa, or Dalmanutha and Magdala and Migdal-Nunia, and still less
about setting out for Bethsaida and arriving at Gennesareth. I have done these
things too often myself. Transcriptional errors, too, were as easy in those days
as printers' errors (or authors' errors) are today. I have just read in a diocesan
magazine that Nathaniel came from Canada of Galilee. Two extra letters may
easily slip into or out of a strange place-name."

By way of conclusion, the Diocesan Gazette *reviewer quotes an illustrative passage
from Carrington's text, in which he has summarized some of the dominant features
of the Gospel:*

"Mark is primarily a narrative," he wrote. "Its subject is 'the beginning of the
gospel' which had swept the world by the time that it was written. Through
its pages walks the figure of Jesus Christ, 'from the Baptism to the Passion.'
It places Him in His cultural and social milieu; the whole countryside comes
to life as He walks through it; the whole city is stirred when He enters it.
The narrative has continuity, motion and drama. It is full of animated figures.... He holds the centre of the stage, of course; but He is inseparable from

---

* Carrington might well have added the more usual "Kaska" to this list.

the fellowship or household of the Twelve, which He forms around Him and to which He commits everything. This association is preserved to the very end ..."

In 1930, while still at Bishop's, Carrington had published The Sign of Faith, *a book designed, as the author stated, "to present English Christianity ... so as to appeal to boys and girls." The Dean wished, as his biographer put it, "to help them see the great adventure of Christianity ..." It appears that the same impulse still infused his writings 30 years later.*

38

"The Church Back Home"
1962

W*ith the decline of the Anglican popula-
tion in the Diocese of Quebec, more and more parishes, especially in rural districts, are
struggling to survive. Many a parish History, such as the one prepared to celebrate the
centenary of Christ Church, Valcartier, observes the disappearance of its founding families among the present congregation. Recalling the original pew holders in Christ
Church, the chronicler remarked: "Upon reading this list of names we realize the
changes time brings to a community. Some of the older residents of Valcartier may have
heard their fathers talk about these families. But to the present generation many of the
names have disappeared entirely from the parish, entire families having died or moved
on to other parts of the country." Yet, former parishioners may continue to feel strong
ties with the churches they have left, and wish to keep in touch with the "church back
home."*

*Those parishioners who have "stayed on" have become increasingly aware of the
need to ensure that their church and churchyard are provided for should membership
drop below the critical number. The parish of Brookbury, for example, as part of its
120th anniversary celebrations, struck a committee "to establish the St. John's Church
and Cemetery Endowment Fund with the Incorporated Church Society of the Diocese of Quebec to ensure future maintenance of this property against the possible time
when few of the descendants will remain in this locality. Parishioners and relatives of
former parishioners have been contacted and the response has been most gratifying."*

The following selection, printed in the Quebec Diocesan Gazette *for June
1962, touches on the special associations particular churches may have for distant friends
and families. It is titled "The Church Back Home."*

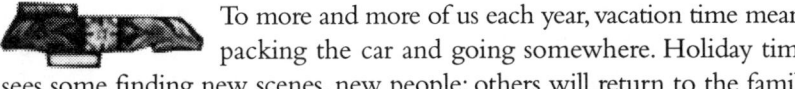 To more and more of us each year, vacation time means
packing the car and going somewhere. Holiday time
sees some finding new scenes, new people; others will return to the familiar surroundings of earlier days. Every year some of us decide to go back to
the places where our families had their beginning in this country, although
we ourselves may be two or three or more generations removed from the
family home. Often we have kept in touch with these older communities

through news of the church there, the news most often is to the effect that the steeple needs repairing or the cemetery a new fence. Former residents are exceptionally generous in contributing to the maintenance of "the old Church back home," as many a church in the Diocese bears witness.

What a disappointment, then, awaits these interested and generous donors, when they plan the summer trip to include "St. Mary's, where Grandfather was baptized, and where Great-uncle Dan rang the bell for fifty-six years—and where our fifty dollars has helped to repair the foundation laid by an even earlier generation." If the visitors arrive during the week, or at almost any hour on Sunday excepting the hour of Divine Service, they will find the little church back home locked and barred, the graveyard securely padlocked. To make enquiries at the neighbouring houses will elicit uncomprehending stares, or at best, a vague direction to ask Old Man Jennings at the white house two miles back. Gone with the fleeting hours of daylight are the hopes of visiting the church, rambling through the graveyard, getting a glimpse of the family entries in the old record books. What rejection is more chilling than the rejection of a Church's locked door?

Once back in the car and on the way again, our travellers agree that the church has to be guarded against vandals, that the graveyard, if left unfenced, will become a pasture or a parking lot—in short "they" are quite right in keeping it all under lock and key. But at the same time, the rebuff is there, and the question nags: Why are we treated like this when we really belong? What harm can we do that they have locked us out??

Perhaps this year it will be different. Perhaps this year when we go back, we shall find the church open and ready to welcome us. Or perhaps we shall find a notice tacked to the door, telling us who has the keys and where he may be found, where the records are kept, and when the next Service will be held. Perhaps some church organization or some school boy or girl at home for the holiday, will be interested enough in the whole congregation of the church, past and present, near and far, to offer this welcome to those who have long looked forward to their summer visit to the Church back home.

The history of Holy Trinity Church, Denison's Mills, published to celebrate its hundredth anniversary, tells the tale of many a rural parish in the Diocese:

Now, in the year 1975, when our church will be one hundred years old, we are trying to think back ... to the time when this lovely old church was built, and to the families who gave of their best to make it what it is and has been.

Surely it behooves us to look forward, to do our part to make and keep it what our forefathers hoped it would be.... Because of the few families left in the community, that belong to the church, we realize that it is impossible to have regular services, but our hope is that the two services a year may continue for a long time. Perhaps, we may celebrate another special anniversary."

A layperson wrote "The Church Back Home," and, not surprisingly, it is the laypeople of the Diocese who have striven to preserve the material heritage of the Church. Although church land was usually the gift of a parishioner or purchased with local funds, traditionally the Diocese has required that church property be vested in the Bishop or, later, in the Church Society. When numbers drop and parish assessments are not paid, the usual recourse is to close a church. Not infrequently the land is sold and the church demolished, a decision made at Diocesan level. Sometimes Government funding may save a church—Christ Church, Frampton, is now a museum, St Matthew's, Quebec, a municipal library. More often, however, it is local organizations, founded for that special purpose, that intervene. The Old North Church Cemetery Association of Hatley, for example, was officially constituted in 1992, but had been busy for some years in painstakingly restoring the utterly neglected resting place of the Township's founding fathers. It is to such organizations, more often than not, that the credit must be given in the preservation of whatever may remain of the "church back home."

39

Relations With Other Communions:
Arvida, La Tuque, and Richmond
1964

D*espite the pessimistic note sounded in Bishop Brown's January Letter, 1964, this was a euphoric time in the Diocese. The various communions around the world displayed a new openness towards one another. Parish after parish sent news to the* Diocesan Gazette *of their outreach to, or invitations from, other denominations with which their previous contact had been minimal. The February issue contains several articles that give evidence of the efforts being made by Anglicans, Roman Catholics, and other denominations to reach a deeper understanding of one another. One of these items concerned Arvida:*

During the Annual Week of Prayer for the Unity of the Church a service of an unprecedented nature was held, January 19th, in the Auditorium of the Recreation Hall in Arvida.

The service, which began at 8 p.m. was conducted in both French and English (with no translations) and was presided over, jointly by the Rev. Eric Caulfield, Rector of the Anglican Church, the Rev. Jack Richardson, United Church Minister, and Abbé Paul Tremblay, Priest of the Roman Catholic Church. Congregations from all the churches in the district attended.

The Hall, which holds 600 people, was filled to overflowing; 150 persons were turned away.

A second item on the same page described a television programme on the subject of "the Anglican Church, its Liturgy, Prayer-life and Worship" aired on the local channel shortly before Arvida's ecumenical service. Footage taken in St George the Martyr Anglican Church was followed by a discussion, in French, between M. Yves Jobin of CKRS-TV and the Rector of St George's, together with one of the latter's parishioners. Later, the group was joined by Fr Roméo Bouchard of the Jonquière Classical College. "The above program," the article concluded, "was a unique opportunity of sharing our common heritage with Christians of other traditions and was a magnificent preamble to the Ecumenical Service which followed on Sunday the 19th."

Also printed in the February issue was the following letter from the Rector of St

Andrew's Church, La Tuque:

After having read the Vision Report from Thetford Mines, where it is expected that there will be a gradual but noticeable drop in the number of church families in the next 10 years, one thing struck me. What are we, as a diocese (which is likely to witness a similar drop in numbers) doing to live on better terms with our French majority? Such questions come to mind as: How many of our clergy can speak French and use it? Do we know our Roman clergy in our own communities? Have we attempted to meet them socially—in their homes? For example, have we paid courtesy calls in the Week of Prayer for Church Unity, or did we call on the day of the death of the last Pope and offer sympathy? Do we as congregations isolate ourselves against contacts with French people, except at work and in stores, etc.?

Comments or even articles on this aspect of church life would be beneficial. I know that at least two clergy have given French addresses on the church to French service clubs. I feel sure that the French pamphlets are a step in the right direction. I hope that someone will undertake a translation of the Eucharist in our revised Prayer Book in French soon.

These are all encouraging signs which we should foster. Could we hear from others on this subject?

The French pamphlets mentioned were a Diocesan initiative designed to promote good relations and mutual understanding with French-speaking Quebecers by providing information on the Anglican Church. The third in the series, entitled Les Anglicans et l'unité, *had appeared in December 1963, and could be purchased through Church House at five cents a copy.*

The two clergy who had addressed French service clubs, were Canons S. A. Meade (in 1962), and S. W. Williams (in 1963); both spoke at the invitation of the Richelieu Club, the one in Thetford Mines, the other in Grand'Mère.

The complete text of Canon Meade's address entitled "L'Écumenisme" appeared (in the original French) in the 1962 Summer issue of the Diocesan Gazette. *The two French-language dailies reporting on the event noted that this was the first time a non-Roman Catholic had been invited to speak before a branch of the Richelieu Club. The vote of thanks on this occasion was proposed by Abbé J. P. Gravel, Curé of the Parish of St-Alphonse. Canon Williams' talk, which also emphasized that "il existe maintenant un réel climat d'amitié entre les églises," is reported in the November 1963 issue of the same paper.*

It should be no surprise that a plea for greater understanding among communions should come from La Tuque, a parish that has had an ecumenical flavour from the beginning. La Tuque itself, which had been little more than a trading post, received its real impetus with the establishment there of the Brown Company, from Berlin, New Hampshire. The Brown family, who were Baptists themselves, made provision for religious services in La Tuque both for the Protestant and for the Roman Catholic population. Among the Protestants it happened that the Anglican Church was the first to offer a clergyman for the region, and as the Company was largely footing the bill for the incumbent's stipend, it was stipulated that, whoever he might be, his ministry should be appropriate for a population that would include Methodists, Baptists, Presbyterians, and others. The churchmanship at La Tuque has continued to reflect the spirit of this initial arrangement.

To avoid the implication that mutual appreciation and respect between members of different communions was centred in the newer northern communities, the following item, which appeared in the Sherbrooke French-language daily La Tribune, *25 September 1964, offers a striking instance from the Eastern Townships:*

Les catholiques de Richmond ont participé, jeudi, à une cérémonie liturgique d'un caractère tout à fait inusité. La messe de requiem chantée dans l'église de la paroisse Ste-Famille ce jour-là, en effet, l'était pour le repos de l'âme d'un pasteur protestant décédé quelques jours plus tôt, le révérend Hugh Imrie Apps.

Cet événement vaut d'être souligné parce qu'il était extrêmement rare, jusqu'à récemment du moins, qu'un office religieux catholique soit célébré à la mémoire d'un membre d'une autre confession religieuse. Nous devons voir là la manifestation d'un esprit nouveau qui honore ceux qui ont pris cette initiative et, d'une façon générale, tous ceux qui sont entrées de cœurs et de fait dans l'esprit œcuménique.

Nous ne sommes aucunement étonnés qu'un tel précédent soit créé dans les Cantons de l'Est. Sans vouloir nous livrer à une louange excessive, nous vous reconnaîtrons que depuis longtemps, catholiques et protestants ont appris à vivre côté à côté, et se coudoyer et à se respecter mutuellement.... Feu le révérend Apps jouissait de l'estime de tous les citoyens de Richmond sans distinction de croyances religieuses. Tous admiraient le respect de la conscience d'autrui qu'il avait su développer en lui à un haut degré. Il est disparu tôt, en pleine activité. Nous formons le vœu qu'il jouisse de la récompense promise aux hommes de bonne volonté et que son exemple demeure comme une inspiration vivante pour tous ceux qui ont eu l'avantage d'entrer en contact avec lui.

40

The Church as the Voice of Conscience:
The Environment
1975

I n the 1970s, the Diocese of Quebec *made strong public representations on environmental issues, particularly those surrounding the James Bay Power Corporation's plans for development in Northern Quebec. This project, as Bishop Matthews asserted, was not only "disturbing the ecological balance of the region," it was also "affecting the lives of 6,000 Native people who have occupied the territory for literally thousands of years—"*

Consequently, at the national level, a "counter-challenge" on behalf of the Native People was offered by the Anglican Church. As Matthews announced to the Diocesan Synod of 1973, the Primate—who regarded the issue as a priority—had "set up a Committee of Concern and appointed one of our own Priests, the Rev. Lynn Ross, as the National Liaison Officer to relate the concerns of the Native people to the concerns of the James Bay Power Corporation. As your Bishop I am proud that not only have I been given the privilege of serving on this committee, but also the opportunity to share a Priest of our Diocese with the National Church."

 You will note [Matthews' Charge continued], that nowhere have I claimed that in our view the James Bay project should be abandoned. Our concern is to protect and uphold the rights and needs of our Native people. If these can be served through the development, well and good. We are committed to the belief that the development must not be carried out at the expense of the Native people. One of them very simply put the problem in a nutshell. "You people," he said, "want to flood a big part of our garden. How would you like us to come and flood a big part of yours?"

By the 1960s and 70s, concern for the environment had become widespread. Even in the 1930s, however, such leaders in the Church as Bishop Carrington were pointing to ecological problems and urging that they be examined. In September 1935, on his return from his first circuit of the Gaspé and the Lower North Shore, Carrington had voiced his alarm over what he had seen. The cod fishery had failed almost completely

that season; help was "badly needed among the hardy fishermen of Labrador or many will not have enough to eat during this coming winter," he warned. This was, moreover, no isolated problem. In an interview with the Quebec Chronicle Telegraph, *the Bishop had urged what the paper described as "the interesting suggestion" that "a scientific study should be made of the causes with a view, if possible, to their removal."*

At the 1975 Diocesan Synod, when the Diocese (and the whole Canadian Church) was in a ferment over such issues as Church union and the ordination of women, Bishop Matthews chose once again to direct attention to environmental issues. His Charge, couched in metaphorical terms, examined his theme from the perspective of current priorities, including those of the Church.

The following is an excerpt from the beginning of the Bishop's Charge to the 62nd (Ordinary) Session of the Synod of the Diocese of Quebec, delivered on Friday, 16 May, in McKinnon Hall, Bishop's University. Even through the medium of the printed page, one can sense the forceful and at the same time méchante *quality that made the Bishop so effective at the grassroots level, as well as so unsettling to the hierarchy.*

In the Name of God, Father, Son and Holy Spirit. Amen.

Most of you have observed little children playing in those small plastic inflatable pools many parents provide during summer days. The children begin by quietly sitting together in the pool, tiny bucket and spade in hand. Tentatively they flip finger to water; they dip and pour it on their feet and legs; then over their heads; then over each other. At this point things begin to get rough. Their voices rise. Hands and feet pound. They jump up and down and prance around the pool. Water, water everywhere. Buckets fly, spades disappear. It is a kind of ritual war dance.

Then comes the first hurt. Wails. Recrimination. Vengeance. Finally mother. She may upbraid them. Scold or spank them. She may counsel them. Perhaps whisk them off to bed. It depends on her—and them.

Eventually, the almost empty pool limply lies deserted, toys broken and bent—another tragic ending.

My friends, those children are like people everywhere. That plastic pool [is] our world, the water and toys natural resources. We know perfectly well that one of these days there will be nothing left but the empty despoiled earth deserted, our broken playthings forgotten. The war dance over.

And what about Mother. I mean Mother Church: What is she doing about it? I think she is doing more than she used to, but not nearly as much as she should. Mother Church spends such a lot of time and energy getting a regular face-lift, replenishing her wardrobe, mulling over her list of eligible guests for her next supper party, she is in danger of becoming so preoc-cupied with her own affairs that she grows insensitive to what's going on in the plastic pool in her own backyard.

It is not clear that the children need their Mother to help them in their relationships one with another and with their environment. I think this is to be a prime concern of Mother Church. People do a lot of talking about our common humanity—the global village. Resolutions are passed and memo-rials circulated. And that is good as far as it goes. But the church needs to move beyond that. Our noble expressions of lofty sentiments have meaning only in the reality of personal relationships. St. John pointed this out long ago when he said, "you cannot love God unless first you love your neigh-bour." In the global village *everyone* is your neighbour.

In an editorial published in September 1934, during Bishop Lennox Williams' epis-copate, the editor of the Quebec Diocesan Gazette *had sounded much the same note: the Church must not remain aloof. It must involve itself actively in those issues touching any branch of the social order.*

The Church aims at the reform of the social order, and it tries to bring it about primarily by changing the lives of individuals.... The Church gives its support, and often leads the way in efforts to bring about a better state of things by legislation and education, but it knows that the great need is a change of heart and therefore its chief aim and most important task is to send out into the world men and women filled with the knowledge of God and on fire with the Spirit of Christ.

41

"A Voluminous Correspondence": A Bishop's Christmas Letter 1985

Bishop R. F. Brown died on his 88th *birthday, five years after his retirement as Assistant Bishop of Montreal and fourteen years after relinquishing his office as eighth Lord Bishop of Quebec. His obituary, written by Canon John D. R. Franklin, paid tribute among other things to the former Bishop's gift for friendship: "[I]t was typical of Russel," he wrote, "that his friends were never forgotten, and later in his parishes and his Diocese he never failed to remember them. I am told that his Christmas mailing list contained over five hundred names, and for each card he added a personal note."*

Canon Harold Brazel, a former Quebec Diocesan Archivist and former Rector of the Parish of Thetford Mines, has thoughtfully placed several of Bishop Brown's Christmas letters, directed to himself, in the Archives. The most recent of these, sent from Fyfield Manor, Oxford, England, the Bishop's last place of residence, is dated 1985.

It is a printed letter with spaces left for the name of the person addressed as well as for the signature, but the substance of the text is so direct and personal that the whole has the effect of a private communication meant for an individual. One cannot fail to be struck by the patience and strength, as well as the humour, with which Brown was enduring debility and pain while he composed his Seasonal Greeting.

 Dear Harold,
... A few months ago, it seemed unlikely that I should be writing this letter. The ulcerated condition of my left leg was so severe that an emergency amputation was necessary. So I am writing this letter with mingled feelings of thanksgiving for many prayers: and wonder as to what ministry remains for me. In the meantime I have the joy of writing to you again. I have been back at home since early October and am learning the art of walking with a prosthesis and hopefully with an artificial limb....

And now for a lighter side! In the earlier part of the year, when I was able to move about, while staying with Richard [his son] and Denise at Blackheath, I took the opportunity to revisit Madame Tussaud's Waxworks in London ... After moving from one display after another I entered the Royal Salon. Here the attendant at the entrance, noticing my limp, suggested that I might like to rest on a nearby sofa, which I did—close to the effigy of the Black Prince. Those of you who are familiar with the exhibits may recall that there are a few sofas scattered about, on some of which may be seen a figure in everyday dress which turns out, after scrutiny, to be an effigy. Well, a minute or so after I sat down, I thought I might pose as an effigy. I did so and for the next half-hour or so had a very amusing time. As the crowds milled by in ones, twos or threes, they would stop and stare at me—*was I real or an effigy?* I came under great scrutiny and sometimes a finger was poked at me just to see! It was great fun.... Every now and again I would break the spell by blinking an eye to the great amusement of the onlookers. It was fun all round. Well, so much for that!

There follows, in a large shaky hand, several lines of personal greetings "to you & Phoebe [Mrs Brazel]—I hope she is keeping better—& that all prosper—though I realise numbers [of Church members] must be down." After alluding to a further note he had enclosed to a parishioner, which he asks his correspondent to deliver by hand, he concludes with wishes for "Christmas Joy." It is signed simply, "Russel Brown."

42

Tributes and Celebrations:
The Cathedral of the Holy Trinity
1825 and 1993

I*n June 1825, when Bishop Jacob Moun-tain's body was brought for burial to the Cathedral that he had built, the coffin was "covered with black cloth and ornamented with black furniture." It was "received by the Reverend Clergy in their surplices, over which they wore black scarfs." There were in attendance representatives from the State, the Military, the Judiciary, and the Bar, as well as "a long train of respectable citizens in deep mourning." The Cathedral was "very full." After the first part of the service had been "gone through in a most sol-emn and impressive manner, the body was removed from the center aisle and depos-ited in a vault on the left side of the communion table, when the remainder of the service was read." Although contemporary newspaper accounts of the funeral give few details, it is likely that the interior of the Cathedral was draped in black. Remote as they were from the scene of these funeral rites, the churchwardens of St John's Church, Bath, in Upper Canada, procured "twenty-seven yards of bombazella, seven and one-half yards of crepe, and a yard of black velvet" in evidence of their mourning for the Bishop.*

In January 1993, a Requiem Eucharist "in Celebration of the Life and Min-istry" of Bishop Allen Goodings was held at the Cathedral. The building was crowded with people of all faiths, and many had travelled a great distance to be present at the service. The interior of the Cathedral, whose splendid restoration had been begun during Bishop Goodings' episcopate, was a blaze of white and gold. In the eye of anyone attending this ecumenical, bilingual service, neither the brightly-coloured vestments of the clergy nor the streetwear of the laypeople suggested any of the sombreness once as-sociated with services for the dead.

The centrepiece of the celebration was a Tribute to the former Bishop, delivered by the Ven. Robert A. Bryan, Archdeacon of the North Shore. The following is drawn from his text:

Last evening I watched a video tape which had been made in February 1985 during Allen Goodings' win-ter visitation on the Quebec North Shore. On the tape was a segment of the Bishop addressing the elderly at the Dr. Hodd Pavillion, the old people's home at

Harrington Harbour. With humility, he remarked, "Many of you in this room are much older than I. You have a lot more wisdom and I suspect that you can teach me a lot of things about the meaning of our Faith"—This was an example of Allen's direct and open way of communicating with all of us.

He loved his annual visitation on the lower North Shore, and the people loved to see him come. When we would land the airplane at a village in the evening, friends would appear at the cockpit door and call out, "Come right up, Bishop, we've boiled the kettle and we'll have a cup of tea."

"Thank you. I'll be there in a minute—I must help button up the plane"—then, lying on his back on the snow underneath the engine, he would button up the engine tent and then, standing on a fuel drum, help secure the wing cover, mittens off in -25° C cold.

In the morning, he would appear at the plane, driving a borrowed snowmobile—"Now then, Bob, what can I do?"

He always pitched in and never complained. He possessed great physical strength as well as spiritual strength. I remember seeing him years before in a photograph in his study, sitting with his Lancashire County rugger teammates—his eyelid drooped a bit from an opponent's errant kick.

His sense of humor was infectious. One morning after a weather layover in Natashquan, en route to St. Clement's Mission, we stood before the owner of the small hotel ready to pay our bill. Allen was first in line—the owner cupped his hand, leaned over and said, "For you Bishop, it's 20 dollars off the bill." I was next—the owner cupped his hand again and whispered to me, "For you Archdeacon, it's 10 dollars off."

From then on, Allen loved to tease me—"From now on, Bob," he would say, "I pay the entire bill and we'll get the full discount."

When I telephoned my nephew in Ottawa the day Allen died, I asked what had happened—my nephew said, "He suffered an aneurism and then I think that his heart finally failed." However, I knew that although his heart might have stopped, it never failed.

Let us pray....

In Jacob Mountain's time, there were close ties between Church and State. When news of the Bishop's death reached the Lieutenant Governor, he issued the following dispatch, dated 18 June 1825, from his residence, the Castle St Lewis in Quebec. It serves as a tribute in its turn:

With sentiments of the deepest concern, the Lieutenant Governor notifies to the public the demise, on the night of Thursday last, of the Right

Reverend the Lord Bishop of Quebec. In adverting to the unaffected piety, extended charity, and long residence in this Province of the late Bishop, the Lieutenant Governor conceives he only anticipates the unanimous feelings of this community, when he announces his desire, that every practicable degree of respect and veneration should be manifested on this most distressing occasion, to the memory of this excellent and lamented Prelate.

PLATE 20 *This window, executed by the N.T. Lyon Glass Co. of Toronto, fills the east window of St. James' Church, Kenogami. It was dedicated by Bishop Lennox Williams on 10 October 1926.*

Appendix A: Clergy List

The following is a list of clergy known to have served within the area of the present Diocese of Quebec, 1759-1993.

Ordination dates, particularly of those serving temporarily in the Diocese, may not be complete. Ordinations known to have been performed by bishops of the Diocese of Quebec are marked with an asterisk.

asst = assistant; BCS = Bishop's College School; CS = Church Society; LR = Lay Reader; pa = missionary to / in parts adjacent; (Q) = Quebec City; (S) = Sherbrooke; (SPG) = missionary of the Society for the Propagation of the Gospel in Foreign Parts; TM = Travelling Missionary; UCC = United Church of Canada

Name	Dates of Ordination		First Post	Date
	Deacon	*Priest*	*in Diocese of Quebec*	*of 1st post*
Abraham, Charles John	1951★	1952	Labrador	1951
Abraham, Philip Selwyn	1922	1923	asst Cathedral	1928
Absalom, Hugh Pryse	1936	1937	Compton & Rector King's Hall	1949
Adams, Thomas	1874	1875	Principal Bishop's & Rector BCS	1885
Adamson, William Agar	1824	1843	Cathedral	1851
Adcock, William Alfred (SPG)	1888★	1891★	Fitch Bay	1888
Alexander, James Lynne (SPG)	1829★	1832★	Leeds	1831
Alflatt, Malcolm Edward	1966	1968	New Carlisle	1977
Allder, Harold Goring	1905	1906	Thetford	1916
Allen, Aaron Anthony (SPG)	1852★	1853★	Missionary of CS & to Quarantine Station	1852
Allen, Cecil	1908★	1909★	asst Sherbrooke	1909
Allen, Frederick Wayne	1965	1967	asst St Peter's (S)	1965
Allen, James Roger	1928	1929	1st North Shore, then chaplain BCS	1932
Allnatt, Francis John Benwell (SPG)	1864	1865	Drummondville	1864
Almond, John McPherson	1896★	1897★	Tabatière Labrador	1896
Amberry, J.			BCS	1876
Anderson, John (SPG)	1828★	1829★	asst at Quebec & pa	1828
Anderson, Richard (SPG)			Upper Ireland	1839
Anderson, William (SPG)	1834★	1835★	St Peter's (Q)	c1835
Andrén, August			asst Waterville, to Swedish pop.	1896
Anido, John David Fosdyke	1940	1941	St Clement's Labrador	1947
Ansley, Amos (SPG)	1824★	1826★	Berthier & Riv. du Loup	1833

Name	Dates of Ordination		First Post	Date
	Deacon	*Priest*	*in Diocese of Quebec*	*of 1st post*
Apps, Hugh Imrie	1942★	1942★	Leeds	1942
Archbold, George (SPG)	1823★	1824★	asst Cathedral & TM	1823
Archer, William Lawrence	1907	1908	TM Transcontinental Railway, La Tuque	1909
Armstrong, Garry Robert	1968	1969	St Clement's Mission	1973
Armstrong, Louis Olivier	1874★	1875★	Brompton: 1st as LR	1873
Arnold, Robert			asst Trinity (Q)	1859
Arnold, William (SPG)	1826★	1827★	New Carlisle	1826
Atkinson, James	1897	1898	Newport	1905
Atthill, Richard	1838★		curate Trois-Rivières	1839
Awcock, Alec Mervyn	1954★	1955★	curate Cathedral	1954
Badgley, Charles Howard	1864	1868	Rector BCS	1870
Bailey, Gregory Evan	1982	1983	chaplain Sherbrooke Hosp.	1989
Balfour, Andrew (SPG)	1832★	1833★	Baie des Chaleurs	1833
Balfour, Andrew Jackson (SPG)	1869★	1872★	Levis	1869
Balfour, Charles Wilfred	1900★	1901★	asst St Maurice	1900
Ball, Josiah (SPG)	1878		Labrador	1887
Ball, Thomas Leander (SPG)	1865★	1866★	N Inverness	1865
Bareham, Alfred	1879	1880	Trinity (Q)	1886
Barnes, James Henry	1914	1915	Trinity (Q)	1919
Barnett, James	1929★	1930★	Labrador	1930
Barnett-Cowan, Alyson Mary	1975	1979★	Schefferville	1978
Barnett-Cowan, Bruce Edgar	1978★	1979★	Magdalen Islands	1977
Barton, William	1896★	1897★	asst Megantic Co.	1896
Bastow, William Salisbury	1908		asst Sherbrooke	1912
Bayley, John	1986★		[died soon after ordination]	
Bayne, Norman Melrose	1893★	1894★	Peninsula	1893
Beattie, Thomas Low Forbes	1937	1938	Kirkdale	1949
Beck, Charles Beauclerk			asst master BCS	1902
Beaufoy, Mark Raymond	1936	1937	Waterville	1948
Bedford-Jones, Harold Hudson	1893	1894	Principal Bishop's	1920
Belden, David Leon	1968★	1969★	Malbay	1967
Belford, Hubert Orser Newcomb	1901	1902	Danville	1916
Belford, James Frankland Beatty	1898	1899	Windsor Mills	1907
Belford, William James	1936★	1937★	Grosse Isle Magdn Is	1936
Belleville, Robert Chambers	1985★	1985★	Port chaplain (Q)	1985
Bennett, Thomas Edward	1943★	1944★	Magdn Is: 1st as LR	1942
Bernard, Walter Charles (SPG)	1884★	1885★	Bury	1884
Berry, Oscar	1928★	1930★	Peninsula: 1st as LR	1927
Beverley, Alton Ray	1907	1908	Trinity (Q)	1910
Bidwell, Edward John	1891	1892	Headmaster BCS	1906
Bigg, Henry Reginald	1898	1899	St George Beauce	1900
Binet, William (SPG)	1853	1854★	Portneuf & Bourg Louis	1853
Birtch, Robert Sydney (SPG)		1853★	West Frampton	1853
Bishop, Charles Eugene	1895★	1896★	Tabatière Labrador	1895
Bishop, Thomas Harveyson	1956	1957	Drummondville	1968
Blaylock, Thomas (SPG)	1874★	1877★	Malbay	1874
Blick, John Harold Leslie	1963	1964	St Clement's East	1966

Name	Dates of Ordination		First Post in Diocese of Quebec	Date of 1st post
	Deacon	*Priest*		
Blizzard, William Terry	1975★	1977★	Marbleton	1976
Blyth, Richard	1959	1960	Magdalen Islands	1969
Bochus, Ian Lawrence	1956★	1957★	Inverness	1956
Boggs, Ernest	— UCC —		associate minister Harrington Aylmer Sound & Chevery	1974
Bonnard, John Maurice	1956	1957	Principal Indian Residential School, LaTuque	1968
Boon, Nelson Leonard	1990	1990★	asst St Clement's Centre	1990
Boston, Harry	1942	1943	Valcartier	1955
Botwood, Edward	1860	1862	curate St Michael's (Q)	1865
Bown, Charles Ebenezer Sharman	1918★	1919★	Kingsey	1918
Boydell, James (SPG)	1867★	1868★	asst St Matthew's (Q)	1868
Boyle, Felix (SPG)	1851★	1852★	Magdalen Islands	1851
Bradshaw, John McIntyre	1886	1889	Shigawake	1902
Brandwood, Herbert	1934	1940	chaplain BCS	1960
Bradley, John Edward	1970	1970	asst St Matthew's & St Michael's (Q)	1972
Brazel, James Harold	1970★	1970★	St Paul's (s) & the Advent	1970
Brennan, Alfred M. St John	1878★		curate St Matthew's (Q)	1878
Brett, John Henry Macklem	1931	1932	Malbay	1938
Brett-Perring, Claud Shays	1941★	1942★	Lake Megantic as LR	1937
Brewer, John Samuel	1899	1900★	asst St Mathew's (Q)	1899
Briggs, Solomon			Portneuf	1856
Brock, Isaac	1852	1853	co-Rector Sherbrooke	1873
Brooke, Henry Arthur	1892★	1893★	Peninsula	1892
Brooke, John		1733	Chaplain to Forces (Q)	1760
Brooks, Charles Henry (SPG)	1892★	1893★	Barnston	1892
Brotherwood, Nicholas Peter	1983	1984	Quebec Lodge	1986
Brown, Clement Decimus (SPG)	1880★	1881★	Shigawake	1880
Brown, James Russell	1943	1944	Drummondville	1956
Brown, Joseph	1832★	1832★	asst Quebec	1832
Brown, Robert Wyndham (SPG)	1880★	1881★	asst Melbourne	1880
Brown, Russel Featherston	1933	1934	St Peter's (s)	1940
Browne, Ethelbert George Burges	1901	1902	asst Sherbrooke	1903
Bruce, Guy Oliver Theodore	1903	1904	asst St Paul's (Q)	1907
Brun, Emile Ulysses		1897★	Ste-Ursule	1897
Bryan, Robert Arthur	1957	1958	St Clement's Mission	1960
Buckland, Alfred Wellington	1897	1898	Portneuf	1910
Bull, Edward	1913	1916	asst Sherbrooke	1922
Bunbury, Walter Shirley Gibson	1904	1906	asst Sherbrooke	1907
Burges, Henry Francis (SPG)	1826	1827	curate Trois-Rivières	1833
Burgett, Arthur Edward	1897	1898	chaplain to Bishop & Hon 2nd asst Cathedral	1906
Burke, John Elson	1957★	1958★	curate Cathedral	1957
Burrage, Henry George (SPG)	1848★	1850★	Hatley	1849
Burrage, Robert Raby (SPG)	1819★	1820★	Point Levi & master of Royal Grammar Sc. (Q)	1819
Burt, Henry Chadwick	1898	1899	St Paul's (Q)	1904

Name	Dates of Ordination		First Post in Diocese of Quebec	Date of 1st post
	Deacon	*Priest*		
Burwell, Adam Hood (SPG)	1827★	1828★	Lennoxville	1827
Butler, Alfred James Agard	1901	1905	chaplain BCS	1919
Butler, John (SPG)		1843★	Kingsey	1843
Butt, Frank Charles	1981	1981	Trois-Rivières Portneuf	1988
Buxton, Digby Hugh	1941	1942	Lac St-Jean	1954
Caffin, George Fordyce Crawford	1900	1901	Johnville	1904
Callis, Philip	1900★	1901★	TM at Quebec	1900
Cameron, John Murchison	1928	1929	Trinity (Q)	1953
Campbell, Charles Cadogan	1939★	1940★	Cape Cove	1939
Campbell, Thomas	1820★	1821★	asst Quebec & pa	1820
Cane, Geoffrey Brett Salkeld	1973★	1980	Trinity (Q): 1st as Youth Worker	1973
Carden, Richard Arthur		1854★	asst curate Quebec	1853
Cardwell, Robert	1912	1913	Sandy Beach	1928
Carr, John Frederic	1868★	1870★	Durham	1869
Carrington, Philip	1918	1919	Dean of Divinity, Bishop's	1927
Carroll, Francis Davis Ward	1903★	1904★	2nd asst Cathedral	1903
Carry, John (SPG)	1850★	1850★	TM to Quarantine Station &c.	1850
Carson, Reginald Arthur	1952★	1952★	Fitch Bay	1952
Cassap, William Henry	1900	1901	East Angus	1906
Cattarns, Henry Richard	1911★		asst master BCS	1911
Caulfield, David Eric	1954	1955	Murdochville	1958
Chaderton, William			St Peter's (Q)	1835
Chambers, James (SPG)	1875★	1877★	Magdalen Islands	1875
Chapman, Thomas Shaw (SPG)	1848★	1849★	TM to Destitute Settlemts & Quarantine Station	1848
Chase, Benjamin Otis	1965		Border Ministry	1967
Cheesman, Charles Henry Saunders	1951	1952★	Valcartier	1953
Cheshire, Howard Stanley	1912★	1913★	Transcontinental Rlwy	1912
Cheverton, William Henry	1921★	1922★	Labrador Harrington	1921
Childs, Sidney	1916	1917	acting Dean of Divinity, Bishop's	1935
Chowne, Alfred William Holland	1873	1875	Rivière du Loup & Quarantine Station	1876
Christie, William Douglas McLaren	1935★	1936	Bury	1935
Church, William Harold Morrison	1932	1933	Domestic Chaplain & Diocesan Missionary	1937
Clark, Rodney Andrew	1993★		curate St Michael's & St Matthew's (Q)	1992
Clarke, Herbert Lewis	1945	1946	lecturer & asst Dean of Divinity, Bishop's	1952
Clinton, William de Witt	1954★	1955	Schefferville	1954
Cloutier, Jacques André	1988★	1988★	asst Lennoxville	1988
Coates, Glenn Curwood	1979★	1980★	Magdalen Islands	1979
Coglan, James (SPG)		1829★	TM & asst chaplain to Garrison (Q)	1829

Name	Dates of Ordination		First Post in Diocese of Quebec	Date of 1st post
	Deacon	*Priest*		
Cole, Robert Henry	1883	1884	asst St Matthew's (Q)	1887
Coles, John Lister	1891	1892	Valcartier	1908
Coleman, Arthur Edmund	1927	1928	Dean of Cathedral	1957
Coleman, Stanley Harold	1923	1924	Leeds	1926
Coleman, William Robert	1942	1943	Dean of Divinity, Bishop's	1950
Colley, Edward	1849	1854	to Bradore Bay & Blanc Sablon from Nfld	1849
Colston, Robert Waller (SPG)	1879★	1880★	Portneuf	1879
Comfort, John	1931★	1932★	asst St Peter's (S)	1931
Cook, Allen Francis	1957	1959	New Carlisle	1991
Cooke, Frank Bradshaw	1926★	1927★	Bourg Louis	1926
Cookesley, Frederick John (SPG)	1862★	1863★	Labrador Blanc Sablon	1862
Coombs, John Ames	1949	1950	curate Cathedral	1949
Corey, Hollis Hamilton Ambrose	1908★	1909★	Labrador Mutton Bay	1909
Cornell, Frederick Widmer			East Angus	1904
Cornwall, John (SPG)			asst Cathedral	1848
Corvan, James Hamilton (SPG)	1869	1870	Coaticook & Hereford	1872
Cowling, Robert Arthur	1903★	1904★	Lake St John & Chicoutimi	1903
Cox, Joseph Churchill (SPG)	1866	1871	Brompton & Windsor	1890
Crosse, Silas (SPG)		1857★	Cape Cove & Percé	1856
Crouse, Robert Darwin	1954	1955	asst prof. of Divinity, Bishop's	1960
Crowfoot, Alfred Henchman	1904	1905	Dean of Cathedral	1927
Cusack, Edward (SPG)	1837★	1838★	Gaspé Bay, Percé & pa	1837
Cuttell, Colin	1937	1938	Levis & 2nd Domestic Chaplain (Q)	1942
Crowther, Ronald	1953	1954	Valcartier	1958
Dalziel, John (SPG)	1849★	1849★	Eaton	1849
Darnell, Henry Faulkner			Stanstead	1860
Davis, William Wallace	1931	1932	Coaticook	1936
Debbage, James Benjamin (SPG)	1868★	1869★	asst St Peter's (Q)	1868
De Gruchy, William	1905	1906	Grindstone Magdn Is	1910
DeHoop, Thomas Anthony	1968	1969	LaTuque	1972
De La Mare, Francis (SPG)	1850★	1851★	Gaspé Basin	1850
Delisle, Jacques		1993★	hon. asst Greater Parish of St Francis of Assisi	1993
De Montmollin, Francis			Quebec	1767
De Mouilpied, Joseph (SPG)	1856	1860★	Malbay	1859
Denton, Henry Charles Armytage	1926	1928	asst Cathedral	1931
Derry, Paul	— UCC —		Sept-Iles	1990
Devitt, Thomas Gardner	1899	1900	Hatley	1907
de Vries, Sybren A.	1955	1957	Port chaplain (Q)	1981
De Wolf, James Edward	1939	1940	Priest & Principal, LaTuque Indian Residential School	1963
Dicker, John Hamilton	1932★	1934★	asst Cathedral	1933
Dickerson, Richard Keith	1960	1960	Georgeville	1982

Name	Dates of Ordination		First Post	Date
	Deacon	*Priest*	*in Diocese of Quebec*	*of 1st post*
Dickson, Herbert Augustus (SPG)	1891★	1892★	Randboro	1893
Dickson, John Stanley Bishop	1896★	1897★	Entry Island Magdn Is	1896
Dinzey, Joseph (SPG)	1857	1858	Compton & Principal	
			Ladies College	1871
Dodman, Donald Andrew	1968	1970	Schefferville	1974
Dodwell, G.			Harrold Prof. Bishop's	1863
Doolittle, Lucius (SPG)	1828★	1829★	Baie des Chaleurs	1828
Dorman, Milton Forrest	1964★	1965★	Peninsula	1964
Driscoll, John Campbell (SPG)			Louiseville, Nicolet &c.	1822
Drolet-Smith, Frances Jane Wall	1982★	1984★	St Clement's East, student	1979
Drolet-Smith, Paul Warren	1981★	1982★	St Clement's Mission East	1981
Dudley, James Elliott	1984★	1985★	chaplain BCS	1981
Dumbell, George William	1868		St Peter's (s)	1898
Dumont, Marcel	1990★	1992★	hon. asst Cathedral	1990
Dunn, Andrew Hunter	1864	1865	5th Lord Bishop	1892
Dunn, Ernest Arthur	1894★	1895★	St Paul's (Q)	1894
Dunn, Harold Curling	1908	1910	Domestic Chaplain	
			with Montmorenci &c.	1913
Dunn, William Coombe	1918	1919	Malbay	1928
Durrett, Lionel Payne	1962	1963	Cookshire	1961
Dutton, Arthur William	1899★	1900★	Way's Mills	1899
Duval, Vernon Lawrence	1947		asst Kenogami	1948
Eames, Joseph (SPG)	1885★	1886★	Labrador	1885
Eardley-Wilmot, Charles Revell	1903	1904	St Paul's (Q) L Beauport	
			Montmorenci & asst (Q)	1908
Early, W. Townsend (SPG)			Stanstead	1870
Eisenhauer, Harris Charles	1921	1923	Melbourne	1926
Elias, Louis	1955★	1955★	Inverness	1955
Ellens, George Frederick	1953	1954	lecturer Bishop's	1957
Emery, Charles Philip (SPG)	1855★	1856★	Upper Ireland	1855
Etherington, Edward John	1893	1894	Trinity (Q)	1896
Evans, Francis	1826★	1827★	curate Trois-Rivières	1826
Eustace, Donald John	1964★	1965★	East Angus	1964
Fairbairn, Alan	1967★	1967★	Windsor	1965
Fairhead, Arthur Gerald	1956	1957	Trinity (Q)	1961
Falloon, Daniel (SPG)	1841★	1842★	Melbourne	1849
Farrar, Walter	1888	1892	Assistant Bishop to Dunn	1910
Faulconer, William Gower (SPG)	1881	1881	St Sylvester	1886
Feilde, Matthew Smithers	1801★	1804★	Precentor Cathedral	1804
Fenwick, Algernon Clavering	1911	1913	Cape Cove	1947
Ferguson, Christopher Mackie	— UCC —		Saguenay Lac St-Jean	1978
Ferris, William Hull	1973★	1973★	St Paul's River	1973
Fitzhugh, Francis Coulburn	1956★	1956★	curate St Matthew's (Q)	1956
Fisk, Charles James	1953★	1954★	curate St Peter's (s)	1953
Flanagan, John (SPG)	1839★		Leeds	1843
Fleming, Charles Bernard (SPG)	1829★	1830★	Shipton & Melbourne	1830
Fletcher, Walter Raémond	1972	1975★	Malbay	1973
Ford, John Francis Stewart	1935★	1946	West Sherbrooke	1942

Name	Dates of Ordination		First Post in Diocese of Quebec	Date of 1st post
	Deacon	*Priest*		
Forde, Richard Augustus	1911	1912	Sandy Beach	1927
Foreman, Sydney Robert	1944★	1945★	Kingsey	1944
Forest, Charles (SPG)	1846★	1847★	Bury	1846
Forster, Harold Theodore Gibson	1939	1941	chaplain, BCS	1953
Forsyth, William Thomas (SPG)	1883★	1884★	Sandy Beach	1883
Forth, David Selwyn	1956	1957	asst prof. of Divinity, Bishop's	1960
Fortin, Octave (SPG)	1865	1865	missionary to Indians St Francis district	1867
Foster, John (SPG)	1862★	1863★	TM Barford & Hereford	1862
Fothergill, Gerald Rowland	1905	1906	Transcontinental Rway LaTuque	1908
Fothergill, Matthew Monkhouse (SPG)	1857★	1859★	TM St Francis district	1857
Fothergill, Roland John	1887★	1888★	curate St Paul's (Q)	1887
Fox, Charles Maxwell (SPG)			asst Trinity (Q)	1863
Franklin, John Douglas Reginald	1940	1941	Shigawake & Port Daniel	1948
Franklin-Watson, Franklin	1903	1905	Drummondville	1921
Frohmann, Charles			curate Cathedral	1886
Fuller, Hume Samuel (SPG)	1876	1879	Bury	1887
Fyles, Thomas W. (SPG)	1862	1864	SPCK chaplain to Immigrants Levis	1883
Gauffreau, Elliot Francis	1956	1957	Hereford from Colebrook NH	1964
Gauthier, Jean Baptiste			Ste-Ursule	1896
Gay, John Lenoir (SPG)			TM of CS	1861
Genge, David	1956	1957	Marbleton	1968
Genge, Mark	1951	1952	Marbleton	1969
Gibb, William Davis	1977★		non-stipendiary deacon St Matthew's (Q)	1977
Gibbins, Henry de Beltgens	1891	1892	Principal Bishop's	1906
Gibaut, John St Helier	1984★	1984	St Clement's Centre	1984
Gifford, Algernon	1849	1850	Labrador from Forteau	c1849
Gilbert, Charles Francis Langton	1914	1917	2nd asst St Peter's (S)	1914
Godwin, Aubrey Eric Walter	1935★	1935★	Peninsula	1935
Gomery, Henry	1884	1885	Gaspé	1916
Goodfellow, Henry Groves	1924	1925★	West Sherbrooke	1926
Goodings, Allen	1959	1959	Dean & Rector Cathedral	1969
Gourley, Robert Leslie	1939★	1940★	Riverbend & Kenogami	1939
Graham, Donald Percy	1951	1954	Harrington Harbour	1959
Grasett, Henry James	1834★	1835★	asst Quebec & pa	1834
Gray, William Thomas	1936★	1936★	Johnville	1936
Greer, Francis Howard Kelley	1952	1953	chaplain, BCS	1962
Guerout, Narcisse (SPG)	1839★	1840★	Louiseville & pa	1839
Gustin, William Alfred	1897★	1898★	asst Ireland	1897
Haensl, Charles Lewis Frederick	1826	1826	Trinity (Q): Evening Lecturer	1853

Name	Dates of Ordination		First Post in Diocese of Quebec	Date of 1st post
	Deacon	*Priest*		
Hale, Edward K.	1964★		Scotstown	1962
Hamilton, Charles	1857★	1858★	curate Quebec	1857
Hamilton, Charles Chetwood	1875★	1877★	curate St Matthew's (Q)	1876
Hamilton, George	1873★	1875★	asst St Matthew's (Q)	1873
Hamilton, Harold Francis	1900	1901★	asst St Matther's (Q)	1900
Harding, George Thompson (SPG)	1875★	1876★	Durham	1876
Hare, Michael	— UCC —		Trois-Rivières-Portneuf	1990
Hardy, Thomas Woodburn	1949★	1950★	curate St Peter's (S)	1949
Harper, Edward James (SPG)	1881★	1883	Melbourne	1882
Harper, Henry Samuel Braughall	1936★	1937★	Ireland	1936
Harrington, George	1921★	1922★	Lorne: 1st as LR	1919
Harrison, Ernest Wilfrid	1940	1941	Waterville & N Hatley	1953
Harrison, John William	1903	1904	New Carlisle	1918
Hart, Eric	1926★	1928★	asst Magdalen Islands	1926
Harte, Henry Swinton	1895★	1896★	Stanstead & Beebe	1895
Harvey, Richard James (SPG)	1877★	1879★	Shigawake	1877
Hatch, Edwin			Rector High School (Q)	1863
Hatch, James Edgar	1888★	1890	St Matthew's (Q)	1888
Hawes, Charles M.			Border Ministry	1970
Hawes, Howard John Richard	1973★	1974★	Harrington Harbour	1975
Heaton, George			curate Trois-Rivières	1860
Heisland, Hobart Hertzle	1955	1955	Hereford from Colebrook NH	1955
Hellmuth, Isaac (SPG)	1846★	1846★	Prof. of Hebrew & Rabbinical Lit., Bishop's	1845
Hepburn, Channell Galbraith	1911★	1912★	asst St Matthew's (Q)	1911
Hepburn, James (SPG)	1870★	1872★	Labrador	1871
Heron, J.E.			Port Daniel	1920
Heron, Robert	1920★	1921★	asst Sherbrooke	1921
Hesketh, Harold	1915	1915	Trinity (Q)	1938
Hewton, Richard W. (SPG)	1884★	1885★	Ireland	1884
Hibbard, Gerald Fitzmaurice	1891	1893	Montmorency	1894
Hibbard, Hubert James Fitzmaurice	1933★	1934★	Stanstead	1933
Hicks, Bradley Charles Alfred	1979★	1980★	Eaton-Dudswell: 1st as LR	1979
Higginson, Alexander Boyd	1900	1901	asst St Peter's (S)	1905
Hill, John Moran	1952★	1952★	Riverbend	1951
Hinton, Donald McIntosh	1990★		hon. asst St Michael's (Q)	1990
Hitch, Allen Thomas	1968★	1968	Magdalen Islands	1968
Hobart, Charles Hampden	1913★	1914★	Mutton Bay	1914
Hobart, Vere Edward	1910★	1911★	asst Sherbrooke	1911
Hobbes, Robert Henry	1957		asst St Peter's (S)	1959
Hodson, John E.	1911	1912	Port Daniel	1919
Hollas, George Basil	1949	1950	Magdalen Islands	1984
Hooper, G. H.			Bourg Louis	1871
Hornby, Raymond Sefton	1921★	1923★	Kingsey	1921
Horner, David	1887	1889	Durham	1891
Houdin, Michael (SPG)			Chaplain 48th Regt	1759
Hough, William (SPG)		1826★	New Carlisle	1825

Name	Dates of Ordination		First Post in Diocese of Quebec	Date of 1st post
	Deacon	*Priest*		
Houghton, Philip Glenn	1971	1972	Trinity (Q)	1981
Housman, George Vernon	1844	1845	curate Cathedral	1858
Howard, John Alexander	1962	1963	Drummondville	1973
Humphries, Edward Hefferton	1914	1915	Kingsey	1923
Hunt, Desmond Charles	1942	1943	Trinity (Q)	1943
Hunter, John Norreys	1894★	1895★	Grindstone Magdn Is	1894
Hurst, George Stackley	1949	1950	Hereford from Colebrook NH	1952
Husband, Edgar Bell (SPG)	1888★	1889★	St Sylvester	1888
Hutchison, Eric William	1955	1955	Forestville	1955
Hutchison, George Malcolm	1955	1957	curate Cathedral	1959
Hutchison-Hounsell, Christine	1992	1993★	St Clement's Centre	1992
Hutchison-Hounsell, Lyndon	1992	1993★	St Clement's Centre	1992
Ievers, Henry Wilton	1908★	1909★	Magdalen Islands	1908
Innes, George Mignon	1862	1863	asst Cathedral	1865
Irving, George Charles			Rector BCS	1865
Jackson, Christopher (SPG)	1803	1804	Hatley	1830
Jackson, Edmund			Marbleton	1895
James, John Paul	1960	1961	Saguenay	1971
Jackson, John (SPG)	1800★	1801★	Evening Lecturer (Q)	1800
Jellicoe, Sidney	1933	1934	Dean of Divinity, Bishop's	1952
Jenkins, John Hea (SPG)	1855★	1856★	West Frampton	1855
Jenkins, Louis Charles (SPG)		1822★	asst Quebec & pa	1822
Jensen, Clarence Henry	1947★	1948★	curate St Peter's (s)	1947
Jensen, Raymond Ernest	1959★	1960★	Trinity (Q)	1988
Jervis-Read, Robert Shelland	1950	1951	St Paul's (s)	1957
Jewell, Frederick Elmer	1929	1931	Portneuf & Bourg Louis	1964
Johnson, Moody Bernard	1913★	1914★	Georgeville & Fitch Bay	1913
Johnson, Thomas (SPG)	1815	1817	Hatley	1819
Johnston, John (SPG)	1838★	1840★	New Carlisle	1838
Jones, Albert	1915	1916	Inverness	1918
Jones, Gilbert Basil	1918	1919	Dean of Divinity, Bishop's	1936
Jones, James Wellesley (SPG)	1858★	1859★	Drummondville	1859
Jones, Maxwell C. M.	1938	1939	Bury	1966
Jones, Septimus (SPG)	1854	1856★	Cape Cove	1854
Jones, William (SPG)	1843★	1844★	curate Eaton	1844
Joyce, Peter Donald	1979★	1980★	Valcartier	1980
Judge, Arthur Horner (SPG)	1882★	1883★	Cookshire	1882
Jungers, Albert Kenneth	1974	1975	New Carlisle	1984
Kay, William Henry			asst St Matthew's (Q)	1873
Keddie, Lawrence Earle	1992	1993★	Magdalen Islands	1992
Keefe, Kenneth Bernard	1940	1942	St Michael's (Q)	1953
Kelley, Arthur Reading	1906	1907★	asst St Matthew's (Q)	1906
Kelley, Brian Scott	1957★	1958★	St Maurice Mission	1957
Kemp, Albert Edward	1946	1947	Trinity (Q)	1949
Kemp, John (SPG)	1847★	1848★	Bury	1847
Kendrick, Grover Edward	1956★	1956★	Inverness	1956
Kennedy, Walter Howard Frere	1955★	1956★	St Peter's (s)	1955

Name	Dates of Ordination		First Post	Date
	Deacon	*Priest*	*in Diocese of Quebec*	*of 1st post*
Ker, Matthew (SPG)	1841	1845	Sandy Beach & Malbay	1858
Ker, Robert	1877	1878	Trinity (Q)	1880
Kerr, Isaac Newton	1893★	1894★	Labrador	1893
Kidd, Donald Worcester	1939	1940	Valcartier	1948
King, Charles Grant	1904	1905	Thetford	1923
King, Ernest Augustus Willoughby (SPG)	1870★	1873★	St Matthew's (Q)	1870
King, William (SPG)	1840★	1840★	asst Bury	1840
Kingston, Peter Bradley	1951★	1952★	Magdalen Islands	1951
Knagg, Richard (SPG)			Stanstead	1819
Knight, Robert (SPG)	1835★	1836★	TM among Destitute Settlers in Quebec & pa	1835
Knox, Thomas Stephen	1951★	1952★	curate St Matthew's (Q)	1951
Lacey, Vincent Corbet (SPG)	1890★	1892	Melbourne	1890
Lack, Walter Frederick	1909	1911	Leeds	1930
Lampman, Paul Everett	1993	1993★	Magdalen Islands	1990
Laws, Harold Stewart	1909★	1910★	asst Labrador	1909
Leather, Robert	1958	1959	Hereford border ministry	1974
Larivière, Louis Vitalien	1880	1880	to Abenaki at Pierreville	1881
Lefevre, Clement Fall (SPG)	1821	1823★	Sherbrooke	1822
Legge, Arthur Ernest Edgar	1913	1914	Marlleton	1921
LeGallais, Frederick George (SPG)	1900★	1901★	Mutton Bay	1901
LeMoignan, Alfred Stanley	1927★	1928★	Anticosti	1927
Lewis, Charles Thomas	1891	1892	Melbourne	1899
Lewis, Owen Gurney	1908★	1909★	TM Lake St John	1908
Lewis, Richard (SPG)	1848★	1849★	Portneuf & Bourg Louis	1848
Lindsay, Sydenham Bagg	1910	1911	curate St Matthew's (Q)	1918
Lloyd, Frederick Ebenezer John (SPG)	1882	1886★	Levis	1885
Lloyd, Thomas	1923★	1924★	Melbourne	1924
Lloyd, Thomas Henry			asst Cathedral	1897
Lloyd, William Valentine (SPG)	1850★	1851★	Leeds & pa	1850
Lobley, Joseph Albert	1863	1864	Principal Bishop's	1877
Lockhart, John Samuel Ingram			Domestic & Examining chaplain to Bp Stewart	c1831
Loiselle, Herbert Octavius	1894	1895	Ste-Ursule	1918
Lokhorst, G.	— UCC —		Team Ministry of Eaton-Dudswell	1973
Lonsdell, Richard (SPG)	1839★	1840★	Kingsey	1839
Loucks, Edwin	1858★	1862	asst Lennoxville	1858
Love, Archibald Thomas	1908★	1909★	Port Daniel	1908
Lund, F. E.			asst Waterville, to Swedish population	1896
Lundy, Francis James (SPG)	1837★	1838★	Point Levi	1838
Lyster, William Gore (SPG)	1856	1859★	Hope & Port Daniel	1858
Maccarther, John Goodwin (SPG)	1864		Bourg Louis	1865
MacCleary, Thomas	1926★	1928★	Bourg Louis	1926
MacDonald, Ian Alexander				

Name	Dates of Ordination		First Post	Date
	Deacon	*Priest*	*in Diocese of Quebec*	*of 1st post*
Robertson	1901	1902	East Angus	1912
Machin, Thomas (SPG)	1849★	1849★	curate Sherbrooke	1849
Mackie, George			Quebec	1836
Mackie, Robert	1942★	1943★	TM under Board in Quebec	1942
Magill, George John (SPG)	1858★	1859★	Stoneham & Lac Beauport	1858
Mainer, John Graham Colin	1945★	1945★	asst Lake St John	1945
Maning, Parsons James (SPG)	1839★	1840★	TM St Giles & Broughton	1843
Mansbridge, Horatio Prideaux (SPG)	1883★		Brompton & Windsor	1883
Marshall, Frank William	1949	1949	Hereford from Colebrook NH	1949
Marston, James Guy	1940★	1940★	asst St Peter's (s)	1940
Mate, Martin	1952	1953	Cookshire	1964
Mathers, Richard (SPG)	1869★	1872★	St Peter's (Q)	1869
Matheson, Selkirk Hugh	1986	1986	Greater Parish of Gaspé	1992
Matthews, Ruth Helenor	1973★	1977★	Forestville	1970
Matthews, Timothy John	1932	1933	Coaticook	1940
May, Edward Geoffrey	1894	1895	asst Cathedral	1898
McCulloch, Robert Lindo	1956	1957	Danville, Asbestos, Kingsey Falls & Denison's Mills	1973
McCullough, Brian Duncan	1971	1971	Valcartier	1971
McGreer, Arthur Huffman	1909	1910	Principal Bishop's	1922
McIllmurray, John Barron	1966★	1967★	Sept-Iles	1971
McKeown, John (SPG)	1848★		Frampton	1847
McLaren, Albert Victor	1909	1911	Sandy Beach	1929
McMillan, William George	1969	1971	St Clement's East	1975
McQueen, Kenneth George	— UCC —		Grand'Mère & Shawinigan	1977
Meade, Sydney Albert	1940★	1940★	St Clement's Mission	1940
Meloche, William Joseph Bertram	1938	1938	Baie Comeau	1944
Merrett, James Douglas	1973	1974	Dean & Rector Cathedral	1988
Merrick, William Chad (SPG)	1849★	1850★	East Frampton	1850
Merriman, Ramsay Owen	1962	1963	curate Lennoxville	1962
Metzger, Curtis	1986★	1986★	asst Cathedral & Trinity (Q)	1985
Mills, Joseph Langley			chaplain to Forces (Q) & Evening Lecturer Cathedral	1815
Milne, George (SPG)	1841★	1842★	Baie of Chaleurs	1841
Mitchell, Frederick William	1926	!927	Johnville	1930
Mitchell, Robert (SPG)	1861★	1862★	Stoneham & Lac Beauport	1861
Moffatt, Edward Knowler	1913	1914	East Angus	1918
Moir, Malcolm Edward	1973★		perpetual deacon Trois-Rivières	1973
Mombert, Jacob Isidore		1858★	asst Trinity (Q)	1858
Moncada, Antonio	— UCC —		Harrington Harbour &c.	1972
Montgomery, Colin Roger	1927	1928	Magdalen Is	1930
Moore, Arthur Henry	1895★	1896★	Randboro	1895
Moore, Marilyn June	1980★	1980★	Sept-Iles	1979
Moorhead, William Henry	1911★	1912★	asst Port chaplain & asst Cathedral	1911

Name	Dates of Ordination		First Post in Diocese of Quebec	Date of 1st post
	Deacon	*Priest*		
Morrell, John Keith	1991★	1992★	asst curate Coaticook	1991
Morgell, Crosbie			Domestic & Examining chaplain to Bp Stewart	1826
Morrill, Garth Roy	1959★	1960★	North Shore	1959
Morris, Charles John (SPG)	1840★	1841★	Gaspé Bay	1840
Morrison, James Dow	1869★		Magog	1868
Mortimer, Francis Charles	1914★	1917★	Harrington Harbour	1914
Mountain, Armine Wale	1846★	1847★	TM District of Quebec & chaplain Grosse Ile	1846
Mountain, George Jehoshaphat	1812★	1814★	asst Cathedral	1812
Mountain, Jacob	1774	1780	Bishop of Quebec	1793
Mountain, Jehoshaphat (SPG)	1778	1779	asst Trois-Rivières	1794
Mountain, Salter Jehoshaphat	1793	1796★	curate & rector Quebec	1797
Murphy, Maurice William	1939	1940	Trinity (Q)	1941
Murray, George Henry Andrews (SPG)	1889★	1890★	Melbourne	1889
Neal, John Vernon	1968	1969	New Carlisle	1970
Nesbitt, Thomas Edward	1970		Coaticook	1975
Nevitt, Robert Barrington			Bourg Louis	1910
Newton, Christopher W.	1950	1951	Labrador Mission	1952
Nichol, Alexander Frederick George	1923★	1924★	Leeds	1924
Nicolosi, Gary Gabriel	1983★	1984★	Malbay	1983
Nicholson, William Henry			chaplain Grosse Ile	1918
Nicolls, Gustavus George	1879	1881	curate St Matthew's (Q)	1882
Nicolls, Jasper Hume	1844	1845	Principal Bishop's	1845
Noble, William Thomas (SPG)	1876	1877	Trinity (Q)	1891
Norman, Arthur (SPG)	1827★		asst Quebec	1827
Norman, Frederick Taylor	1925	1925	St Peter's Limoilou	1960
Norman, Richard Whitmore	1852	1853	Dean & Rector Cathedral	1888
Norie, Frederick Burton	1889	1891	curate St Matthew's (Q)	1893
Norris, Gerald Leigh	1953★	1954★	Peninsula	1953
Norwood, Joseph William (SPG)	1871	1873	Magdalen Islands	1885
Nutter, Bruce Dunstan	1984	1985	Magdalen Islands	1985
Oakley, Arthur John	1905	1906	Richmond	1917
Ogilvie, John (SPG)	1749	1749	chaplain of 60th Regiment, at Quebec with Amherst	1761
Onyewuchi, Rufus Chukwuemeka	1974★	1975★	Baie Comeau	1974
Ottiwell, Arthur Vivian	1934	1935	St Matthew's (Q)	1936
Owen, Ronald Roy	1977★		Hereford	1977
Parker, George Henry (SPG)	1863	1864	Kingsey	1866
Parkin, Edward (SPG)			Sherbrooke	c1829
Parkin, Edward Cullen (SPG)	1844★	1845★	Valcartier	1845
Parkinson, Edwin	1930	1931	Malbay	1941
Parnther, David Bernard (SPG)	1840★	1841★	St Giles	1840
Parrock, Richard Arthur	1893★	1894★	Domestic Chaplain at Bishopthorpe to Bp Dunn	1893
Parry, Horace Weston	1925★	1926★	Missionary, unattached	1925

Name	Dates of Ordination		First Post in Diocese of Quebec	Date of 1st post
	Deacon	*Priest*		
Patterson, Curtis	1977★	1978★	Harrington Harbour	1977
Patterson, Ellwood Harold	1944★	1945★	Leeds	1944
Peabody, Gordon Shepard	1965★	1965★	Malbay	1965
Peacock, Gerald Vernon	1952★	1953★	curate Cathedral	1952
Peacock. Patricia Ellen	1985★	1985★	chaplain BCS	1985
Pearse, Arthur Henry (SPG)	1855	1856	Portneuf & Bourg Louis	1858
Peart, Malcolm	1904	1905	Gallup Hill, Melbourne	1923
Peirce, Roy Willis	1944★	1946★	St Maurice	1944
Pell, George Russell	1975	1976	chaplain Bishop's & Champlain Regional College	1978
Pennefather, Thomas (SPG)	1850★	1851★	1st as LR Abbotsford; then Bourg Louis & St Catherine	1850
Pepperdene, Liddon Max Muller	1926	1927	Trinity (Q)	1930
Percival, H. Spencer			Sawyerville	1916
Percy, Gilbert (SPG)	1832	1833	St Paul's (Q)	1850
Perkins, Arthur Raymond	1937★	1938★	Magdalen Islands	1937
Perry-Gore, Walter Keith	1961	1962	New Carlisle	1971
Petry, Henry James (SPG)	1854	1855	asst Levis, New Liverpool & Bergerville	1858
Phillips, Samuel Henry			asst Trinity (Q)	1867
Pike, Stuart	1988★	1989★	Wakeham & York	1988
Pilcher, Norman Donald	1938★	1939★	asst Kenogami	1938
Piper, Geoffrey	1986★	1988★	Eaton-Dudswell: 1st as LR	1986
Plaskett, Francis	1904★	1905★	asst Labrador	1905
Plees, Robert George (SPG)	1841★	1842★	St Peter's (Q)	1847
Plimpton, Hollis	1988★	1988★	Parish of Victoria	1988
Plummer, Alfred Harold	1912★	1912	Shigawake	1917
Porter, William Newington	1934	1935	New Carlisle	1955
Presnail, William Robert	1985★	1986★	Trois-Rivières	1984
Price, William	1885★	1886★	Westbury	1885
Prout, John William Charles	1895	1896★	Magdalen Islands	1895
Provis, William Frank	1983★	1986★	asst Coaticook	1983
Pye, George Peter	1897★	1898★	Labrador	1897
Rakale, David	1934	1936	temp. licence Lennoxville & Sherbrooke	1963
Radley-Walters, George (SPG)	1878★	1879★	Malbay	1880
Radley-Walters, Sydney	1909★	1911★	asst Malbay	1909
Rawson, Christopher Wright	1866★	1867★	asst Cathrdral	1871
Ray, Douglass Ellicott	1974★	1976	Fitch Bay	1975
Raymond, William Ober	1905	1906	prof. of English, Bishop's	1929
Read, Philip C.	1873	1874	Rector BCS	1877
Reed, Ernest Samuel	1931	1932	Rector & Archdn of Gaspé	1946
Reeve, Ronald E.	1950	1951	Church of the Advent (s) & lecturer Bishop's	1954
Reeves, Arthur William	1914★	1915★	Sawyerville	1914
Reid, Charles Peter (SPG)	1835★	1836★	Compton	1840
Reinhardt, Theodore	1965	1967	Port Daniel	1970
Rexford, E. I.	1876	1894	Quebec without charge	1887

Name	Dates of Ordination		First Post in Diocese of Quebec	Date of 1st post
	Deacon	*Priest*		
Reynolds, Henry Dunbar	1854★	1855★	New Liverpool	1854
Rennison, Geoffrey	1954	1955	St Paul's (s)	1964
Richardson, Thomas (SPG)	1864★	1864★	Bury & Lingwick	1864
Richmond, John Pettener (SPG)	1860★	1861★	TM Barford	1860
Richmond, William (SPG)	1858★	1859★	Compton	1858
Ridley, John	1881	1883	asst Cathedral	1884
Riopel, Solomon (SPG)	1868★	1869★	curate St Matthew's (Q)	1868
Ripper, Sydney Richard	1949	1950	Portneuf	1955
Roberts, Charles	1861★	1862★	Bourg Louis: 1st as LR	1861
Roberts, Derek Francis Madden	1948	1949	Compton, Milby & chaplain King's Hall	1952
Robertson, Alexander Hume	1887★	1888★	Randboro	1887
Robertson, David (SPG)	1827★	1830★	chaplain to Garrison (Q)	1855
Robins, George	1916	1917	Sandy Beach	1924
Robinson, Thomas Robinson	1956	1957	Trinity (Q)	1966
Robinson, William Beauclerk	1840★	1841★	TM District of Quebec	1840
Robson, John W.	1949	1950	Malbay	1962
Roe, Henry (SPG)	1852★	1853★	Ireland, Inverness & pa	1852
Roe, Peter (SPG)	1877★	1878★	Brompton & Windsor	1876
Rollitt, Charles (SPG)	1844★	1845★	TM of CS District of Quebec	1845
Ross, Blair William	1987★	1987★	curate Victoria Parish	1987
Ross, Dean Ellwood	1974★	1981★	asst Lennoxville	1972
Ross, Edward George William (SPG)			Rivière du Loup en bas, Kamouraska & pa	1842
Ross, George McLeod (SPG)	1827★	1828★	Drummondville	1827
Ross, Lynn Curtis	1968★	1969★	Schefferville	1969
Ross, Reginald Ivan	1905	1905	Ste Ursule	1906
Ross, William Moray (SPG)	1854★	1855★	Lower Inverness & Nelson	1854
Rothera, Joseph (SPG)	1889★	1891★	Leeds	1889
Rowcliffe, Robert Gay	1930★	1931★	Inverness	1931
Rowe, Joseph Samuel			Inverness	1916
Rowe, William James	1918	1919	Port Daniel	1931
Rowland, Adam			Upper Ireland	1870
Roy, Edward			Pierreville: Abenaki Mission	1877
Roy, Ernest Raymond	1902★	1903★	East Angus	1902
Roy, Jean-Jacques	1874	1887	Ste-Ursule	1904
Roy, Philias Rufus	1907★	1908★	asst Labrador	1907
Rudd, James Sutherland (SPG)			Missionary to Quebec	1800
Rudd, Thomas (SPG)	1888★	1889★	Randboro, Newport	1888
Russell, Edward Charles			curate Sherbrooke	1917
Ryott, Robert Garner	1904	1906	curate Sherbrooke	1928
Sadler, William Alan	1956	1956	asst prof. Bishop's	1964
Salt, Alfred Lewis	1951★	1952★	Sawyerville	1951
Salt, Richard John	1974★	1977★	1st as Youth Worker	1971
Sandeman, Arthur Alister Malcolm	1939	1940	asst Cathedral	1942
Sandy, Joseph	1976★		Matimekosh	1976
Sauerbrei, Claude	1924	1925	lecturer Bishop's	1927
Scarth, Archibald Campbell (SPG)	1857	1858	asst Lennoxville	1859

Name	Dates of Ordination		First Post	Date
	Deacon	*Priest*	*in Diocese of Quebec*	*of 1st post*
Schmitt, Edward Joseph	1969	1970	Coaticook	1971
Schmitt, Kathleen Mary Speegle	1972★		non-stipendiary asst Coaticook	1972
Scott, Elton	1923	1924	prof. Pastoral Theology Bishop's	1935
Scott, Frederick George	1884★	1886	Drummondville	1887
Scratch, Gordon Alfred Clare	1970★	1970★	chaplain Bishop's	1970
Seaborn, Robert Lowder	1934	1935	Dean & Rector Cathedral	1948
Seaman, Justus John Smith	1903★	1904★	Grand' Mère	1904
Seaman, William Frederick	1905★	1906★	Grand' Mère	1906
Secord, Joseph Alward	1945	1950★	Inverness	1950
Seeley, Maxwell Horman Ward	1913	1914	Thetford Mines	1924
Sewell, Edmund Willoughby (SPG)	1824★	1827★	asst Cathedral & TM	1824
Sewell, Henry Doyle (SPG)	1837★	1838★	TM District of Quebec & pa	1837
Shaw, Gerald Keith Gregg	1967	1968	Gaspé & Sandy Beach	1978
Sherman, Louis Ralph	1912	1913	Dean & Rector Cathedral	1925
Shires, Robert John	1913★	1914	LaTuque	1917
Short, Robert (SPG)	1825★	1827★	asst Quebec & pa	1827
Short, Robert Quirke (SPG)	1783	1787	Trois Rivières	1801
Shortt, Jonathan (SPG)	1832★	1834★	asst Quebec & pa	1832
Shreve, Richmond	1874	1875	St Peter's (s)	1902
Silva-White, Cyril Percy	1935	1936	curate St Peter's (s)	1946
Simpson, John Edward Francis	1844★	1845★	St Paul's (Q)	1845
Simpson, Samuel Hoare (SPG)	1848★	1849★	New Ireland	1848
Sisco, Frederick Alan	1913★	1914★	Lorne	1913
Slater, Robert H Lawson	1924	1925	Georgeville	1971
Smith, Buxton Birbeck	1869	1871	Sherbrooke	1883
Smith, Frederick Augustus (SPG)	1850△	1851△	Malbay, Sandy Beach & Peninsula	1850
Smith, Janet P.	1989★	1990★	St Clement's Mission West	1989
Smith, Lennox Ingall	1888	1889	asst Cathedral	1899
Smith, Remington Rocksborough	1900	1901	Dean of Divinity Bishop's	1921
Smith, Richard	1981	1982	Chaleur Bay Parish	1993
Smith, Ronald David Roy	1972★	1973★	Murdochville	1971
Smith, Wallace Westwood	1922	1925★	Magdalen Islands	1925
Smyth, Phyllis	— UCC —		Saguenay	1971
Snow, Norman Henry	1911★	1912★	asst Transcontinental Rway LaTuque	1911
Sowerbutts, Crompton	1907		asst Valcartier	1907
Spackman, Ailsa	1983★	1985★	asst Gaspé	1983
Spackman, Peter John	1966	1967	Sept-Iles	1975
Standfast, William Duncan	1897	1899	Headmaster BCS	1909
Stavert, Alexander Bruce	1964★	1965★	Schefferville	1964
Steele, Howard Douglas	1882	1882	chaplain Grosse Ile	1895
Stevens, Albert (SPG)	1875★	1876★	Hereford	1875
Stevens, Cecil Gardner	1911★	1912★	1st as asst New Carlisle, then asst Mutton Bay	1911
Stewart, Charles Henry (SPG)			curate Sherbrooke	1854

Name	Dates of Ordination		First Post in Diocese of Quebec	Date of 1st post
	Deacon	*Priest*		
Stewart, Charles James (SPG)	1798	1799	Hatley	1817
Stewart, Douglas Allan Bernard	— UCC —		Grand'Mère & Shawinigan	1983
Stringer, Alexander	1952	1953	Sept-Iles &c.	1959
Stone, Glenn	1984★	1985★	Valcartier	1984
Strong, Samuel Spratt (SPG)	1835★	1836★	Acting Chaplain to the Forces Quebec	1836
Stuart, Henry Coleridge (SPG)	1871★	1874★	asst St Matthew's (Q)	1871
Suddard, John (SPG)			District of Gaspé	1819
Sutherland, George J. (SPG)	1890★	1891★	Labrador	1890
Sutton, Edward George (SPG)	1844★	1845★	TM for CS	1844
Sweet, John Hales Sweet (SPG)	1873★	1874★	Stoneham	1873
Sykes, Horace William	1905	1906	1st Shawinigan, then Fitch Bay	1915
Sykes, James Samuel Sr (SPG)	1855	1855	chaplain: Marine Hosp & Immigrants, Port of Q & Jail	1861
Sykes, James Samuel Jr (SPG)	1872★	1875★	Levis	1872
Tannar, John Colin	1900★	1901★	asst Ireland	1900
Tambs, Robert Caspar (SPG)	1865★	1866★	TM with Grosse Ile & Saguenay	1866
Taylor, Alfred (SPG)			St Sylvester	1885
Taylor, Humphrey John	1943	1944	Saguenay	1947
Taylor, Jonathan (SPG)	1821★	1822★	Township of Eaton	1821
Taylor, William F. Jr	1961	1961	Hereford from Colebrook	1961
Templeman, Evered Marsh Wigram	1888	1890	asst St Matthew's (Q)	1906
Thomas, William David Charles	1958	1959	Murdochville	1961
Thomas, William Morley House	1939	1940	Valcartier	1947
Thompson, Ernest	1948	1949	team ministry Coaticook	1985
Thompson, Joseph Henry	1848	1849	prof. of Divinity & Hebrew Bishop's	1855
Thompson, Isaac Martin (SPG)	1871★	1874★	Brompton	1871
Thompson, Matthew George	1886★	1887★	Levis	1886
Thompson, Norman John	1912	1914	asst Cathedral	1922
Thompson, William Linton			Stanstead	1857
Thomson, Heather Joan	1977★	1979★	chaplain Alexander Galt	1978
Thorndike, Charles Faunce	1866	1867	asst Cathedral	1869
Thornloe, George (SPG)	1874★	1875★	Stanstead	1874
Thornloe, James (SPG)	1866★	1868★	TM Bishop's College	1866
Thorp, Charles (SPG)	1867	1869	Bury	1875
Tocque, Philip (SPG)	1851	1854	Hopetown	1864
Toosey, Philip	1765	1765	asst Quebec	1785
Torrance, John S. (SPG)	1839★	1840★	asst St Paul's (Q)	1839
Townshend, David William	1984	1985	Schefferville	1987
Trotman, Charles			curate Cathedral	1886
Tucker, Nevil Francis	1938	1939	Sawyerville	1952
Tulk, Arthur Edmund	1903	1904	Kingsey	1926
Tunstall, James Marmaduke (SPG)			TM Quebec &c.	1788
Turney, William Charles	1915	1916	Chicoutimi & Arvida	1925
Turpin, Reginald Matthew	1942★	1942★	asst Kenogami	1942

Name	Dates of Ordination		First Post in Diocese of Quebec	Date of 1st post
	Deacon	*Priest*		
Vachell, Harvey		1836★	curate Quebec	1835
Van Linge, Jakob (SPG)	1849★	1850★	West Frampton	1849
Vallis, Hubert Arthur	1950	1951	Magdalen Islands	1973
Vaughan, Edward Richard	1964★	1965★	Lac St-Jean	1964
Veyssière, Legère Jean–Baptiste Noel			Trois-Rivières	1767
Vial, Frank Gifford	1897★	1898★	Stanstead & Beebe	1897
Vial, William Stephen (SPG)	1859★	1860★	Inverness	1859
Vibert, Arthur John	1904★	1905★	asst Labrador	1904
Von Iffland, Anthony Aaron (SPG)	1862★	1863★	Portneuf	1862
Voyer, Pierre	1988★	1988★	asst Cathedral	1988
Wainwright, Richard (SPG)	1864	1867★	Labrador	1864
Wait, William Wade	1838★	1840★	Portneuf & Bourg Louis	1840
Waitt, Thomas Brace	1888	1891	Principal Bishop's	1905
Walker, Robert Holdsworth	1859	1860	Rector BCS	1867
Walker, Walter Ernest	1938★	1939★	East Angus, Marbleton & Malbay	1937
Walshe, Anthony Crawford			Acton Vale	1861
Walters, John (SPG)	1866	1867★	Magdalen Islands	1866
Ward, Edward Cecil	1930★	1931★	1st North Shore, then Bourg Louis	1931
Ward, James Grant	1902★	1903★	asst Labrador	1902
Ward, Norman Reginald	1913★	1914★	Marbleton	1913
Ward, Robert Grant (SPG)	1859★		asst Inverness	1859
Warder, Richard Cartwright	1926	1927	Durham & Melbourne	1938
Warren, Archibald Ralph	1910★	1911★	Sandy Beach	1910
Washer, Charles Briggs (SPG)	1871★	1874★	Inverness	1871
Watkins, Benjamin	1884	1885	prof. of Classics, Bishop's	1891
Watson, Benjamin	1897★	1899★	asst St Matthew's (Q)	1899
Watson, Gordon Spencer	1943★		Baie Comeau	1943
Way, Max B.			Sandy Beach	1928
Wayman, John Wright	1899★	1900★	Johnville	1899
Weagant, George Edwin	1902★	1903★	St Maurice & Lac St-Jean	1902
Weary, Edwin C. (SPG)	1882	1885	Rivière du Loup	1889
Webster, Frederick Mather (SPG)	1879★	1880★	Labrador	1879
Webster, Richard Webster Boot			Trinity (Q)	1878
West, Ronald William	1985★	1986★	St Clement's West	1986
Westman, Linton George	1959★	1959★	Fitch Bay & Tomifobia	1958
Whatham, Arthur Edward	1884	1885	Ways Mills	1895
Wheeler, William Thomas	1903★	1904★	Barford	1903
White, Crispin Michael	1965	1966	Labrador	1968
White, Gavin Donald	1953	1954★	asst St Matthew's (Q)	1953
White, Isaac Patrick (SPG)	1843★		TM for CS Dist of Quebec	1843
Whitehouse, David	1966	1967	Trinity (Q)	1975
Whiteley, William Marshall	1896	1899	Port Daniel	1916
Whitlow, Brian William	1938	1939	chaplain & Classics BCS	1946
Whitney, James Pounder	1883	1885	Principal Bishop's	1900
Whitten, Andrew Trew (SPG)	1843★	1844★	Leeds	1846

Name	Dates of Ordination		First Post in Diocese of Quebec	Date of 1st post
	Deacon	*Priest*		
Whittenbury-Kaye, Ronald Dinwiddie	1928★		Upper St Maurice Mission	1928
Wickes, William	1850★	1851★	TM with Grosse Ile	1851
Wilford, Vaughan McLean	1955★	1955★	Windsor Mills	1955
Wilken, Alan Gillies	1909	1910	asst Cathedral	1919
Wilkinson, Bathurst George	1891★	1892	prof. of Pastoral Theology Bishop's	1892
Williams, C. S. (SPG)			Rivière du Loup	1821
Williams, James William	1852	1853	Rector BCS	1857
Williams, Lennox Waldron	1885★	1886★	asst St Mathew's (Q)	1885
Williams, Sydney Waldron	1929	1930	asst Cathedral	1931
Williams, Tegid Aneurin (SPG)	1884	1886	Dudswell	1889
Wilson, Ernest King	1893★	1894★	Hall's Stream	1893
Winckley, Alfred Reginald Thorold	1889	1890	East Angus	1908
Withycomb, John			asst St Peter's (Q)	1916
Wood, Samuel Simpson (SPG)		1819★	Drummondville	1819
Wood, Sidney	1932★	1932★	Lorne	1932
Woolryche, Alfred James (SPG)	1855★	1856★	Stoneham & Lac Beauport	1855
Wright, Henry Enoch (SPG)	1891★	1892★	East Angus	1891
Wright, Robert William Ellegood	1890	1891	Georgeville	1895
Wurtele, Louis Campbell (SPG)	1859★	1861★	TM of CS	1859
Yates, Narcissus Peter	1886	1887	lect. in Hebrew, Bishop's	1891
Young, James Leversedge	1959★	1960★	Windsor Mills	1959
Young, John Vernon	1913★	1914★	Junior Immigration chaplain	1913
Zillman, John Herman Leopold			Portneuf	1889
Zion, William Potts	1956	1957	asst prof. Bishop's	1963

Appendix B: Consecration List

Consecrations and Deconsecrations in the Diocese of Quebec 1793-1993

The following headings are those employed in the *Register of Consecration of Churches, Burial Grounds &c in the Diocese of Quebec*, preserved at Church House, Quebec.

In the entries which follow, the "Place or Mission" is further identified by county or district placed immediately afterwards within square brackets. Figures bracketed thus {} are the entry numbers in the *Register;* the absence of such a number indicates that the Act was not recorded there.

B. G.=Burial Ground; Ch=Church; Cmty=Cemetery; Cpl=Chapel

Much further information, including a record of services held in school-houses or private homes as well as consecrated buildings is contained in a compilation by the Rev. Canon Harold Brazel, former Diocesan Archivist, and deposited in the Diocesan Archives in Lennoxville.

Place or Mission	{}	What Consecrated [Episcopal Act]
Acton Vale [Bagot]	{92}	Church & B. G.
Adderley [Megantic]	{235}	Church & B. G.
Agnes [Megantic]	{104}	Church
	{193}	lots in B. G.
Amherst Island Magdalen Is	{79}	Church & B. G.
Arvida [Chicoutimi]	{363}	Church
	{421}	Ch Deconsecrated
	{422}	Church
Asbestos [Richmond]	{358}	Church Dedicated
	{369}	Church
Ascot Corner [Sherbrooke]	{225}	Church
	{356}	Ch Deconsecrated
Aubert Gallion: see *St Georges-de-Beauce*		
Ayer's Cliff [Stanstead]	{197}	Church
	{288}	Church

Name of Church &c	By Whom	Date	Remarks
St Mark's	J. W. Williams	1873 Apr. 25	*one annual service as of 1993*
St Luke's	J. W. Williams	1880 Sept. 20	*closed 1949; sold*
St Barnabas'	J. W. Williams	1891 May 31	
	A. H. Dunn	1905 May 30	
St Augustine's	J. W. Williams	1869 July 31	*closed before 1916; demolished*
St George the Martyr	P. Carrington	1952 May 11	
St George the Martyr	T. J. Matthews	1974 Nov. 1	*returned to Aluminum Co. & First United Church use*
St John of the Saguenay	T. J. Matthews	1974 Nov. 1	
All Saints'	P. Carrington	1949 Jan. 2	
All Saints'	P. Carrington	1955 June 12	*deconsecrated 1975 Dec. 13*
Ch of the Holy Comforter	J. W. Williams	1876 June 2	
Ch of the Holy Comforter	P. Carrington	1948 May 21	
St George's	A. H. Dunn	1906 Dec. 8	*church building moved to Ayer's Cliff from Perryboro*
St George's	L. W. Williams	1922 Oct. 1	

Place or Mission	{}	What Consecrated
		[Episcopal Act]
Baie Comeau [Saguenay]	{336}	Church
	{385}	B. G.
Barachois, Malbaie [Gaspé]	{129}	Church
	{130}	B. G.
Barford	{184}	Church
Barnston [Stanstead]	{260}	Church
	{314}	Ch Deconsecrated
Beattie's Settlement [Megantic]	{123}	Church
Beaupré [Montmorency]		Chapel Dedicated
Beebe [Stanstead]	{238}	Church
	{416}	Ch Deconsecrated
Beebe Plain: see *Beebe*		
Bergerville: see *Sillery*		
Bishop's Crossing: see *Bishopton*		
Bishopton: see *Dudswell Centre*		
Black Lake [Megantic]	{172}	Church Dedicated
Bourg Louis [Portneuf]	{33}	Church & B. G.
Bown (Bury) [Compton]	{24}	Church & B. G.
	{143}	Church
Bury [Compton]	{310}	B. G.
	{329}	Addition to B. G.
Bradore [Duplessis]	{410}	Church
Brilliant Cove [Gaspé]	{308}	Church
	{437}	Ch Deconsecrated
Brompton [Richmond]	{91}	Church
Bromptonville [Richmond]	{204}	Church
	{293}	Ch Deconsecrated
Brookbury [Compton]	{23}	Church & B. G.
Broughton [Beauce]	{57}	Church & B. G.
Bury Robinson [Compton]	{32}	B. G.
	{68}	Church
	{250}	B. G.
	{212}	Church
	{215}	B. G.
	{323}	B. G.
Cacouna [Temiscouta]	{83}	Church
	{252}	Church
Campbell's Corners [Inverness]	{239}	Church
Canterbury [Compton]	{139}	Church

Name of Church &c	By Whom	Date	Remarks
St Andrew & St George	P. Carrington	1938 Aug. 7	
St Andrew & St George	R. F. Brown	1963 May 31	
St Paul's	A. H. Dunn	1895 July 20	*closed*
	A. H. Dunn	1895 Aug. 3	
[St Laurence's]	J. W. Williams	1876 —	*"no record survives"; demolished*
Christ Church	J. W. Williams	1889 June 15	
Christ Church	L. W. Williams	1928 June 9	*discontinued 1919; sold, demolished*
St Matthew's	A. H. Dunn	1893 Dec. 15	*deconsecrated 1954 July 2; sold*
	P. Carrington	1953 Sept. 23	*closed; "probably 1966"; not in Register*
All Saints'	J. W. Williams	1881 Nov. 1	
All Saints'	T. J. Matthews	1974 May 19	*sold*
St Peter's	A. H. Dunn	1893 June 9	*sold and demolished in 1930*
St Bartholomew's	G. J. Mountain	1852 Aug. 20	
St Thomas'	G. J. Mountain	1849 Jan. 31	
St Thomas'	A. H. Dunn	1897 Sept. 26	*church burnt 1944*
[St Thomas'?]	L. W. Williams	1927 Oct. 6	*listed in Register merely as "Bury"*
St Thomas'	P. Carrington	1936 Sept. 9	
St Christopher's	T. J. Matthews	1972 March 5	
St John's	L. W. Williams	1926 July 31	
St John's	A. Goodings	1985 June 17	
Christ's Church	J. W. Williams	1872 Nov. 1	*deconsecrated 1975 May 11*
St Lawrence's	A. H. Dunn	1908 May 3	
St Lawrence's	L. W. Williams	1924 May 15	*demolished*
St John's	G. J. Mountain	1849 Jan. 30	
St Luke's	G. J. Mountain	1857 Oct. 11	*"closed circa 1900"; demolished*
	G. J. Mountain	1852 June 27	
St Paul's	J. W. Williams	1864 July 3	
	J. W. Williams	1885 Oct. 7	
St Paul's	A. H. Dunn	1910 Sept. 18	
	A. H. Dunn	1912 May 12	
	L. W. Williams	1932 May 24	*listed in Register merely as "Bury"*
St James'	J. W. Williams	1870 Aug 28	
St James the Apostle	C. Hamilton, Bp of Niagara	1886 Aug. 24	*summer church*
Church of the Ascension	J. W. Williams	1882 June 18	*church building moved to Inverness Village in 1925*
Christ's Church	A. H. Dunn	1896 Dec. 11	

Place or Mission	{}	What Consecrated [Episcopal Act]
Cap à l'Aigle, St-Étienne-de-Mal Baie [Charlevoix]	{199}	Church
	{287}	Church
Cape Cove [Gaspé]	{36}	Church & B. G.
	{245}	Church
	{326}	B. G.
Carr's Settlement [Compton]	{191}	B. G.
Chandler [Gaspé]	{342}	Church
	{439}	Ch Deconsecrated
Charny (Chaudière) [Levis]		Church Dedicated
Charleston: see *Hatley*		
Chevery [Duplessis]	{411}	Church
	{419}	B. G.
Clarke City [Saguenay]	{331}	B. G.
	{393}	B. G.
Coaticook [Stanstead]	{66}	Church
	{213}	Church
	{229}	Burial Lots
	{343}	Chapel
	{405}	Cpl Deconsecrated
Coaticook North [Stanstead]	{97}	Church
	{344}	Ch Deconsecrated
Compton [Compton]	{48}	Church
	{254}	Church
	{108}	B. G.
Compton Tnsp [Compton]	{275}	B. G.
Cookshire [Compton]	{3}	Church
	{236}	Church
	{112}	B. G.
Corner of the Beach [Gaspé]	{118}	Church
	{119}	B. G.
	{328}	Addition to B. G.
Cranbourne [Dorchester]	{414}	B. G. Deconsecrated

Name of Church &c	By Whom	Date	Remarks
St Peter's on the Rock	A. H. Dunn	1907 Aug. 11	*summer church*
St Peter's on the Rock	L. W. Williams	1922 Aug. 6	*summer church*
St James'	G. J. Mountain	1853 Aug. 18	
St James'	J. W. Williams	1884 July 10	
St James'	L. W. Williams	1934 Aug. 17	
	A. H. Dunn	1904 Sept. 12	
St George's	P. Carrington	1942 Aug. 23	
St George's	A. Goodings	1986 Aug. 22	*"sold to Gaspesia Co. (Price Co.)"*
St Matthew's	L. W. Williams	1920 Oct. 3	*shared with Presbyterians; Anglican services ended 1962*
St Michael's	T. J. Matthews	1972 Oct.	*[no day]*
	T. J. Matthews	1974 Oct. 10	
	P. Carrington	1937 July 22	
	R. F. Brown	no date	*[between 1965 Sept. 26 and Oct. 31]*
St Stephen's	J. W. Williams	1863 Oct. 21	*demolished 1908*
St Stephen's	A. H. Dunn	1911 Jan. 15	
[in Mt Forest Cemetery]	J. W. Williams	1878 June 18	*"H. Cutting, Mrs Thompson, Dr Ives, Rev. J. Foster"*
The Holy Spirit	P. Carrington	1942 Oct. 10	Bishop Mountain Hall
The Holy Spirit	R. Jervis-Read, for A. Goodings	1968 Oct. 8	
Christ's Church	J. W. Williams	1875 June 13	
Christ's Church	P. Carrington	1942 Dec. 18	
St James'	F. Fulford, Bp of Montreal	1855 June 29	*demolished*
St James the Less	J. W. Williams	1887 Sept. 2	
	J. W. Williams	1891 Dec. 11	
	J. W. Williams	1868 Sept. 25	
St Peter's	C. J. Stewart	1830 Feb. 2	*listed as Eaton in Register*
St Peter's	J. W. Williams	1880 Oct. 17	
[Union Cemetery Co.]	A. H. Dunn	1893 June 19	
St Luke's	A. H. Dunn	1893 July 21	*closed by 1969*
St Luke's	A. H. Dunn	1893 July 21	
	P. Carrington	1936 Aug. 28	
[St James']	T. J. Matthews	1973 Sept. 25	*incorrectly listed as "St George's" in Register; no record of consecration; remains and gravestones taken to Christ Church Cemetery, Frampton West; church (never consecrated) sold 1927*

Place or Mission	{}	What Consecrated
		[Episcopal Act]
Cumberland Mills [Beauce]	{82}	Church & B. G.
Danville [Richmond]	{257}	Church
	{176}	Church Dedicated
	{201}	Church
	{138}	Lot
	{154}	6 lots in B. G.
Denison's Mills [Richmond]	{166}	Church
Ditchfield [Compton]	{101}	Church
Dixville [Compton]	{249}	Church
Dolbeau [Lake St John]	{362}	Joint Ch Dedicated
	{390}	Community B. G.
Drummondville [Drummond]	{19}	B. G.
	{31}	Private B. G.
	{73}	Church
	{330}	"new Cemetery"
Dudswell: see Marbleton		
Dudswell Centre [Wolfe]	{289}	B. G.
	{228}	Church
Dudswell Corner: see Dudswell Centre		
East Angus [Compton]	{110}	Church
	{445}	Ch Deconsecrated
Eaton Corner [Compton]	{4}	Church
	{69}	B. G.
	{131}	Chapel
	{434}	[Ch] Dedicated
Entry Island [Magdalen Is]	{179}	Church Dedicated
	{302}	B. G.
	{366}	Church
Eustis [Sherbrooke]	{175}	Church Dedicated
Fitch Bay [Stanstead]	{262}	Church
Forestville [Saguenay]		Church Dedicated
Frampton East: see Hemison		
Frampton West [Dorchester]	{15}	Church

Name of Church &c	By Whom	Date	Remarks
St Paul's	J. W. Williams	1870 Feb. 3	*summer church*
St Augustine's	J. W. Williams	1888 May 17	*church burnt "1894 or 1895"*
St Augustine's	A. H. Dunn	1896 Dec. 6	
St Augustine's	A. H. Dunn	1907 Sept. 1	
["in Protestant Graveyard"]	A. H. Dunn	1896 Dec. 7	*Blaylock family lot*
[in "Danville Cemetery"]	A. H. Dunn	1900 Oct. 4	
Holy Trinity	J. W. Williams	1875 Sept. 29	
St John the Baptist	J. W. Williams	1890 June 27	
St Cuthbert's	J. W. Williams	1884 Oct. 7	
Dolbeau Community Ch	P. Carrington & J. MacKay (UCC)	1951 Jan. 20	*closed*
	R. F. Brown & K. G. McMillan (UCC)	1965 May 22	
	G. J. Mountain	1846 Aug. 22	
	G. J. Mountain	1852 June 24	*R. N. Watts family*
St George's	J. W. Williams	1867 Feb. 6	
St George's	P. Carrington	1937 June 19	
	L. W. Williams	1923 June 22	
Ch of the Good Shepherd	J. W. Williams	1877 Dec 11	*church moved to Bishop's Crossing (Bishopton) in 1916*
Christ Church	J. W. Williams	1892 Jan. 13	
Christ Church	Lynn Ross, for A. B. Stavert	1993 Sept. 12	
St Paul's	C. J. Stewart	1830 Feb. 3	*listed as Eaton in Register; "burned down" c. 1893*
	J. W. Williams	1864 Sept. 29	
St Andrews Chapel	A. H. Dunn	1895 Oct. 3	*also listed under {174} with same data*
St Andrew's	R. F. Brown	1969 July 4	*"sold for a dwelling" in 1970*
[All Saints']	A. H. Dunn	1900 July 31	
	L. W. Williams	1925 July 26	
All Saints'	P. Carrington	1953 Aug. 16	
Christ's Church	A. H. Dunn	1896 Nov. 5	
St Matthias'	J. W. Williams	1889 June 20	
Trinity Church	P. Carrington	1955 June 19	*(not listed in Register) deconsecrated 1979 Oct. 28 by A. Goodings*
Christ Church	G. J. Mountain	1844 Feb. 12	*restored with the aid of a Québec Gvt grant in 1985; one service held annually*

Place or Mission	{}	What Consecrated [Episcopal Act]
Gallup Hill [Richmond]	{45}	Church
	{51}	B. G.
	{233}	B. G.
	{231}	B. G.
	{216}	B. G. (addition)
	{360}	Ch Deconsecrated
Gascons [Bonaventure]	{136}	Church & B. G.
	{220}	Church
Gaspé [Gaspé]	{34}	Church & B. G.
	{246}	"Church on old site"
	{211}	Church
	{339}	Church Dedicated
	{346}	Church
Gaspé South: see *Wakeham*		
Georgeville [Stanstead]	{234}	Church
Gould [Compton]	{67}	Church
	{132}	Church
	{396}	Ch Deconsecrated
Grand Bay [Bagot]	{240}	B. G.
Grand' Mère [Champlain]	{178}	Church Dedicated
	{195}	Church
	{202}	Church
	{300}	Ch Deconsecrated
	{301}	[new] Church
Grant's Settlement: see *Wakeham*		

Name of Church &c	By Whom	Date	Remarks
St John's	G. J. Mountain	1855 Jan. 24	*listed under Melbourne in Register*
	G. J. Mountain	1856 June 3	*listed under Melbourne in Register*
St John's	J. W. Williams	1879 June 28	*listed under Melbourne; 1876 Aug. 24 inserted under 'Remarks' in Register*
St John's	J. W. Williams	1879 June 28	*listed under Melbourne; notation June 27 inserted under 'Remarks' in Register*
"of St John's"	A. H. Dunn	1912 Aug. 31	*listed under Melbourne in Register*
St John's	P. Carrington	1950 July 6	*sold to Pentecostal Church and moved to Lennoxville*
St Philip's	A. H. Dunn	1896 Aug. 12	
St Philip's	A. H. Dunn	1913 Aug. 21	
St Paul's	G. J. Mountain	1853 Aug. 14	*listed as Gaspé Basin in Register*
St Paul's	J. W. Williams	1884 July 13	*listed as Gaspé Basin in Register*
St Paul's	A. H. Dunn	1910 Aug. 28	*"burnt"*
St Paul's	P. Carrington	1941 June 29	
St Paul's	P. Carrington	1944 Aug. 20	
St George's	J. W. Williams	1880 June 17	*notation 1867 Nov. 13 inserted under 'Remarks' in Register*
St Peter's	J. W. Williams	1864 July 2	*listed under Lingwick in Register*
St Peter's	A. H. Dunn	1895 Dec. 13	
St Peter's	R. F. Brown	1966 July 3	*sold*
	J. W. Williams	1882 Sept.4	*notation 1858 Aug. 12 inserted under 'Remarks' in Register*
St Stephen's	A. H. Dunn	1899 Nov. 5	*church "moved and enlarged 1900"*
St Stephen's	A. H. Dunn	1905 July 16	*"moved to McGibbon Street in 1906"*
St Stephen's	A. H. Dunn	1907 Oct. 13	*remarks in Register question that there were two consecrations—{195 & 202}—but QDG confirms that there were two*
St Stephen's	L. W. Williams	1924 June 11	
St Stephen's	L. W. Williams	1924 June 11	

Place or Mission	{}	What Consecrated [Episcopal Act]
Grindstone [Magdalen Is]	{78}	Church & B. G.
	{277}	Church
	{361}	Church Dedicated
	{431}	Ch Deconsecrated
Grosse Ile Quarantine Station [Montmagny]		Church
Grosse Isle [Magdalen Is]	{248}	Church
	{316}	Church
	{335}	B. G.
	{432}	Addition to B. G.
Halesboro [Portneuf]	{13}	Church & B. G.
Hall's Stream [Compton]	{124}	Church
Hardwood Hill Windsor [Richmond]		
	{106}	Church
Harrington Harbour [Saguenay]	{148}	Church
	{365}	Church
Hatley [Stanstead]	{7}	B. G.
		Church
	{8}	Church & B. G.
	{84}	B. G.
	{207}	B. G.
	{352}	Addition to B. G.
Hemison [Dorchester]	{14}	Church
	{226}	Church
Hereford [Compton]	{85}	B. G.
	{86}	Church
Hopetown [Bonaventure]	{120}	Church & B. G.
	{401}	Addition to B. G.
Ile d'Orléans [Montmorenci]	{90}	Church
Ile Maligne [Lac St-Jean]	{353}	Joint Church

Name of Church &c	By Whom	Date	Remarks
St Luke's	J. W. Williams	1869 July 27	
St Luke's	L. W. Williams	1918 July 17	*burnt 1946*
St Luke's	P. Carrington	1953 Aug. 13	
St Luke's	A. Goodings	1980 Sept. 11	*church sold*
St John the Evangelist			*no record of consecration*
Holy Trinity	J. W. Williams	1884 July 27	*notation 1884 March 1 inserted under 'Remarks' in Register; church destroyed in 1922*
Holy Trinity	L. W. Williams	1928 July 27	
Holy Trinity	P. Carrington	1938 July 10	*listed in Register under Grosse Ile South*
Holy Trinity	A. Goodings	1982 Sept. 17	
Christ Church	G. J. Mountain	1843 March 12	*listed as Portneuf (Halesboro) in Register; one service per annum*
St Paul's	A. H. Dunn	1894 Jan. 23	*closed; church moved to Canaan, Vt, for use under same dedication*
Grace Church	J. W. Williams	1891 June 16	*closed in 1909 and demolished; lumber probably used in the construction of St George's, Windsor Mills*
Christ's Church	A. H. Dunn	1898 June 26	
Christ's Church	P. Carrington	1953 July 17	
	C. J. Stewart	1834 July 10	*listed under Charleston in Register*
Old North Church			*built 1817-8, no record of consecration; demolished 1928*
St James'	C. J. Stewart	1834 July 13	
	J. W. Williams	1870 Sept. 18	*listed in Register under Charleston*
	A. H. Dunn	1909 June 13	
	P. Carrington	1947 Oct. 5	
St Paul's	G. J. Mountain	1844 Feb. 11	*listed in Register under Frampton East*
St Paul's	J. W. Williams	1876 June 25	
	J. W. Williams	1871 June 26	
All Saints'	J. W. Williams	1871 June 26	
St James'	A. H. Dunn	1893 July 28	
St James'	R. F. Brown	1967 June 8	
St Mary's	J. W. Williams	1872 July 14	*listed incorrectly in Register as St James'; opened for occasional use*
Emmanuel	P. Carrington & S. MacKay (UCC)	1948 Feb. 29	

Place or Mission	{}	What Consecrated [Episcopal Act]
	{388}	Ch Deconsecrated
Inverness North: see *Rectory Hill*		
Inverness South [Megantic]	{307}	Church
	{76}	B. G.
Island Brook [Compton]	{224}	Church
Johnville [Sherbrooke]	{312}	B. G.
Kawawachikamach (Schefferville) [Duplessis]	{440}	Church
Kegaska [Duplessis]	{208}	B. G.
	{279}	B. G.
	{334}	Addition to B. G.
	{376}	Ch & Addn to B. G.
	{418}	B. G.
Kenogami [Chicoutimi]	{272}	Church
	{398}	Ch Deconsecrated
	{297}	B. G.
	{306}	B. G.
Kingsey [Drummond]	{18}	Church & B. G.
	{232}	B. G.
	{217}	B. G.
Kingsey Falls [Drummond]	{258}	Church
Kinnear's Mills [Megantic]	{74}	Church & B. G.
	{151}	Church
Kirkdale [Drummond]	{11}	Church

Name of Church &c	By Whom	Date	Remarks
Emmanuel	R. F. Brown	1964 June 12	*sold*
Ch of the Ascension	L. W. Williams	1926 Oct. 24	*listed in Register under Inverness Village; church (moved from Campbell's Corners in 1925) was reconsecrated and reopened for worship on 28 Jan. 1926*
	J. W. Williams	1867 July 30	*listed as Christ Church in Register*
St John's	J. W. Williams	1876 March 19	*notation 1874 Jan. 16 inserted under 'Remarks' in Register; closed 1944*
"Libby Farm"	L. W. Williams	1917 Oct. 17	*listed as Milby Johnville Mission in Register; "Owner of land Celina Libby"*
St John's	A. Goodings	1987 May 20	*Naskapi Band Church*
	A. H. Dunn	1909 June 22	*listed in Register as Kegashka Bay Northern Beach Labrador*
	L. W. Williams	1919 June 29	*listed in Register as Kegaska River Labrador*
	P. Carrington	1937 Aug. 7	*listed in Register as Kegashka*
St Philip's	P. Carrington	1959 July 6	*listed in Register as Kegashka*
	T. J. Matthews	1974 Oct. 10	
St James'	L. W. Williams	1917 Aug. 19	
St James'	Eric Caulfield, for R. F. Brown	1966 Nov. 13	*now a museum*
	L. W. Williams	1925 May 24	
	L. W. Williams	1926 Oct. 11	
St Paul's	G. J. Mountain	1846 Aug. 12	*summer church*
	J. W. Williams	1879 June 28	*notation 1876 Apr. 8 inserted under 'Remarks' in Register*
Maplewood Cemetery	A. H. Dunn	1912 Sept. 1	
Christ Church	J. W. Williams	1888 June 3	*"Deconsecrated 1976 by T. J. Matthews"; sold*
St Mark's	J. W. Williams	1867 July 29	
St Mark's	A. H. Dunn	1899 Nov. 30	*now a summer church*
Holy Trinity	G. J. Mountain	1840 Feb. 22	*listed in Register as Trinity Church; church later used as church hall when new church was consecrated in*

Place or Mission	{}	What Consecrated [Episcopal Act]
	{77}	B. G.
	{88}	Church
	{122}	B. G.
	{150}	"Private lot"
	{189}	lot in B. G.
	{317}	B. G.
Lake Beauport [Quebec]	{103}	Church
Lake Megantic: see *Agnes*		
L'Anse au Brilliant: see *Brilliant Cove*		
L'Anse aux Gascons: see *Gascons*		
La Baie: see *Grand Bay*		
La Tabatière [Duplessis]	{382}	Church
La Tuque [Champlain]	{349}	Church
		Chapel Dedicated
L'Avenir [Drummond]	{87}	Church
	{94}	B. G.
	{121}	Church
Lawrence [Compton]	{340}	Church
Lawrence Colony: see *Lawrence*		
Leeds [Megantic]	{10}	Church
Lemesurier: see *Beattie's Settlement*		
Lennoxville [Sherbrooke]	{5}	Church
	{21}	Church
	{55}	College Chapel
	{171}	Chapel Dedicated
	{203}	Oratory
	{227}	B. G.
	{378}	Chapel Dedicated
Levis [Levis]	{29}	B. G.
	{70}	Church
	{415}	Ch Deconsecrated
	{125}	B. G.
	{386}	Ch Deconsecrated

Name of Church &c	By Whom	Date	Remarks
			1872
"to Trinity Church"	J. W. Williams	1868 Sept. 28	listed in Register as Durham Upper Kirkdale
Holy Trinity	J. W. Williams	1872 May 24	listed in Register as Durham Kirkdale
north side of Holy Trinity	A. H. Dunn	1893 Oct. 9	
	A. H. Dunn	1899 May 30	Mrs Mary Anne White of Melbourne
"Part of lot no 6"	A. H. Dunn	1904 July 18	"belonging to Anne Jane Breadon"
	L. W. Williams	1928 June 17	
St James'	J. W. Williams	1891 May 21	
St Andrew's	R. F. Brown	1961 July 11	
St Andrew's	P. Carrington	1945 Apr. 29	
St Anne's	R. F. Brown	1963 Sept. 8	Indian Residential School; recorded in Synod Journal, not entered in Register
St Paul's	J. W. Williams	1871 Dec. 12	
	J. W. Williams	1874 Sept. 20	
St Paul's	A. H. Dunn	1893 Oct. 8	closed 1925; demolished
St Lawrence's	P. Carrington	1941 Sept. 12	
St James'	G. J. Mountain	1838 Feb. 18	one service (ecumenical) per annum
St James'	C. J. Stewart	1830 Feb. 10	"taken down"; wood used in original Bishop's College building
St George's	G. J. Mountain	1847 Oct. 25	
St Mark's	G. J. Mountain	1857 July 1	Bishop's College
[St Mark's]	A. H. Dunn	1892 Oct. 4	Bishop's College
of the Venerable Bede	A. H. Dunn	1908 March 11	Divinity House, dismantled
Malvern Cemetery	J. W. Williams	1877 May 17	notation Nov. 1877 under 'Remarks' in Register
St Martin's	P. Carrington	1959 Oct. 11	Bishop's College School
	G. J. Mountain	1851 Sept. 8	listed under Point Levis
Holy Trinity	J. W. Williams	1865 Sept. 29	
Holy Trinity	T. J. Matthews	1973 Oct.12	demolished
Holy Trinity	R. F. Brown	1963 June 9	headstones and remains removed to Mount Hermon Cemetery, Sillery

Place or Mission	{}	What Consecrated [Episcopal Act]
Lingwick: see *Gould*		
Limoilou (Quebec City) [Quebec]	{303}	Church
	{444}	Ch Deconsecrated
Little Gaspé [Gaspé]	{62}	B. G.
	{266}	Church
Little Metis, St-Octave-de-Métis		
[Rimouski]	{200}	Church
Long Point of Mingan [Saguenay]	{134}	B. G.
Loretteville [Quebec]	{282}	Church
	{395}	Parish Hall Dedicated
Lorne [Richmond]	{243}	Church
	{355}	Ch Deconsecrated
	{102}	B. G.
Louiseville: see *Rivière-du-Loup-en-haut*		
Lower Ireland [Megantic]	{42}	Church & B. G.
	{253}	Church
Magog [Stanstead]	{93}	Church
Malbaie [Gaspé]	{53}	Church & B. G.
	{117}	Church
	{285}	B. G.
	{338}	Addition to B. G.
Maple Grove [Megantic]	{41}	Church
	{75}	Church & B. G.
	{242}	Tower & Chancel
	{159}	Church
	{198}	Addition to B. G.
Marbleton [Wolfe]	{46}	Church

Name of Church &c	By Whom	Date	Remarks
"new St Peter's"	L. W. Williams	1926 Jan. 25	
St Peter's	Richard Blyth, for A. B. Stavert	1993 Apr. 18	*sold, demolished; memorial wall plaques removed to St Michael's, Sillery*
"of St Peter's Church"	G. J. Mountain	1859 July 22	
St Peter's	J. W. Williams	1889 July 26	*serving as Ecumenical Chapel in the Forillon National Park*
St George's	A. H. Dunn	1907 Aug. 25	*summer church*
	A. H. Dunn	1896 July 14	
St Paul's	L. W. Williams	1920 June 11	*furnishings came from St Paul's Mariners Chapel which was deconsecrated in 1920*
beneath St Paul's Ch	R. F. Brown	1966 Mar. 20	
Ch of the Epiphany	J. W. Williams	1883 May 16	
Ch of the Epiphany	P. Carrington	1948 May 21	*demolished*
	J. W. Williams	1890 July 2	
Christ's Church	G. J. Mountain	1854 Feb. 15	*demolished after 1883; new church consecrated 1887*
Christ's [Church]	J. W. Williams	1887 Jan. 9	*notation 17 March 1884 in Register under 'Remarks'; now summer church*
St Luke's	J. W. Williams	1874 June 21	
St Peter's	G. J. Mountain	1856 Aug. 17	
St Peter's	A. H. Dunn	1893 July 20	
	L. W. Williams	1922 June 29	*listed in Register as Mal Bay*
St Peter's	P. Carrington	1938 Aug. 24	*listed in Register as Malbay*
Holy Trinity	G. J. Mountain	1854 Feb. 14	*listed in Register under Upper Ireland*
Holy Trinity	J. W. Williams	1867 July 30	*listed in Register as Ireland*
Holy Trinity	J. W. Williams	1882 Dec. 10	*listed in Register as "Maple Grove (South Ireland)"*
Holy Trinity	A. H. Dunn	1902 June 20	*listed in Register under Upper Ireland; now summer church*
	A. H. Dunn	1907 June 6	
St Paul's	G. J. Mountain	1855 Feb. 14	*listed in Register under Dudswell*

Place or Mission	{}	What Consecrated [Episcopal Act]
	{61}	B. G.
	{397}	Additional B. G.
Melbourne: see *Gallup Hill*		
Melbourne Ridge [Richmond]		
	{157}	Church
Métis: see *Little Metis*		
Milby [Sherbrooke]	{95}	B. G.
	{96}	Church
Montmorenci Falls [Quebec]	{192}	Church
Murdochville [Gaspé]	{377}	Curch Dedicated
Murray Bay [Charlevoix]	{177}	Church
	{341}	Church "closed"
Mutton Bay [Saguenay]	{135}	Church
	{324}	Church
	{332}	B. G.
New Carlisle [Bonaventure]	{37}	B. G.
	{52}	Church
	{140}	Church
	{408}	Addition to B. G.
	{424}	Chapel
	{425}	Addition to B. G.
	{442}	Addition to B. G.
New Liverpool [Levis]	{12}	Church & B. G.
Newport Point [Gaspé]	{127}	Church
	{389}	Ch Deconsecrated
	{128}	B. G.
New Richmond [Bonaventure]	{400}	Church Dedicated
	{413}	Church

Name of Church &c	By Whom	Date	Remarks
"of St Paul's Church"	G. J. Mountain	1858 July 4	*listed in Register under Dudswell*
St Paul's	R. F. Brown	1966 Sept. 22	
St Saviour's	A. H. Dunn	1901 Oct. 22	*closed 1920; demolished*
	J. W. Williams	1875 June 11	
St Barnabas'	J. W. Williams	1875 June 11	
St Mary's	A. H. Dunn	1904 Nov. 13	*gift to the Redemptorist Fathers as a Chapel of Perpetual Prayer for Christian Unity; transfer not recorded in Register*
St Philip's	P. Carrington	1959 June 19	
St Anne's	C. Hamilton, Bp of Niagara	1899 July 26	
St Anne's	P. Carrington	1942 July 26	*had been summer church; latter entry in Register under Pointe-au-Pic*
St Clement's	A. H. Dunn	1896 July 23	
St Clement's	L. W. Williams	1932 July 24	
St Clement's	P. Carrington	1937 Aug. 1	
	G. J. Mountain	1853 Aug. 24	
St Andrew's	G. J. Mountain	1856 July 31	
St Andrew's	A. H. Dunn	1897 Aug. 23	
St Andrew's	R. F. Brown	1970 June 30	
Jubilee Chapel of the Blessed Virgin	A. Goodings	1979 Oct. 10	*added to St Andrew's Church; its earlier dedication (31 Aug. 1936 by P. Carrington) not noted in Register*
St Andrew's	A. Goodings	1979 Oct. 10	
St Andrew's	A. Goodings	1989 Sept. 6	
Christ's Church	G. J. Mountain	1841 Sept. 9	*"[Both] Deconsecrated Oct. 17 '75"; church sold as a house; remains and headstones removed to Mount Hermon Cemetery, Sillery*
St Peter's	A. H. Dunn	1895 July 16	
St Peter's	"by Rural Dean," for R. F. Brown	1964 Nov. 16	*demolished*
	A. H. Dunn	1895 July 16	
		1862 May 24	
St Mary Magdalen	T. J. Matthews	1973 July 1	

Place or Mission	{}	What Consecrated [Episcopal Act]
Nicolet [Nicolet]	{17}	Church & B. G.
North Hatley [Stanstead]	{142}	Church
	{350}	Chapel
	{367}	Chapel Dedicated
Old Fort Bay [Duplessis]	{373}	B. G.
	{407}	Church
Old Harry [Magdalen Is]	{270}	B. G.
	{276}	Church
Orleans, Island of: see *Ile d'Orléans*		
Parent [Champlain]	{368}	Chapel Dedicated
Paspebiac [Bonaventure]	{20}	Church & B. G.
	{281}	Church
	{364}	Church
	{441}	Ch Deconsecrated
Peninsula [Gaspé]	{247}	Church
	{267}	B. G.
	{114}	[Chancel of] Ch
	{315}	B. G.
Percé [Gaspé]	{65}	Church & B. G.
	{209}	[Chancel of] Ch
Perryboro [Compton]	{109}	Church
	{137}	B. G.
	{152}	Chancel of Ch
Pointe Bleue [Lac St-Jean]	{265}	B. G.
	{113}	Church
	{384}	Ch Deconsecrated
	{149}	B. G.
Pointe-au-Pic: see *Murray Bay*		
Point St Peter [Gaspé]	{26}	B. G.
	{404}	B. G. Deconsecrated
Port Daniel [Bonaventure]	{81}	Church & B. G.
	{205}	Church
	{383}	B. G.
Portneuf [Portneuf]	{255}	Church
	{327}	B. G.

Name of Church &c	By Whom	Date	Remarks
St Bartholomew's	G. J. Mountain	1846 Aug. 4	*demolished 1916*
St Barnabas'	A. H. Dunn	1897 Sept. 10	
St George's	P. Carrington	1945 July 30	1st Quebec Lodge
St Peter's	P. Carrington	1954 July 27	2nd Quebec Lodge
	E.S. Reed, Bp of Ottawa	1957 July 21	
St Peter's	R. F. Brown	1970 Feb. 2	
	L. W. Williams	1915 July 17	
St Peter's by the Sea	L. W. Williams	1918 July 19	
	P. Carrington	1955 Feb. 2	R.C.A.F. Station; *closed*
St Peter's	G. J. Mountain	1847 Sept. 29	
St Peter's	L. W. Williams	1919 July 27	
St Peter's	P. Carrington	1952 Oct. 12	
St Peter's	Peter Spackman, for A. Goodings	1989 July 25	*sold*
St Matthew's	J. W. Williams	1884 July 15	
	J. W. Williams	1889 July 27	
St Matthew's	A. H. Dunn	1893 July 16	
	L. W. Williams	1928 July 13	
St Paul's	G. J. Mountain	1862 May 24	
St Paul's	A. H. Dunn	1909 July 18	*chancel added in 1908*
Church of the Advent	J. W. Williams	1891 Dec. 13	
	A. H. Dunn	1896 Oct. 15	
St George's	A. H. Dunn	1899 Dec. 2	*"formerly Church of the Advent"; church later moved to Ayer's Cliff*
	J. W. Williams	1889 July 7	
St John the Divine	A. H. Dunn	1893 July 12	
St John the Divine	Eric Caulfield, for R. F. Brown	1963 May 10	
	A. H. Dunn	1898 July 13	
Private, Johnson family	G. J. Mountain	1850 June 23	*month corrected from July in Register*
	Gordon S. Peabody, for R. F. Brown	1967 Oct. 25	
St James'	J. W. Williams	1869 Aug. 14	
St James'	A. H. Dunn	1908 Aug. 9	*incorrectly listed as St George's in Register*
	R. F. Brown	1962 Sept. 24	
St John the Evangelist	J. W. Williams	1888 May 30	*notation 1869 Nov 20 inserted under 'Remarks' in Register*
St John the Evangelist	L. W. Williams	1934 Oct. 28	*listed under Halesboro*

Place or Mission	{}	What Consecrated [Episcopal Act]
Quebec City [Quebec]	{1a}	Cathedral
		Chapel [opened]
	{6}	Chapel
	{284}	Cpl Deconsecrated
	{168}	Church
	{295}	Ch Deconsecrated
	{16}	Chapel
	{22}	B. G.
	{64}	Chapel
	{111}	Church
	{156}	"Chancel & Organ Chamber"
	{438}	Ch Deconsecrated
		Chapel Dedicated
Quebec City: see also *Bergerville, Limoilou, Ste Foy* and *Sillery*		
Randboro [Compton]	{251}	Church
	{375}	Ch Deconsecrated
Rapide Blanc [Champlain]	{374}	Church Dedicated
	{403}	Dedication Removed
Rectory Hill [Megantic]	{47}	Church & B. G.

Name of Church &c	By Whom	Date	Remarks
Holy Trinity	Jacob Mountain	1804 Aug. 28	*Portneuf in Register Rededicated after restoration 1993 Jan. 23 by A. B. Stavert*
Trinity		1825 Nov. 27	*no record of dedication or consecration in Register; building sold, congregation moved to Ste-Foy in 1960*
St Paul's (Mariner's Chapel)	C. J. Stewart	1832 June 3	
St Paul's (Mariner's Chapel)	L. W. Williams	1921 June 10	*furnishings went to St Paul's, Loretteville*
St Peter's	G. J. Mountain	1844 Oct 18	*"Sentence in Bishop's Archives"; church burnt in great Quebec fire of 1845 and rebuilt on new site in 1846*
St Peter's	L. W. Williams	1924 Nov. 19	*see new St Peter's under Limoilou*
All Saints	G. J. Mountain	1844 Nov. 1	*attached to the Bishop's residence, located in the Cathedral Close*
"for Strangers"	G. J. Mountain	1848 Nov. 2	*listed as Charlesbourg Road*
St Luke's	G. J. Mountain	1859 Dec. 7	The Marine Hospital; *"Building closed by Government"*
St Matthew's	A. H. Dunn	1892 Nov. 1	*earlier building burnt in Quebec fire of 1845; no listing of earlier consecration*
St Matthew's	A. H. Dunn	1901 Oct. 13	
St Matthew's	A. Goodings	1979 June 17	*given to the city of Quebec, June 1979; serving as a municipal library*
The Holy Spirit	A. H. Dunn	1892 Sept. 22	Bishopthorpe, *rue d'Auteuil; consecration not noted in Register; sold in 1971*
[St Matthew's]	J. W. Williams	1886 July 7	*listed as Randborough in Register*
St Matthew's	P. Carrington	1958 Feb. 2	
St Paul's	P. Carrington	1957 Sept. 28	
St Stephen's	G. J. Mountain	1855 May 4	*listed under Inverness in Register; "burnt"*

Place or Mission	{}	What Consecrated [Episcopal Act]
	{194}	Church
	{427}	Ch Deconsecrated
	{430}	Addition to B. G.
Richmond [Richmond]	{9}	Church
	{50}	B. G.
	{230}	B. G.
	{153}	Church
	{214}	B. G.
	{271}	B. G.
	{391}	Chapel Dedicated
Riverbend [Lac St-Jean]	{359}	Joint Church
River David [Yamaska]	{44}	[Private] B. G.
Rivière-du-Loup [Temiscouata]	{206}	Church & B. G.
Rivière du Loup en-bas [Temiscouata]	{144}	Church
	{294}	Ch Deconsecrated
Romaine, Labrador [Saguenay]		
	{186}	B. G.
St Augustine River [Duplessis]		
	{370}	Church
	{402}	Church
St-Georges-de-Beauce [Beauce]		
	{56}	[Private] B. G.
	{268}	Church
	{409}	Ch Deconsecrated
St-Giles [Lotbinière]	{43}	Church
	{60}	B. G.
St Margaret's Range St-Sylvestre East [Lotbinière]	{58}	Church & B. G.
St-Malachie: see *Hemison*		
St-Patrice [Lotbinière]	{38}	Church

Name of Church &c	By Whom	Date	Remarks
St Stephen's	A. H. Dunn	1905 June 19	*listed incorrectly in Register as Inverness Richmond Hill*
St Stephen's	M. Awcock, for A. Goodings	1979 Oct. 28	
St Stephen's	A. Goodings	1980 May 4	*listed in Register as Inverness Rectory Hill*
St Anne's	C. J. Stewart	1834 July 20	
St Anne's	G. J. Mountain	1856 June 2	
St Anne's Church	J. W. Williams	1879 June 27	*notation 1875 Apr. 5 inserted under 'Remarks' in Register*
St Anne's	A. H. Dunn	1900 May 20	
	A. H. Dunn	1911 Oct. 22	
	L. W. Williams	1915 Oct. 24	
The Redeemer	R. F. Brown & Graham Ban (UCC)	1965 May 26	Wales Home
Trinity	P. Carrington & J. MacKay (UCC)	1950 July 2	*closed*
J.G.C. Wurtele & family	G. J. Mountain	1854 Oct. 20	
St Bartholomew's	A. H. Dunn	1908 Aug. 18	*closed in late 1980s*
St Michael & All Angels	A. H. Dunn	1897 Oct. 3	
St Michael & All Angels	L. W. Williams	1924 Aug. 8	*closed 1925 and demolished*
Mission of St Clement's	A. H. Dunn	1903 June 29	
St Augustine's	P. Carrington	1955 July 19	
St Augustine's	R. F. Brown	1967 Oct. 1	
Pozer family	G. J. Mountain	1857 Oct. 8	*listed in Register as St George, Aubert Gallion*
St Peter's	J. W. Williams	1889 Aug. 25	*notation 1877 July 10 inserted under 'Remarks' in Register*
St Peter's	A. Goodings, for R. F. Brown	1970 Oct. 20	*demolished 1970*
Trinity Church	G. J. Mountain	1854 Feb. 17	*demolished; "Last service 1911 July 20"*
	G. J. Mountain	1857 Oct. 15	
St John the Evangelist	G. J. Mountain	1857 Oct. 12	*listed in Register as St Margaret, St Giles; "services dropped 1889"; demolished*
St David's	G. J. Mountain	1854 Jan. 31	*listed in Register as St Sylvester–St Patrick; "closed 1890"; demolished*

Place or Mission	{}	What Consecrated [Episcopal Act]
St Paul's River Labrador [Duplessis]	{187}	Church
	{392}	Church Dedicated
	{372}	B. G.
	{426}	Church
St-Romuald: see *New Liverpool*		
St-Sylvestre West [Lotbinière]	{59}	B. G.
	{241}	B. G.
	{39}	Church
Ste-Catherine [Quebec]	{274}	Church
Ste-Foy [Quebec] *"Quebec Ste Foy"*	{380}	Church Dedicated
Ste-Ursule [Maskinongé]	{155}	Church
	{387}	Ch Deconsecrated
Sand Hill [Compton]	{105}	B. G.
	{237}	Church
	{412}	Land Re-consecrated
Sandy Beach [Gaspé]	{54}	Church
	{273}	Church
	{63}	B. G.
	{280}	B. G.
	{325}	B. G.
	{433}	Addition to B. G.
Sawyerville [Compton]	{181}	Sanctuary Dedicated
Schefferville Knob Lake [Duplessis]	{379}	Church Dedicated
	{417}	Church Dedicated
Scotstown [Compton]	{259}	Church
	{219}	Chancel
	{443}	Ch Deconsecrated
Sept-Iles [Saguenay]	{381}	Church Dedicated
	{399}	Church
Shawinigan Falls [St-Maurice]	{180}	Sanctuary Dedicated

Name of Church &c	By Whom	Date	Remarks
St Paul's	A. H. Dunn	1903 July 13	*demolished Sept. 1965*
St Paul's	R. F. Brown	1965 Sept. 26	*listed in Register as St Clement's Mission (East) St Paul's River Saguenay*
St Paul's	E.S. Reed, Bishop of Ottawa	1957 July 21	
St Paul's	A. Goodings	1979 June 20	
	G. J. Mountain	1857 Oct. 14	*listed in Register as St Sylvester*
	J. W. Williams	1882 Oct. 8	
St George's	G. J. Mountain	1854 Feb. 1	*listed in Register under St Sylvester–St Giles; "closed 1919"; demolished*
St Thomas'	G. J. Mountain	1852 Aug. 19	*closed 1906; demolished*
Trinity	R. F. Brown	1960 Nov 3	*listed in Register under*
All Saints'	A. H. Dunn	1901 Oct. 7	
All Saints'	R. F. Brown	1963 June 30	*demolished 1963*
	J. W. Williams	1891 June 5	*name written as Sandhill in Register*
St Luke's	J. W. Williams	1880 Oct. 18	*name written as Sandhill in Register; notation 1880 Feb. 27 inserted under 'Remarks' in Register*
	T. J. Matthews	1973 May	
St John the Evangelist	G. J. Mountain	1856 Aug. 19	
St John the Evangelist	L. W. Williams	1917 July 22	*burnt 1992*
	G. J. Mountain	1859 July 23	
	L. W. Williams	1919 July 24	
St John's	L. W. Williams	1932 Sept. 18	
St John's	A. Goodings	1983 May 8	
of Mission Hall	A. H. Dunn	1902 May 10	
St Peter's	P. Carrington	1960 May 22	*"closed 9 Dec. 1990"*
St John's	T. J. Matthews	1974 [no date]	*"replacing Indian Chapel demolished 1973"; in Register listed under "Schefferville Indian Village"*
St Alban's	J. W. Williams	1888 Oct. 3	*listed in Register as Scotts' Town*
St Alban's	A. H. Dunn	1912 Dec. 15	
St Alban's	A. B. Stavert	1992 Nov. 4	*sold*
All Saints'	R. F. Brown	1961 June 4	
All Saints'	R. F. Brown	1967 Apr. 16	
St John the Evangelist	A. H. Dunn	1901 May 12	

Place or Mission	{}	What Consecrated [Episcopal Act]
	{196}	B. G.
	{347}	Church
	{429}	Ch Deconsecrated
Sheldrake [Saguenay]	{147}	B. G.
Sherbrooke [Sherbrooke]	{1}	Church & B. G.
	{348}	Church
	{436}	Ch Deconsecrated
	{40}	Church
	{158}	Church
	{263}	Church
	{100}	B. G.
Shigawake [Bonaventure]	{80}	Church & B. G.
	{269}	Church
	{337}	Addition to B. G.
Sillery [Quebec]	{167}	Church
	{25}	Mt Hermon Cmty
	{28}	Mt Hermon Cmty
	{30}	Mt Hermon Cmty
	{89}	Mt Hermon Cmty
	{107}	Mt Hermon Cmty
	{133}	Mt Hermon Cmty
	{160}	Mt Hermon Cmty
	{188}	Mt Hermon Cmty
	{210}	Mt Hermon Cmty
	{218}	Mt Hermon Cmty
	{221}	Mt Hermon Cmty
	{283}	Mt Hermon Cmty
	{291}	Mt Hermon Cmty
	{292}	Mt Hermon Cmty
	{311}	Mt Hermon Cmty
	{322}	Mt Hermon Cmty
South Durham [Drummond]	{98}	Church
	{145}	Church
	{428}	B. G.
Spooner's Pond Kingsey [Drummond]	{99}	Church

Name of Church &c	By Whom	Date	Remarks
	A. H. Dunn	1905 July 16	*described as "part 627 Parish of St Flore"*
St John the Evangelist	P. Carrington	1944 Oct. 15	
St John the Evangelist	A. Goodings	1980 Jan. 13	
	A. H. Dunn	1898 June 18	
St Paul the Apostle	C. J. Stewart	1830 Jan. 31	*demolished 1844*
St Paul the Apostle	P. Carrington	1944 Nov. 19	*listed in Register as Sherbrooke–Westward;*
St Paul the Apostle	T. J. Matthews, for A. Goodings	1985 Apr. 5	*sold; in use as Roman Catholic church*
St Peter's	G. J. Mountain	1854 Feb. 10	*demolished 1900*
St Peter's	A. H. Dunn	1902 March 18	*this church is the successor of the 1830 St Paul the Apostle and of St Peter's*
Ch of the Advent	J. W. Williams	1889 June 23	
"Urnwood Cemetery"	J. W. Williams	1890 June 22	*lot numbers are specified in Register*
St Paul's	J. W. Williams	1869 Aug. 14	*in Register written as "Chigouac (Shigawake)"*
St Paul's	L. W. Williams	1915 July 11	
St Paul's	P. Carrington	1938 Aug. 19	
St Michael's	G. J. Mountain	1856 Sept. 16	*in Register under "Quebec, Quebec"*
1/2 lot &c, Private Parties	G. J. Mountain	1849 Aug. 16	
lots, Private Parties	G. J. Mountain	1851 Aug. 16	
lots, Private Parties	G. J. Mountain	1852 June 16	
lot, Private	J. W. Williams	1872 June 11	*C. V.M. Temple*
lot, Private	J. W. Williams	1891 Sept. 7	*W. H. Carter*
lot, Private	A. H. Dunn	1896 June 4	*S. W. Drum*
lot, Private	A. H. Dunn	1903 Jan. 15	*Vesey Boswell*
cemetery lot	A. H. Dunn	1903 Sept. 17	*"belonging to Vesey Boswell Esq"*
lot	A. H. Dunn	1910 May 5	*"lot, Dr Colin Charles Sewell"*
lot	A. H. Dunn	1912 Oct. 29	*Charles Mills Teakle*
lot	A. H. Dunn	1914 Sept. 9	*Mrs James F. Wilson*
lot	L. W. Williams	1920 Sept. 22	*"Lafferty Lot"*
lot	L. W. Williams	1923 Oct. 8	*"Balfour Lot"*
lot	L. W. Williams	1923 Nov. 2	*"Teakle Lot"*
lot	L. W. Williams	1928 March 2	*"Fothergill Lot "*
lot	L. W. Williams	1932 Apr. 29	*"Rhodes Lot "*
St James'	J. W. Williams	1875 June 22	*listed in Register as "Durham, South"*
St James'	A. H. Dunn	1898 Feb. 9	
St James'	A. Goodings	1979 June 4	
Christ Church	J. W. Williams	1890 June 19	*deconsecrated in 1945, not in Register; demolished*

Place or Mission	{}	What Consecrated [Episcopal Act]
Springbrook: see *Frampton West*		
Stanhope [Stanstead]	{264}	Church
	{394}	Ch Deconsecrated
Stanstead [Stanstead]	{222}	Church
Stoneham [Quebec]	{71}	B. G.
	{72}	Church
Styles Island Mutton Bay [Saguenay]		
	{126}	B. G.
Sydenham Place: see *Kingsey*		
Thetford Mines [Megantic]	{173}	Church Dedicated
	{318}	B. G.
	{371}	Church Dedicated
Three Rivers [St Maurice]	{2}	Church
	{146}	B. G.
Tingwick [Arthabaska]	{256}	Church
	{354}	Ch Deconsecrated
	{296}	B. G.
Tomifobia [Stanstead]	{351}	Church Dedicated
	{420}	Ch Deconsecrated
Trois-Rivières: see *Three Rivers*		
Trout Brook: see *Tingwick*		
Upper Durham: see *L'Avenir*		
Upper Ireland: see *Maple Grove*		
Valcartier [Portneuf]	{321}	B. G.
	{406}	Addition to B. G.
Wakeham [Gaspé]	{35}	Church & B. G.
	{115}	Church
	{116}	B. G.
	{319}	B. G.

Name of Church &c	By Whom	Date	Remarks
St Paul's	J. W. Williams	1889 June 28	
St Paul's	S. Meade, for R.F. Brown	1965 Oct. 31	*"Given to Dixville School For Retarded Children"*
[Christ Church]	J. W. Williams	1875 Dec 5	*notation 1864 Apr. 12 inserted under 'Remarks' in Register; originally consecrated as Church of Grace*
	J. W. Williams	1866 June 17	
St Peter's	J. W. Williams	1866 June 17	
	A. H. Dunn	1894 July 10	
[St John the Divine]	A. H. Dunn	1893 June 9	
	L. W. Williams	1930 May 31	
St John the Divine	P. Carrington	1956 June 7	
St James'	C. J. Stewart	1830 Feb. 21	*remarks in Register cite Stewart's SPG report as evidence of consecration*
	A. H. Dunn	1898 May 22	
St Paul's	J. W. Williams	1888 May 15	*notation 1859 Apr. 11 inserted under 'Remarks' in Register*
St Paul's	P. Carrington	1948 May 21	*demolished*
	L. W. Williams	1925 May 8	*listed in Register under Trout Brook*
St Andrew's	P. Carrington	1946 May 14	
St Andrew's	T. J. Matthews	1974 Oct. 27	
	L. W. Williams	1931 May 3	*no record of consecration of church [Christ's Church] in Register*
Christ's Church	R. F. Brown	1969 June 15	
St James'	G. J. Mountain	1853 Aug. 15	*listed as Gaspé Basin in Register*
St James'	A. H. Dunn	1893 July 18	*listed as Gaspé South in Register*
"of St James' Church"	A. H. Dunn	1893 July 18	*listed as Grant's Settlement Gaspé South in Register*
	L. W. Williams	1930 Aug. 31	*listed as Gaspé Bay South in Register*

Place or Mission	{}	What Consecrated [Episcopal Act]
Waterville [Compton]	{49}	Church & B. G.
	{244}	B. G.
Way's Mills [Stanstead]	{261}	Church
	{190}	B. G.
Westbury [Sherbrooke]	{223}	Church
	{367}	Ch Deconsecrated
	{313}	B. G.
Windsor Mills [Richmond]	{278}	Church
	{423}	Ch Deconsecrated
Wolf Bay Labrador [Duplessis]		
	{290}	B. G.
	{333}	Addition to B. G.
York [Gaspé]	{141}	Church
	{286}	B. G.
	{320}	Church
	{435}	Addition to B. G.

Name of Church &c	By Whom	Date	Remarks
St John the Evangelist	G. J. Mountain	1855 Sept. 11	
	J. W. Williams	1883 Oct. 22	
Ch of the Epiphany	J. W. Williams	1889 June 18	
"Drew burying ground"	A. H. Dunn	1904 Sept. 10	*"Given to Church by A. A. Drew"*
St Thomas'	J. W. Williams	1875 Dec. 7	*notation under 'Remarks' appears as* 2 Dec.
St Thomas'	P. Carrington	1948 May 21	
	L. W. Williams	1917 Oct. 23	
St George's	L. W. Williams	1918 July 9	*entry in Register lists both Grace Church and St George's; some lumber used to build St George's probably came from Grace Church, Hardwood Hill*
St George's	A. Fairbairn, for T. J. Matthews	1977 July 16	*church sold to "French Baptists"*
	L. W. Williams	1923 July 2	
	P. Carrington	1937 Aug. 5	*spelled Wolfe Bay in Register*
St Andrew's	A. H. Dunn	1897 Sept. 1	
	L. W. Williams	1922 July 2	*listed in Register as "York (Sandy Beach)"*
St Andrew's	L. W. Williams	1930 Sept. 1	
St Andrew's	A. Goodings	1984 June 3	

Maps

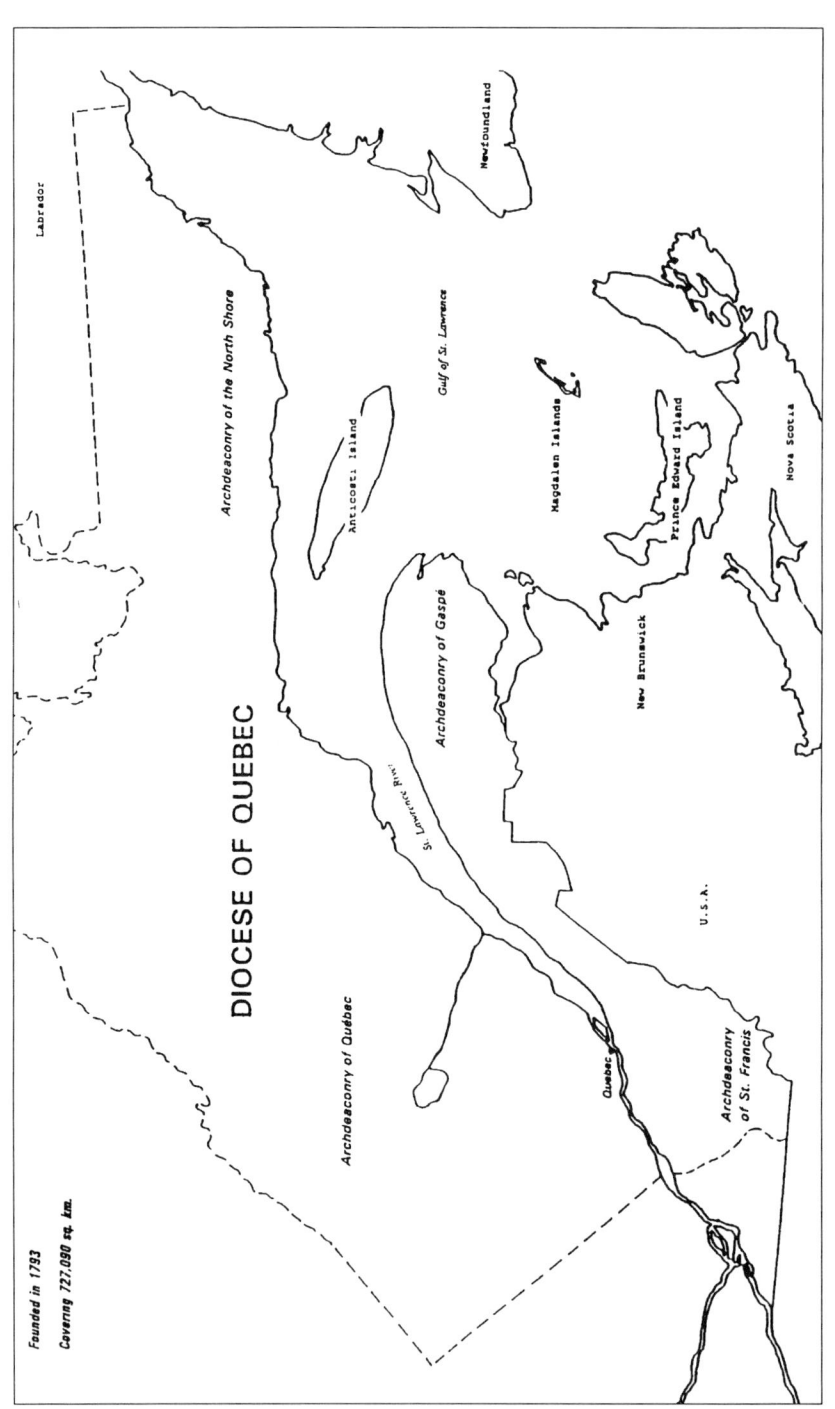

Founded in 1793

Covering 727,090 sq. km.

DIOCESE OF QUEBEC

Labrador

Newfoundland

Archdeaconry of the North Shore

Anticosti Island

Gulf of St. Lawrence

Magdalen Islands

Prince Edward Island

Nova Scotia

Archdeaconry of Gaspé

New Brunswick

St. Lawrence River

Archdeaconry of Québec

U.S.A.

Québec

Archdeaconry
of St. Francis

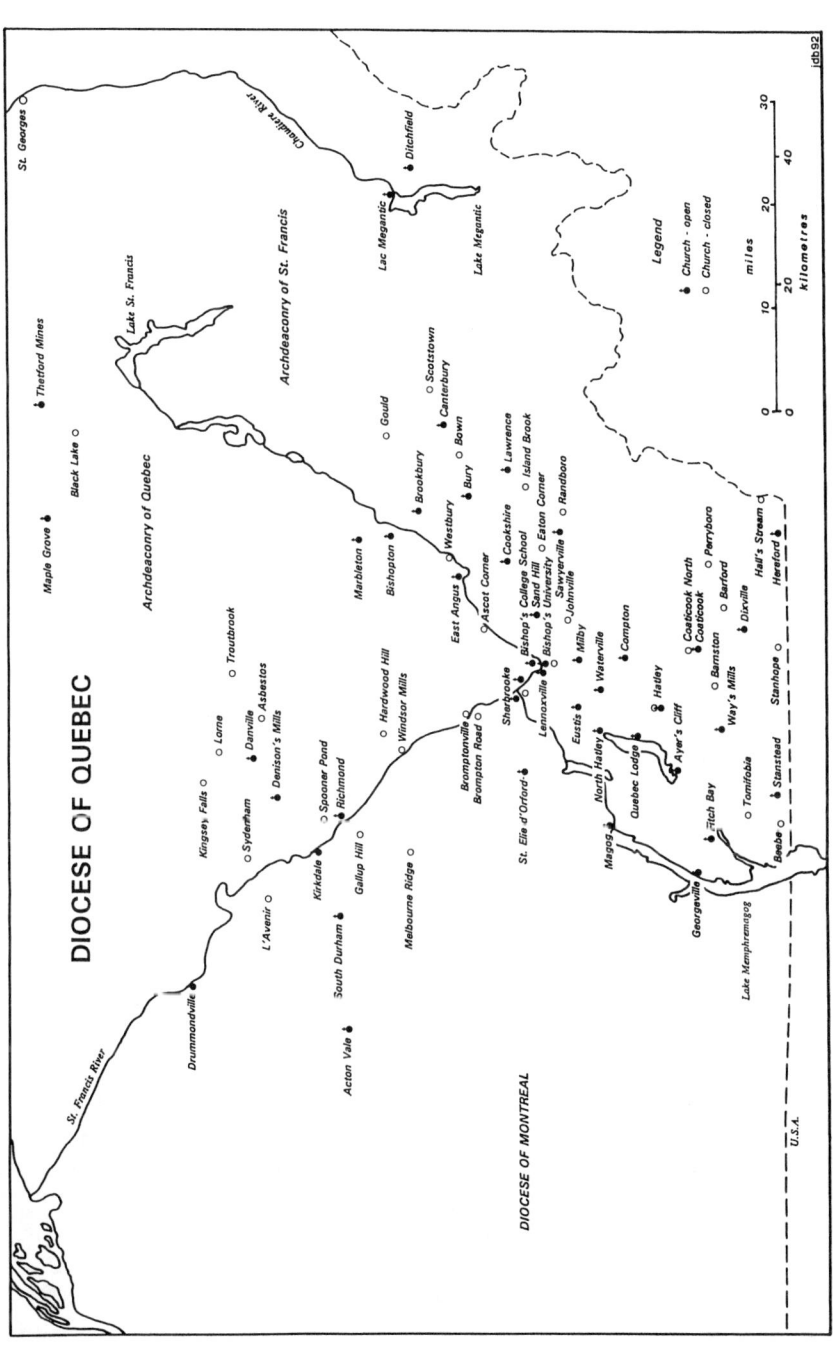

DIOCESE OF QUEBEC

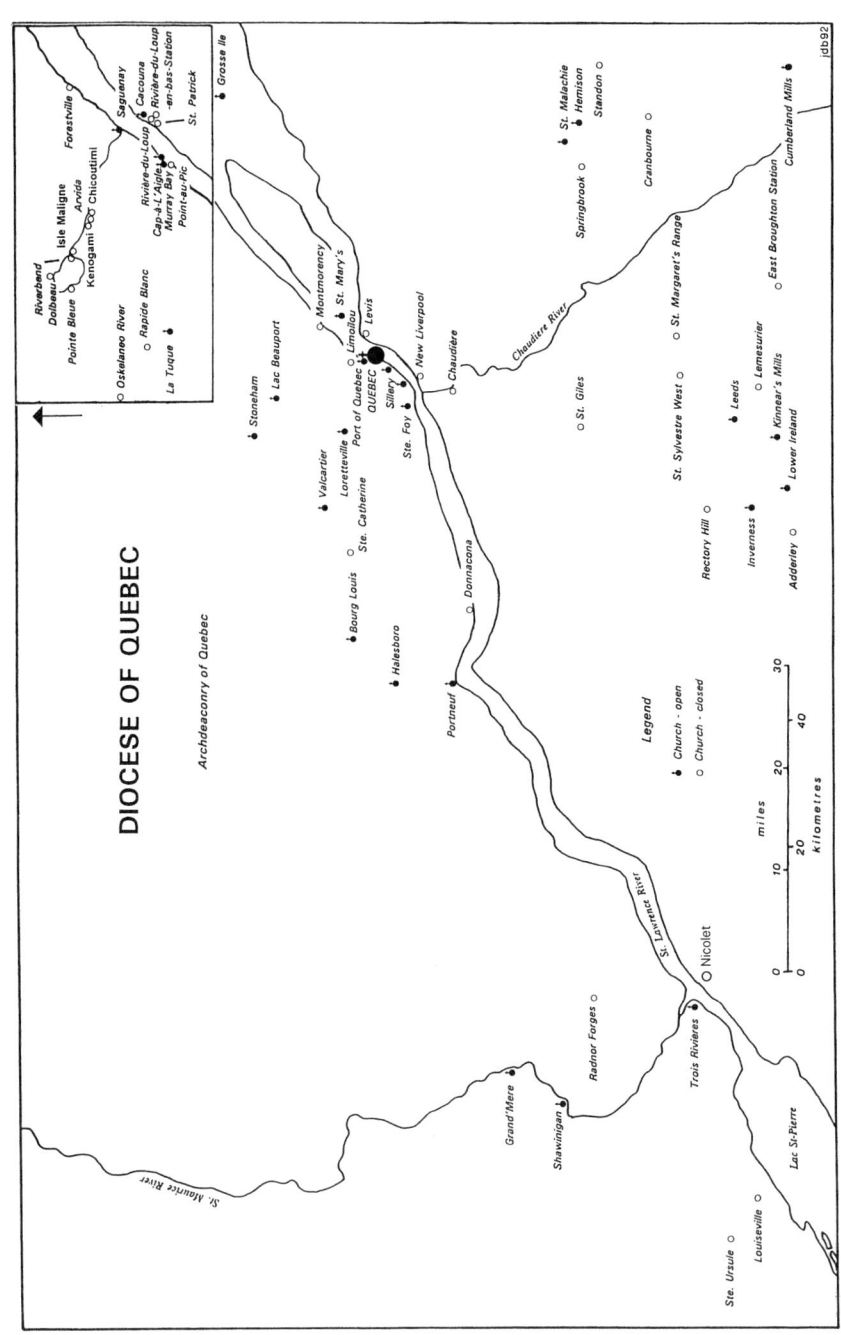

DIOCESE OF QUEBEC

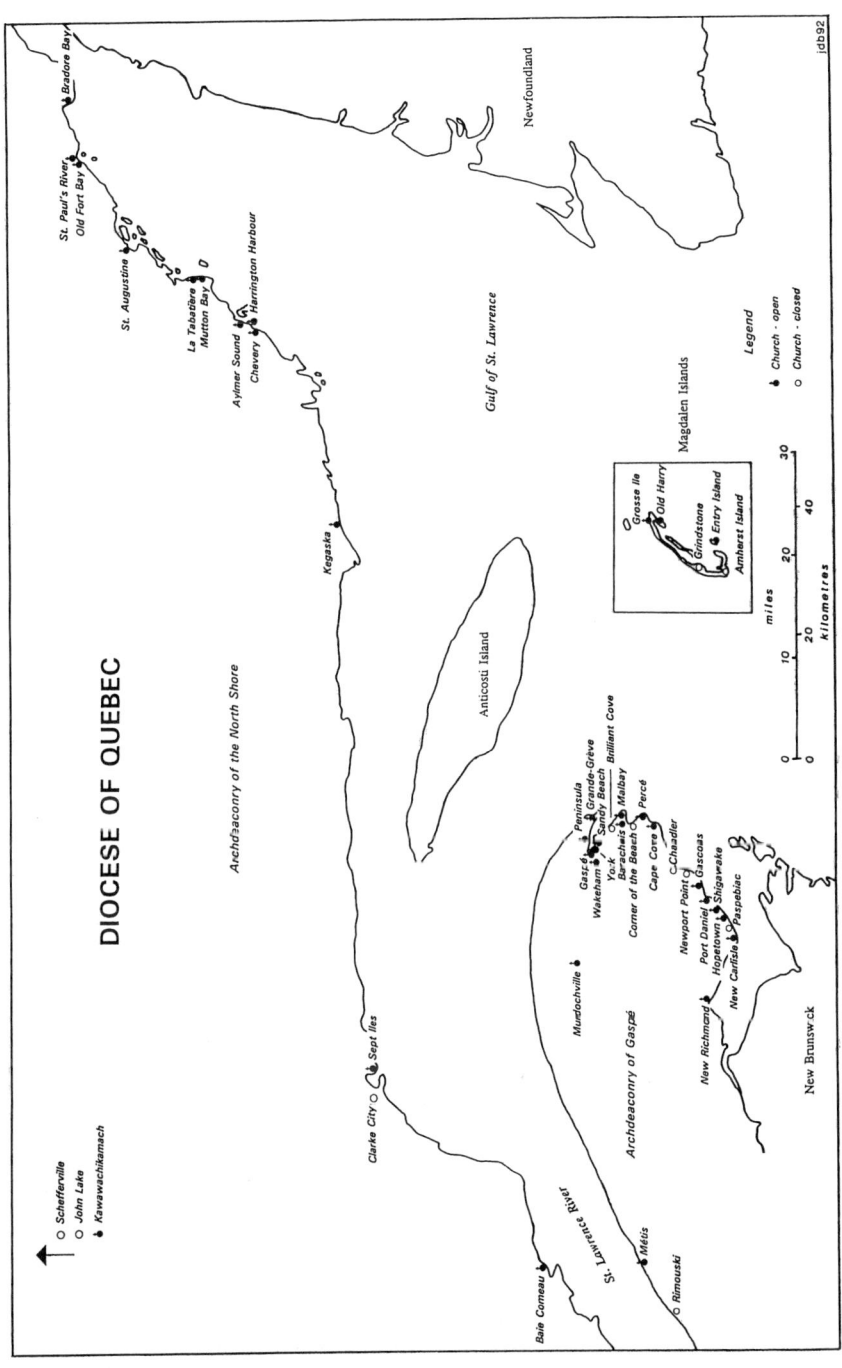

DIOCESE OF QUEBEC

Notes to Chapters

Chapter I: "This Late Acquisition to the Crown"

15   *"the total & unaccountable neglect ... for a long series of years,"* Lambeth Palace Archives (hereafter LPA), Moore Papers, "Foreign," I, ff 138-152, Jacob Mountain to Archbishop Moore, 13 June 1803.

15   *Murray pointed a sharp contrast ... with our laws, religion, and customs,"* quoted in Ernest Hawkins, *Annals of the Diocese of Quebec* (London, 1849), 11-12.

16   *"It would be more agreeable ... selected for Colonial service,"* Hawkins, *Annals of the Diocese of Quebec*, 11.

16   *another church historian ... "the great Canadian theme,"* H. H. Walsh, *The Christian Church in Canada* (Toronto, 1956), 1.

16   *In June of that year ... as chaplains to the British forces.* For the names of 14 of these chaplains, see H. C. Stuart, *The Church of England in Canada, 1759-1793* (Montreal, 1893), 7.

16   *General Montcalm ... nobility of soul,"* A.R.M. Lower, *Colony to Nation*, 4th ed. (Don Mills, Ont., 1964), 62.

16   *The first Anglican service ... not a very pretty question,* Carrington, *The Anglican Church in Canada: A History* (Toronto, 1963), 35-6.

17   *On 23 October 1759, he wrote anxiously ... at New Rochelle, New York,* [C.F. Pascoe], *Classified Digest of the Records of the Society for the Propagation of the Gospel in Foreign Parts 1701-1892* (London, 1893), 136.

17   *"the discharged soldiers ... [can] marry & bury in French,"* LPA, SPG Papers, II, ff 25-6, Extracts from letter, Frances Brooke to Bishop Terrick, 24 Jan. 1765.

17   *On 27 December ... as much my desire as theirs,"* LPA, Fulham Papers, I, ff 110-111, Extract from a letter, Murray to Rev. Dr Bearcroft, Secretary of SPG, 1761, filed with Petition, undated, to Rev. D. Bruton.

17   *Indeed, the "Chief Justice ... prejudiced against our faith and Religion,"* LPA, Fulham Papers, I, ff 106-7, Petition, undated, to Rev. D. Bruton.

17   *"a very unfortunate ... policy ... by the authorities,"* Carrington, *The Anglican Church in Canada*, 36. See also Lucien Lemieux, *Histoire du catholicisme québécois: Les années*

difficiles (1760-1839), I (Montréal, 1989), 20-1.

18   *with generous Government stipends*; each was paid £200 annually by the Crown. A report on the stipends of the Anglican clergy in 1790 shows Chaplains to the Garrison receiving £115.5.0 annually, and SPG Missionaries, paid partly by the Society and partly by Government, receiving from £100 to £150 annually. See Stuart, *The Church of England in Canada, 1759-1793*, 87-9.

18   *The Governor dispatched a curt letter … imposed upon them*; LPA, Fulham Papers, I, ff 161-2, Extract from a letter from Carleton to the Earl of Hillsborough, 21 July 1768.

18   *He also informed the Bishop … to be got the better of,"* LPA, Fulham Papers, I, ff 163-6, Carleton to Bishop Terrick, 13 Aug. 1768.

18   *Dr Brooke, for example, … without any Allowance for the same,"* LPA, Fulham Papers, I, ff 163-6, Sir Guy Carleton to Bishop Terrick, 13 Aug. 1768. At one time Murray voiced complaints about Brooke's involvement in idle disputes at Quebec, for a brief account of which see Carl F. Klinck, ed., *The History of Emily Montague* (Toronto, 1961), vi.

19   *"To conciliate their Affections … Administration of Justice,"* LPA, Fulham Papers, I, ff 163-6, Sir Guy Carleton to Bishop Terrick, 13 Aug. 1768.

19   *De Montmollin seems to have insisted … keep ours with Roman Catholics,"* LPA, Fulham Papers, I, ff 161-2, Carleton to the Earl of Hillsborough, 21 July 1768.

20   *On the eve of the Revolution … the right of citizenship,"* Alec R. Vidler, *The Church in an Age of Revolution: 1789 to the Present Day* (Harmondsworth, Middlesex, 1974), 12.

20   *In England … the Roman Catholics … even a royal veto,"* Vidler, *The Church in an Age of Revolution*, 42-3.

20   *Centuries of distrust … "without being known as Catholics,"* Owen Chadwick, *The Victorian Church: Part One 1829-1859*, 3rd ed. (London, 1987), 282.

20   *In sharp contrast … with two French bishops,* see Walsh, *The Christian Church in Canada*, 40, 46-7. Walsh traces this "full-blown diocesan organization" back as far as 1637.

21   *"Elsewhere in the history of Christianity … survive as a state,"* Chadwick, *The Victorian Church*, 8.

21   *The founders of New England … they had despaired,"* Paul Johnson, *A History of Christianity* (London, 1976), 421.

23   *"The want of Bishops (in America) … part of its Constitution,"* see *A Sermon Preached Before the Incorporated Society for the Propagation of the Gospel in Foreign Parts, … on Friday February 20, 1767 By … John Lord Bishop of Landaff* (London, 1767); this sermon occasioned a number of pamphlets printed in the Thirteen Colonies, both for and against it. It is quoted, with comments, in Thomas Bradbury Chandler, *An Appeal to the Public, In Behalf of the Church of England in America* (New York,

1767), x-xi, for example. See also Charles Chauncy, *A Letter To a Friend, Containing, Remarks on certain Passages in a Sermon Preached, By the Right Reverend ... Lord Bishop of Landaff, ... In which the highest Reproach is undeservedly cast upon the American Colonies* (Boston, 1767).

23   *The Church of England hierarchy ... a favourite appointed,"* Frederick V. Mills, *Bishops By Ballot: An Eighteenth-Century Ecclesiastical Revolution* (New York, 1978), 214.

24   *"Quebec being [a Roman Catholic] Episcopal See ... unavoidably suffer by it,"* LPA, SPG Papers II, ff 28-9, copy of a letter: Des Vœux to Pechell, 6 Apr. 1765.

24   *Dean Tucker of Gloucester ... than take a Voyage to England?"* LPA, SPG Papers II, ff 28-9, Queries relating to the Introduction of Episcopacy into America ... by Dean Tucker of Gloucester to the Bishop of London, June 1765.

25   *From his arrival at Halifax ... would be most the effective,"* Brian Cuthbertson, *The First Bishop: A Biography of Charles Inglis* ([Halifax], 1987), 94.

26   *but, on 1 June "was driven ... whalers and fishermen,"* Carrington, *The Anglican Church in Canada,* 49.

26   *At "Gaspé and Pierce Island ... the clergy and a curious multitude,"* see "Bishop of Nova Scotia's Minutes of Voyage to Quebec" in A. R. Kelley, *The Church of England in Quebec 1759-1791: A Compendium of Church and State Papers* (Quebec, 1937), 44. Inglis appears to have gone ashore at three different settlements, on 1, 3, and 4 June.

26   *On the same day, ... more churches than they needed,"* Cuthbertson, *The First Bishop,* 106.

27   *"[I] did not understand one twentieth ... that there should be any,"* see "Bishop of Nova Scotia's Minutes of Voyage to Quebec" in A. R. Kelley, *The Church of England in Quebec 1759-1791,* 46. Here and elsewhere, by "Canadian," Inglis means French Canadian.

27   *His injunctions to the clergy ... of life and morals,* Inglis's 14 "Injunctions Given to the Clergy of the Province of Quebec ..." are printed by Stuart, *The Church of England in Canada, 1759-1793,* 73-5.

27   *"4,000 Canadians ... were among the communicants,* "Bishop of Nova Scotia's Minutes of Voyage to Quebec" in A. R. Kelley, *The Church of England in Quebec 1759-1791,* 45.

27   *130 confirmed ... and some dissenters,"* Cuthbertson, *The First Bishop,* 109.

28   *In 1765, Frances Brooke ... music & shew,"* LPA, SPG Papers, II, ff 25-6, Extract from Mrs Brooke's Letter to Bishop Terrick, 14 Jan. 1765.

28   *When (in 1893) the Rev H. C. Stuart ... and the roar of artillery,"* Stuart, *The Church of England in Canada, 1759-1793,* 6.

28   *In 1934, Lennox Williams ... said to be a Missionary Diocese,"* L. Q. [Lennox Williams], "St Clement's Mission: Canadian Labrador," *Quebec Diocesan Gazette* (hereafter *QDG*) (July, 1934), 27.

28   *Even before leaving Britain ... £500 from his own income,* Stuart, *The Church of England in Canada, 1759-1793,* 101-2.

29   *Meanwhile, Bishop Inglis, as soon as he heard ... American-bred Divines,"* Cuthbertson, *The First Bishop,* 115-16.

29   *Lord Dorchester's candidate ... as Mrs Simcoe described him in 1791,* see *Mrs. Simcoe's Diary,* Mary Quayle Innis, ed. (Toronto, 1978), 40 (entry for 1 Dec. 1791).

29   *In a Memorial, dated 13 March 1793 ... establishments in the new Townships,"* Stuart, *The Church of England in Canada, 1759-1793,* 103.

31   *Pretyman's "close friendship ... in accordance with [Pretyman's] advice,"* Thomas R. Millman, *Jacob Mountain, First Lord Bishop of Quebec* (Toronto, 1947), 16.

31   *To a clergyman ... in that New-world,"* LPA, SPG Papers II, ff 28-9, copy of a letter: Des Vœux to Pechell, 6 Apr. 1765.

31   *"to be Bishop ... during his natural life,"* Letters Patent erecting the Provinces of Lower Canada and Upper Canada into a Bishop's See, 28 June 1793. See Quebec Diocesan Archives (hereafter QDA) A-1, 16.

31   *An attempt ... made in the recent Constitutional Act ... jurisdiction of the Bishop of Nova Scotia,"* 31 Geo. iii, cap. 31, ss. 35-42.

32   *As Carrington asserts ... provided for in this way,"* Carrington, *The Anglican Church in Canada,* 53.

32   *It may be argued ... to be the National Church" in Canada,* Stuart, *The Church of England in Canada, 1759-1793,* 91.

32   *it has been equally maintained ... failed to make this crystal clear,* Walsh, *The Christian Church in Canada,* 135.

32   *Although the provision of land ... of fierce political controversy,"* Carrington, *The Anglican Church in Canada,* 53.

33   *When Jacob Mountain arrived from England ... to be their proper places,"* Walsh, *The Christian Church in Canada,* 135.

33   *"If he had come to the Canadas ... resource, and outstanding ability,"* Millman, *Jacob Mountain, First Lord Bishop of Quebec,* iii. It is made clear, however, that Mountain's achievements were significant, particularly in the field of education.

33   *When the latter was erected in 1850 ... reincorporated into the Diocese of Quebec,* Letters Patent Erecting the Diocese of Montreal, 18 July 1850; Letters Patent limiting the size of the Diocese of Quebec, 18 July 1850; and Order-in-Council for inclusion of St Francis District of Quebec; see QDA A-4, 33-a and 33-b; A-4, 34.

35   *Although some 32,000 immigrants from abroad ... passed on to the United States,"* Helen I. Cowan, *British Immigration Before Confederation* (Ottawa, 1968), 14.

35   *"Notwithstanding ... will still more perplex him,"* Adam Fergusson, *Practical Notes Made During a Tour in Canada, and a Portion of the United States in* MDCCCXXXI, 2nd ed. (Edinburgh, 1834), 260.

36   *Furthermore, Upper Canada ... "a society basically similar to that of England,"* G. P. deT. Glazebrook, *The Church of England in Upper Canada 1785-1867* (n.p., 1982), 11.

36   *"Most of the Church of England missions ... out of the limits of the diocese,"* A. W. Mountain, *A Memoir of George Jehoshaphat Mountain* (Montreal, 1866), 344-5.

36   *the Rev. Louis Wurtele ... the Diocesan assessment] of this Mission,"* *Twenty-fifth Report of the Incorporated Church Society of the Diocese of Quebec* (1867), 26.

37   *The Rev. C. B. Washer's account of his mission ... old enough to go away,"* *Sixtieth Report of the Incorporated Church Society of the Diocese of Quebec* (1902), 44.

37   *"Of course I was faced with the problem ... it will reach the old level,"* "Archbishop's Letter," *QDG* (April, 1960), 2.

38   *painted as "snobbish and wealthy ... in the deep bush,"* Glazebrook, *The Church of England in Upper Canada 1785-1867*, ii.

39   *While, as Nancy Christie suggests ... "need not be adapted to colonial circumstances,"* "'In These Times of Democratic Rage and Delusion': Popular Religion and the Challenge to the Established Order 1760-1815," in *The Canadian Protestant Experience 1760-1990*, George A. Rawlyk, ed. (Burlington, Ont., 1990), 16.

39   *"Despite the fact that many English-speaking ... be a minority religion,"* Christie, "'In These Times of Democratic Rage and Delusion,'" 10.

Chapter II: Branches of the Vine

41   *"Since the time of its first foundation in North America ... would be foolish,"* A. R. Kelley, "The Changing Name of the Church," *Journal of the Canadian Church History Society* (hereafter *Journal of the CCHS*) (Dec. 1964), 69-74.

42   *"As nationalistic feeling grew ... l'église episcopale du Canada,"* John G. McCausland, *Counting Myself Happy: Vignettes of the 60-year Ministry of John G. McCausland, SSJE, 1927-1987* (Toronto, 1989), 106.

42   *"considerable resistance ... he may deem appropriate,"* *Journal of the Seventieth (Ordinary) Session of the Synod of the Diocese of Quebec* (1987), 24-5. The Rev. Ray Jensen of LaTuque and the Rev. Canon Edward Vaughan of Trois-Rivières, the mover and seconder of the Resolution, were both serving in predominately French-speaking regions.

42   *"Going from one clergyman to another ... is a good one,'* Paul Ferris, *The Church of England,* rev. ed., (Harmondsworth, Middlesex, 1964), 14 and 16-17.

43   *Once inducted, an incumbent ... even within the English Church,* Walter Alison Phillips,

ENGLAND: RELIGION, *Encyclopædia Britannica,* 11th ed.(hereafter *EB*), (New York, 1911), IX, 420-1.

43   *The Church of England claims ... the end of the sixth century ... to contain sound doctrine,"* William Hunt, CHURCH OF ENGLAND, *EB,* IX, 442-3.

44   *I John Butler ... [signed] John Butler,* QDA, B-52, Diocese Book: Subscriptions 1843-1850.

44   *I Edwin Weary ... [signed] Edwin Weary,* QDA, B-52 (C): Book of Subscriptions, I, 1889-1907.

45   *Although the Thirty-nine Articles ... 'historical interest' in the Church today,* Ferris, *The Church of England,* 11-12.

45   *"attempted [finally] to define those standards ... for so many centuries,"* Carrington, *The Anglican Church in Canada,* 187-8.

45   *It is highly gratifying ... ineffectual to convey their feelings, A Sermon Preached Before the Incorporated Society for the Propagation of the Gospel in Foreign Parts ... February 16, 1821 ... Together with the Report of the Society for the Year 1820* (London, 1821), 114.

46   *neither churches nor Prayer Books ... a good teacher of sacred music,* Transcript by James Reid of the Letters of C. J. Stewart, text following letter 39 (19 Feb. 1819), Eastern Townships Archives (hereafter ETA), Bishop's University, Lennoxville.

46   *Jacob Mountain, while on a confirmation tour ... you would have wept outright,"* Jacob Mountain to Susanna Brooke, 22 Aug. 1809, QDA, Unbound MSS, Jacob Mountain Letters (Private and Personal), Case T, Folder 3.

46   *"[It] is mainly through the Prayer Book ... its special tradition,"* Carrington, *The Anglican Church in Canada,* 289.

46   *It was not because of an absence of differences ... was the prayer book,* Glazebrooke, *The Church of England in Upper Canada 1785-1867,* iii.

47   *Perhaps the most important question ... to arrive at those decisions,"* "Liturgy in the Diocese of Quebec: Statement Approved,"*QDG* (March, 1985), 1 (words in bold appear as printed in the original).

47   *"requesting the appointment of a commission ... and its literary style,"* "Report of the Diocesan Executive Council," *Journal of the Seventy-first (Ordinary) Session of the Synod of the Diocese of Quebec* (1989), 43.

47   *the Prayer Book Society of Canada ... only one branch,* personal letter from Graham Eglington of the PBSC to the present writer, 8 Dec. 1992, in response to an enquiry on the number of the Society's members within the Diocese of Quebec. A branch was formed in Port Daniel, Gaspé, in 1994.

48   *"to postpone the pressure for reform ... a generation earlier than they were,"* Vidler, *The Church in an Age of Revolution,* 33-4.

48   *"dry, commonsensical ... wealth went unchallenged,"* Vidler, *The Church in an Age of Revolution,* 40 and 35.

48   *Since the accession of the Hanoverian line ... celebrated infrequently,* William Hunt, CHURCH OF ENGLAND, *EB,* IX, 450. It is worth noting that this passage is quoted verbatim (although without identification of its source) in an article on the Church printed in the *QDG* (Sept. 1932), 19.

48   *Cathedral music ... only one in fact existed,* Sydney H. Nicholson, *Quires and Places Where They Sing* (London, 1932), 48.

48   *His children knew him ... along the road of duty,* James Anthony Froude, "The Church of England Fifty Years Ago," *Short Studies on Great Subjects* (New York, 1883), 158.

49   *"ill-regulated ... religious emotion,"* ENTHUSIASM, *sb* 2, *OED.*

49   *He was, as his son George recalled ... decorum in sacred things,"* [G. J. Mountain] "Memoir of the Late Bishop of Quebec," *The Christian Sentinel, and Anglo-Canadian Churchman's Magazine* (Jan. & Feb. 1827), 7.

49   *"jealously concerned ... rather than theologically, High Church,"* Vidler, *The Church in an Age of Revolution,* 35.

49   *"with the spiritual interests ... than a Missionary Bishop of Canada,"* quoted by Millman, *Jacob Mountain,* 278.

49   *"the respectable establishments ... of the Church of Rome,"* Jacob Mountain to Archbishop Moore, 13 June 1803, LPA, Moore Papers, "Foreign," I, ff 138-152.

49   *compact between Church and State,* for a useful analysis of this relationship, see J.L.H. Henderson, "The Abominable Incubus: The Church as by Law Established," *Journal of the CCHS* (Sept. 1969), 58-66.

49   *To the modern reader ... of the greatest respectability here,"* Millman, *Jacob Mountain,* 109-10 and n. 29. Jackson was ordained in 1800 and received a Government salary of £100. His appointment as Domestic Chaplain to the Bishop was in 1808. In 1811 he was appointed to Sorel; see Thomas R. Millman, *Life of Bishop Stewart* (London, Ont., 1953), 204.

49   *the dignity of a Dean and Chapter at Quebec,* Jacob Mountain to Archbishop Moore, 13 June 1803, LPA, Moore Papers, "Foreign," I, ff 138-152.

51   *It was to government ... never to have a substantial existence,* Millman, *Jacob Mountain,* 58-9.

51   *if not exactly "asleep,"... rousing itself into activity,"* Vidler, *The Church in an Age of Revolution,* 40.

51   *The Tractarians saw the Church ... the divine right of anointed kings,"* Geoffrey Faber, *Oxford Apostles: A Character Study of the Oxford Movement* (Harmondsworth, Middlesex, 1954), 81.

51   *"an important exponent of Anglican theology ... Evangelicalism and Liberalism,"* D. C. Masters, "Bishop's University and the Ecclesiastical Controversies of the Nineteenth Century (1845-1878)," *Canadian Historical Association Reports* (1951), 36.

52   *Roe could still value ... amply shows,* see Roe's memorial sermon, preached in St Peter's Church, Sherbrooke, and printed in the *Sherbrooke Gazette*, 16 Nov. 1888.

52   *After conceding that "there is not ... I never will be,* Henry Roe, *A Letter to the Congregation of St. Matthew's Chapel, Quebec; in Answer to the Rev. Dr. Percy's Letter on 'Tractarianism,'* (Quebec, 1858), 7 and 20; QDA, index 346, bound with other ephemera in *Pamphlets Quebec 1819-1927*.

52   *"I shall not suffer myself ... there I bide the Issue,"* 5-page printed pamphlet of Gilbert Percy's Letter to the Editor, dated 13 May 1858, in *The Quebec Gazette*, (n.p., n.d.), 1; QDA, B-62, bundle 17.

53   *To them the Scriptures ... Protestant Missions throughout the world,"* Faber, *Oxford Apostles,* 82. For a wider view with particular reference to Canadian Evangelicalism extending to other demoninations, see Michael Gauvreau, "Protestantism Transformed: Personal Piety and the Evangelical Social Vision 1815-1867," *The Canadian Protestant Experience*, 48-97.

53   *Isaac Hellmuth was a member ... Bishop's College,* see D. C. Masters, "Bishop's University and the Ecclesiastical Controversies of the Nineteenth Century," 38; Masters suggests that Hellmuth does not seem to have had any appreciable influence on "the theology of the university."

54   *identified ... Stewart with the Evangelicals,* H. H. Walsh, *The Christian Church in Canada,* 147; *Jacob Mountain ... "the least appearance of enthusiasm,"* Jacob Mountain to Susanna Brooke, 22 Aug. 1809, QDA, Jacob Mountain Letters (Private & Personal), Index 123, Case T, folder 3; *"difficult to attach ... stream of tradition,"* T. R. Millman, *Life of Stewart*, 169-70.

54   *a powerful and earnest sermon ... frequency of receiving the Sacraments,* J. W. Williams, *The Christian Ministry: Its Duties and Responsibilities* (Quebec, 1888), 6; *Pamphlets Quebec 1819-1927,* QDA, index 346.

54   *Very often, that spiritual character ... converting souls to God,* J. W. Williams, *The Christian Ministry: Its Duties and Responsibilities*, 8-9.

55   *To think of the Oxford Movement itself ... not visible things,"* Faber, *Oxford Apostles*, 92.

55   *The original Tractarians ... observing its directions,"* Vidler, *The Church in an Age of Revolution,* 157.

55   *In it "they were delighted to find ... were correctly understood,"* Owen Chadwick, *The Victorian Church: Part One,* 212.

55   *With fresh eyes ... 'said or sung,'* see Christopher Headon, "Developments in Canadian Anglican Worship in Eastern and Central Canada 1840-1868," *Journal of CCHS* (June 1975), 33 *et passim*.

55   *altar lights, vestments, ... and auricular confession,* Vidler, *The Church in an Age of Revolution,* 157-8.

55   *In the famous* Lincoln Judgment ... *from the date of its delivery,"* Lewis Tonna Didbin, THE LINCOLN JUDGMENT, *EB,* XVI, 713.

57   *"those who had been led ... obtained in most churches,"* Percival Jolliffe, *Andrew Hunter Dunn: Fifth Bishop of Quebec, A Memoir* (London, 1919), 30.

57   *As to a Processional Cross ... when on the spot,* Jolliffe, *Andrew Hunter Dunn,* 30-1.

57   *"and many difficulties ... R. A. Parrock,* Jolliffe, *Andrew Hunter Dunn,* 108.

58   *We do not think it the part ... to accede to any of their requests,* Printed letter to F. G. Scott, from R. Campbell, Charles J. Pigot, John Hamilton *et al.,* Feb. 1909 together with Scott's reply, dated 12 Feb. 1909; QDA, B-46: "Cathedral." These two sheets, which appear to have been printed to give publicity to the efforts the petitioners had made to resolve the situation, are otherwise undated.

59   *"no splendour of decorative ritual ... the risen Lord and His Church,"* see "The State of the Church," *S. Matthew's Church Merssenger,* vol. IV, no. 13 (Jan, 1908), 2-3, (copies in QDA). Scott himself edited the paper which every parishioner received free of charge.

59   *Other parishes have resisted ... wafer bread,* some churches on the Lower North Shore supplied their priest with leavened bread for the Eucharist (which was acceptable according to the Prayer Book) whereas their priest would accept wafer bread only. He observed that the people were willing to *receive* wafer bread, probably because that was all that he would consent to consecrate. This occurred in the 1930s; see parish papers held at Harrington Harbour.

59   *As to the manner of conducting service ... committed to his charge,* Journal of the Synod of the Church of England in the Diocese of Quebec, Twentieth Session (1893), 20-21.

60   *"I attended the Cathedral ... I changed to Trinity"* [Eva Jane Lloyd], "Letter to Auxilia," *QDG* (Sept. 1964), 4.

60   *It will be the aim of the Committee ... for promoting unity,* E[ardley]-W[ilmot], "Oxford Movement Centenery," *QDG* (July 1932), 27.

61   *"an iconoclast ... wearing a religious label,"* Colin Cuttell, *Philip Carrington: Pastor, Prophet, Poet* (Toronto, 1988), 53.

61   *More than one of Carrington's ordinands ... any extreme of churchmanship,* I am grateful to the Rev. Ray Jensen for this information.

61   *Carrington's epithet ... no party man,"* Carrington, *The Anglican Church in Canada,* 155, for example.

61   *"the new theology," ... "state-church Anglicanism,"* McCausland, *Counting Myself Happy,* 22.

61   *Far from endorsing Modernism … for legends to arise,"* Cuttell, *Philip Carrington*, 46-7.

63   *what was called a 'biblical theology' … faith and its corollaries,"* Vidler, *The Church in an Age of Revolution*, 274.

63   *Carrington's positive, energetic presence … Visitations and excursions,* The Lent issue of the *QDG*, 1953, for example, contains three pieces by Carrington: "The Archbishop's Letter," 9 and 32; "The Manchester Bell," 12 and 24; and "More New Translations: The Four Gospels: by E.V. Rieu," 22-4.

63   *[T]he consciousness of faith … in peace as in war,* A.V. Ottiwell, "With No. 8 Canadian General Hospital," *QDG* (June 1946), 16.

63   *considerable matter for reflection.* The following articles all appeared in the *QDG*: W. R. Coleman, "A Message For Lent," (Lent 1952), 10-11; A.E.E. Legge, "The Marks of the True Shepherd," (Autumn 1950), 13 and 29-30; A. M. Ramsay as summarized by J. R. Brown, "The Bible and the Ministry of the Word," (Christmas 1959), 22-5.

63   *The Rector of Drummondville … Forward Movement pamphlet,* Christians and Jews; see J. R. Brown, "Christian Teaching and Antisemitism," *QDG* (Lent 1958), 23-4 and 29. Biographical information on Brown appeared in *QDG* (Spring 1958), 36.

64   *"strongly reminiscent of heresy trials,"* Michel Despland, "The Process of Secularization," *One Church, Two Nations?* Philip LeBlanc and Arnold Edinborough, eds., (Don Mills, Ont., 1968), 126.

64   *Although he contributed … enough at the time.* The earlier of these two pieces predated Harrison's appointment to the Editorial Board: see E. W. Harrison, "Christmas: Natural and Supernatural," *QDG* (Christmas 1953), 11; "The Unjust Steward," (Lent 1958), 33-4 and "General Synod High Spots and Low Spots," (Fall 1959), 8. These represent a very small fraction of Harrison's signed contributions; he remained on the board under Bishop Brown's episcopate until his departure for the GBRE, Diocese of Toronto, in 1962.

64   *"such controversial topics as … the so-called 'new morality,'* see cover of Ernest Harrison's *A Church Without God* (Toronto, 1966). This book, originally to have been titled *Mother Church Is Dead and Gone—What do the Children do Now?* attacked the relevance of the Church. See also McCausland, *Counting Myself Happy*, 113-114.

64   *While Carrington's churchmanship … "Evangelical Catholic,"* Cuttell, *Philip Carrington*, 48.

64   *changing approach to forms of worship … the Liturgical Movement,* N. D. P[ilcher], "Our Lenten Preparation: Participation in Christ," *QDG* (Feb. 1963), 1; "How a Youth Group Worded Our Liturgy," *QDG* (Jan. 1967), 2, and (Feb. 1967), 3; "Some Opinions and Ideas: Comments on 'A Twentieth Century Folk Mass," *QDG* (Nov. 1965), 1 and 3; "Sing Praises Lustily With a Good Courage: Folk Mass at St Peter's [Sherbrooke]." *QDG* (Jan. 1966), 1. From September 1965 to November 1966 the *QDG* carried a monthly feature entitled "Liturgical Changes and Ecumenical Experiments."

64   *Articles on clergy working closely ... psychiatric needs of their parishioners,* W.S.F. P[ickering], "To Visit the Rector or the Psychiatrist," *QDG* (Sept. 1962), 4; *spiritual care-givers ... hospital staff,* "Doctors and Clergy Brought Closer Together," *QDG* (Oct. 1962), 1; *Bishop's ... first university in Canada ... for divinity students,* "Clinical Pastoral Training For Divinity Students," *QDG* (May 1963), 2.

64   *It is no longer adequate ... reach out to his flock,* W. P. Z[ion], "The Place of Psychology in Theological Training," *QDG* (Jan. 1965), 3.

65   *"A strong case can be made ... of honest human inquiry,"* J.D.F. A[nido], "Theological Education and the Parishes," *QDG* (Jan. 1965), 3.

65   *In 1963, the Canterbury Association ...* Honest to God, B[arbara] H[oult], "Canterbury Association—Bishop's University," *QDG* (Sept. 1964), 2.

65   *Perhaps in deference ... sympathy and encouragement,"* E[ve] A. P[ennington], "Not Berton But His Book, *QDG* (Feb. 1965), 3.

65   *Prominent American sociologist of religion ... 'an ecclesiastical* Fanny Hill,*"* John G. Stackhouse, "The Protestant Experience in Canada Since 1945," *The Canadian Protestant Experience 1760-1990,* 210.

65   *In Quebec City, a layman ... "Uncomfortable Spew?"* F. W. S[lingerland], "Uncomfortable Spew?" *QDG* (March 1965), 3-4.

65   *If all the so-called 'stumbling blocks ... would appeal to anybody at all,"* J.D.R. F[ranklin], "Christianity Today," *QDG* (Nov. 1963), 4.

65   *Though **particulars** may differ ... than your thoughts,"* Sidney Jellicoe, "Ordination Sermon," *QDG,* (June 1965), 3-4. Text printed in bold as in original. Although he was not one of the diocesan clergy at the time, the Rev. Professor Ronald E. Reeve's contribution of a series of three articles to the *Diocesan Gazette,* entitled "Current Trends in Theology" should be noted here as well; see *QDG* (Sept. 1967), 1; (Oct. 1967), 1 and 4; and (Nov. 1967), 1 and 4.

66   *Both Church Music ... Architecture,* H. I. A[pps], "Music in Church: Prelude, Interlude, Postlude," *QDG* (Dec. 1962), 1 and 3, (Jan. 1964), 4, (Summer 1964), 4; J. R. Brown, "Inside Your Church," *QDG,* (Sept. 1961), 1, and J. E. B[urke], "Not a Perishable Home," *QDG* (Sept. 1964), 1, (Oct. 1964), 3, (Dec. 1964), 4.

66   *but perhaps the most striking ... for the holy dead,* S. R. R[ipper], "Churches and Ceremonial or Ritual and Rubrics," *QDG* (Sept. 1963), 3, (Oct. 1963), 1, (Nov. 1963), 1, (Dec. 1963), 1, and (Jan. 1964), 3.

66   *"An Anglican, Rivière du Loup, ... important members of the Anglican Church."* Both items are found under the heading "Editor's Desk: Readers Opinions," *QDG* (March 1964), 4.

67   *He has the right to expect ... but not any more,* T. J. M[atthews], "Liturgically Speaking," *QDG* (March 1967), 3.

67   *"I understand this cleric's preoccupation ... the way it is,"* T. J. M[atthews], "Liturgically Speaking," 1.

69   *In 1892, within three weeks ... and meeting his people,* Dunn landed 11 September 1892. By 29 September he had begun his tour with a confirmation in Barnston; see *Journal of the Synod of the Church of England in the Diocese of Quebec, Twentieth Session* (1893), 13-17.

69   *"he was struck, first and foremost ... strong Prayer-Book Church-people,"* Jolliffe, *Andrew Hunter Dunn,* 85.

Chapter III: The Road to Autonomy

71   *the seeming unwillingness of its adherents ... rather than look to the State for aid,"* for the parallel situation in the Diocese of Toronto, see Robert Merrill Black, "Stablished in the Faith: The Church of England in Upper Canada 1780-1867," in *By Grace Co-Workers: Building the Anglican diocese of Toronto 1780-1989,* Alan L. Hayes, ed. (Toronto, 1989), 32.

71   *The American Methodists ... in the states had already done,* Carrington, *The Anglican Church in Canada,* 81.

71   *Following the American Revolution ... proper respect for British institutions,"* Walsh, *The Christian Church in Canada,* 5.

72   *In 1801, after consultation with Bishops Mountain and Inglis ... each £150 received from the Government,* H. P. Thompson, *Into All Lands: The History of the Society for the Propagation of the Gospel in Foreign Parts 1701-1950* (London, 1951), 145-6.

72   *"In 1832 ... was thus thrown upon the Society,"* see SPG pamphlet: *Summary Account of the Society for the Propagation of the Gospel in Foreign Parts Corrected to October 1847* (London [1847]), 4-5.

72   *Until Bishop G. J. Mountain's death ... by vote of the Imperial Parliament,* see SPG pamphlet: *Return of the Number of Colonial Bishops, Stating the Salaries of Each, and the Sources Whence Those Salaries Are Derived* ([London,] 1855), 60.

73   *The cause of the people of Paspebiac ... and the Society, A Sermon, Preached ... on Friday, February 18, 1803; ... An Abstract of the Proceedings of the Society* (London, 1803), 52; this item is mistakenly listed under "Upper Canada."

73   *With respect to the voluntary contributions ... exceeded the income by £5710 7s 6d,* see *The Report of the Committee Appointed to Prepare A Concise Statement, For Public Information, of the Objects, Transactions, and Resources of the Society for the Propagation of the Gospel in Foreign Parts* (London, 1828), 5.

74   *Soon after Bishop Stewart was promoted ... on the part of the clergy,* Diary of James Reid, Vol. 23, entry for 31 Dec. 1849, Montreal Diocesan Archives (hereafter MDA).

74   *to a neighbouring clergyman "request[ing] ... Civil Secretary's Office, Quebec,"* Stewart to Reid, 7 Jan. 1828, Stewart Letters, Reid Collection, Vol. II, QDA.

74   *"I wish you w^d write ... which they may publish,"* Stewart to Reid, 25 Nov. [1829], Stewart Letters, Reid Collection, Vol. II, QDA.

74   *In December 1840 ... his third letter that year,* C. P. Reid to A. M. Campbell, 7 Feb. 1840, USPG Archives, C/CAN/LC2, 101; the same to John Russel (Treasurer of the SPG), 14 Sept. 1840, 102; the same to A. M. Campbell, 31 Dec. 1840, 103.

75   *The Church edifice ... handsomely painted,* C. P. Reid to A. M. Campbell, 31 Dec. 1840, USPG Archives, C/CAN/ LC2, 103.

75   *In the Diocese of Quebec ... with excellent fruit,* see *Report of the Society for Promoting Christian Knowledge, with an Account of the Receipts and Expenditure from April 1819, to April 1820* (London, 1820), 108-9.

76   *"500 Bibles ... in aid of the funds of the* SOCIETY *and the schools,"* see *Report of the Society ... 1827* (London, 1828), 37-8.

76   *You may know [Pye explained] ... voted £20 to aid the building,* SPCK Archives, Society Minute Book, Vol. 68, 90.

77   *According to Pye's report ... built the church in two months,"* Sixtieth Report of the Incorporated Church Society of the Diocese of Quebec ... 1901* (1902), 73-4.

77   *In 1908, the SPCK donated books ... cost the congregation £1.1.8,* SPCK Archives, Society Grant Book, No. 20, 356-7, 362, 387-8.

77   *An annual grant of £500 ... a* <u>College</u> *at* <u>Lennoxville</u>*,"* SPCK Archives, Society Minute Book, Vol. 41, meeting of 6 Dec. 1842, 542.

77   *In 1847, it voted an additional sum ... from other quarters,"* SPCK Archives, Society Minute Book, Vol. 43, meeting of 6 July 1847, 58.

77   *the endowment ... Pastoral Theology in 1892,* SPCK Archives, Society Grant Book, 1924-1961, 162; this entry, for £1000, appears to have been carried forward; it is dated in the margin "April '92." The page, headed "Quebec," carries no other item.

77   *To establish a fund from which ... came to no more than £10,500,* Thompson, *Into All Lands,* 248.

77   *This sum was paid ... valued at $53,341.59,* see *Jubilee Memoir of the Church Society of the Diocese of Quebec 1842-1892* (Quebec, 1892), 8.

77   *"in augmenting the incomes ... at once, $3,000 a year,"* Henry Roe, *Story of the First Hundred Years of the Diocese of Quebec* (Quebec, 1903), 52.

79   *Although Mountain's leadership ... the Christian life for that,"* quoted by A. W. Mountain, *A Memoir,* 439.

79   *and, like Bishop Stewart ... believer in self-help,* In 1832 Stewart urged self-help in his charge to the clergy, and in 1833 sent a circular to all congregations asking

them to support their own rectors; see Glazebrooke, *The Church of England in Upper Canada*, 18.

79   *In 1888 the SPG again reduced ... in strength and confidence,* see Thompson, *Into All Lands*, 249.

79   *Such [he reminded the Synod] ... has not been unfruitful,* see *Journal of the Synod of the Church of England in the Diocese of Quebec, Eighteenth Session* (1888), 16-7.

79   *In 1893, Archdeacan Henry Roe ... of the missionary by the Diocesan Board,* J. Langtry, *History of the Church in Eastern Canada and Newfoundland* (London, 1892), 66-7. [While this description of the Quebec system is useful, Langtry is generally unreliable, especially in the early period, and should be used with caution.]

80   *As far as I know ... called there 'The Quebec system,'* Carrington, *The Anglican Church in Canada*, 134-5.

80   *Whenever the Diocesan Board finds ... refunded to the Board by the mission,* "Canons: Diocese of Quebec" IX, 5, *Journal of the Synod of the Church of England in the Diocese of Quebec, Twentieth Session*, 66.

80   *Dunn, who "fully understood ... had been a particular care of the Society,* Thompson, *Into All Lands*, 249; for Dunn's remarks, see "Bishop's Address," *Journal of the Synod of the Church of England in the Diocese of Quebec, Twentieth Session*, 18.

81   *"in positions of isolated power ... personal attributes,"* Glazebrooke, *The Church of England in Upper Canada*, 144.

81   *In 1832, when the annual ... new energy to the church's administration,"* T. R. Millman, "Beginnings of the Synodical Movement in Colonial Anglican Churches with Special Reference to Canada," *Journal of the CCHS* (No. 1, 1979), 6.

82   *Like the SPCK, the Church Society ... all matters relating to the endowment of the same,"* see "Constitution of the Church Society of the Diocese of Quebec, Adopted at a General Meeting of the Society, duly convened at Montreal, on the 21st July, 1842," *Annual Report of the Church Society of the Diocese of Quebec, 1843* (Montreal, [1843]), 9 11.

83   *One sermon at least ... until a sermon shall have been so preached,* see "General By-laws of the Corporation of the Church Society of the Diocese of Quebec," adopted ... 1845, *Third Annual Report of the Incorporated Church Society of the Diocese of Quebec, 1845* (Montreal, [1845]), 10.

83   *This no doubt provoked some grumbling.* Early in 1849, the Rev. C. P. Reid, then incumbent at Compton, wrote to his father complaining about "the proceedings of the Church Society," see the Diary of James Reid, entry for 10 Jan. 1849, MDA.

84   *The Secretary reports having been present ... in addition to the sum above reported,* see *Ninth Annual Report of the Incorporated Church Society of the Diocese of Quebec* (Quebec, 1851), 17.

85   *Elgin had incurred … Most Anglicans were Tories.* See, for example, the entry for 1 Oct. 1849 in the journal of the Rev. Ernest Hawkins, Secretary of the SPG, who had just completed a tour of the Diocese of Quebec and was being entertained in Quebec City by several members of the Central Board and Lay Committee of the Church Society. He recorded that at a dinner party on that date, Lord Elgin was universally condemned, especially for his handling of the Rebellion Losses Bill earlier that year; "MS Journal of the Rev. Ernest Hawkins of His Tour in Canada and America 1849," USPG Archives.

85   *some of the Diocesan clergy … was the leader of this movement;* for Bethune's circular to the clergy, dated 9 Oct. 1849, together with an account of the meetings held in Montreal, see the MS Letterbook of James Reid, 58-9 and 72-4, parish papers of Bishop Stewart Memorial Church of the Holy Trinity, Frelighsburg, Que.

85   *"It is thought, in some quarters," … against the proceeding,"* G. J. Mountain, *Thoughts on "Annexation," in Connection With the Duty And the Interest of Members of the Church of England; and as Affecting Some Particular Religious Questions* (Quebec, [1849]), 15-16.

85   *In our own particular case in this Province … than such a tendency as this,* see *Journal of the Synod of the United Church of England and Ireland in the Diocese of Quebec, Third Session* (1861), 15-17.

86   *The Conference of Bishops … to "meet together in synod,"* see *Minutes of a Conference of the Bishops of Quebec, Toronto, Newfoundland, Fredericton and Montreal, Holden at Quebec, From September 23rd to October 1st, 1851,* reprinted in A. W. Mountain, *A Memoir,* 292-9.

87   *The remaining bishops … ecclesiastical as well as civil,"* see the account of the Bishop's visit to England in A. W. Mountain, *A Memoir,* 303-317; see also Carrington, *The Anglican Church in Canada,* 115.

87   *Canadian synodical government … several good studies,* for example, T. R. Millman, "Beginnings of the Synodical Movement in Colonial Anglican Churches with special reference to Canada, *Journal of the CCHS* (XXI, 1, 1979), 3-19; Bentley G. Hicks, "Synodical Government Within Canadian Anglicanism: Retrospective Implications," *Journal of the CCHS* (Oct. 1991), 123-40; H.R.S. Ryan, "The General Synod of the Anglican Church of Canada," *Journal of the CCHS* (Apr. 1992), 7-128.

87   *According to Article 9 … for a choice to be made,* see "Appendix," *Journal of the Synod of the United Church of England and Ireland, in the Diocese of Quebec, Fourth Session* (1862), 54-7.

87   *More than one full day was consumed … "which was carried by all standing,"* see *Journal of the Synod of the United Church of England and Ireland, in the Diocese of Quebec, Special Session* (1863), 14 *et passim.*

89   *On Williams' death in 1892 … while Hamilton had sunk to two,* for the record of balloting see *Journal of the Synod of the Church of England in the Diocese of Quebec, Special Session* (1892), 13-24.

91   *In 1909 ... be provided for the coadjutor,* see *Journal of the Synod of the Diocese of Quebec, Twenty-eighth Session* (1909), 117-8.

91   *Dunn obviously hoped ... the 'necessity' of such a course of action,* see *Journal of the Synod of the Diocese of Quebec, Special Session* (1910), 17-22.

91   *In June 1911 ... and Synod went on to other business,* see *Journal of the Synod of the Diocese of Quebec, Twenty-ninth (Ordinary) Session* (1911), 19-38. Although Dunn presided at the opening session of Synod, Ferrar took the Chair that evening, underscoring his apparent position as natural successor.

91   *The second failure ... who are not members of this Diocese,* see *Journal of the Sixty-third and Sixty-fourth (Ordinary) Sessions of the Synod of the Diocese of Quebec* (1977), 13-21.

92   *On this occasion everything possible ... during the pauses between some of the ballots,"* see *Journal of the Sixty-third and Sixty-fourth (Ordinary) Sessions of the Synod of the Diocese of Quebec,* 22, notes 2 and 3.

92   *at the electoral Synod following each ... on the fifth,* see *Journal of the Synod of the Diocese of Quebec, Special Session* (1915), 13-14; and *Journal of the Sixty-third and Sixty-fourth (Ordinary) Sessions of the Synod of the Diocese of Quebec,* 25-8.

92   *The procedures laid down at the 1990 synod ... favoured election by default,* see "Procedures for the election of a Coadjutor Bishop," *QDG Special Supplement* (Sept. 1990), 4; *Journal of the Seventy-second (Ordinary) Session of the Synod of the Diocese of Quebec* (1990), 18-24.

93   *I shall not lay stress ... Very sincerely yours, Lennox Williams,* quoted in Owsley Robert Rowley, *The Anglican Episcopate of Canada and Newfoundland* (London, 1928), 259.

93   *By resolution of the 1990 Synod ... alternatives to the existing process,"* *Journal of the Seventy-second (Ordinary) Session of the Synod of the Diocese of Quebec,* 28.

93   *On 29 October ... twenty-one (21) years,"* *Journal of the Synod of the Diocese of Quebec; Thirty-third (Ordinary) Session* (1920), 23; for the text of the canon, see "Appendix O," *Journal of the Synod of the Thirty-sixth (Ordinary) Session of the Synod of the Diocese of Quebec* (1926), 97; "The Report of the Committee to Whom was Referred the Question of Extending to Women the Privilege of Membership to Vestries," *Journal of the Synod of the Diocese of Quebec, Thirty-third (Ordinary) Session,* 79-81, states the arguments *against* admitting women to Vestries.

93   *In his Charge ... of giving women representation in the Synod,"* "Synod Proceedings," *QDG* (July, 1934), 24.

95   *a resolution adopted at the Lambeth Conference ... is to be brought into effect,"* "The Bishop's Charge," *Journal of the Fortieth (Ordinary) Session of the Synod of the Diocese of Quebec* (1934), 54.

95   *the subject of extending the franchise ... Lay: for 29, against 21,"* see *Journal of the Forty-eighth (Ordinary) Synod of the Diocese of Quebec* (1951), 23; the three synods referred

to are the 46th, 47th and 48th, held in 1947, 1949 and 1951 respectively; there had been a similar resolution at the 1945 synod.

95   *In 1953 Archbishop Carrington remarked ... have been elected as members,"* "The Lord Archbishop's Charge: Women's Work" *Journal of the Forty-ninth (Ordinary) Session of the Synod of the Diocese of Quebec* (1953), 35.

95   *He might also have mentioned that women ... to represent the Diocese of the Yukon,* Carrington, *The Anglican Church in Canada,* 283.

95   *In 1963 and 1965 ... and Dr D. C. Masters,* see *Journal of the Fifty-fourth (Ordinary) Session of the Synod of the Diocese of Quebec* (1963), 28; and *Journal of the Fifty-fifth (Ordinary) Session of the Synod of the Diocese of Quebec* (1965), 27.

95   *and Bert Meade had died,* T. M., "In Memoriam: Sidney Albert Meade," *QDG* (Sept. 1961), 4.

95   *Bishop Brown welcomed the first ... desirable innovation,* "The Bishop's Charge," *Journal of the Fifty-fourth (Ordinary) Session of the Synod of the Diocese of Quebec* (1968), 44-5.

96   *We consider with you ... has admitted women delegates,* "Report of the Committee on the Lord Bishop's Charge," *Journal of the Fifty-fourth (Ordinary) Session of the Synod of the Diocese of Quebec,* 48.

96   *In 1969, the Diocese sent ... committees of the Anglican Church of Canada,* Jane Corkran, "Youth Observer at Synod," *QDG* (Oct. 1969), 1. General Synod was held from 18-26 August in Sudbury; other Diocesan representatives were Messrs H. H. Gibaut and H. A. Simons, the Rev. David Thomas, the Ven. T. J. Matthews and Bishop R. F. Brown.

96   *Women's names began to appear ... the Diocesan Council for Social Service;* in 1968, of five lay members, two were women; by 1974, of eight, seven were women; in 1987, all (seven) were women.

96   *a statement of sentiment ... because they deal with human lives,* "Youth Synod, Resolutions to Diocesan Synod," *Journal of the Sixty-first (Ordinary) Session of the Synod of the Diocese of Quebec* (1974), 49. By resolution of the 1989 Synod, provision was to be made "for a process to change its governing legislation to provide for the election or appointment of two youth delegates from each Deanery to be full members of Diocesan Synod"; *Journal of the Seventy-first (Ordinary) Session of the Synod of the Diocese of Quebec* (1989), 25.

97   *Although General Synod had made provision ... youth delegates at home,* see *Journal of the Seventy-first (Ordinary) Session of the Synod of the Diocese of Quebec* (1989), 25; and *Journal of the Seventy-second (Ordinary) Session* (1990), 28.

97   *"The next step," ... of order and self-government,* Carrington, *The Anglican Church in Canada,* 126.

97   *The [General] Synod's members ... a change in diocesan representation at General Synod,* Ryan, "The General Synod of the Anglican Church of Canada: Aspects of Constitutional History," 108-110.

98   *it was shown in debate that ... equal representation from each diocese,* "Representation issue unresolved," *Anglican Journal* (Sept. 1992), 9A.

Chapter IV: Within and Without

99   *It is to be regretted ... for peace and prosperity in every community,* see *A Sermon Preached Before the Incorporated Society for the Propagation of the Gospel ... on Friday, February 16, 1821 By ... Herbert, Lord Bishop of Peterborough* (London, 1821), 132-3.

99   *a visit to Melbourne in 1846 ... "eleven varieties" of sects,* Hawkins, *Annals of the Diocese of Quebec,* 249-50.

101   *Upon the presumption ... we have no right to compromise them,* C. J. Stewart to J. Reid, 8 May 1832, Stewart Papers, QDA; the church in question was that at Stanbridge Mills in the present Diocese of Montreal.

101   *It was easy to foresee ... that which his office obliges him to do,* "A Pastoral Letter to the Clergy and Laity of the Diocese of Quebec, Upon the Question of Affording the Use of Churches and Chapels of the Church of England, For the Purpose of Dissenting Worship By George J. Mountain" (Quebec, 1845), 4-7.

103   *Although I hold such marriages in much abhorrence ... as perplexing as it is painful,* G. J. Mountain to A. H. Pearse, 3 Feb. 1859, Diocesan Papers, B-2, 48, f. 142, QDA. In 1902, General Synod enacted a Canon on the prohibited degrees of marriage and, in 1907, Bishop Hunter Dunn transmitted two copies of a table setting them out to every incumbent, who was to post one in each of his churches, see "The Bishop's Charge," *QDG* (July 1907), 85-6.

104   *on speaking with one of the Church wardens ... situated like those of Cape Cove,* George Milne to G. J. Mountain, 24 June 1861, Diocesan Papers, B-3, 49, f. 32, QDA.

105   *After just six years ... "according to their abilities and usefulness,"* Millman, *Life of Stewart,* 101; see also Appendix C, 181-2, which lists the catechists (exclusive of Indian catechists) serving in the Diocese of Quebec under Stewart, in many cases with their postings and remuneration.

105   *On reference to my Report ... during the time of the Services,* John Eden to C. J. Stewart, 5 July 1836, Diocesan Papers, B-6, 52, f. 31, QDA.

106   *Despite these hardships and trials ... 52 candidates for confirmation,* [John Eden to G. J. Mountain,] "Return of Sunday Schools, Reading Stations &c. from 1 July 1934 to 30th June 1935," Diocesan Papers, B-6, 52, f. 28, QDA.

106   *Once persuaded to accept the principle ... throughout his whole episcopate,"* see Millman, *Life of Stewart,* 102.

106   *Where there is no hope of advancement ... it has not been my good fortune to find it,* LPA, Moore Papers, "Foreign," I, ff 138-152, Jacob Mountain to Archbishop Moore, 13 June 1803.

107   *Between 1914 and 1994 ... remained for no more than a year,* see clergy list provided by Byron Clark, *Anglican Mission of Magdalen Islands: 140th Anniversary,* 32.

107   *"In 1970, the Faculty of Divinity ... specific preparation for Holy Orders,"* Sidney Jellicoe, "Bishop's University—Faculty of Theology: Report for the Academic Year 1969-70," *Journal of the Fifty-seventh (Ordinary) Session of the Synod of the Diocese of Quebec* (1970), 78.

107   *The Lord Bishop of Quebec transmits to the Society ... at the disposal of the Bishop,* see *A Sermon Preached Before the Incorporated Society for the Propagation of the Gospel in Foreign Parts, ... on Friday, February 16, 1816 ... By George Henry, Lord Bishop of Chester* (London, 1816), 47.

108   *Until 1828 ... the inevitable interruptions of a clerical household,"* A. R. Kell[e]y, "Theological Education in the Early Days," *QDG* (Sept. 1942), 14.

108   *Eager as he was to recruit local candidates ... pursuing another line of life,"* see leather notebook endorsed "Society's Students, Accepted Candidates & Aspirants not fully recognized," among "Ven. G. J. Mountain Gaspé Papers," Index 124, Case 2, folder 12, QDA.

108   *The first seminary within the boundaries ... at a salary of £100 a year,* Legge, *The Anglican Church in Three Rivers,* 56.

108   *Henry Roe, one of the original ... College staff in his own person,"* T. R. Millman, ed., "Reminiscences of the Earliest Lennoxville Days [by Henry Rowe]," *Journal of the CCHS* (Sept. 1971), 39.

108   *the College came to exercise a "considerable influence ... were either graduates or members of the faculty,* D. C. Masters, "Bishop's University and the Ecclesiastical Controversies of the Nineteenth Century," 42. This is not to say that the Evangelical party had no influence on church affairs in the Diocese of Montreal. In 1869, it managed to secure the succession of an outside Evangelical candidate to the episcopate; moreover Montreal's Diocesan Theological College, founded in 1873, was financed by, and under the control of, the Evangelical laity of that diocese.

109   *described the College in 1928 ... and other spiritual exercises,"* McCausland, *Counting Myself Happy,* 12 and 25.

109   *Dean Jellicoe, in announcing to Synod ... to such small numbers,* see *Journal of the Fifty-seventh (Ordinary) Session of the Synod of the Diocese of Quebec* (1970), 78.

109   *While I am certain that it is God's will ... in these present days,* McCausland, *Counting Myself Happy,* 173-4.

110   *The startling repercussions of Vatican II ... into the vanguard of ecumenism,"* Carlo Falconi, *The Popes in the Twentieth Century,* quoted by Vidler, *The Church in an Age of Revolution,* 271.

110   *Confederation was seen by many Protestant leaders ... for what became in 1925 The United Church of Canada,"* Phyllis D. Airhart, "Ordering a New Nation and Reordering

Protestantism 1867-1914," *The Canadian Protestant Experience*, George A. Rawlyk, ed., 99-100; George Johnson, "The Future of Ecumenism in Canada," in LeBlanc and Edinborough, eds., *One Church, Two Nations?* 180-2.

110   *Another matter which I hope is frequently engaging ... and the Churches of the East*, see QDG (July 1907), 84-5.

111   *After the fusion of denominations ... the Principles of Union*, John Gwynne-Timothy, "The Evolution of Protestant Nationalism," in LeBlanc and Edinborough, eds., *One Church, Two Nations?* 43; Gwynne-Timothy was a member of the General Commission of Church Union.

111   *"From each of these assemblies ... a revolution in the ecumenical movement,"* George Johnson, "The Future of Ecumenism in Canada," *One Church, Two Nations?* 183. See also [R. F. Brown] "Bishop's Letter," QDG (Feb. 1964), 2, in which he discusses the W.C.C. meeting and Vatican II in some detail.

111   *Under the headline "Brotherhood in Action!" ... a service in St James Church [Trois-Rivières]*, see QDG (Mar. 1965), 1; in all there are six ecumenical features and four photographs on this front page.

113   *Pope Leo XIII's Encyclical ... by Archdeacon Henry Roe in 1897*, Henry Roe, *The Continuity of the Church of England and the Papal Encyclical Apostolicæ Curæ* (Quebec, 1897), 3-87. This pamphlet, according to its preface, was published by Resolution of Diocesan Synod.

113   *Whatever regulations the Church of Rome may see fit ... in the Roman Catholic Church*, see *Journal of the Thirty-ninth (Ordinary) Session of the Synod of the Diocese of Quebec* (1932), 62.

114   *It is incorrect to state that "I advised" ... this point was made in the article*, "Understanding and Co-operation At Riverbend," QDG (Nov. 1968), 1; the title, printed as a headline, seems singularly inappropriate.

114   *Trinity, it should be noted ... held services on alternate Sundays*, [Philip Carrington,] "My Summer," QDG (Autumn 1950), 15.

114   *Canon Ralph Latimer and Dr Robert Craig ... among those in attendance*, see *Journal of the Fifty-seventh (Ordinary) Session of the Synod of the Diocese of Quebec*, 26.

114   *As you will have seen from the agenda ... with our brethren of the United Church*, see *Journal of the Fifty-seventh (Ordinary) Session of the Synod of the Diocese of Quebec*, 40.

115   *in a Memorial to Synod ... Principles of Union agreed upon by this Church,"* see *Journal of the Fifty-seventh (Ordinary) Session of the Synod of the Diocese of Quebec*, 108-9.

115   *If Jesus is the Man for Others ... Ordains priests and Ordains bishops*, see *Journal of the Fifty-eighth (Ordinary) Session of the Synod of the Diocese of Quebec* (1971), 41.

115   *Faced with the problem of supplying a resident priest ... and continues to the present day."* Bishop Matthews granted four such special licences to ministers of the United Church, and Bishop Goodings granted five. Currently, Bishop Stavert has licenced one of his own clergy to minister jointly to an Anglican-United Church congregation (at Trois-Rivières). I am grateful to the Ven. Richard Blyth, Archdeacon of Quebec, for explaining to me the intricacies of this practice.

116   *Discussion about "the admission of women ... instituted in the primitive Church,"* "The Encyclical Letter," QDG (Oct. 1920), 102-3.

116   *A good deal is being both said and written to-day ... yet it needs to be said,* Christopher Cheshire, "The Ministry of Women," reprinted from *The Commonwealth* in QDG (Feb. 1920), 21, 23, and 24.

117   *At 10.30 a.m. in the Cathedral ... and even a mother-in-law,* see QDG (Oct. 1960), 1. The article is unsigned.

117   *When the discussion was opened to the meeting ... could never have the charge of a parish,* "Women Discuss Their Church Role at Congress," QDG (Oct. 1963), 4.

118   *I realize that some of you are deeply disturbed ... less than 10 years ago!* see *Journal of the Sixtieth (Ordinary) Session of the Synod of the Diocese of Quebec* (1973), 37.

118   *At the request of the clergy, the vote ... the result of the debate,"* see *Journal of the Sixty-first (Ordinary) Session of the Synod of the Diocese of Quebec* (1974), 20-1.

118   *Bishop Matthews conducted the Opening Devotions ... which he had written,"* see *Journal of the Proceedings: Anglican Church of Canada 27th Session General Synod, Quebec 1975* (Toronto 1975), M-1.

118   *The open arms with which ... in the business sessions of Synod,* Harold F. Appleyard, "A Guest's Impression," QDG (Summer 1975), 4.

119   *On 6 March 1977 ... ordained her to the priesthood,* "Historic Event in Drummondville," QDG (Apr. 1977), 2; Joyce Hibbert, "The Rev. Ruth Matthews at Drummondville," QDG (Summer 1977), 1.

120   *In August 1963, the city of Toronto ... and the organization required to meet them,"* see "Plans for Congress" and "Congress Theme," QDG (Sept. 1962), 1.

120   *Briefly, the Congress came to the conclusion ... and to live up to them,"* J[ames] L. Y[oung], "Congress Report from Rev. J. L. Young," QDG (Sept. 1963), 1.

120   *"to promote mutual fellowship ... of the New Hebrides to Trois-Rivières,"* "Diocese Welcomes Congress Delegates," QDG (Summer 1963), 1.

120   *Besides visiting Quebec City ... in the form of pulp wood and minerals,"* see "Visitor from Congress," QDG (Sept. 1963), 1, and J. E. D[eWolf], "Dedication of LaTuque Indian Residential School Chapel," QDG (Oct. 1963), 1.

121   *If English and French [in Canada] ... and what we have is superstition,* quoted in "Father Rakale Returns to South Africa," *QDG* (May 1964), 4.

121   *"But if this relationship is to grow ... We must share information and plans,"* Leslie [Stradling], "Message from Johannesburg," *QDG* (Sept. 1964), 1.

121   *The one I would particularly suggest ... they will be well able to support it,* "Anglican World Mission: Suggestions from the Bishop of Johannesburg," *QDG* (Oct. 1964), 1.

123   *Of the seven churches under his care ... very little from these people financially,"* J. K. Rakale, "Letter from South Africa," *QDG* (Dec. 1964), 1.

123   *I thank you again ... the new church when it is completed,* "Letter From the Rev. J. K. Rakale," *QDG* (Feb. 1965), 1.

123   *By the time the partnership was brought to a close ... and All Saints, Stilfontein,* see *Journal of the Fifty-seventh (Ordinary) Session of the Synod of the Diocese of Quebec,* 52.

124   *Ties and contacts between the two dioceses ... his own arrest and imprisonment,* see *Journal of the Fifty-ninth (Ordinary) Session of the Synod of the Diocese of Quebec* (1972), 28.

124   *We share in common ... sparsely settled as is our own,* John Morrell, "Companion Diocese Program Inaugurated," *QDG* (Nov. 1991), 1.

124   *a notice of motion ... as long as the principle was retained,"* see *Journal of the Fifty-seventh (Ordinary) Session of the Synod of the Diocese of Quebec* (1970), 33-4. The mover of the original motion was the Rev. J. L. Young, the seconder the Rev. D. Thomas.

125   *Although at first it was thought that an appendix ... held in Quebec City—in 1905,* Carrington, *The Anglican Church in Canada,* 223.

125   *In the matter of Prayer Book revision ... by issuing 'special forms' for use,* Jolliffe, *Andrew Hunter Dunn,* 135.

125   *In 1909, the members of the Committee ... an intensely conservative spirit,"* W. J. Armitage, *The Story of the Canadian Revision of the Prayer Book* (Toronto, 1922), 25.

125   *Two years later ... be taken at the present time,"* Armitage, *The Story of the Canadian Revision of the Prayer Book,* 31.

126   *General Synod accepted a draft revision ... as the accepted basis for further revision and enrichment,"* Armitage, *The Story of the Canadian Revision of the Prayer Book,* 102 and 103-5.

126   *Particularly noteworthy were the parts ... high in scholarship in the Canadian Church"),* Armitage, *The Story of the Canadian Revision of the Prayer Book,* 32, 109, and 63.

126   *the historic display "of every Prayer Book ... Anglican Congress in 1963,* "Every Anglican Prayer Book To Be Displayed," *QDG* (Jan. 1963), 1.

126   On two separate occasions ... fundamentally the old Prayer Book, Carrington, *The Anglican Church in Canada*, 290.

127   *The aim [of the revision] ... it pulled together very well*, Cuttell, *Philip Carrington*, 140.

127   *the following day, 3 September ... the successor of the 1662 Prayer Book*, McCausland, *Counting Myself Happy*, 111.

127   *In contrast to previous ventures ... the "token Evangelical presence."* I am grateful to the Rev. Dr Ronald E. Reeve for information on this subject.

128   *As a glance at the national newspaper ... will amply demonstrate*, see, for example, *Anglican Journal* (Dec. 1991), which contains a feature article (p. 1); a news item from "Around the World" (p. 4); and a letter to the editor (p. 8); also March 1992, with feature story (pp. 1, 10-11) and related article (p. 10).

128   *During the 1980s, a number of well-prepared articles ... featured prominently among its pages*, Daphne Stanford, "The Church and Unemployment, part I," *QDG* (Sept. 1984), 3; Gary Nicolosi, "The Church and Unemployment, part II," (Oct. 1984), 3-4; Marilyn Moore, "Capital Punishment Today: The Case Against the Death Penalty" (Oct. 1986), 6-7; James V. Scott, "Why Kill People Who Kill People to Show That Killing People Is Wrong?" (May 1987), 6-7; Patricia Peacock, "Report on Family Violence Presented to Diocesan Synod," (Dec. 1987), 6-7.

128   *During the same period ... with issues surrounding sexual orientation,"* I am grateful to the editor of *Integrator* for supplying these observations. The priest whom he quotes served in the Diocese in the early 1980s and made these comments privately. With the exception of a motion (emanating from one of the Deanery Boards) presented to Diocesan Synod in 1979, there is virtually *no* mention of sexual orientation in any official statement by the Diocese of Quebec.

128   *At Diocesan Synod in 1987 ... for consideration and action,"* see *Journal of the Seventieth (Ordinary) Session of the Synod of the Diocese of Quebec* (1987), 25-7. The original motion was proposed by the Rev. Ronald Smith, seconded by the Rev. T. C. Reinhardt.

129   *Unfortunately the DEC Reports ... any submission on the subject,* see "Appendix 3: "[Report of] Diocesan Executive Council," *Journal of the Seventy-first (Ordinary) Session of the Synod of the Diocese of Quebec* (1989), 42-3; and "Appendix 15: Report to Synod 1990, Diocesan Executive Council," *Journal of the Seventy-second (Ordinary) Session of the Synod of the Diocese of Quebec* (1990), 69-71.

129   *According to an article covering a three-part lecture series ... was his practice in such cases,* see Chris Ambidge, "Challenged and Challenging at the Cathedral," *Integrator* (Summer 1993), 4-5.

Chapter V: Meeting the Challenge

131   *"People brought ashore opposite church ... to die on his road,* quoted in A. W. Mountain, *A Memoir*, 260-261.

131   *Charles Forest ... appealed to his Bishop for relief,* Charles Forest to G. J. Mountain, 9 June 1847, Grosse Isle, "Diocesan Papers," B-6, 52, f. 157, QDA.

133   *the Bishop "suggested it to such ... first in the turn himself,"* A. W. Mountain, *A Memoir,* 257.

133   *Of the 17 clergy ... Three others died,* see MS Chronicles of the Diocese of Quebec, Vol. II, under 1847, QDA.

133   *Deeply as we must deplore ... the words of life and peace?* quoted in A. W. Mountain, *A Memoir,* 264, 265-6.

134   *As the reports were heard and discussed ... a changed social order,* "4th Annual Clergy Workshop," *QDG* (Nov. 1978), 4.

134   *In his Episcopal Charge, Bishop Bruce Stavert ... the training and support of lay ministry,* "Episcopal Charge: Synod 1993," *QDG* (Nov. 1993), 3-4.

135   *Frampton, Broughton, Ireland, Inverness ... the Liturgy & a printed Sermon,* Leather-covered notebook titled "Society's Students, Accepted Candidates & Aspirants not formally recognized," 32-3, Unbound MSS, Index 124, Case 2, Folder 12, QDA.

136   *I spend every Tuesday in Black Lake ... the constant change,* Philip Callis to A. H. Dunn, 31 Jan. 1910, Correspondence of A. H. Dunn, B-51, QDA.

136   *the role of "lay readers formally commissioned ... the travel plans of distant clergy,"* W.F.T., "Parish Notes: All Saints', Hereford," *QDG* (Apr. 1963), 2. See also G. E. [Kendrick], "The Anglican Parish of Coaticook (Part II)," *QDG* (Summer 1962), 4, which recounts that on the sudden death of the Rev. W. J. Rowe of St Stephen's, services were carried on during the eight-month interval before a successor was appointed, largely by Mr S. A. Meade, layreader.

137   *During the years we worked together ... for lack of a minister,* T[imothy] M[atthews], "Herbert Arthur Simons," *QDG* (Jan. 1984), 1. In recognition of his involvement with the layreaders, Mr Simons was appointed first warden of the Diocesan Order of Layreaders.

137   *Be so good as to tell Mr Lindon ... as soon as it will be convenient,* C. J. Stewart to James Reid, 25 Nov. 1819, Stewart-Reid Letters, I, QDA. Following Bishop Jacob Mountain's representations to the SPG, the Society did, however, authorize Lindon "to draw upon their Treasurer for £90," see G. J. Mountain to James Reid, 22 June 1820, Reid-G. J. Mountain Papers, QDA.

137   *"useful and fancy articles ... in connection with the Church of St Barnabas,"* see *St. Barnabas, North Hatley: Our Story 1894-1979* (n.p., [1979]), 42.

138   *In Trois-Rivières, for example, ... the 'Three Rivers Rectory Endowment Fund,'"* Legge, *The Anglican Church in Three Rivers,* 69-72.

138   *The first undertaking of the Ladies' Guild of St John's, Brookbury ... the inside of the Church,"* Rowell and Lapointe, *Township of Bury: Canton de Bury 1836-1986,* 12.

138   *In the "Treasurer's Book" of the Ladies Guild of St Peter's-by-the-Sea ... including four brushes*, MS "Treasurer's Book, Ladies Guild of Old Harry," 1916-1938, collection of Byron Clark.

139   *"fire attributed to the act of vandals ... gratefully received and carefully recorded*, "Fire Destroys Hall," *QDG* (Summer 1960), 3; W.M.H. Thomas, "Letters to the Editor," *QDG* (Summer 1961), 4.

139   *A Chancel Guild ... to be planted near the church*," Records of "St Michael's Chancel Guild" (MS notebook), i 7 d-1, St Michael's Parish Papers, Sillery.

139   *At Grosse Isle on the Magdalen Islands ... care for, clear and fence the burial ground*, see *Anniversary Newsletter of the Magdalen Islands Mission 1850-1975* (n.p., 1975), 20; and MS "Vestry Minutes, Holy Trinity, Grosse Isle, 1952-1972" (Xerox), entry for 31 Jan. 1965, collection of Byron Clark.

139   *An extract from the 1891 Vestry Minutes of St Barnabas Church, Lake Megantic ... by the ladies of the Guild*," typescript, "Saint Barnabas Anglican Church, Lake Megantic 100th Anniversary: Excerpts from the Vestry Minutes from 1891 to 1991," entry for 1891 [italics mine].

141   *St Stephen's Ladies' Guild, Coaticook, ... improvements to all church property*," G[rover] E[dward] K[endrick], "Parish Notes: The Anglican Parish of Coaticook 1862-1962," *QDG* (June 1962), 2.

141   *The initials 'W.A.' ... in the church and in society*, Alyson Barnett-Cowan, "The Bishop's Messengers: Harbingers of the Ordination of Women," *Journal of the CCHS* (Oct. 1986), 76.

141   *At a meeting of the St Matthew's Branch of the W.A. ... were able to attend*," W.A. Minute Book, 1886-8, St Matthew's (Quebec) Parish Records.

141   *In nearby Sillery, ... the management of the lantern*, Records of the St Michael's W.A., i 7 a-1, St Michael's Parish Papers, Sillery.

142   *The W.A. not only enlisted the support ... a parish in the diocese of Quebec*," "Historic Event in Drummondville: Induction of the Rev. Ruth Matthews," *QDG* (April 1977), 2.

142   *dedicated exclusively to the help of Clergymen ... Mutton Bay Nursing Home in the Canadian Labrador*," [Mrs Winfield], "The Association of Church Helpers," *QDG* (March 1935), 27.

142   *The fifty-first Annual Meeting ... their support in the coming year*, Olive Boswell, "The fifth [sic] Report of the Association of Church Helpers," *QDG* (March 1943), 24.

143   *Judging from its Minute Book ... "being used at night for smoking*," MS Minute Book of the St Michael's Quebec Branch of the Church of England Men's Society, 1913-17, i 7 e-1 St Michael's Parish Papers, Sillery.

143   *The Eastern Townships Churchman's Association ... its income to Parochial objects,"* A[rthur] E. E. L[egge], "Parish Notes: Coaticook," *QDG* (March 1932), 8-9.

143   *In 1963, responding to an alarming decline ... from the Layman's Ordination Fund,* "Bishop's Letter," *QDG* (Jan. 1963), 2; H. H. Gibaut, "Report of the Laymen's Ordination Fund," *Journal of the Fifty-fourth (Ordinary) Session of the Synod of the Diocese of Quebec* (1963), 76; and H. H. Gibaut, "Report of the Laymen's Ordination Fund," *Journal of the Special Session of the Synod of the Diocese of Quebec* (1969), 70-1.

143   *The three-day Stewardship Conference ... in the* Diocesan Gazette, J. G. M[arston], "Continuing Stewardship," *QDG* (June 1964), 1.

143   *Initially open only to boys ... have had Servers join the Order,"* see W.H.M. C[hurch], "Quebec Diocesan Order of Servers Annual Report," *QDG* (March 1962), 4, and "Letter to the Editor," *QDG* (May 1962), 4; W.H.M. C[hurch], "New Venture Proves Successful: Report on First Diocesan Server's Camp," *QDG* (Christmas 1951), 21; Harold Church, "Quebec Diocesan Order of Servers—Report to Synod 1977," *Journal of the Sixty-third and Sixty-fourth (Ordinary) Sessions of the Synod of the Diocese of Quebec* (1977), 65-6.

144   *Little publicity [he pointed out] ... who can take services in Cree,* see *Journal of the Forty-fourth (Ordinary) Session of the Synod of the Diocese of Quebec* (1943), 39.

144   *It was a wonderful thing to see that chapel ... the congregation of Christ's flock,'* "Archbishop's Letter," *QDG* (Christmas 1958), 9.

145   *The Naskapis [he pointed out] ... a tremendous one for them in countless ways,* "Bishop's Letter," *QDG* (Feb. 1963), 2. Bishop Brown's letter uses the older spelling "Nascopi" which I have normalized to avoid confusion.

145   *"Although the Naskapi people have for many years ... in a fire that destroyed their home,* Bruce Stavert and Lynn Ross, "Joseph Sandy, Deacon: A Tribute, *QDG* (Apr. 1978), 4. See also Donald A. Dodman, "Naskapi Ordination," *QDG* (May 1976), 1; and Peter Spackman, "Tragedy at Matimekosh," *QDG* (Apr. 1978), 1.

145   *I appreciate the invitation to speak to this Synod ... Thank you for listening,* "Presentation by Chief Joe Guanish," *Journal of the Seventy-first (Ordinary) Session of the Synod of the Diocese of Quebec* (1989), 85-6; also "Chief Joe Guanish brings concerns to Synod," *QDG* (Nov. 1989), 3.

146   *The War-torn Flags that hang in the Sanctuary ... at the battles of Quatre Bras and Waterloo,* [A. H. Crowfoot,] *The Cathedral of the Holy Trinity, Quebec: A Perambulation* (n.p., 1947), 26-8.

146   *The doors of the Cathedral are closed ... the organ playing the National Anthem,* "The regimental Colours in the Cathedral," *QDG* (May 1916), 58.

147   *I think it right to name to your Grace ... quite friendly and pleasant,* LPA, F. Temple Papers, Official Letters 1900: Foreign , Vol. 42, ff 20-1, A. H. Dunn to F. Temple, 1 Jan. 1900.

148   *On 3 January 1915 (the National Day of Intercession) ... our Empire and our allies are fighting,"* "Prayers For Victory," *QDG* (Feb. 1915), 22-4.

148   *The April issue contained some stirring verses ... the hearts of our men are wide open,* S. C. Lowry, "Your King and Distant Countries Need You," and "Letter from a Chaplain with Our Soldiers at the Front," *QDG* (Apr. 1915), 46 and 39-40, respectively. Compare the latter with F. G. Scott, *The Great War as I Saw It* (Toronto, 1922), 39-41.

148   *at the request of Sir William Price ... to the Prime Minister of the Province of Quebec,* see *Journal of the Synod of the Diocese of Quebec: Thirty-first (Ordinary) Session* (1916), 39-41.

149   *I have ordained no one else ... for the Clergy to enlist as combatants,* see *Journal of the Synod of the Diocese of Quebec: Thirty-first (Ordinary) Session,* 52, 54, 58 and 66. See also a letter read to the clergy at this Synod in which the Chief Press Censor cautions the clergy against announcing any war news "based upon private telegrams, or letters," 59-60.

149   *At this moment our thoughts ...* all *the churches in the Diocese for private prayer,* see *Journal of the Synod of the Diocese of Quebec: Thirty-second (Ordinary) Session* (1918), 69-71.

150   *45 percent of the Canadian troops ... among the religious denominations,* see *Synod Journals* for 1916, 65-6, and for 1918, 69.

150   *By 1918 the number of Diocesan clergy "serving with the colours" ... little or no loss has been suffered,"* see *Journal of the Synod of the Diocese of Quebec: Thirty-second (Ordinary) Session* (1918), 59 and 55.

150   *We must get a really new and better world ... to win the world for Christ,* see *Journal of the Synod of the Diocese of Quebec: Thirty-third (Ordinary) Session* (1920), 35.

151   *Until his resignation in 1935 ... arms trade and "selfish Nationalism,"* see, among many others "The Bishop's Letter," *QDG* (Mar. 1928), 1-3; (Jan. 1932), 1-2, and "Pastoral Letter," (Mar. 1935), 1-3.

151   *The present generation ... in a very limited sense true of nations,* "Editorial," *QDG* (July 1934), 3.

151   *War is hateful to the Christian soul ... "injustices in the Treaty of Versailles,"* [Philip Carrington] "Psalm 53:1," *QDG* (Sept. 1939), 13 and 15.

151   *Twice within a quarter of a century ... blindness and selfishness and sin,* "Editorial," *QDG* (Sept. 1939), 6; Eardley-Wilmot, in speaking of war, actually uses the phrase "a judgement sent by God," 8.

152   *The tiny Anglican community of Entry Island ... died in the prison camps there,* Wm C. Dunn, "Royal Rifles War Memorial Church," *QDG* (Sept. 1945), 26; the Entry Island Honour Roll appears in *Anniversary Newsletter of the Magdalen Islands Mission 1850-1975,* 27.

152   *The Municipality of Bury ... would not survive,* Rowell and Lapointe, *Township of Bury:*

Canton de Bury 1836-1986, 32. The largest number of Hong Kong veterans also came from Bury, 31 in number; Nina Rowell, "Service Honours Hong Kong Veterans," *QDG* (Mar. 1992), 3.

152   *The Rev. A. E. Tulk ... the second in 1945,* "Two Brothers Make Supreme Sacrifice," *QDG* (Apr. 1945), 20-1.

152   *With the end of hostilities ... 72 of whom were Anglicans,* "Discharged Service Personnel and War Brides," *QDG* (Feb. 1947), 12.

152   *One of the expectations ... to a deeper awareness of God,* A.V. Ottiwell, "The Church and Discharged Men and Women from the Forces," *QDG* (Feb. 1947), 13. See Ottiwell's earlier comments on the subject in chapter II, 63.

153   *The United and Anglican Churches ... of which church involvement was a component,* John G. Stackhouse, Jr, "The Protestant Experience in Canada Since 1945," *The Canadian Protestant Experience*, 200-1 and 206.

153   *St. Paul's, the Mariner's Chapel ... by Stewart in 1832.* This chapel, at Munn's Cove, flourished "during the palmy days of the square timber industry," and served those employed by it as well as the sailors manning the fleets of square-riggers bound to and from Quebec, see "Old St. Paul's Chapel of Quebec," *QDG* (Sept. 1932), 18.

154   *Last February ... were properly clothed for the winter,* Glenn Stone, "Ministry of International Outreach at Port of Quebec," *QDG* (Feb. 1993), 1.

154   *In 1888, for example, a major altercation ... thought necessary to publish the correspondence,* from mid-November 1888 until late January 1889 at least seven of these letters appeared in the Quebec *Morning Chronicle*.

154   *Despite this discomfiture ... until his retirement in 1908,* SPCK Archives, Minute Book, Vol. 57, 259, entry for 2 Oct. 1883.

155   *(such as 'Operation Shoebox' ... were filled and distributed,* Glenn Stone, "Ministry of International Outreach at Port of Quebec," *QDG* (Feb. 1993), 1; and Glenn Stone, "Missions to Seamen," *QDG* (Nov. 1993), 8.

155   *From the beginning of August ... has yet been held in any of the camps,* G. R. Fothergill, "District News: Transcontinental Railway," *QDG* (Oct. 1908), 122-3.

156   *One of the six Unemployment Camps ... to meet this challenge, too,* see, for example, *QDG* (Nov. 1934), 6, and (Jan. 1935), 8.

156   *On 5 March 1829 ... the names of 53 children,* see "Register of the Female Orphan Asylum—Opened March 5th 1829," QDA, File 126.

157   *Madam, I am apprehensive that the Ladies ... in appearance she is younger,* G. J. Mountain to Mrs E. Sewell, 2 April 1829, QDA, File 126.

157   *for the May Minutes record ... had left the Asylum,* QDA, File 126, "Secretary's Book, Female Orphan Asylum 1829," [10 and 12].

157   *Mary Mountain, as her private correspondence ... lest they should do without,* Masters and Masters, *Ten Rings on the Oak,* 92-3.

158   *born at Nicolet ... not the means of affording her there,* Memorandum endorsed "Mr Trigge 13th Oct 1829," QDA, File 126.

158   *Two of the members ... send their votes by letter,* they were Anne Stewart and Mary Mountain, both of whose letters are dated 7 Nov. 1829, the former voting against admission, the latter in favour; QDA, File 126.

158   *but as their spokesman pointed out ... and had abandoned her,* "Extract from the proceedings of the Military Asylum Committee respecting the transfer of orphans to the F. O. Asylum, Jan 1843," and "Register of Children Transferred from the Military Orphan Asylum to the Quebec Orphan Asylum, 5 February 1843," QDA, File 126.

158   *When the Finlay Asylum ... took charge of its management,* see "Finlay Home Marks 100 Years," *QDG* (Nov. 1962), 4. Unlike the Female and Male Orphan Asylums, the Finlay had the advantage of an endowment. An interesting article on the Home's chapel appeared in *QDG* (Feb. 1947), 22 and 32.

159   *20th [Dec.] Visited. And was pleased ... 25th. All at Church and well,* "Visitor's Book 1836," [91], QDA, File 126. Miss Pike's Report inserts the account of 21 December *after* 25 December and of Christmas Eve as part of 20 December; for clarity's sake these entries have been reordered chronologically.

Notes & Sources: Illustrations

Plate 1a   *The Royal gift of 1766* (QDG, Summer 1959, p. 24). These pieces were executed in 1763 by Thos Hemming and sent three years later to Quebec under custody of General James Murray. Although the chalice and credence paten have remained with the Parish of Quebec and continue to form part of the Cathedral plate, sometime after the arrival of the second Royal gift the flagon and smaller paten disappeared. In 1942 the plate was reassembled for the first time in more than a hundred years on the discovery that two other pieces, identifiable by their hallmarks and the arms and cipher of George III, were to be found in the parish of St Armand East, Frelighsburg, having been in use there as long as anyone could remember. As early as 1816, in fact, the curate of the parish, in his Report to the Bishop, had stated that one of his churches possessed "a Paten and Flagon of plate," but that the other (St Armand West) had only "a crystal cup, Decanter, and a common Dining plate for the bread." After the pieces were reunited, the integrity of the set established, and photographs taken, the flagon and paten were returned to Frelighsburg.

Plate 1b   *The Royal gift of 1804.* This double set, made especially for the Cathedral by Messrs Rundle and Bridge, Silversmiths to His Majesty, consists of a pair of massive silver candlesticks, two flagons, two chalices, two patens, one credence paten, and one octagonal alms dish. All the pieces bear the arms of the donor and of the diocese, together with the I.H.S. in a glory, or a dove on a triangle in a glory, emblematic of the Trinity. Bishop J. W. Williams found a mistake in the Latin which recorded the gift in an inscription on the patens: "the word 'accommodatum' ... spelt with only one 'm.' By way of rectifying the error he had a line, indicative of abbreviation, placed over the 'm'" (see Crowfoot, *The Cathedral of the Holy Trinity*, 30).

Plate 2   *Bishops of the Diocese in the 19th Century* (QDG, Jan. 1901, facing 2). This delightful montage (a reconstruction of the original) is accompanied by the comment that because "not many Colonial Dioceses can lay claim [in 1901] to have had a 'Century of Bishops,' for, in the year 1801, outside the British Isles, there were, in the British Empire, only the two Bishops of Nova Scotia and Quebec ... we [the editors of the *Diocesan Gazette*] thought we could not offer our readers a better illustration, with which to usher in the New Century, than a group of Portraits of these five Prelates, who, in the providence of God, have been called to preside, as Chief Pastors, over the destinies of the English Church in our Diocese, during the past one hundred years."

Plate 3   *Bishops of the Diocese in the 20th century* (photographs courtesy of the QDA).

Plate 4   *St James' Church, Trois-Rivières* (Gaspé Deanery G.A. Scrapbook, 1951, 96). Although the first Anglican incumbent was placed at Trois-Rivières in 1768, the land

and endowment of the present church did not pass to the Bishop of Quebec until 1823. The Recollets, the original proprietors, appear to have remained in residence in the monastery until 1777, "after which the buildings were converted to Governmental purposes, the church becoming part courthouse and part storeroom, and the monastery a hospital at first and a gaol, with sheriff's offices, afterwards" (Legge, *The Anglican Church in Three Rivers*, xiv).

Plate 5a   *Interior of the Cathedral of the Holy Trinity* (QDG, Feb. 1897, facing 14). The old practice of decorating churches with freshly-cut boughs for Christmas continued to be widespread in the diocese. The Church of St James, Lac Beauport, still retains a set of wooden threading-tools, probably designed by some local workman, for binding the branches together before fastening them in place around the sanctuary.

Plate 5b   *Consecration and Enthronement of the Rt Rev. Lennox Williams* (*Journal of the Synod of the Diocese of Quebec, Special Session*, 1914, facing 24). Present are, Top Row: left to right, Rev. Canon F.J.B. Alnatt, Ven. A. J. Balfour, Rev. Phillip Callis, Rt Rev. E. J. Bidwell, Bishop of Kingston, Rev. R. A. Parrock, Rt Rev. John C. Farthing, Bishop of Montreal, Rev. Aghapios Gholam, Priest Greek Orthodox Church, Rev. Sophronios Beshara, Deacon Greek Orthodox Church. Lower Row: left to right, Rt Rev. W. Lennox Mills, Bishop of Ontario, Rt Rev. Lennox Waldron Williams, Bishop of Quebec, His Grace Charles Hamilton, late Archbishop of Ottawa, Rt Rev. Clare L. Worrel, Bishop of Nova Scotia and Acting Metropolitan, Abp Germanos of Baalbek, in the Patriarchate of Antioch, an Archbishop of the Greek Orthodox Church, Rt. Rev. F. Courtney, late Bishop of Nova Scotia. In his sermon that evening, the Bishop of Montreal pointed to the presence of Archbishop Germanos and his attendants, guests of the Bishop-elect, both at the Service and in the Procession, as "an object lesson in the essential unity of the Church of Christ" (*loc. cit,* 25). A copy of this photograph hangs in many a vestry in the diocese to this day.

Plate 6   *The earliest format of the* Quebec Diocesan Gazette (QDG March 1900, cover). The *Diocesan Gazette* is the second "official" Diocesan publication to be produced "under the sanction of the Bishop"; the earlier one, the *Canadian Ecclesiastical Gazette*, had been published from 1850 to 1853, during G. J. Mountain's episcopate, under joint authority of the Church Society and the Diocese of Quebec. The present, larger format of the *Diocesan Gazette* first appeared with the 1960 January issue, volume LXVII. It conformed with the *Canadian Churchman* (now the *Anglican Journal*), which from that date has been mailed out with the *Diocesan Gazette* to Anglicans on parish lists.

Plate 7   *Advertising carried in the* Quebec Diocesan Gazette (QDG May 1899, fly leaf). All three of the advertisements shown here appear to be church-related, but local hotels, grocers, coal merchants, druggists, laundries, and "sanitary plumbers," for example, are also represented among advertisers this same year. Until the 1950s, Anglican clergy could enjoy the facilities offered by The Clergy House of Rest at Cacouna for a vacation and time of study during the summer months. To "secure the Guest of the House that freedom and liberty of action to which they are entitled," a notice posted in the building proclaimed, "an established Rule ... forbids except on special occasions, and with the approval of the Master of the House—the admission of Ladies to the hospitality of the House" (see James T. Sweeny, *Québec Pilgrimage*, 59).

Plate 8a   *Landing Bishop A. H. Dunn at Pointe Bleue Rocks* (QDG, Sept. 1905, facing 118). The S.S. *Colon* was lent for the occasion by B. A. Scott, Esq., to transport the Bishop and his party from Roberval to Pointe Bleue and back.

Plate 8b   *At the Church of St John the Divine, Pointe Bleue* (QDG, Sept. 1905, facing 118). Accompanying articles mention that, in the interval between the taking and the publishing of this photograph, "Old Charlie," the interpreter, had died, and Maggie Robertson, in addition to acting as cook for the missionary and keeping the church fresh and clean, had taken on the role of interpreter as well (QDG, 118-119).

Plate 9a   *Bishop Bruce Stavert and the Rt Rev. Narciso Ticobay.* The *Diocesan Gazette* published a Special Supplement in December 1991 on the Companion Diocese Program in which the Covenant, signed on 24 September 1991 by the two Bishops, was printed in full.

Plate 9b   *Visiting parishioners: Harrington Harbour* (private collection).

Plate 10a   *A komatik, St Augustine River* (Gaspé Deanery G.A. Scrapbook, 1951, 69). This photograph of the Rev. Sydney Meade was taken on a return visit to his old parish; he had been in sole charge of the Canadian Labrador from 1941 to 1944. Today the snowmobile has largely replaced the dogsled for overland travel here.

Plate 10b   *The M. V. Hollis Corey* (private collection). The vessel is flying the flag of the Anglican Church of Canada, adopted in 1955.

Plate 11a   *Congregation at Christ Church, Brompton* (Gaspé Deanery G.A. Scrapbook, 1951, 152). In the year of its consecration, Christ Church, Brompton, was "the first and only Protestant place of worship in the Township ... a plain, but well proportioned, and very attractive wooden building, 50 ft x 25 ft inside, with porch and bell turret, and having sittings for 120 persons" (*The Thirty-first Report of the Incorporated Church Society ... for 1872*, 16). In 1873 the missionary in charge served congregations at Windsor, Brompton Church, Brompton Falls, and Hardwood Hill; Brompton Church attendance was then, on average, about 40 (*The Thirty-third Report of the Incorporated Church Society ... for 1874*, 44-5).

Plate 11b   *After a Service of Holy Communion near Wolf Bay* (private collection). On the Lower North Shore, most families have traditionally left the villages during summer to fish from the outside islands, and what ministry they have received during that season sought them out by boat or by plane at their camps.

Plate 12a   *A. Y.P.A. Conference* (Gaspé Deanery G.A. Scrapbook, 1951, 16). This event was the second of two week-end Conferences at Quebec Lodge in 1945, the later held from Friday, 31 August, to Monday, 3 September, for which about 40 were in residence. The Rev. Sydney Meade and Mrs Meade served as Dean and Hostess. Archbishop Carrington, who took part in both conferences, spoke to this group on the history of the diocese; "particular[ly] helpful for the young people present was his vivid word picture of our new fields of endeavour like Arvida, Baie Comeau, and the Upper St Maurice Mission" (QDG, Sept. 1945, 12 and 24).

Plate 12b *Senior Girls' Camp, Fort Haldimand* (Gaspé Deanery G.A. Scrapbook, 1951, 259). The Fort Haldimand Camp Log Book preserves the signatures of 23 campers, divided among five patrols (the Wanderers, Forget-Me-Nots, Bluebirds, Fence Busters and Spitfires) for this particular group. The staff of eight included a Matron (Vera J. Reed), Guider (Mary Fish), Swimming Instructress (June Walton), Handicrafter (Rita Franklin), Program Director (Fredi Meade), Chaplain (Sydney Meade), and two Cooks (Drusa E. Patterson and Diana M. Miller). A Chapel Log records the names of all the girls who read the Lessons. Mattins and Evensong were sung daily; the theme chosen for this session was "To Be a Pilgrim."

Plate 13 *Diocesan G.A. Guides: Malbay, York and Sandy Beach* (Gaspé Deanery G.A. Scrapbook, 1951, 21). The book profiles 12 other Diocesan G.A.s including those at East Angus, Drummondville, Grosse Isle (Magdalen Islands), Melbourne, and Mutton Bay. The Scrapbook, hand-written and illustrated with photographs and sketches, measures 28 cm by 37 cm, and contains 260 pages. Its stout plywood boards are held in place by three stove bolts, and the cover is decorated with the arms of the diocese in enamel and gold paint. I am most grateful to Mrs Fredi Meade for the loan of this unique volume.

Plate 14 *Shawinigan Falls* (Gaspé Deanery G.A. Scrapbook, 1951, 92).

Plate 15 *Compton* (Gaspé Deanery G.A. Scrapbook, 1951, 203).

Plate 16a *The Mission to Seamen, Port of Quebec.* This pre-fabricated building was opened for use in September 1991.

Plate 16b *The A.C.W. bi-centennial quilt.* The squares were each designed and executed by a different A.C.W. across the diocese. Once completed, the squares were arranged and assembled by St George's A.C.W. in Lennoxville. Co-ordinated by Mrs Winnie Jellicoe, the project was completed and ready for display at major diocesan and parish events throughout the bi-centennial year.

Plate 17 *Memorial tablet to the Rev. William Chaderton.* A close examination shows that the sixth and seventh lines of the tablet had first been inscribed "in the zealous discharge of his *ardent* duties ..." but were subsequently corrected to read "... of his *arduous* duties ..." The original St Peter's Chapel was destroyed in the great Quebec fire of 1845, but was rebuilt the following year. It was within this second chapel that Chaderton's tablet was soon to be erected. In 1924, the old building on St Valier Street was deconsecrated and a new church built in Limoilou. The plaque was removed and remounted. When this last St Peter's was deconsecrated and demolished in 1993, Chaderton's tablet, with a number of others, was carried to St Michael's, Sillery, where this photograph was taken.

Plate 18 *Diocesan Publications: pamphlets in French.* This particular pamphlet, *Les Anglicans et l'unité*, contains eight pages and treats the subject of ecumenism under the following headings: "Notre unité dans le Christ," "Où commence l'unité?" "L'Appel anglican à tout le peuple chrétien," "Les Anglicans et les Églises orthodoxes," "Les Anglicans et les Églises protestantes," "Tentatives de réunion," "Les Anglicans et les Catholiques romains," "Le Conseil mondial des Églises," and "La Vocation de l'Église anglicane."

Plate 19   *Sketch map of St Clement's Mission* (QDG, Apr. 1916, facing 42). A note on the illustrations for the April issue mentions that "the cuts" of this sketch and a photograph of Corey himself "in travelling costume" were supplied by the *Canadian Churchman*, for which publication he had supplied them.

Plate 20   *The East Window of St James' Church, Kenogami* (QDG, Nov. 1926, facing 7). Sir William Price, President of Price Brothers Company Limited, had been accidentally killed on 2 October 1924 at Kenogami "while conducting an inspection of a landslide which had occurred on the previous evening and endeavoring to make plans for the safety of his men." After nine days of search, his body was recovered and interred in Kenogami on a hill overlooking the Saguenay River. In a personal tribute published in the *Diocesan Gazette*, Bishop Lennox Williams pointed to Sir William's many benefactions. Those to the Church included providing for some years "the entire salary and cost of travelling expenses of a General Missionary," and "the whole cost" of a Mission Boat for St Clement's Mission (QDG, Dec. 1924, 28 and 31).

Sources: Windows

1 *Clergy Wives,* "Extracts from letter, Frances Brooke to Bishop Terrick, 24 Jan. 1765," LPA, SPG Papers, II, ff 25-6;. G[race] I. M[arston], "The Role Of The Clergy Wife in The Parish," *QDG* (May 1962), 1 and 4; E. M., "Clergy Wives Entertained at East Angus," *QDG* (May 1960), 2; "Quebec Diocesan Youth Conference/Preliminary Announcement," *QDG* (Jan. 1935), 17, and "Quebec Diocesan Youth Conference," *QDG* (Sept. 1935), 16; [W.H.M. Church,] "Gwendolyn S. Carrington," *QDG* (Jan. 1984), 1. The five clergy families in which both husband and wife were ordained are the Barnett-Cowans, the Drolet-Smiths, the Hutchison-Housnells, the Schmitts, and the Spackmans.

2 *Relations With Other Communions: Trois-Rivières,* see *Journal of the Fifty-Ninth (Ordinary) Session of the Synod of the Diocese of Quebec* (1972), 19; Jacob Mountain to Susanna Brooke, 15 July 1794 in H. C. Stuart, *Episcopate of Dr Jacob Mountain,* 34 and 38-45, MS Volume, File 332, QDA (The accents in Stuart's transcription of the Supérieure's letter to Bishop Mountain have been normalized).

3 *"A Sermon Preached at Quebec,"* Jacob Mountain, *A Sermon Preached at Quebec, On Thursday, January 10th, 1799; Being the Day Appointed For a General Thanksgiving* (Quebec, 1799), iii-iv, vii-xi, 7-8, 10, 16 and 18; Vidler, *The Church in an Age of Revolution,* 33-5; J. Mountain to G. J. Mountain, 31 October 1814, quoted in A. W. Mountain, *A Memoir,* 31-2; "Memoir of the Late Bishop Mountain," *The Christian Sentinel,* (Jan. & Feb. 1827), 7.

4 *A Family Excursion,* Letter from Jacob Mountain to unspecified addressee, Quebec, 31 Oct. 1804, QDA, Unbound MSS., Index 23, case T, folder 3; A. W. Mountain, *A Memoir,* 12-13.

5 *The SPG and the Search for "Proper Clergymen to Go Abroad,"* [Pascoe], *Classified Digest of the Records of the Society for the Propagation of the Gospel,* 136-141; SPG *Annual Report, 1811,* (London, 1811), 42-3 and 45; Carrington, *The Anglican Church in Canada,* 74; Thompson, *Into All Lands,* 146. "Editorial," *QDG* (July 1932), 4; *Journal of the Thirty-ninth (Ordinary) Session of the Synod of the Diocese of Quebec* (1932), 39.

6 *To Declare For the Church,* letters 7 and 25, "Transcript of Bishop Stewart's Letters," ETA, Bishop's University; letter from C. J. Stewart to James Reid, 2 July 1817, and the same to the same, 29 Oct. [1819], QDA, Stewart-Reid Letters; C. M. Day, *History of the Eastern Townships* (Montreal, 1869), 213; "Complaint Against Mr Knagg, being a copy of a deposition before the magistrate," 11 Feb. 1824, QDA, Unbound MSS, Index 124, case 2, folder 12 "Gaspé Papers"; letter from John Gallie to Jacob Mountain, 12 Feb. 1824, and "Extract from a letter of the Archdⁿ of Quebec respecting Gaspé," 4 April 1825, in the same file; *Christ Church, Stanstead, Quebec: One Hundred Years of Witness* (n.p., [1958]), 5; Pascoe, *Classified Digest of the Records of the SPG,* 871.

7 *The Church and the Benefits of Education,* "Present Strength of Revd Mr Doty's School at Three Rivers 5th Septr 1816," in Legge, *The Anglican Church in Three Rivers,* 43; Diocesan Papers, B-24, f 7, QDA; SPCK *Annual Report* for 1830, 38-40; letter from C. P. Reid to J. B. Meilleur, 31 Mar. 1845, E0013, Art 290, loc 1A18 - 1202B, letter 1368, and the same to the same, 4 Dec. 1854, Art 337, 1A18- 3104B letter 1838, Education, lettres reçues, ANQ; J. W. Williams, *Self-Education: A Lecture,* (Quebec, 1864) bound in *Pamphlets: 1819-1927,* QDA.

8 *The "Duties of Visitation and Confirmation,"* letter from Jacob Mountain (senior) to Jacob Mountain (junior), Quebec, 25 March 1821, QDA, Unbound MSS., Index 23, case T, folder 3; the same to Bathurst, [London], 17 Dec. 1816; Reports of the SPG for 1820, 101, and 1821, 134-5.

9   *"The Late Awful Visitation of the Cholera Morbus,"* Bilson, *A Darkened House*, 24; G.
     J. Mountain, *A Retrospect of the Summer and Autumn of 1832: Being a Sermon Deliv-*
     ered in the Cathedral Church of Quebec, on Sunday, the 30th December, in that Year, By
     the Venerable G. J. Mountain ... With an Appendix ... (Quebec, 1833), 5-6, 8, 11-13,
     21, 25, and 32.

10   *A Ministry in French*, see *Regulations Respecting the Chapels and the Districts or Chapelries*
     Attached to Them, in the Parish of Quebec, no.V; an endorsement on the copy in the
     QDA suggests that these regulations remained in force until 31 Dec. 1859; [G. J.
     Mountain,] *The Church in the Colonies ... 1843 and 1844, Part II* (London, 1846),
     29; *A Sermon Preached Before the Incorporated Society for the Propagation of the Gospel*
     ... by Charles James, Lord Bishop of Chester ... Together with the Report of the Society for
     the Year 1826 (London, 1827), 111; [Henry Christmas,] *The Emigrant Churchman in*
     Canada by a Pioneer of the Wilderness, 2 vols. (London, 1849), I, 48; Francis De La
     Mare to G. J. Mountain, 12 Feb. 1849, QDA, Diocesan Papers, B-6, f. 82; Pierre
     Simon, William Simon, Abraham Lenfesty and Philip Tourgis to G. J. Mountain,
     8 Nov 1850, QDA, Diocesan Papers, (B-6), f. 93; [sender's name cut away] to G.
     J. Mountain, 17 Feb. 1851, QDA, (B-51), mistakenly filed among the corre-
     spondence of A. H. Dunn; A. W. Mountain, *A Memoir*, 74-5; see Robert Merrill
     Black, "Anglicans and French-Canadian Evangelism 1839-1848," *Journal of the*
     CCHS (April 1984), 20-22 *et passim*; *Second Annual Report of the Colonial Church &*
     School Society for the Diocese of Quebec, Canada (Quebec, 1859), 11, and *Fourth*
     Annual Report of the same (Quebec, 1861), 19; George Gale, *Historical Sketch of*
     Trinity Church (Quebec, 1925), 9; W[illiam] Wickes, "Church Society: Journal of
     Travelling Missionary (May to November)," *The Canadian Ecclesiastical Gazette*
     (Quebec, 11 Dec. 1851), 50; "Consecration of All Saints' Ste Ursule," *QDG*
     (Nov. 1901), 140; S. W. W[illiams], "All Saints Church, Ste Ursule Falls," *QDG*
     (Jan. 1963), 3-4 and "An Account of the deconsecration of the church at Ste
     Ursule Falls, June 30th which appeared in the French Press," *QDG* (Sept. 1963),
     2; "Anglican Pamphlets in French," *QDG* (Sept. 1963), 2; *Journal of the Sixty-sixth*
     (Ordinary) Session of the Synod of the Diocese of Quebec (1979), 27; "Anglicans in
     Mission funds enable Ministry in French," *QDG* (Feb. 1986), 1; "Francophone
     Anglican Speaks to Church Society of Quebec," *QDG* (June 1985), 1;
     "Francophones' report urges evangalization [sic]," *Anglican Journal* (Feb. 1993), 3;
     Mary Nemeth, Nora Underwood and John Howse, "The Religion Poll," *Maclean's*
     (12 April, 1993), 36; the Anglican Church's submission to the B&B Commission
     is quoted in Philip LeBlanc and Arnold Edinborough, eds, *One Church, Two Na-*
     tions? xiii; "Waterville," *Fifty-fifth Report of the Incorporated Church Society of the*
     Diocese of Quebec, 1897, 116-7.

11   *Famine and Quarantine*, [Famine Relief] *The Berean* (Quebec), 4 Feb. 1847, also 11
     Feb., 18 Feb., and 25 Feb.; "Aid ... From C. E.," *The Quebec Gazette*, 17 May and
     letter from G. M. Douglas to A. C. Buchanan, 11 June 1847; letter from Arch-
     bishop of Dublin to G. J. Mountain , 8 June 1847; the same to the same, 10 July
     1847; Letter from Scottish relief agency, Edinburgh, to G. J. Mountain 2 June
     1847; "Irish Famine Fund," Index 124, Unbound Papers, Case 2, Folder 17,
     QDA; [names of those who died at sea] *The Morning Chronicle* (Quebec) 30 Oct.
     1847; Missionary Register, Anglican Travelling Missionaries, District of Quebec
     (microfilm 4M00-0478A), ANQ; letter to G. J. Mountain from Charles Forest, 9
     June 1847 and letter from G. J. Mountain to A. W. Mountain, 12 June 1847,
     "Diocesan Papers," B-6, 52, f. 157, QDA; A. W. Mountain, *A Memoir*, 256-9; [C.
     P. Reid contracts typhus], reprinted from the *Montreal Courier* by *The Berean*, 28
     Oct. 1847.

12   *The Travelling Missionary*, May Harvey Drummond, *The Grand Old Man of Dudswell:*
     Being the Memoirs of the Rev. Thos. Shaw Chapman (Quebec, 1916), 50-7; D. C.
     Masters, *Bishops: The First Hundred Years,* 7.

13   *"Pilgrims & Proselytes,"* Flint, *John Strachan,* 13, 19; letter to G. J. Mountain from Isaac Hellmuth, 27 March 1854, "Diocesan Papers," D-22, f. 45, QDA; Ernest R. Roy, "The Roy Family's Debt to the Bible", I-II *QDG* (Fall 1958), 28-30, and (Christmas, 1958), 22-3; Edgar Andrew Collard, "William Turnbull Leach," *Dictionary of Canadian Biography,* XI, 502-4; Henry Roe, ed., *Memoir of Rev. Canon Scarth, and Annals of His Parish* (Sherbrooke, 1904).

14   *A Second Chance in a New World,* Susannah Moodie, *Roughting it in the Bush* (Toronto, 1962), 27; letter from William Gore Lyster to G. J. Mountain, 30 Mar 1858, "Diocesan Papers," B-3, 49, f 14, QDA; the same to the same, 21 Apr. 1858, f. 16; the same to the same, 10 May 1858, f. 23; the same to the same, 17 May 1858; Short to the same, 27 June 1859, f. 31; *The Eighteenth Report of the Incorporated Church Society of the Diocese of Quebec, 1859,* 15-16; H[enry] R[oe], "In Memoriam: William Gore Lyster," *QDG* (Mar. 1902), 36-8.

15   *A Difficult Birth: Quebec's First Synod,* A. W. Mountain, *A Memoir,* 286-99 and 370; G. J. Mountain, "A Pastoral Letter to the Clergy and Laity of the Diocese of Quebec," 23 Dec. 1852; *Statutes of the Province of Canada,* 19 & 20 Vic. cap. 14; T. R. Millman, "Beginnings of the Synodical Movement in Colonial Anglican Churches with special reference to Canada," *Journal of the CCHS* (1979), 8-9; *Report of the Proceedings of the Meeting of the Bishop, Clergy and Laity of the Diocese of Quebec, Held at the National School House, Quebec, on the 24th June, 1858, Taken from the "Quebec Mercury" of the 26th of that Month; Together with Certain Articles From that Journal, and Others, Bearing Upon the Subject of Synodical Action* (Quebec, 1859), *passim*; George Gale, *Historical Sketch of Trinity Church* (Quebec, 1925), 8-9; and *Proceedings of the Synod of the United Church of England and Ireland in the Diocese of Quebec ... in the year* MDCCCLIX (1859), 20-21, 30-33, and 50.

16   *Waiting For the Minister to Call*; Armine W. Mountain, *A Memoir,* 387-91; letter from J. P. Richmond to G. J. Mountain, dated Easter, 1862, Diocesan Papers, B-10, 56, f 86, QDA; the same to the same, 11 Aug. 1862, Diocesan Papers, B-10, 56, f. 90; "Priest Takes Wings," *QDG* (Summer 1960), 1; J[ohn] E. B[urke], "St. Clement's Mission 1861-1961" *QDG* (Oct. 1961), 1 and 4; Robert A. Bryan, "Chairman's Message," *QLF* [Quebec-Labrador Foundation] *Annual Report 1992,* 2-3; Robert A. Bryan, "Aunt Lizzy," typescript, 4 pp. For a similar use of "Aunt" and "Uncle," elsewhere in the Diocese, see "In Memoriam: Magdalen Islands" on the death of "Uncle Dan" and "Aunt Suz" McLean of Entry Island, *QDG* (Oct. 1962), 4; Hollis H. A. Corey, "Labrador Revisited," *QDG* (Fall 1952), 19-20; "The Missioner," *QDG* (Nov. 1962), 1; Frances E. O. Monck, *My Canadian Leaves: An Account of a Visit to Canada in 1864-1865* (London, 1891), 202-4 and 335-6. Catherine Julia Botwood, wife of the Rev. Edward Botwood, died, aged 25 years 4 months, at St John's, Newfoundland, and was buried in the Hall plot of the Mount Hermon Cemetery, Sillery (Section F 64), together with three Botwood children. The earliest of these four gravestones, that of Mary Hall Botwood, is inscribed "died at Forteau Labrador," 19 March 1863.

17   *Selling the Pews,* Church Temporalities Act, VI Vict., cap. 32, ss. 2 and 7; letter to G. J. Mountain from Robert Cowling and C. H. Tambs, Bury, 5 July 1862, "Diocesan Papers," QDA B-2, f. 86; D. C. Masters, *Bishop's University: The First Hundred Years,* 6-7; Nina Rowell and Mariette Lapointe, *Township of Bury: Canton de Bury 1836-1986,* (n.p., 1986), 12; R. W. Norman, *Free and Unappropriated Seating in Churches* ([Quebec, 1890]), 5; Jolliffe, *Andrew Hunter Dunn: A Memoir,* 118; Valcartier Vestry Books, QDA; Valcartier Churchwardens' Reports, QDA "Diocesan Papers," B-35, f. 47; *One Hundred Years: A History of Christ Church Valcartier,* (n.p., [1945]), 19-20; G. J. Mountain, "Circular to the Clergy of the Diocese of Quebec, no. 2," 4 Feb. 1851, printed in *The Canadian Ecclesiastical Gazette* (13 Feb. 1851), 69-71.

18   An *"Augustinian" Ordinand,* W. G. Cookesley, *Memorial Sketch of Frederick John Cookesley* (London, 1867), 40-2, 65-6, 76-8 *et passim;* A. W. Mountain, *A Memoir,* 419; letter from [no name] to G. J. Mountain, 5 Nov. 1862, QDA, B-23, Diocesan Papers.

19   *Questions of Ritual,* D. C. Masters, *Bishop's University: The First Hundred Years,* 5-6. letter from Jasper Nicolls to J. W. Williams, Bishop's College, 21 Jan. 1868, QDA B-38, "Bishop Williams' Correspondence" file; Chadwick, *The Victorian Church, Part I: 1829-1859,* 212 and 495-501; letter from M. Z. Nesbett to J. W. Williams, 16 Dec. 1875, QDA B-38, "Bishop Williams' Correspondence" file.

20   *Parish Endowments,* letter to J. W. Willims from H. W. Trigge, Nicolet, 31 March, 1868; the same to the same, Nicolet, 5 Feb. 1868; and O. Fortin to the same, St Francis, 14 May 1868; also Report of Committee on Nicolet Endowment Fund, 30 June 1873 all in QDA, B-38 "Bishop Williams' Correspondence" file; *Annual Reports of the Incorporated Church Society of the Diocese of Quebec* for 1843, 1845, 1848, and 1870; Testimonials of Joseph de Mouilpied, "Diocesan Papers", B-11, f. 91.

21   *Expanding the Church,* SPCK Minute Book, Vol. 58, 81-2, proceedings of meeting held 6 May 1884, SPCK Archives, London, England; "Dudswell Road Church in account with the Revd Wm King," Sept. 1849, QDA, Diocesan Papers, B-2, f. 81.

22   *A Parish Complaint: Grindstone,* see Byron Clark, *Anglican Mission of Magdalen Islands 140th Anniversary 1850-1990,* 15-16, 32-3; letters from J. W. Williams to Chas Leslie, Quebec, 19 May 1886; J. Norwood to J. W. Williams, Grindstone, 26 May 1886; and James Cassidy to the same, Entry Island, 24 June 1886, QDA B-39, "Bishop Williams' Correspondence" file. See also *Forty-Sixth Report of the ... Church Society, 1887* (1888), 75-7, and *Forty-Eighth Report ..., 1889* (1890), 96-7.

23   *A Parish Complaint: Drummondville;* letters from F. G. Scott to J. W. Williams, Drummondville, 4 Nov. 1887, and F.J.B. Allnatt to the same, 31 Mar. 1885, QDA B-39, "Bishop Williams' Correspondence" file; the Resolution from St. George's Church in Vestry assembled, 11 Apr. 1887, is in the same file. See also *Forty-Fifth Report of the Incorporated Church Society of the Diocese of Quebec,* 1886 (1887), 54-6, and *Fifty-Fifth Report ...,* 1896 (1897), 54-5.

24   *Visitation By Land and Sea,* "An extract from the Magazine 'THE NET' dated January 1, 1888," QDA, "Files-Bishops," J. W. Williams, typescript [*Paragraphing has been introduced to break up Stevens' almost solid text*]; *Reports of the Incorporated Church Society of the Diocese of Quebec, 1887,* 68-9.

25   *A Ministry to the Native People;* H. C. Stuart, *Church of Saint John the Divine ...,* MS volume, file 376, QDA; Arthur E. E. Legge, *The Anglican Church in Three Rivers, Quebec 1768-1956* (n.p., 1956), 100-1, 112. A. R. Kelley, *The Church of England in Quebec 1759 to 1791,* 75.

26   *"The Missionary Work of All Church Women,"* Report of the Meetings Held in Montreal, Sept. 9th and 10th, 1886, Called By the Provisional Committee Which Was Authorised By the Board of Missions For the Purpose of Organizing a Woman's Auxiliary ... (Montreal, 1886), 11-12, 27-8; Carrington, *The Anglican Church in Canada,* 182; "Auxiliary Notes: Quebec Diocese," and Jane M. Price, "The Woman's Auxiliary," *Monthly Letter Leaflet Issued By the Woman's Auxiliary to Missions,* (April, 1890), 21-4; "Missionaries Letters," *Monthly Letter Leaflet* (May, 1890), 47-8; *Our Fifty Years: 1886-1936* (n.p., [1936]), 5; "Bishop's Letter," *QDG* (Feb. 1963), 2.

27   *"The Quebec Cathedral Imbroglio,"* Joliffe, *Andrew Hunter Dunn: A Memoir*, 88-9; T. H. Norris and G. Veasy, "The Quebec Cathedral Imbroglio" (Quebec, 1894); "Circular No. 7," The Protestant Churchmen's Union and Tract Society (Toronto, 1894); W. T. Noble, "A Remonstrance: An Open Letter to the Lord Bishop of Quebec," 2nd ed. ([Toronto, 1894]); W. T. Noble, "An 'Open Letter' to the Archbishop of Ontario With Appendix" (Quebec, 1896); R. J. Hewton and C. R. Jones, "A Lay Reply to Rev. W. T. Noble's Open Letter to the Lord Bishop of Quebec (Hatley, 1894), the above pamphlets are all to be found in QDA, B-46. See also the collection of contemporary newspaper cuttings in the Wurtele Scrapbooks, IV, Archives of the McCord Museum of Canadian History, M18889, 35-8, 92, 247.

28   *Church Lighting,* letter from Dumbell to the Superintendent of the Electric Light Co., 27 Dec. 1897, St. Peter's Parish Papers, Sherbrooke, Que.; A. W. Mountain, *A Memoir,* 194. See *QDG* (Feb. 1963), 2, for a photograph of the interior of the Church of the Epiphany, Way's Mills, with its original oil lamps still in place.

29   *The Church at War,* "Visitation Charge," *QDG* (July 1914) 81, and "Day of Intercession," (Sept. 1944), 105; F. G. Scott, *The Great War as I Saw It* (Toronto, 1922), 15, 38, 95-6 and 117; F. G. Scott, *Lift Up Your Hearts* (Toronto, 1941), 4, 22. *[I wish to thank Mr A. Addie of Quebec City for bringing* Lift Up Your Hearts *to my attention.]*

30   *The* Glad Tidings, letter from A. E. Burgett to A. H. Dunn, 19 Feb. 1913, B-16, QDA; "Interesting Letter From the Rev. F. G. LeGallais," *QDG* (Dec. 1920), 124; W. G. Horwood, "The People of the Labrador," *QDG* (Jan. 1927), 25-7; "The Editor's Page," *QDG* (Sept. 1947), cover photograph of *Glad Tidings III* and 7; "Bishop's Letter," *QDG* (Summer 1961), 2 and (Sept. 1961), 2; D. Percy Graham, "Let's Build a Boat," *QDG* (Oct. 1961), 4; "Stop Press," *QDG* (Nov. 1961), 1; "Mission Boat," *QDG* (Apr. 1962), 4; D. P[ercy] G[raham], "The Lord Bishop Commissions the Hollis Corey," *QDG* (Nov. 1962), 1; W. H. Cheverton, "Labrador," *Eighty-third Report of the Incorporated Church Society of the Diocese of Quebec, 1924,* 82-4; Copy of letter from Sydney Meade to P. Carrington, 4 Aug. 1944, 4-5, Harrington Harbour Parish Papers; Outstations Register, Nov. 1939—Nov 1948, Harrington Harbour Parish Papers; Log Book of the Glad Tidings III, June 1969—Sept 1961, QDA; Personal Diary of R. L. Seaborn, 12-18, photocopy (original in private collection), QDA; A. W. Mountain, *Memoir,* 390.

31   *Faith of Our Fathers (and Mothers),* L. W. Williams, "Bishop's Letter," *QDG* (May 1932), 1-3.

32   *The Voice of Conscience:* The Quebec Diocesan Gazette, [C. R. Eardley-Wilmot], "Editorial," *The QDG* (Jan. 1934), 3-4; [C. R. Eardley-Wilmot], "Editorial," *The QDG* (July 1934), 3; "The Manufacture of Arms by Private Firms," *The QDG* (Jan. 1935), 29; *Journal of the Fortieth (Ordinary) Session of the Synod of the Diocese of Quebec* (1934), 65; "Pastoral Letter, Lent 1935," *The QDG* (Mar. 1935), 1-2.

33   *Vestry Books,* Vestry Book for Paspebiac, 1933-1954 in QDA; A. W. Mountain, *A Memoir,* 74.

34   *Parish Traditions and "Church Ceremonial,"* A. R. Beverley, *Trinity Church Quebec: A Historical Sketch* (Quebec, 1911), 19; Harrington Harbour Parish Papers, "Christ Church, Harrington Harbour," typescript: undated and unsigned, 1, 8-9, and "St. Clement's Mission, An Appreciation" signed by Claude S. Brett-Perring, undated, 9.

35   *Youth Work in the Diocese,* Junior Girls' Camp Logs for 1949 and 1951, *Fort Haldimand Camp,* MS Book, (no page numbers), private collection; N. M., "The Anglican Girls' Camp," *QDG* (Sept. 1942), 25; P. C., "Anglican Boys," *QDG* (Jan. 1943),

17-19; N. Machin, "The Camp Site at North Hatley," *QDG* (Aug. 1943), 18; "Fort Haldimand to Become Youth Camp," *QDG* (Apr. 1948), 17; J[ames] L. Y[oung], "New Camping Venture," *QDG* (Oct. 1962), 3.

36   *Mission to Industry,* W. W. Davis, "Seven Islands and Knob Lake," *QDG* (Autumn 1951), 17-18; "Parish Notes: Seven Islands," *QDG* (Summer 1956), 17-18; Robert Shorten, "Some Memories of Sept Iles and the Iron Ore Project," undated typescript; Timothy Matthews, "Greetings from Bishop Timothy Matthews to the Congregation and Friends of All Saints' Anglican Church ..." undated typescript [1985]; letter from Charles H. S. Cheesman and Robert K. Shorten to the Anglican and United Church congregations of Seven Islands, 25 Oct. 1955; letter from Christina Bobbitt to the author, 10 Mar. 1993.

37   *Bringing the Gospel Home,* S. M., "Book Review: *According to Mark,*" *QDG* (Sept. 1961), 4; Cuttell, *Philip Carrington: Pastor, Prophet, Poet,* 50, 56, 67; Carrington, *According to Mark: A Running Commentary on the Oldest Gospel* (Cambridge, 1960).

38   *"The Church Back Home,"* E[ileen] M[atthews], "The Church Back Home," *QDG* (June 1962), 3; E[thel] M[artin], "120th Anniversary: St. John's Church, Brookbury," *QDG* (Oct. 1962), 3; *One Hundred Years: A History of Christ Church Valcartier,* 23; *Holy Trinity Church, Denison's Mills: The Hundredth Anniversary, 1875-1975* (n.p., [1975]), 23.

39   *Relations With Other Communions: Arvida, La Tuque and Richmond;* "Bishop's Letter," *QDG* (Jan. 1964), 2; "Unique Services Held in Arvida" and "Ecumenical Experiment in Arvida," *QDG* (Feb. 1964), 2; "Readers Opinions," *QDG* (Feb. 1964), 4; "Ecumenity—L'Ecuminisme," *QDG* (Summer 1962), 1 and 4; "Il existe maintenant ..." *QDG* (Nov. 1963), 2; "French Pamphlet No. 3," *QDG* (Dec. 1963), 4; "Tribute to Rev. Hugh I. Apps," *QDG* (Nov. 1964), 4. *["Readers Opinions" appears as printed; the item from La Tribune—probably printed with transcriptional errors—has been normalized.]*

40   *The Church as the Voice of Conscience: The Environment,* "Bishop's Charge," *Journal of the Sixtieth (Ordinary) Session of the Synod of the Diocese of Quebec* (1973), 34-5; *Journal of the Sixty-Second (Ordinary) Session of the Synod of the Diocese of Quebec* (1975), 39; "Labrador," *QDG* (Sept. 1935), 19-20; [C. R. Eardley-Wilmot] "Editorial," *QDG* (Sept. 1934), 5.

41   *"A Voluminous Correspondence,"* printed letter from Russel Brown to Harold Brazel, 1985, QDA, "Files—Bishops: R. F. Brown"; John Franklin, "Obituary: Russel Featherstone Brown (1900-1988)," *The Record* (Sherbrooke), 17 Feb. 1988, 10.

42   *Tributes and Celebrations,* [Robert A. Bryan,] "A Tribute: Delivered by the Ven. Robert A. Bryan, Archdeacon of the North Shore at the Requiem Eucharist in Celebration of the Life and Ministry of Bishop Allen Goodings, Quebec, Quebec, January 9, 1993," typescript; "Memoir of the Late Bishop of Quebec," *The Christian Sentinel, and Anglo-Canadian Churchman's Magazine* (Jan. & Feb., 1827), 16-17; Glazebrooke, *The Church of England in Upper Canada,* 110.

Index